Lessons of Economic Stabilization and Its Aftermath

Lessons of Economic Stabilization and Its Aftermath

edited by
Michael Bruno
Stanley Fischer
Elhanan Helpman
and
Nissan Liviatan
with
Leora (Rubin) Meridor

The MIT Press
Cambridge, Massachusetts
London, England

This book was set in Palatino by The MIT Press and was printed and bound in the United States of America.

Library of Congress Cataloging-in-Publication Data

Lessons of economic stabilization and its aftermath / edited by
Michael Bruno . . . [et al.].
     p.   cm.
     Papers from a conference held at the Mishkenot Sha'ananim Music
Center in Jerusalem, Jan. 1990, and sponsored by the Bank of Israel
and the Inter-American Development Bank.
     Includes bibliographical references and index.
     ISBN 0-262-02324-5
     1. Economic stabilization—Congresses.   2. Economic stabilization—
Latin America—Congresses.   3. Economic stabilization—Israel—
Congresses.   4. Economic stabilization—Turkey—Congresses.
5. Economic stabilization—Yugoslavia—Congresses.   I. Bruno,
Michael.   II. Bank Yisra'el.   III. Inter-American Development Bank.
HB3732.L47 1991
338.9—dc20   90-22153
                                                                CIP

Contents

Acknowledgments

This detailed comparative analysis of the post-stabilization experiences of eight economies is the outcome of a two-day conference held at the Mishkenot Sha'ananim Music Center in Jerusalem at the end of January 1990. The project was initiated by Enrique Iglesias, President of the Inter-American Development Bank (IDB), who suggested to Michael Bruno that the Bank of Israel host a conference, co-sponsored by the IDB, at which some Latin American countries' most recent stabilization experiences would be compared with one another and with the experience of Israel. Five Latin American countries were chosen (Argentina, Bolivia, Brazil, Chile, and Mexico), and it was agreed that Turkey and Yugoslavia would be important additions. Coincidentally, the scheduling of the conference matched the 35th anniversary of the Bank of Israel.

Michael Bruno asked the other editors of this volume to serve as a Program Committee; we then drew up a list of proposed authors and formal discussants (after consulting other experts, notably Rudiger Dornbusch and Jacob Frenkel, and Miguel Urrutia of the IDB). The individual members of the Program Committee carried out a thorough pre- and post-conference refereeing process for all the papers and the comments. In the latter phase and in the scientific editing of this book the editors were skillfully assisted by Leora Meridor, Deputy Director of the Research Department at the Bank of Israel.

The conference was jointly financed by the IDB and the Bank of Israel. The administrative arrangements were efficiently coordinated by Raphy Meron, Director of International Relations at the Bank of Israel.

As in the case of the Toledo Conference (which led to the volume *Inflation Stabilization*, published by The MIT Press in 1988), the participants in this conference included several policy makers and advisers from the countries being discussed—notably Juan L. Cariaga, Minister of Finance of Bolivia at the time of the stabilization plan; José Luis Machinea, former Governor of the Bank of Argentina; Persio Arida, who participated in the design of the Cruzado plan in Brazil (Central Bank Governor Bucchi was in the audience); Guillermo Ortiz, now Deputy Minister of Finance of Mexico; Mitja Gaspari, Deputy Governor of the National Bank of Yugoslavia (Governor Vlatkovic was in the audience); and some of the editors of this volume who were involved in the Israeli stabilization program. Several of the participants are top economists and officials in the International Monetary Fund, the World Bank, or the IDB. With the exception of few experts and a few policy makers who could not attend, the list of participants is probably the most appropriate one that could have been drafted for such a conference. It made the discussion from the floor no less interesting than the formally prepared papers.

We wish to thank the institutions and the many individuals who made the publication of this volume possible. The first vote of thanks goes to the IDB, and especially to Enrique Iglesias, who not only initiated the conference and personally followed its preparation but who also, in his wise opening remarks at the conference, set the content and tone of the proceedings. Several people at the Bank of Israel actively and ably helped Raphy Meron on the organizational side, notably Andrew Aber, Marina Barda, and Esther Shuminer. Akiva Offenbacher and Miki Eran helped take notes of the general discussion. Saul Hanono helped on the IDB side.

The Music Center at Mishkenot Sha'ananim provided an ideal location for a medium-size, chamber-style seminar of this kind. It helped set the cultural level by staging a performance by two of its most able young musicians on the opening evening of the conference, for which thanks go to Ram Evron, Director of the Music Center.

Aside from Leora Meridor's excellent work as scientific co-editor, Maggie Eisenstaedt, editor at the Maurice Falk Institute for Economic Research in Israel, organized the diverse contributions into a consistent whole as regards language and style (in collaboration with Raphy Meron and assisted by Cliff Churgin). Our thanks also go to her for drawing the figures and getting the manuscript ready for the Press in disk form. Chava Reich labored conscientiously over many of the rough typescripts.

We wish to thank The MIT Press, and in particular Terry Vaughn, for showing keen interest in this volume. The introduction that follows was written at Terry's suggestion.

We end by thanking all the contributors for their collective effort and their patient compliance with the strict editorial instructions, and by expressing our hope that this will be a useful reference work for professionals and also for interested individuals among the general public.

Lessons of Economic Stabilization and Its Aftermath

1   Introduction and Overview

Michael Bruno

In the past two decades a number of countries in Latin America and elsewhere have gone through rather extreme inflationary experiences, largely as a result of internal crises reflecting a failed response to external shocks and mounting debt. While these crises can be attributed to common internal roots, notably large budget deficits, the nature of the inflationary process across countries and over time has varied, and so has the set of required stabilization measures.

The inflationary process in some of these countries, including Bolivia (and more recently Yugoslavia, Poland, and, by default, Argentina and Brazil), has resembled the relatively short but highly explosive European hyperinflations of the 1920s. Under a definition introduced by Cagan (1956), a hyperinflation is one whose rate of price increase exceeds 50% per month. Its shock cure—no gradualist approach could ever work— must be accomplished by orthodox measures involving sharp fiscal and monetary reform.

Cumulative experience of the 1970s and the 1980s has drawn attention to an important intermediate species of high (chronic) inflation which is much more prolonged and more stable. It may typically last 5–8 years and show monthly rates of 5–25%. This characterized the inflation in Argentina, Brazil, and Israel up to 1985 and that in Mexico up to 1987. The quasi-stability of that inflation comes from an inherent inertia, which, in turn, is strongly tied up with a high degree of indexation or with accommodation of the key nominal magnitudes (wages, the exchange rate, and the monetary aggregates) to the lagged movements of the price level. It is the obvious way in which an inflation-prone system attempts to protect itself from the evils of inflation, thus giving inflation a longer lease on life and delaying its more fundamental cure.

Some of the more moderate predecessors of this process appeared in Latin America in the 1950s (Pazos 1972). However, as long as inflation stays below a monthly rate of, say, 5–6% (which corresponds to a two-digit annual rate) its cure can be gradualist. It took the large external shocks of the 1970s to bring about the new species of galloping, yet for a time quasi-stable, inflation in the three-digit annual range. The origin of this process, as of its hyper brother, lies in government finances. Its cure must perforce involve the same sharp orthodox fiscal and monetary measures. Similarly, the very high rate of inflation, as in the case of hyperinflation, makes a gradualist approach too costly if not impossible. Yet there is one major difference between the two processes. Given inflationary inertia, the orthodox cure is necessary but not sufficient. The correction of fundamentals does not by itself remove inflationary inertia, as the most recent Mexican example has shown. Supplementary direct intervention in the nominal process, such as a temporary freeze of wages, prices, and the exchange rate, can substantially reduce the initial cost of disinflation. The two-pronged approach to stabilization, applied to Argentina, Israel, and Brazil in 1985–1986 and later to Mexico, came to be known as the *heterodox* program. Two of these countries, Argentina and Brazil, failed to stabilize, mainly because their fundamentals were not set in place. Both countries have gone into hyperinflation since 1987. In the other two countries, Israel (in 1985) and Mexico (in 1988) the stabilization program has been successful, though structural adjustment is still going on. In the case of Israel, at least, the unemployment cost of disinflation was paid at a later stage.

This volume centers on the comparative experiences of eight countries. Bolivia and Chile represent successful orthodox stabilizations. Argentina and Brazil represent failed or short-lived heterodox experiences. Israel and Mexico are successful heterodox cases. To this list we have added Turkey, which still has chronic, two-digit inflation, and Yugoslavia, which recently moved into hyperinflation and which at the time of the conference introduced a major stabilization program. Had the conference been held a few months later we would probably have included a study of Poland's hyperinflation and stabilization; this case is mentioned only here and in the panel discussion (chapter 11).

Before describing the contents of this book, which deal mainly with the aftermaths of the successful and the failed stabilizations, I will turn to a comparative overview of the basic facts of inflation in these countries in the 1970s and the 1980s. The data are summarized in table 1.1, organized by subgroup and country. Dates of major stabilization efforts appear in parentheses. The first three columns give the average monthly rate of inflation by subperiod. This is followed by the peak monthly rate (and its date). Column 5 indicates the number of months in which inflation exceeded 50% (with the corresponding number for a 25% threshold in parentheses). The last two columns measure the number of years of three-digit annual inflation. The same underlying data (excluding Poland) appear in figure 1.1, with the monthly price level (P) measured in a logarithmic scale on the vertical axis (using 1970 as unit reference). The slope of a country curve at each point measures the monthly inflation rate, $d(\log P)/dt$.

Throughout the 1970s most of the countries in the sample, with the exceptions of Chile and Argentina, were experiencing rather moderate inflation (on the order of 1–2% monthly). Chile underwent a major and rather painful orthodox stabilization in 1975; after that it took over 5 years and another crisis for its inflation to decelerate to a monthly rate of around 1.5%. Argentina tops the inflation league for the period as a whole. Its price level by the end of 1989 was over 10 billion (10^{10}) times the 1970 level. Israel and Brazil split off from the rest of the group in the late 1970s and the early 1980s. Israel stabilized successfully; Brazil's 1986 attempt failed. As the table and the figure show, after the short-lived first Austral (1985) and Cruzado (1986) plans, Brazil and Argentina went from high inflation to hyperinflation, with average and peak monthly rates resembling those of the Bolivian price explosion of 1982–1985.[1] Whereas Bolivia successfully stabilized in early 1986, Argentina's and Brazil's inflation profiles after 1987 show "kinks" in the curves, representing a series of further failures of allegedly "heterodox" shocks.[2] Detailed descriptions of the experiences of four of these countries up to 1987—Argentina, Bolivia, Brazil, and Israel—appeared in *Inflation Stabilization* (MIT Press, 1988).

The three lowest curves in the figure, representing Mexico, Turkey, and Yugoslavia, show moderate inflation until mid-1986. At that time Mexico was already embarking on a correction of "fundamentals," while its inflation was accelerating (see also table 1.1). Its successful heterodox program in January 1988 was a major step forward. After 1986 Turkey continued with a somewhat faster yet moderate two-digit inflation, while Yugoslavia's ill-fated attempts at partial stabilization sent that

Table 1.1
High inflation and stabilization, 1970–89 (monthly percentages and numbers of months and years).

	Average monthly rate[a]			Peak Monthly rate (date) (4)	Number of months with rate > 50% (> 25%) (5)	Number of years with annual rate > 100%	
	1970–79 (1)	'80–85 (2)	'86–'90 (3)			'70–'79 (6)	'80–'89 (7)
Successful orthodox							
Bolivia ('85)	1.4	18.5	2.1	182 (2/85)	9(16)	—	5
Chile ('75)	7.6	1.7	1.4	88 (10/73)	1(1)	4	—
Failed heterodox							
Argentina ('85)	6.8	11.9	19.0	197 (7/89)	5(18)	5	10
Brazil ('86)	2.4	7.9	19.7	84 (2/90)	4(18)	—	8
Successful heterodox							
Israel ('85)	2.6	9.1	1.4	28 (7/85)	-(1)	—	6
Mexico ('88)	1.2	3.9	4.8[b]	15 (1/88)	-(-)	—	3
New members							
Turkey ('80)	1.9	3.3	3.8	21 (2/80)	-(-)	—	1
Yugoslavia ('90)	1.4	3.4	14.5	60 (12/89)	3(7)	—	3
Poland[c] ('90)	0.3	2.6	8.6	77 (1/90)	2(5)	—	2

Source: IFS (IMF).
a. Monthly averages refer to periods from January of the first year to December of the last year except for 1990, for which most data reach only up to January–February.
b. From April 1988 to April 1990 the average monthly rate was 1.7%.
c. Based on annual data up to 1987 and monthly data for 1988–1990.

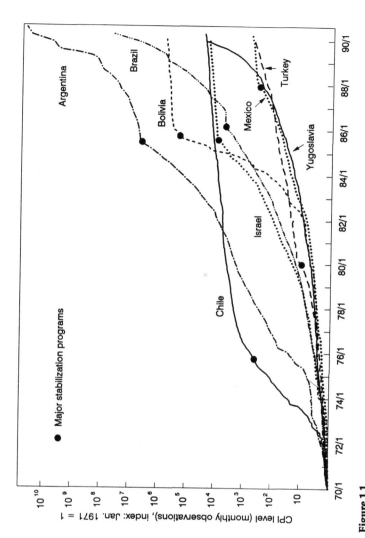

Figure 1.1
Inflation and stabilization in eight countries.

country, too, into hyperinflation. If Poland's data were recorded in the figure, the slope of its curve would look very much like Yugoslavia's in 1988–89, except that the level would be lower, since Poland had a smaller cumulative price increase up to that point.

As a final comment on this comparative overview of the data, I will note one quite remarkable common characteristic of all four relative success stories (Chile, Bolivia, Israel, and Mexico). During the latter part of the 1980s they were all still running rather stable, relatively low, yet significant inflations, with rates on the order of 20% per annum. (Note that all four curves in the figure turn into parallel straight lines.)

High inflation is merely one manifestation of an underlying deep crisis in the real economy. Even a successful price stabilization is in most instances no more than a necessary first step in a more protracted process of structural reform, as is borne out in some of the following chapters, to whose main contents I will now turn.

Chapter 2 starts with an account by Juan Antonio Morales of the post-stabilization experience of Bolivia, whose 1985–86 stabilization program after hyperinflation was analyzed by the same author in *Inflation Stabilization*. Bolivia is one example of the problematic tradeoff in exchange-rate and monetary policy between the maintenance of recently achieved (and rather fragile) price stability and the promotion of external competitiveness and overall economic activity. While Bolivia's price stabilization has become an established fact, persistently low investment rates, especially in the private sector, have kept growth at bay. At the same time, maintaining fiscal equilibrium at the cost of indiscriminate slashing of expenditures on social services has proved politically problematic. Next, exchange-rate policy and variability have maintained the dollarization of the economy longer and kept the remonetization of the economy slower than expected. Finally, not only were the post-stabilization high real interest rates unconducive to growth; in the Bolivian case, as in some others, they contributed to a series of banking crises and a general instability in the financial system.

Chile's post-stabilization experience, which Vittorio Corbo and Andrés Solimano address in chapter 3, is an important reference point. The fiscal shock therapy of 1975–1977 and the experiment with exchange-rate-based stabilization of 1978–1982 have shown the slow pace of convergence to a low-inflation equilibrium if it is not done all at once. The costs of the initial adjustment, in terms of real wage cuts and employment losses, were extremely high, to a degree that could most probably not be sustained in a democratic environment. While stabilization was lengthy and painful, the more recent post-1984 experience is especially interesting since it represents a stage that has probably not yet been reached in the other successful stabilization stories recorded here. Well-functioning goods markets (while adjustment in the labor market was much more sluggish), a competitive real exchange rate (a 50% real devaluation was achieved over 1984–1988, without acceleration in inflation), and a restoration of basic macroeconomic balances (after a deep crisis in 1982–83) have all been conducive to a resumption of non-inflationary growth of both exports and GDP. Chile is now once more one of the fastest-growing semi-industrial economies, and the recently established autonomy of its central bank may help keep inflation low and may reduce it further. The lesson from this experience is that, once relative stability is achieved and the rules of the game are clear, investment and growth will eventually recover, although slowly.

Failure of stabilization is usually due to a lack of correction of the fundamental imbalances that brought about the crisis in the first place. The aftermath of a failed shock stabilization is not the same as a fresh start or a first major stabilization, because the credibility problem worsens with each failure. These lessons are brought out by the detailed analyses of the post-stabilization experiences of Argentina (by Daniel Heymann in chapter 4) and Brazil (by Eliana Cardoso in chapter 5). The Austral Plan in Argentina, which was a professionally well-conceived program, managed for a while to steer the economy away from hyperinflation but was clearly insufficient to achieve permanent stability. A deficient tax system and the absence of a permanent, socially acceptable cut in expenditures were certainly the greatest hindrances to the success of the first and the subsequent attempts at stabilization. Underlying that failure were the lack of a social consensus and the absence of a political leadership that could credibly express its preference for sustainable stabilization, the way it did in the Israeli, Mexican, and Bolivian examples. Successive failures have eroded government credibility, first under Alfonsin and subsequently under Menem. By the end of 1989 the very survival of the domestic currency was being questioned.

Cardoso presents two models of the Brazilian economy in chapter 5. In the first she tackles the problem of a price freeze without a deficit cut, showing that it will increase price variability. The second model addresses the inflationary effect of external credit rationing when the government has a large external debt. Brazil's Cruzado plan, even more than Argentina's Austral plan, lacked the necessary fiscal and monetary scaffolding. As is pointed out in Arida's discussion of Cardoso's paper, when inflation resurges after a failed program, a new indexation regime, based on more frequent wage readjustments, is put in place in an effort to achieve a "fair" income distribution, and a higher inflation is then required to reinstate the same real variables (such as the real exchange rate).

The comparison of the Argentinian and Brazilian experiences forms the subject of chapter 6, authored by Miguel Kiguel and Nissan Liviatan. The most interesting feature of such a comparison is the contrast between the difference of the two inflation profiles before the 1985–86 programs and their remarkable similarity afterward. Before, inflation was higher and more unstable, and had a clearer fiscal nature, in Argentina than in Brazil. Afterward, these differences disappeared as the two countries underwent similar inflation-stabilization cycles of increasing amplitude. A program of price and wage controls (inaccurately termed a "heterodox" shock), which temporarily stabilized prices (see the small ripples in the curves for Argentina and Brazil after 1986 in figure 1.1), was followed by a new price explosion. The authors analyze these successive cycles, stressing the role of expectations and the anticipation of government actions by firms and workers. These accentuate the instability of price behavior under the new inflationary "regime." The damage that such a policy inflicted on the credibility of nominal anchors is separate from the problem of fiscal credibility. Once hyperinflation ensued, no return to wage and price freezes as part of a stabilization package could be envisaged.

The book then turns to the two successful heterodox stabilization programs. By mid-1987, Israel's stabilization seemed an almost perfect success. Stabilization was achieved at relatively low real transition costs, inflation was stabilized at a low level, and at the same time output and productivity growth in the first two years were unusually high. In retrospect, this fast growth looks more like a one-time spurt, as the economy subsequently went into a deep two-year slump which led to a substantial rise in unemployment in the course of 1989.

Michael Bruno and Leora Meridor analyze these developments in chapter 7, showing that although some unanticipated events may have deepened the recession, its main cause lay in the slow recuperation from the distortive effects of 15 years of inflation. The dominant cause of the output slump on the supply side came from excessive increases in real wages; high initial real interest rates and a heavier tax burden on the business sector also contributed. These were in large part endogenous to the post-stabilization process. Such a cycle, we now know, has been observed in many other historical stabilization episodes, notably in Europe in the 1920s. Israel's case also illustrates the slow post-stabilization restructuring process going on in the real economy and in the financial system. The persistence of 15–20% inflation in spite of the slump remains an enigma. Structural factors, a slow learning process in the wage and exchange-rate policy game, and the lack of an absolute anti-inflation conviction on the part of the political leadership and the business community may provide part of the explanation.

Mexico's case, described in detail by Guillermo Ortiz in chapter 8, provides a very important addition to our understanding of the two-pronged approach to the stabilization process. Although its problems deepened in the wake of the 1982 debt crisis, Mexico responded earlier than other countries by correcting its fundamental internal and external imbalances, as well as by carrying out the required restructuring. On the one hand, the case of Mexico illustrates the point that orthodox measures are necessary but not sufficient to extricate an economy quickly from the high-inflation syndrome. The successful "Pacto de Soledaridad" of December 1987 provided the complementary answer for the disinflation package which in Israel, at 500% inflation, had to be carried out all at once. But the case of Mexico also shows, in contrast to the case of Israel, that an early awareness by a determined political leadership of the depth of the crisis, before annual inflation hits 200%, may help a country to avoid some of the more painful adjustments afterward. A more severe external crunch, motivating quick action, and a more flexible labor market, cushioning the internal shock, have certainly also helped a lot. While Mexico has exhibited the familiar post-stabilization high real interest rate as well as the real-appreciation syndrome, so far a deep recession has been avoided. Implementation of a bold structural adjustment program, including privatization of state-owned enterprises and vigorous deregulation and liberalization of external trade, has substantially enhanced the government's credibility. Moreover, these measures may also explain why, in spite of relatively high real interest rates and a real appreciation, private investment and renewed growth have been taking place amidst ongoing stabilization.

Turkey and Yugoslavia, though they are very different cases, were both included in this conference under the heading of new high-inflation countries or the "early warning signals" of high inflation. In chapter 9 Dani Rodrik analyzes Turkey's experience in the 1980s, after the country extricated itself from a severe foreign-exchange crisis, negative growth, and a brief spurt of three-digit inflation. In the course of the 1980s the Turkish economy achieved a remarkable transformation from an inward to an outward orientation, with very substantial export growth and a comfortable balance of payments. Yet, after some success in the early 1980s, inflation remains unconquered, and the budget of the public sector is out of control as a result of extrabudgetary funds which can be used and abused for discretionary purposes. Inflation was rekindled under the dual influence of fiscal deficits and a shrinking base for the inflation tax, and its stability was hampered by a premature process of financial liberalization. Turkey illustrates the case of a loss of nominal anchors, for the sake of sustaining export competitiveness and growth, as the exchange rate, money, wages, and prices chase one another in an upward-drifting inflationary process. In many ways this is a repetition of the Israeli and Brazilian experiences of the 1970s.

The case of Yugoslavia, described by Velimir Bole and Mitja Gaspari in chapter 10, is of interest not only because it presents another example of how the introduction of wage and price controls in the absence of fiscal and monetary reform can send a country directly into hyperinflation. The novel aspect for the present study is the special nature of hidden public-sector deficits, which have their institutional analogues in other Eastern European economies. In Yugoslavia, the deficit and the public debt were hidden in the quasi-fiscal function of the central bank, which supplied subsidized credit to enterprises and also absorbed foreign-exchange losses while acting as a financial intermediary for foreign loans. The problem is further accentuated by the particular way in which the rest of the banking system operates, under the directives of self-managed enterprises. In the absence of financial accountability at the level of individual enterprises, this system acts as a channel for the collectivization of losses. The chapter concentrates on the analysis of the effects of this institutional setup on the inflationary process.

Considerable institutional reform measures were undertaken by Markovic's government. The bold, comprehensive stabilization package introduced at the end of 1989 is mentioned only briefly at the end of the chapter. Until mid-1990 the program seems to have been very successful in halting inflation—at the cost, however, of serious disruptions in the real economy. The case of Yugoslavia is an especially tricky one, owing to the political upheavals in that country's federal political structure. It is interesting to note, though, that an initially credible stabilization program may at least temporarily serve as a consensus-enhancing catalyst, playing a role similar to that of the otherwise disunited "national unity government" of Israel in 1985. The cumulative historical experience of the other countries recorded in this volume makes it prudent to await subsequent developments in Yugoslavia and to gain sufficient perspective before a more serious evaluation is made. The same could probably be said for the recent Polish stabilization experience, had it been included in this volume.[3] Both of these cases, and those of other Eastern and Central European economies, could form an interesting subject for the next conference on stabilization.

This volume ends with a panel discussion entitled "What's New Since Toledo?" The invited speakers were Guido Di Tella, Stanley Fischer, Jacob Frenkel, and Nissan Liviatan. There was considerable participation from the floor. The discussion centered around the main general issues surveyed here and provides further insight into several of them. There is no doubt that the experience accumulated since 1987 has deepened our understanding of the complexity of the stabilization process and has shed new light on old problems. It has also uncovered new problems and identified post-stabilization patterns of behavior which those of us present at Toledo in 1987 could not have predicted.

It is important to stress that this volume centers on the actual experiences of countries and on some of the general lessons that could be drawn from them. It is not a treatise on the economic theory of sharp stabilization. The latter is a legitimate separate, though clearly connected, subject of scientific enquiry. Quite a few of the participants in this conference have added, elsewhere, to the burgeoning theoretical literature on the subject.[4] This volume should serve as an important contribution not only to future policy making but also to its enhancement by further theoretical generalization.

Acknowledgments

I wish to thank Stan Fischer, Elhanan Helpman, Nissan Liviatan, and Leora Meridor for helpful comments on a draft of this chapter.

Notes

1. All three are remarkably similar to the profiles of the major European hyperinflations of the 1920s. Hyperinflation lasted 4 years in Germany (peaking at 30,000% for September 1923) and 3 years in Austria, Hungary, and Poland (with monthly peaks between 100% and 300% taking place over a year before the German peak). For an analysis of the shock stabilizations of these four countries see Sargent 1982. That historical experience inspired the planners of the sharp stabilizations of 1985–1986.

2. The term is certainly a misnomer in this case, since the subsequent programs of Argentina and Brazil may have been "hetero" but had little orthodoxy (i.e., fiscal stabilization) in them. See discussion below and chapters 4–6.

3. For a recent account of the Polish reform see Lipton and Sachs 1990.

4. For a sample of relevant recent contributions see Alesina and Drazen 1989; Bruno 1988; Bruno and Fischer 1990; Calvo and Vegh 1990; Dornbusch 1988; Helpman and Leiderman 1988; Kiguel and Liviatan 1989; Persson and Wijnbergen 1988.

References

Alesina, A., and A. Drazen. 1989. Why Are Stabilizations Delayed? NBER Working Paper.

Bruno, M. 1988. "Econometrics and the design of economic reform." *Econometrica* 57, no. 2: 275–306.

Bruno, M., and S. Fischer. 1990. "Seigniorage, operating rules and the high inflation trap." *Quarterly Journal of Economics* 105, no. 2: 353–374.

Cagan, P. 1956. "The monetary dynamics of hyperinflation." In *Studies in the Quantity Theory of Money*, M. Friedman, ed. (University of Chicago Press).

Calvo, A. G., and C. A. Vegh. 1990. Credibility and the Dynamics of Stabilization Policy: A Basic Framework. Mimeograph, IMF.

Dornbusch, R. 1988. Notes on Credibility and Stabilization. NBER Working Paper 2790.

Helpman, E., and L. Leiderman. 1988. "Stabilization in high inflation countries: Analytical foundations and recent experience." In *Carnegie Rochester Conference Series*, K. Brunner and A. Meltzer, eds., volume 28 (North-Holland).

Kiguel, M. A., and N. Liviatan. 1989. The Old and the New in Heterodox Stabilization Programs: Lessons from the Sixties and the Eighties. Mimeograph, World Bank.

Lipton, D., and J. Sachs. 1990. "Creating a market economy in Eastern Europe: The case of Poland." *Brookings Papers on Economic Activity*.

Pazos, F. 1972. *Chronic Inflation in Latin America*. Praeger.

Persson, T., and S. van Wijnbergen. 1988. Signalling, Wage Controls and Monetary Disinflation Policy. Seminar Paper 406, Institute for International Economic Studies, University of Stockholm.

Sargent, T. 1982. "The ends of four big inflations." In *Inflation: Causes and Effects*, R. E. Hall, ed. (University of Chicago Press).

2

The Transition from Stabilization to Sustained Growth in Bolivia

Juan Antonio Morales

The Bolivian stabilization program of August 1985 is already more than four years old and is the only survivor of the four such programs initiated around the same time in Latin America. Moreover, price stability has been sturdy enough to withstand severe external shocks.

But the good results of stabilization have been followed by only a very modest recovery of output growth, and the employment picture is still blurred. Bolivia has not caught up with the GDP losses of the early 1980s, nor has it been rewarded as yet, in terms of improvement of living conditions, for the policies it adopted. In the public's perception, as witnessed by press editorials, the crisis unleashed in 1982 is not over yet, although significant progress is acknowledged.

The features of the stabilization program are by now well documented (see, e.g., Sachs 1986, 1987; Bernholz 1988; Pastor 1988; Morales 1988a, 1988b). It suffices to remember that the program relies on exchange-rate unification, supported domestically by tight monetary and fiscal policies and externally by a significant debt alleviation. Also, the program dismantled most price controls. Since Bolivia suffered a true case of hyperinflation between 1984 and 1985, different in many ways from the chronic high inflations of its neighbors, the means of control were also different.

A major aim of the paper is to provide a thorough description of the post-stabilization macroeconomy as well as some indications of the unsolved problems. The maintenance of stabilization dominates the attention of Bolivian policy makers. Other manifestations of macroeconomic disequilibrium, that may imperil price stability in the future, have received somewhat less recognition. In addition, the medium-term problems in the aftermath of stabilization have their own characteristics that need to be analyzed in some detail. They have to do with the tradeoffs between: domestic price stability, external competitiveness and level of economic activity; stability of the private financial system and macroeconomic stability; low inflation now and high inflation later; and fiscal equilibrium now and loss of tax revenues later. The most important medium-term problem, although not unrelated to the ones mentioned above, is the establishment of attractive conditions for the resurgence of private investment.

1. Background: The Results of Stabilization to Date

Inflation

The inflation rates measured by the percentage changes in the Consumer Price Index (CPI) and the Wholesale Price Index (WPI) generally exhibit low values starting from the second quarter of 1986. Since then, the inflation rates in almost every quarter have stayed below 5%. The exceptional periods were the second quarters of 1986 and 1988 and the last two quarters of 1989. Changes in the official exchange rates (and in the parallel market for foreign exchange) have a similar pattern, with even lower rates (table 2.1, lines A1–A3, and figure 2.1).

The program not only ended the hyperinflation but was robust enough to withstand the adverse shocks to the external (and fiscal) accounts produced by the severe drop in Bolivia's export prices (table 2.1, line A5) and by the arrears by Argentina on payments for its purchases of natural gas from Bolivia.

Wages in the private sector have been increasing steadily since the third quarter of 1986; their real values show a very strong recovery and were, in the third quarter of 1989, 72% higher than at the end of 1985 (table 2.1, lines A4 and D3). There are no comparable data for wages in the public sector; the comments below are based on fragmentary information. Wages in the main state enterprises have increased as fast as or faster than in the private sector; however, wages in the central administration, where most public-sector employees work, have very significant lags with regard to both inflation and wages in other sectors.

The Remaining Macroeconomic Disequilibria

The sharpness of the picture of the inflation rate notwithstanding, there are several questions on the nature of Bolivia's stabilization that need further scrutiny.

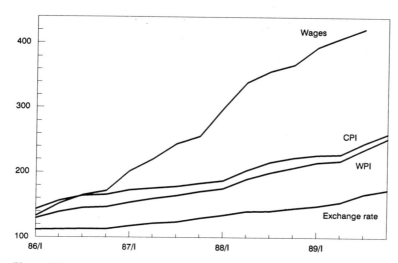

Figure 2.1
Prices, exchange rate, and private-sector wages.

Relatively High Fiscal Deficits

Despite the emphasis on fiscal correction in the Bolivian program of 1985, the consolidated deficits of the non-financial public sector (NFPS), which includes the deficits of the general government and the public enterprises, after an exceptional first year, remained high (table 2.2).[1] Current savings were negative in 1987, and their level for 1988, although positive, was still very low. Note that the budget deficits of the last three years are of the same order of magnitude as the ones of the years immediately preceding the high-inflation years.

The existence of substantial budget deficits does not mean that efforts to control expenditures and raise tax revenues were weak. On the contrary, ceilings on current expenditures of the government and the public enterprises have been very important, but they could not be reduced sufficiently to match the shortfalls in income, especially those resulting from the fall in sales of goods and services abroad. The 1986 tax reform, at whose core was a value-added tax, has shown some promising first results but has not yet been fully implemented. Internal and import tariff revenues, excluding transfers from public enterprises to the government, are still below the levels attained in the 1970s. The low level of economic activity, to which we refer below, has also affected fiscal revenues.

Table 2.1
Financial indicators after the stabilization program.

	Mean 1986–1989	1986 I	II	III	IV	1987 I	II	III	IV	1988 I	II	III	IV	1989 I	II	III	IV
A. Prices, exchange rates and wages (quarterly percentage change rates)																	
1. Consumer prices[a]	6.2	43.6	9.1	4.8	1.1	4.4	1.7	1.5	2.6	2.3	8.4	6.1	3.2	1.9	0.6	7.5	5.9
2. Wholesale prices[b]	6.0	30.0	7.3	4.4	1.2	4.5	3.9	3.0	3.8	2.7	8.2	5.2	3.9	3.9	1.3	7.9	7.2
3. Exchange rates (Bs per U$)[b]	3.5	12.3	0.4	0.5	0.3	4.1	3.4	1.9	4.7	3.6	4.4	0.4	2.9	2.4	4.0	8.0	3.9
4. Private sector nominal wages[c]	10.1	33.4	14.1	8.6	4.1	17.4	9.3	10.7	4.7	16.9	13.6	5.0	2.9	7.4	3.6	3.3	n.a.
5. Export prices[d]	-3.0	-23.2	-2.2	0.0	3.2	-10.5	0.3	-0.3	-5.9	-0.3	-2.3	0.8	-2.2	6.0	5.4	-10.2	n.a.
a. Natural gas[d]	-4.5	-11.2	-0.9	-0.3	1.4	-18.3	-1.2	-0.3	-10.6	-0.3	-8.0	-5.6	-5.8	0.4	11.5	-14.4	n.a.
b. Tin[d]	-2.3	-50.3	-4.8	-2.5	8.5	14.4	0.5	-2.3	3.4	-2.1	1.9	6.7	0.5	14.5	20.4	-18.1	n.a.
B. Money and credit (quarterly percentage change rates)																	
1. Base Money[b]	11.0	-1.5	24.0	18.1	9.6	21.7	12.9	10.7	20.9	0.1	8.6	12.3	30.4	-8.5	1.1	3.1	20.5
2. M1[b]	7.8	-4.7	27.0	11.6	35.3	-0.2	7.5	12.5	14.7	-9.2	8.6	4.4	32.3	-10.5	3.3	-3.4	8.7
3. M3[b,f]	11.5	15.8	43.8	28.3	32.5	17.9	10.0	2.0	11.9	1.0	10.9	8.3	17.9	-0.3	-1.7	8.8	-10.8
C. Dollarized deposits and interest rates (levels at end of quarter)																	
1. Dollarized deposits (% of total commercial bank deposits)[b]	66.0	34.9	42.6	49.6	54.8	67.4	68.1	66.4	67.9	72.7	73.8	73.3	73.9	74.2	74.0	79.2	84.0
2. Annual nominal interest rate for dollarized deposits[b]	15.0	12.3	14.9	14.9	15.0	15.1	15.5	16.0	15.6	15.8	16.0	15.3	14.9	13.9	14.3	15.6	15.1

D. Relative price levels (base 1985/IV = 100)

1. Real exchange rate[e]	90.4	n.a.	95.3	n.a.	n.a.	n.a.	84.2	n.a.	n.a.	91.5	91.1	90.3	93.7	95.9	75.5	n.a.
2. Private-sector real wages[c]	92.9	97.1	100.7	103.7	116.6	125.3	136.5	139.3	159.1	166.8	165.0	164.4	173.4	178.7	171.8	n.a.
E. Consolidated non-financial public-sector deficit (% of GDP)[c,g]	5.2		2.5					7.4					5.7			
F. Balance of payments, current account (% of GDP)[d,g]	−7.9		−9.6					−10.0					−4.3			−2.6

a. Based on basic data from the National Institute of Statistics.
b. Based on basic data from the Central Bank of Bolivia.
c. Based on data from the Unit for Policy Analysis (UDAPE), Ministry of Planning, La Paz.
d. Based on data from International Monetary Fund, International Financial Statistics, August 1989.
e. Estimates of the Unit for Policy Analysis (UDAPE), Ministry of Planning, La Paz; declining values indicate appreciation.
f. Includes dollarized and dollar-linked depostis.
g. Yearly values.

Table 2.2
Consolidated non-financial public sector operations (percent of GDP).

	1984	End of hyper- inflation 1985	1986	1987	1988
1. Total revenues	19.7	25.2	27.5	24.5	26.8
2. Total expenditures	43.3	35.0	30.0	31.9	32.4
a. Interest	2.9	7.1	5.5	4.2	2.9
b. Other expenditures	40.4	27.9	24.5	27.7	29.5
3. Current savings	−11.0	−3.6	1.4	−1.7	1.1
4. Primary deficit $(2b - 1)$	20.6	2.7	−3.0	3.2	2.8
5. Overall deficit $(2 - 1)$	23.5	9.8	2.5	7.4	5.7
6. Financing					
7. External	2.5	4.4	6.0	2.4	5.6
a. Net disbursements	−0.4	0.1	2.2	2.0	3.1
b. Unpaid interest	0.6	3.0	3.9	2.6	3.0
c. Argentinian arrears	2.3	1.2	−0.1	−2.1	−0.5
8. Internal	21.1	5.4	−3.4	5.0	0.1
a. Central bank	20.6	5.2	−4.6	4.3	2.5
b. Floating debt	0.5	0.2	1.1	0.7	−2.4
Memorandum item: Seigniorage[a]	15.1	8.4	2.2	2.1	3.1

Source: Based on data of flows from the Unit for Policy Analysis (UDAPE), Ministry of Planning, La Paz.
a. Defined as $100 \times [H - H(-1)]$ GDP, where H = money base.

The increase in expenditures in 1987 was due to the once-and-for all severance payments to the discharged workers of the state mining enterprises; that year's deficit is thus explained by a structural adjustment and was perceived as such by the public and the international lending institutions. Expenditures as a share of GDP increased again in 1988, to finance a growing investment budget, but, in contrast with 1987, there was a small contribution of current savings.

The overall deficits of the past three years were financed, by and large, by additional external indebtedness, voluntary and involuntary, and by drawing on foreign-exchange reserves. Viewed from another angle, the primary budget exhibited relatively large deficits in the past three years. This, and low seigniorage, imply a *net* (of foreign-exchange reserves) foreign debt/GDP ratio, growing faster than did the excess of the real interest rate *plus* real exchange depreciation over the output growth rate. The question is: how long will this continue, given the fact that current investment rates are very low? The potential fragility of the situation may be anticipated by the public, imperiling stabilization relatively soon.[2] As Makinen (1988, p. 351) warns: "The deficit is being covered by foreign credits, not a reassuring development given the experience of the last thirty years."

Many countries with similar deficits are currently experiencing significantly higher inflation rates. "Normal" budget deficits in Bolivia, however, tend to be larger than in other countries, because a very high proportion of total investment is public: in some years of the 1980s, over 50% of total fixed investment was public, as table 2.7 will show. In general, the recovery of investment is accompanied by some increase in the budget deficit, since current savings are usually not enough to finance public investment. Nonetheless, current savings in the past three years were much too low.

High Deficits in the Current Account of the Balance of Payments

If one looks at the current account, and especially at the trade-account figures in the balance of payments, one notices that the external adjustment has been taken place very slowly (table 2.3). The trade deficits between 1985 and 1988 are explained not only by the fall in exports but also by a surge in imports from their low levels of 1984. The causes of the jump in imports have been hypothesized elsewhere (Morales 1988a). The trade surplus of 1989 is explained by the strong growth of exports of minerals and soybeans.

The current-account deficits were financed by renewed access to foreign financing, by repatriation of capital, and by unidentifiable sources, in which the dishoarding of domestically held dollar bills and the laundering of drug money (the so-called "coca dollars") may be important. Again, as in the case of budget deficits, it is possible to define a "core" trade deficit in a long-term growth perspective, related to the need for counting on net resource transfers from abroad to complement domestic savings (at least until 1997, according to Bolivia, Ministry of Planning, 1989). However, the observed trade deficits of 1986–1988 seem to be higher than the core deficit.

Overvaluation

Before going into the discussion of overvaluation, a short review of the exchange regime may be helpful. The foreign-exchange market is regulated by a Dutch auction mechanism in the central bank, called the *bolsín*. The central bank sets both a floor price and the quantity to be auctioned in each session. Each bidder whose bid exceeds the floor price must pay his bid price. The official exchange rate results from the weighted

Table 2.3
Balance of payments, 1984–1989 (US$ millions).

	1984	1985	1986	1987	1988	1989[a]
1. Trade balance	232.9	−69.4	−117.5	−243.4	−117.4	60.5
Exports FOB	724.5	623.6	556.5	523.8	531.2	723.0
Imports CIF	491.6	693.0	674.0	767.2	648.6	662.5
2. Balance of non-factor services	−18.0	−12.6	−25.0	−16.7	−38.2	−26.0
3. Factor services (net)	−431.2	−362.3	−279.5	−267.7	−252.8	−255.7
4. Net transfers	88.5	80.0	99.0	126.0	137.0	100.3
5. Balance on current account						
a. Non-interest current account	205.0	−54.8	−89.8	−120.7	−31.7	50.9
b. Current account	−127.8	−364.3	−323.0	−401.8	−271.4	−120.9
6. Balance on capital account	−308.9	−230.3	−62.7	226.4	230.4	330.8
7. Exceptional financing	261.8	358.0	359.6	444.7	211.3	103.9
8. Errors and omissions	27.4	179.7	−84.3	−191.1	−102.3	−231.5
9. Overall balance (5b + 6 + 7 + 8)	−147.5	−56.9	−110.4	78.2	68.0	82.3
Memorandum item: Net foreign-exchange reserves	32.7	91.6	216.3	164.9	169.8	18.6

Source: Based on basic data from Central Bank of Bolivia.
a. Preliminary.

average of all accepted bids. Bidders know neither the floor price nor the quantity supplied by the central bank before entering the auction. Their bids (in sealed envelopes and accompanied by banker's checks in Bolivianos) are based on the information provided by the values of those variables in previous auction.

The above description shows that the central bank has several ways of intervening in the *bolsín*, while preserving its image as a market mechanism. A few weeks after the system was implemented, the difference between the official exchange rate and the floor price narrowed to almost nothing, except occasionally. In the rare cases of speculative attacks against the Boliviano, the central bank discreetly increased the amount supplied in the auction in order to align the bid prices with the floor price. Symmetrically, in even more rare cases, the central bank reduced the amount supplied to the auction, to devalue in discrete steps.

Bernholz's (1988) hypothesis that a country following a more expansionary monetary policy than its main trade neighbors will have an undervalued currency was clearly upheld in the parallel foreign-exchange market during the maturation of the hyperinflation. He adds—

from the experience of other stabilizations—that after stabilization the exchange rate should converge to its purchasing-power parity. The Bolivian data posit the question in a slightly different perspective: has stabilization achieved more than a return to purchasing-power parity? In other words, has stabilization led to overvaluation?

Line D1 in table 2.1 seems to provide an affirmative answer to the question above. Significant overvaluation was observed at least until the third quarter of 1988. This assertion is corroborated by the rapid growth in real wages and the CPI of non-tradables in the same period. During 1989, the evolution of the CPI of non-tradables was similar to that of the CPI of tradables. This leads us to believe that overvaluation in that year was similar to the small one of the last quarter of 1988. Lack of data prevents us from reaching more definite conclusions. Note that the number for the second quarter of 1989 is clearly an outlier and may be explained more by events in Bolivia's trade partners than by domestic policy developments.[3] The implications of overvaluation are explored in section 3b.

Low Monetization and High Dollarization
It should be remembered that the hyperinflation caused severe demonetization. Re-monetization after stabilization has been very slow, because the stabilization package depended to a significant extent on a very tight monetary policy. The main instrument of monetary policy is the mandatory deposits of public enterprises with the central bank.

Although the monetary aggregates have grown on average more rapidly than inflation, the pace has not been enough given the initial demonetization. The general rule, when the stabilization program was launched, was that the money base would grow only with the accumulation of foreign reserves. In fact, that principle was not always followed. Even if the strong seasonal effects are discounted, great fluctuations in the rates of growth are observed (table 2.1, lines B1–B3). The expansions and contractions in base money and M1 indicate an active money supply policy, with a reaction function to the inflation rate, with a lag of one period; monetary policy has not been at all accommodating.

The growth in M3, that includes the dollarized deposits, was very strong during 1986 when most of the capital repatriation took place. Ratios of mid-year M1 to GDP were 2.9%, 4.2%, 4.4%, and 5.1% for 1986, 1987, 1988, and 1989, respectively. (Compare these numbers with an average of 9.8% during the 1970s.) Almost as a mirror image of low monetization, dollarization is very significant (figure 2.2). By the end of 1989, 84% of bank deposits were in dollars or in dollar-denominated accounts (see line C1 in table 2.1). In addition, the quantity of dollar bills in circulation in the domestic economy, although not known with precision, is believed to be very significant.

The domestic banking system offers two main types of dollarized deposits, in the form of certificates of deposit (CDs): (1) time deposits in dollars (dollar deposits) and (2) time deposits denominated in Bolivianos but indexed to the official exchange rate (dollar-indexed deposits).

Interest on these deposits is paid in the currency of the deposit, although in both cases they are first computed in dollars. Similarly, the principal is returned in the currency of the deposit, after adjustment to the exchange rate in the case of deposits in Bolivianos. Incidentally, some banks also offer demand deposits and savings passbooks in dollars. The reserve requirement for dollar deposits and dollar-indexed deposits is *currently* identical to the one for time deposits in Bolivianos (10%), and lower than for demand deposits and savings passbooks (20%).

The low degree of monetization after stabilization does not necessarily reflect a low demand for M1, at least initially. No doubt, the institutional change in the domestic banking system, with the reopening of dollar accounts, reduced the demand for M1. But after discounting this factor,

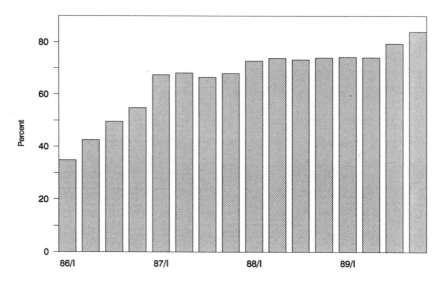

Figure 2.2
Dollarization in the banking system (dollarized deposits in total deposits).

the observed low level of monetization may reflect the short side of a market in disequilibrium rather than any lack of faith in the stabilization program.

In the dollarization process, the effects of repatriation must be distinguished from the effects of portfolio shifts. It should be stressed that the repatriated capital has been placed, almost entirely, in dollar deposits. This is the main explanatory factor in the initial rapid growth of dollarized deposits. Also, after stabilization and the reopening of dollar accounts, some of the dollar bills hoarded by the public inside Bolivia were deposited in the banking system. But after mid-1987, repatriation deaccelerated and dollarization was then essentially caused by portfolio shifts.

In Morales 1989a a regression equation to explain the fall of the ratio of M1 to M3 was estimated. The logarithm of the ratio M1/M3 was regressed on the expected rate of devaluation, the spread of the borrowing rate of interest in dollars in the domestic market over the LIBOR rate, a dummy variable (equal to 0 for months before July 1987 and 1 afterward), and a time trend. All variables had coefficients with the expected signs and were significant at the 5% significance level.[4]

High Interest Rates

Extremely high interest rates have been observed since the implementation of the stabilization program (line C2 in table 2.1 and figure 2.3). For our purposes, the interest rate on dollar transactions will be called the "real" interest rate. *Ex post* real interest rates in Bolivianos are also very high, but they are not discussed—for the sake of simplicity and, more important, because most financial transactions are made in dollars anyway.[5]

After a normal jump in real interest rates following stabilization, a further and important increase occurred in mid-1987. Around the same time, the credit market was segmented, with preferential rates for development loans (mostly to pay for imports of capital goods, services, and inputs) and market rates for working capital, trade, and consumption loans. The development loans, financed almost entirely with foreign resources, were supposed—but failed—to reduce demand pressure on the overall credit market.

Several questions, to which we now turn, are related to the determinants of the very high real interest rates in the market.

The tight monetary policy alluded to above may be a first explanatory factor. A second explanation is given by a country risk premium in the

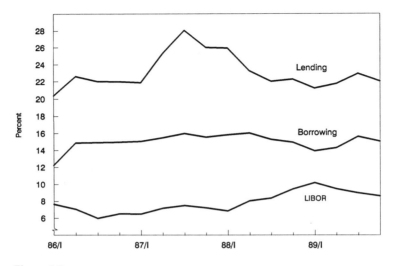

Figure 2.3
Interest rates on dollar transactions.

interest rates, given Bolivia's history of macroeconomic and political instability, its high degree of foreign indebtedness, and the memory of the "dedollarization" measure taken in 1982 (and later repealed). The trouble with this latter argument is that the spread between domestic borrowing rates and international rates *increased* over time, at least until the first quarter of 1988. The risk premium should not have increased as political and macroeconomic stability became established. Moreover, depositors can—and do—hedge against political risks by keeping very-short-term deposits. This observation weakens the risk-premium explanation.

The dynamic behavior of demand provides a third explanation. The demand for loans exhibits a perverse dynamism of its own, with a microeconomic effect of increasing the risk of defaults by banks. Because of forecast and appreciation errors regarding the pace of economic reactivation and the state of the domestic market, many borrowers who had contracted credits at high interest rates found themselves saddled with heavy debts and the need for new loans. The financing of interest payments with new loans caused a ballooning of outstanding debts, and delinquency rates increased rapidly. The proportion of overdue loans in assets (and total loan portfolios) has been unusually high in the past three years (table 2.4).

Table 2.4
Commercial bank portfolios (percent, end-of-period).[a]

	1986	1987	1988				1989			
			I	II	III	IV	I	II	III	IV
Overdue loans/Assets	7.5	8.0	11.4	7.1	10.8	6.3	9.9	7.1	9.8	6.6
Overdue loans/Total loans	n.a.	13.0	18.7	11.4	16.8	9.8	13.9	10.1	13.9	9.0
Overdue loans/Capital	83.4	67.3	111.9	78.4	114.1	61.1	68.4	55.4	81.2	61.2
Refinanced loans/Assets	n.a.	18.0	19.6	21.9	22.0	23.9	26.4	28.7	28.7	28.9
Refinanced loans/Total loans	n.a.	29.2	32.2	35.1	34.1	37.5	36.9	40.8	40.7	39.7
Capital/Assets	8.9	11.9	10.2	9.0	9.5	10.3	14.5	12.8	12.0	10.7
Memorandum item: Lending interest rate for loans in US$ (%)	22.0	29.3	26.0	23.3	22.0	22.3	21.2	21.7	22.9	22.1

Source: Bulletins of the Superintendent of Banks, 1989.
a. Includes only private commercial banks.

The very large spread between the lending and borrowing rates (going back to figure 2.3) is also puzzling. The following, not wholly convincing, explanations have been advanced:

1. The "de-dollarization" measure of 1982 caused banks to suffer severe capital damage. This, together with the deterioration of their portfolios after stabilization, induced many of them to try to (partially) recoup losses out of their performing loans, by charging high interest rates on them.

2. The hyperinflation produced a heavy financial de-intermediation and an extraordinary expansion of "curbside markets." Although substantial progress has been accomplished after stabilization, banks have not yet recovered the scale of their operations before the hyperinflation.

3. The end of the hyperinflation left the banks saddled with large operating costs, coming mainly from overstaffing and overextension of branches. Although banks have significantly trimmed their personnel and closed many branches, they still have to face the costs of maintaining large buildings and other infrastructure in their headquarters. These costs, together with a reduced scale, have been conducive to high unit operating costs.

The large spreads can also be explained by industrial-organization arguments. The domestic commercial banking system comprises only sixteen banks, and hence competition is weak. There is evidence, moreover, of colluded interest-rate fixing. Before 1982, the active presence of a number of branches of large foreign banks provided a more competitive environment, but the regulations on capital movements during the hyperinflation drove many of them away. With the stabilization program, the capital account of the balance of payments has been fully liberalized, but the foreign banks have not returned.

In the past two years, Bolivia has faced two mild banking crises, the first in mid-1987 and the second in mid-1989. The government of Bolivia felt compelled, in 1988, to negotiate a loan with the World Bank to strengthen the private banking sector. A few months earlier, the government had reestablished an independent Superintendent of Banks and Financial Institutions, hoping that this would serve as a timely warning on bank bankruptcies. This institutional reform and the loan averted a further deterioration of the banking system, but the symptoms of frailty remained. During the months of July and August 1989, the banking system was shaken again: the results of the elections prompted a run by depositors. The central bank had to establish a special line of credit to rescue the banks. Fortunately, normalcy was restored by September 1989 and bank deposits have recovered their pre-crisis levels.

The results of my econometric work (Morales 1989a) on the determinants of the interest rates lend support to a combination of tight monetary policy and troubles in the banking sector as the main determinants of high interest rates. The spread of the domestic borrowing interest rate over the LIBOR rate was regressed on its lagged value, the logarithm of M1 (expressed in dollars), and a dummy variable (0 for months before July 1987 and 1 afterward). All variables were significant at the 5% level, except the dummy variable that was significant at the 11% significance level.

Output and Employment

A modest recovery of output has occurred since the second year after stabilization (table 2.5). Small but positive rates of growth of GDP were observed in 1987, 1988, and 1989, following negative rates from 1982 to 1986. Observe, however, the strong recovery in manufacturing and mining in the past two years. Figure 2.4 completes the picture, showing the severe deterioration of living standards until 1986 and the evolution afterward.

It is very hard to come by reliable estimates of unemployment. Numbers initially provided by the Bolivian Ministry of Labor, which showed very high rates of unemployment and which were reported in my previous work (Morales 1988a), have been reviewed by the National Institute of Statistics (NIS), which found significantly lower unemployment rates. The NIS conclusions are based on household data, which are plagued with technical deficiencies. The numbers in line D1 of table 2.5 are based on the original NIS household data, with corrections for consistency, and should be treated as gross estimates.

Regardless of the exact unemployment rate, it is interesting to notice that, in the public's perception—as captured by the pollsters of the major candidates in the May 1989 elections—unemployment appeared to be the most important issue that worried voters. The recovery of employment was the major theme in the electoral campaign.

More than the aggregate loss of jobs, what is clearly identifiable is a change in their quality. As evidence of this change in quality, it has been pointed out that the number of workers enjoying social security and

Table 2.5
Output and employment indicators after the stabilization program.

	1986	1987	1988	1989[e]
A. Rates of growth[a] (annual percentage change rates)				
1. GDP	-2.9	2.1	2.8	2.4
2. Per capita GDP[a]	-5.5	-0.6	0.0	-0.4
3. Per capita private consumption	-2.3	-0.3	-1.5	-0.4
4. Urban labor force	3.7	3.7	4.0	4.0
5. Urban employment[b]	1.7	3.1	4.0	5.5
B. Output indexes (base: 1985 = 100)[a]				
1. GDP	97	99	102	104
2. GDP per capita	94	94	94	94
3. Mining	74	75	106	134
4. Hydrocarbons	96	97	101	104
5. Manufacturing	102	106	110	113
6. Agriculture and livestock	95	95	96	93
7. Construction	92	91	102	110
8. Electricity, gas, and water	104	98	102	107
9. Services	100	104	103	104
C. Export volumes (base: 1985 = 100)[c]	105	97	98	n.a.

D. Urban employment[b]				
1. Unemployed as percent of labor force	12.9	13.4	13.4	12.2
2. Workers affiliated with social security system (thousands)	319	268	n.a.	n.a.
3. Counterfactual: potential affiliations with social security system (thousands)[d]	356	369	384	399
4. Difference between D3 and D2	37	101	n.a.	n.a.
5. Difference D4 as percent of potential affiliations	10.3	27.4	n.a.	n.a.
E. Per capita private consumption (base 1985 = 100)	98	97	96	96

a. Computations based on data provided by the National Institute of statistics.
b. Author's estimates based on basic data from the household surveys for the National Institute of Statistics.
c. Source: International Monetary Fund, International Financial Statistics, December 1989.
d. Estimated as the number of affiliations, had the percentage of affiliations in the labor force of 1985 remained constant.
e. Preliminary.

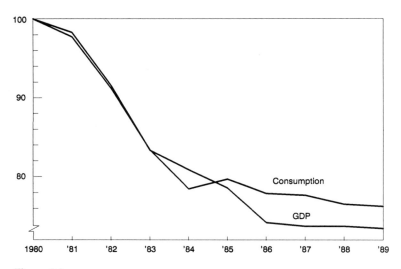

Figure 2.4
GDP and private consumption per capita (index: 1980 = 100).

medical coverage decreased from 343,000 to 268,000 between 1985 and 1987. This difference represented around 6.2% of the urban labor force in 1985.

The loss in jobs (and potential jobs) with social security coverage can be directly attributed to the stabilization program; however, there may have been other causes (of a more structural nature) at work, such as the fall in the terms of trade, the gains in labor productivity in the manufacturing and mining sectors, and, more generally, the transition from a distorted position to a less distorted one (Makinen 1988). The case of dismissals in the mining sector provides the best example of unemployment resulting not from anticipation errors but from the need to face reality, if stabilization was to endure. The solution of the long-term structural problems of the mining sector, including substantial overstaffing and decapitalization, became urgent once the tin market collapsed. The market collapse *and* the stabilization program precipitated the correction that had been postponed for years.

The arguments citing the tin-mining sector can be extended to other sectors. In a society with a large agrarian sector and non-structured (or informal) urban sectors, the unemployment effects of stabilization, based on an analysis of the (expectations augmented) Phillips curve, are of limited relevance. Wage employment, where problems of nominal wage rigidity could be present, is relatively small, and even there labor contracts with very explicit incorporation of expected inflation are not very common. Without denying that some unemployment resulted from anticipation errors, the most clearly identifiable cause of unemployment in the stabilization package was the discharging of about 10% of the labor force in the public sector. Many of the dismissed workers could not be rapidly relocated in other sectors of the economy, for reasons such as age and education.

A very detailed distinction between the unemployment caused by anticipation errors and wage rigidities, on the one hand, and by structural factors, on the other hand, does not seem to be very fruitful for policy design. The fact that stabilization had a hard landing in sectors that needed structural adjustment is of concern for current policy, even for aggregate-demand policy.

2. Further Thoughts on the Bolivian Stabilization

Inflation Low but Above International Levels

Bolivia's inflation, low by Latin American standards, is still significantly higher than the inflation rate in the industrialized countries of the West. The Bolivian pattern, after stabilization, has been one of generally low rates broken by sudden outbursts, usually following strong devaluations and/or hikes in the domestic prices of fuels. This pattern can be traced back to the initial strong overvaluation of the Boliviano after stabilization, to the indexation rules for public prices discussed in section 3b, and, equally important, to external shocks generated in the macroeconomic instability of Bolivia's neighbors (and trade partners).

In an attempt to redress the initial overvaluation, the government increased the rate of crawl of the exchange rate during 1987 and until the second quarter of 1988. Moreover, exchange-rate correction was called for by the rapid depreciations in the neighboring countries undergoing high inflation. During this phase of exchange-rate correction, however, the indexation rule for the domestic prices of oil derivatives was not enforced.

The need to correct the fall in the relative price of fuels became urgent after the warning given by the high budget deficits of 1987 and early 1988. The correction was made in April 1988. This, together with the accumulated depreciation, induced a round of price adjustments across the economy. Relative price adjustments in Peru and Argentina also drove the Bolivian inflation up. The rate of the crawl was reduced in the second half of 1988 to quell inflationary pressures. The slow-crawl policy was continued during the first half of 1989, given the added ingredient of an election year. The banking crisis, following the elections of May 1989, was accompanied by a speculation against the Boliviano that caused a jump in the exchange rate. This jump was followed by increases in the price of fuels, and a new round in price hikes, which lasted until the end of 1989, began.

Real Wages in the Private Sector

Real wages in the private sector have shown a surprising dynamism since the second semester of 1986. Three factors may explain this:

1. Real wages hit an abnormally low level in the first quarter after the stabilization program was launched. Wages could not be sustained at that level for long without disrupting production in a significant way.

2. Major structural changes also explain the rapid increase in real wages. The work force in the manufacturing sector became leaner, productivity increased, and the workers who stayed obtained important wage hikes. With a lag of about one year, the production in the privately owned mines picked up momentum, with more capital-intensive technologies and a smaller work force than before stabilization, and real wage growth ensued. The substantial wage growth in construction can be explained by the active policy of public works financed by the local municipalities and the Social Emergency Fund. The municipalities are the main beneficiaries of the tax reform of 1986. The Social Emergency Fund is a broad program of poverty alleviation financed with international donations.

3. Some enterprises expected a stronger recovery in 1987 and thus acquiesced in the demands of their workers for wage increases. In addition, starting in the first months of 1987 and until the first quarter of 1988, devaluation proceeded at a relatively fast pace (at least faster than right before), affecting expectations. A significant share of the wage increases can be attributed to expectation errors with regard to both the extent of economic reactivation and the rate of devaluation.

The Role of External Finance

The importance of foreign financing and adequate foreign-exchange reserves in the stabilization experiences after hyperinflation has been underscored by several authors (see, e.g., Dornbusch 1988). The Bolivian case is no exception. Indeed, a major objective in the design of the stabilization program was to reestablish relations with official international creditors. As a first measure, the government had to prepare for negotiations with the International Monetary Fund (IMF). It was correctly assumed that the nature of the stabilization program would make it acceptable to the IMF, except for the thorny requirement of resumption of payments (eventually, after rescheduling) to the creditor foreign commercial banks.

While negotiations with the IMF were in progress, the only foreign support that Bolivia received took the form of involuntary lending, with the suspension of its external debt service with the commercial creditors. After a while, the Bolivian efforts at stabilization received full, although slow, support from the official international lending agencies. In June 1986 Bolivia reached a stand-by arrangement with the IMF, the first since 1980, fully nine months after the stabilization program had begun. The IMF waived its requirement of an agreement with the commercial banks. In 1988, Bolivia obtained another loan from the IMF as Enhanced Structural Adjustment Financing (ESAF). Other official creditors, including the Andean Reserve Fund and the World Bank, followed in the IMF's path, with loans to strengthen foreign-exchange reserves. Bolivia also benefited from medium-term and long-term development loans from the Inter American Development Bank, the Andean Development Corporation, the World Bank, and foreign governments. Assistance to the Social Emergency Fund, much of it in the form of donations, was also very important.

Net disbursements in the period 1986–1988 on long-term and medium-term loans amounted to US$518 million; net short-term disbursements and net loans from the IMF totaled around US$100 million (see also table 2.6). The net debt increase in the past three years differs significantly from the net disbursements because of the important reschedulings in the Paris Club of 1986 and 1988. There was also a debt cancellation in 1988 in the form of a debt buy-back from the private foreign banks for US$407 million. A mutual cancellation of outstanding debts between Argentina and Bolivia was agreed to in October 1989. This reduced Bolivia's gross debt by US$720 million.

Net transfers on account of the long-term and medium-term loans to the NFPS became positive in 1986, after having been highly negative between 1982 and 1985. There was a substantial positive net resource transfer in 1986. After that, the transfers declined.

Table 2.6
External public debt indicators, 1985–1988.

	1985	1986	1987	1988
A. Long-term debt (US$ millions)				
1. Stock of debt outstanding and disbursed	3,484	4,064	4,599	4,569
2. Disbursements	133	345	209	258
3. Principal repayments	177	106	74	114
4. Net disbursements (2 − 3)	−44	239	135	144
5. Interest payments	156	100	62	93
6. Total debt service (3 + 5)	333	206	136	207
7. Net transfers (4 − 5)	−200	139	73	51
B. Long-term debt (percent of GDP)				
1. Stock of debt outstanding and disbursed	101.4	101.2	107.2	100.0
2. Disbursements	3.9	8.6	4.9	5.6
3. Principal repayments	5.2	2.6	1.7	2.5
4. Net disbursements	−1.3	5.9	3.1	3.2
5. Interest payments	4.5	2.5	1.4	2.0
6. Total debt service	9.7	5.1	3.2	4.5
7. Net resource transfers	−5.8	3.5	1.7	1.1
C. Short-term debt (US$ millions)	650	765	608	681
D. Operations with the IMF (US$ millions)				
1. Use of IMF credit	51	145	141	145
2. Purchases	0	113	0	61
3. Repurchases	19	30	25	49
E. Total (A1 + C + D1) (US$ millions)	4,185	4,974	5,348	5,395
Memorandum item: GDP in US$ millions	3,434	4,018	4,289	4,571

Source: Dollar values from World Bank, World Debt Tables 1988–89 and 1989–90
editions; dollar GDP estimates by author based on official accounts.

The fresh loans and the debt-service alleviation helped to rebuild foreign-exchange reserves and to finance development projects. Equally important, the resumption of international credits helped to strengthen domestic confidence in the stabilization program.

Repatriation of capital has also been significant since the stabilization plan was announced, as mentioned above. Dollar and dollar-linked time deposits in the banking system grew from $24 million in December 1985 to $490 million by the end of 1989 (around 10.5% of that year's GDP).

The Political Features of Adjustment

The following delimitation of periods in Bolivia's recent history should help in the discussion. The hyperinflation happened during the presidency of Hernn Siles-Zuazo from October 1982 to July 1985. Stabilization began in the last quarter of 1985 and was implemented during Victor Paz-Estenssoro's mandate, which lasted until July 1989. The successor of Paz-Estenssoro, Jaime Paz-Zamora, inaugurated his presidency in August 1989. He continues the economic policy of his predecessor.

The Weakening of the Labor Movement

In spite of its low degree of industrialization, Bolivia has traditionally had a very powerful labor movement, with *de facto* veto power over many government regulations. The fact that the labor unions courageously opposed the military dictatorships of the 1970s and the early 1980s gave them a strong voice during the first government of the transition to democracy.

Not unexpectedly, the domestic adjustments required by the changes in the external environment in 1982–83 were resisted by the unions, since they implied large cuts in real wages. The unions federated in the Confederation of Bolivian Workers (COB) objected to every attempt at stabilization. The Siles-Zuazo administration, facing unbearable social unrest, repeatedly conceded large nominal wage increases financed with seigniorage. This lenient policy explains why, in the eyes of the public, the wage race was the most important source of money expansion.

The stabilization program of August 1985 was at first opposed by the leadership of the COB, but this did not last. The earlier stabilization attempts and the opposition to them both eroded the strength of the unions and provided information on the costs of stabilization relative to the cost of failing to combat inflation. Also, the unemployment that had been building up since the hyperinflation years reduced the militancy of the unions and lent credibility to the threats of dismissals by the employers. Furthermore, the government took some strong measures to control social unrest, including a short-lived state of emergency and the confinement of labor leaders in remote villages for 15 days.

The layoff of 23,000 out of 30,000 miners—the backbone of the labor movement—administered the *coup de grace* to militancy. Since then, the COB officials have had huge difficulties in asserting their leadership: their calls for strikes have gone mostly unheard and have not been followed by the rank and file.

The weakening of the labor movement facilitated the adoption of the drastic stabilization program. The Paz-Estenssoro government did not feel, at any time, the need for a social pact or an incomes policy.

The Pact for Democracy

No less instrumental than the taming of the labor movement was the Pact for Democracy signed between the two main political parties, the Nationalist Revolutionary Movement (MNR) of President Paz-Estenssoro and Nationalist Democratic Action (ADN) of former president General Hugo Banzer. The two parties agreed to carry on the stabilization program proposed by the MNR. In consequence, crucial legislation in support of the program, including the tax reform and the budgets, was readily passed in Congress. Also, the Executive, in the hands of the MNR, was freed from the supervision of Congress and received full powers.

The Pact for Democracy was also helpful in gathering support for the program in the press, as most Bolivian newspapers, radio, and TV stations are owned or controlled by members of ADN.

The stabilization program has gained broad and persistent public support in spite of its admitted cost. In the last elections (held in May 1989), almost four years after the stabilization program went into effect, the three major parties proposed to continue it. They obtained 65.4% of the popular vote and absolute control of Congress.

The Signals to Establish Credibility

Adherence to the announced stabilization policies, external adversities notwithstanding, was the banner of the Paz-Estenssoro government and the most important source of credibility. The tenacity of purpose in maintaining stabilization seems, *ex post*, to have been duly appreciated by the public and the markets.

Commitments on the growth of monetary emission initially provided the nominal anchor in the stabilization program. A drastic reduction in the growth rate of the money base was clearly an identifiable and credible initial move in the government's attempt to stop hyperinflation (Kiguel and Liviatan 1988). Moreover, a tight rein on the issuing of money at the beginning of the program, when virtually all prices in the private sector were fully flexible and when the central bank's reserves were almost nil (US$30 million), was tantamount to fixing the nominal exchange rate in the parallel market and also fixing the official exchange rate, given that exchange-rate unification was a major policy tenet.[6] The situation changed four months after the beginning of the stabilization program, with the constitution of foreign-exchange reserves. At that moment, the government anchored inflation more explicitly on the exchange rate. The exchange-rate regime, initially presented to the public as flexible, then became heavily administered.

The tight money policy needed a complementary fiscal-policy signal. The government found such a signal in a very strong stance with regard to nominal wage increases in the public sector. The government's skirmishes with the public-sector labor unions over nominal wage increases were perhaps the most important signal (certainly more important than tax reform) to the general public of its commitment to maintain stabilization.

Other institutional factors also helped credibility. For instance, the non-market mechanisms of protection against inflation in Bolivia are relatively underdeveloped. Wage-indexation arrangements are nonexistent, and in the financial markets dollarization of assets works differently than the incorporation of expected inflation in the interest rate. This made it easy for the government not to try to cheat the public with surprise inflation. There was no temptation to bypass indexation arrangements, for example, to correct relative prices. In addition, the government could not use inflation to liquidate public debt, since virtually all of it is external.[7]

3. The Resumption of Growth

The Measures of Structural Adjustment

The stabilization program of August 1985 included, or was followed by, ample liberalization of the markets for goods and credit, deregulation of the labor market, and reduction of the size of the state in the economy.

Liberalization of foreign trade has, however, been somewhat hesitant. Between 1985 and 1989 at least four major changes in the tariff schedule have taken place. Tariffs currently have two rates, 17% for most imports and 10% for a list of capital goods. In fact, the tariff status is still very unstable.

Abrupt trade liberalization played a non-negligible role in the immediate aftermath of the stabilization program. As Pastor (1988, p. 24) observes, "import competition, coupled with exchange rate stability, essentially played the role price controls served in the heterodox program of Bolivia's neighbors: domestic producers were constrained from raising prices beyond the exchange rate times the relevant dollar price."

But trade liberalization in the post-stabilization phase, together with other elements in current economic policy, has created other, more structural, problems. Competition from imports has made the price of tradables lag behind those of other goods and services. For instance, the consumer prices of tradable foodstuffs trail behind the prices of non-tradable foodstuffs and the overall consumer price index (Morales 1989b). The clearest case is that of agro-industrial prices and prices of produce from large agricultural estates in eastern Bolivia, which fell substantially relative to other prices. Also, imports that compete with these products registered significant volume increases.

The income losses brought about by liberalization (initially coupled with overvaluation) have created strong pressures on the government by associations of large agricultural producers and industrialists for more protection. The government yielded to some of their demands—for instance, import quotas for sugar and edible oils have been reestablished.

The stabilization program recovered the principle of free contracting in the labor market. This deregulation reduced the employers' costs and administrative hurdles to discharging redundant workers. In another deregulation move, the backward wage-indexation mechanism in force between 1982 and 1985 was completely dismantled. Also, the wage regime was reformed and simplified by consolidating to a basic yearly wage a myriad of bonuses, most of which had been granted during the high-inflation years.[8]

Free contracting has not eliminated all rigidities in the labor market. The significant increases in real wages, discussed in section 2b, can be offered as proof of this assertion.

The previous administration and the new one announced their intention to disinvest, but no significant privatization has yet taken place. Reductions in the size of government have meant, essentially, substantial reductions in the public-sector payroll.

Short-Term Policies to Restore Growth

The Consolidation of Stabilization
The viewpoint of the past two governments was that the preservation of stabilization is a necessary condition for the restoration of growth. A further lowering of the inflation rate is also deemed necessary. Stabilization in a broad sense, that is, with no significant distortions in relative prices, should increase the marginal efficiency of the required new

investments. With the current policies, the government aims at an annual GDP growth of 4–4.5% for the next four years, with a relatively modest (gross) fixed investment/GDP rate of 14%.[9]

The Bolivian government has also been emphasizing that the reduction in uncertainty, brought about by stabilization, will help boost private investment. The resurgence of the manufacturing sector after stabilization is cited as a proof of this assertion. Stability is also seen as a necessary condition for attracting crucial direct foreign investment.

The emphasis on stabilization as a means to achieve growth does not, however, seem obvious. There are frequent proposals in the press, and even in academic circles, for more expansionary domestic demand policies.

The Strengthening of Public Finances

Fiscal equilibrium has top priority on the government's agenda, and fear of inflation is not the only explanation. Public-sector savings are essential for the constitution of local counterpart funds necessary for the disbursement of contracted foreign loans.

Full implementation of the ongoing tax reform is one of the pillars of fiscal policy. The other pillar is the maintenance of the real value of revenues from the public sector's domestic sale of foreign exchange and goods and services. On the other hand, savings that are brought about by lags in wages of civil servants and by slashing spending on education and health are unsustainable. Not only does the government's efficiency suffer, but, worse, this type of policy may negatively affect private investment.

The level of and the changes in the exchange rate have significant revenue implications, since the public sector is a net supplier of foreign exchange to the rest of the economy. The current indexation arrangements of the exchange rate and public prices present some interesting aspects. Bolivia has been *loosely* following a crawling-peg exchange rate and a policy of indexing the price of oil derivatives (and of other publicly provided goods) to the exchange rate of the previous month.[10] With these indexation rules, inflationary shocks (like a stepwise increase in wages, in the exchange rate, or in foreign prices) do have an impact, but the effects on the persistence and the fluctuations of inflation are rather limited. However, as the initial impact on inflation was sometimes large, the authorities tended to skip indexation for long periods. But then, as lags accumulated in the exchange rate and in public prices, the authorities resorted to overindexation until the next shock. Overindexation can take on a precise meaning, as in Morales 1989a. For present purposes, let us simply state that overindexation exists when the factors of indexation are much higher than 100%.

In the presence of overindexation, even if the inflation rate ultimately converges to the international inflation rate (which is not always the case), its persistence may eventually lead to wage indexation or, worse, to disorderly escalating wage increases that will probably be financed by money creation in the public sector. At that point inflation would accelerate. Clearly, this sets limits to the indexation rules.

Last but not least, given the limits of taxation and of revenues from the sale of goods and services, it appears that the big push to reach a sustainable expenditure program and to restore liquidity in the public sector has to come from vigorous moves toward privatization.

Overvaluation Revisited

Although by the end of 1989 overvaluation did not seem to be very important, its implications for Bolivia's activity levels and economic recovery are worth analyzing.

First there is the question of how disruptive overvaluation is for trade flows. Bolivia exports mainly natural gas and minerals, whose prices are either fixed in foreign exchange in international markets (minerals) or result from negotiations within the limits of a bilateral monopoly (sales of natural gas to Argentina). Exchange-rate overvaluation, unless absurdly high, has a minor impact on the profitability and the level of activity of firms in these sectors. But non-traditional exports and the import-competing industries can be severely hurt. For instance, the substantial increase in the supply of smuggled goods is evidence of the impact of overvaluation on the import-competing industries.

Second, it is well known that overvaluation increases speculative demand for foreign exchange and capital flight. But it is also true that capital movements are not independent of the way in which the exchange rate is corrected. A stepwise devaluation of sufficient magnitude can stop speculative movements. But stepwise devaluations are dangerous, especially in view of the experience of the hyperinflation years, during which many of them took place. Moreover, with a discrete devaluation, the *bolsín*, which has worked reasonably well in exchange-rate unification, may lose credibility. A more rapid crawl of the Boliviano in the *bolsín* has its own shortcomings, as has been argued above.

Third, although there is no conclusive empirical evidence, theoretical considerations suggest that the tight monetary policy referred to above, in face of relatively high budget deficits, gives rise to continuous (but how large?) real appreciation of the exchange rate. Also, rapid capital repatriation, prompted by the high interest rates, may have been behind overvaluation in the first two years after stabilization began.

The Behavior of Investment

The crisis of the 1980s has produced a very substantial decline in investment rates (table 2.7). The investment rates in the private sector were particularly low in the past four years.

Low investment rates in the private sector are conventionally explained by the prevailing macroeconomic disequilibria. But the effect of credibility, not on stabilization, but on long-term developments seems as important. Fears of a future reversal of policies still prevail in the private sector. In this context, the persistent weakness of public finances may awaken fears of future confiscatory measures against the private sector through exchange-rate manipulations, punitive taxes, or outright expropriation. Underinvestment and lack of maintenance of social overhead also contribute to the shyness in private investment.

To reactivate the economy and *a fortiori* to resume growth, while at the same time maintaining stabilization, seems significantly more difficult than it was to stop inflation. Even if stabilization, with all its components

Table 2.7
Fixed investment, 1980–1988 (percent of GDP in current Bolivianos).

	Private	Public	Total
1980	7.3	6.9	14.2
1981	4.5	9.5	14.0
1982	5.6	7.4	13.0
1983	3.3	8.4	11.7
1984	3.8	8.4	12.2
1985	2.7	8.1	10.8
1986	2.9	3.2	6.1
1987	2.8	3.1	5.9
1988[a]	2.5	3.2	5.7

Source: World Bank, Bolivia: Country Economic Memorandum, September 1989.
a. Estimated.

including real interest rates convergent to the international ones, is established, it will not suffice, in the words of Dornbusch (1989b), "to provide an *automatic* mechanism of crowding in significant growth." Many other factors are needed, some of which have been discussed above. A generous inflow of foreign resources, full reassurances to domestic private investors that foreign aid will be forthcoming, the creation of a social infrastructure, and the strengthening of the judiciary to avoid uncertainties as to the full enjoyment of property rights are, *inter alia*, the required ingredients for the formation of an optimistic environment for private investment and, ultimately, growth.

Given both Bolivia's natural resources and its structural obstacles, foreign investment is expected primarily in mining and hydrocarbons. A substantial influx of private foreign capital could create a climate in which investment by Bolivians in all sectors of the economy, financed with capital repatriation, will boom. This scenario actually happened in the 1960s, in the medium-term aftermath of the successful stabilization of December 1956.

4. Concluding Remarks

The Bolivian experience quite clearly shows that, in the post-stabilization period following hyperinflation, the combination of heavy doctoring of the exchange rate, tight monetary policy, and limits on the rate of growth of fiscal expenditures on non-traded goods and services can indeed sustain price stability. Price stability obtained in this way is also more resilient than was believed at first. The strong political alliances supporting the program and the renewed access to foreign lending significantly contributed to the maintenance of stability.

While price stability is a fact, the recovery of the Bolivian economy still has a long way to go. Of all the obstacles, the low investment rates, especially those of the private sector, are the most worrisome for the medium-term outlook. It seems that one way in which the pessimistic equilibrium, with low investment, can be broken is by actively attracting direct foreign investment into mining and hydrocarbons. These moves could then be followed by investment by Bolivians financed with repatriated capital.

Another key element for recovery is the formation of savings and the restoration of liquidity in the public sector. Fiscal equilibrium has proved more elusive a goal than originally believed. The maintenance of a remunerative exchange rate and the continuous alignment of public and other prices is essential, together with continuation of the ongoing tax reform, to redress the situation. Privatization may give the needed big push toward a sustainable fiscal equilibrium. On the other hand, the maintenance of fiscal equilibrium by indiscriminately slashing spending on social services is unsustainable in the medium run.

Part of the persistence of a domestic inflation rate above the international level can be explained by the casual way of applying indexation to the exchange rate and public prices. While substantial progress has been made in correcting the initial overvaluation, the question is now: how stable is the situation? There is also the additional problem of the current activist exchange-rate policy having increased undesirable dollarization.

The interest-rate problem is almost as difficult to tackle as the fiscal weakness. It is also as urgent, since a significant share of the instability in the banking system can be attributed to the high interest rates now prevailing. The recurrent banking crises could devastate macroeconomic stability.

Acknowledgments

I am grateful to Nissan Liviatan, Jaime de Melo, Paul McNellis, Gonzalo Chavez, Alfredo Canavese, and an anonymous referee for very useful suggestions on earlier drafts of this article. Gonzalo Castro provided research assistance.

Notes

1. Unfortunately, lack of available data precludes consolidation of the NFPS deficit with that of the central bank. Domestic sales of Certificates of Deposit (CDs) by the central bank to the public, to constitute foreign-exchange reserves, have been taking place in the last two years. Although the CDs command very high interest rates, the small size of the current stock (no more than 1.3% of GDP) makes servicing them low. This service is, of course, one source of the central bank's deficit.

2. My misgivings are supported by the growing literature on intertemporal tradeoffs. See, e.g., Sargent and Wallace 1981, Drazen and Helpman 1988, and Blanchard and Fischer 1989.

3. The figures in table 2.1, line D1, are derived from averages of the official exchange rates and the parallel market exchange rates of the country's trade partners. This procedure abounds with technical difficulties, but the alternatives are even worse.

4. The expected devaluation rate was estimated by a distributed lag of current and past rates of devaluation. The coefficients of the distributed lags were assumed to lie on a second-degree polynomial with a far-end zero restriction. Their sum was found to be significant at the 5% significance level. All the other independent variables were significant at the same significance level.

5. Strictly speaking, the *ex post* real interest rates on dollar operations, valued domestically, will be lower than the "real interest rate" as defined here for convenience, in the presence of exchange-rate appreciation.

6. It seems that, at that moment, the conditions (as discussed, e.g., in Helpman and Leiderman 1988) for the equivalence for exchange-rate management and monetary policy were met.

7. The ratio of external debt to GDP can be reduced, however, with very high inflation that causes lags in the real exchange rate, as may happen in advanced cases of hyperinflation. But in general, external indebtedness allays fears of using inflation for the purpose of debt liquidation. However, expectations of disruptions in net resource transfers from abroad evoked, on occasion, the possibility of rapid exchange-rate depreciation and, hence, inflation.

8. The only bonus that remained was the Christmas bonus. The consolidation, although not crucial for the stabilization package, was more than a cosmetic move, in the sense that it smoothed out the seasonality of cash outlays by the government and private enterprises. Seasonal effects, coupled with an index-ation mechanism for the exchange rate and public prices, could give more persistence to inflation than is desired.

9. See Bolivia, Ministry of Planning, 1989.

10. The rules for indexation of public prices were set out in stabilization decree SD 21060 (August 1985).

References

Bernholz, Peter. 1988. "Hyperinflation and currency reform in Bolivia: Studied from a general perspective." *Journal of Institutional and Theoretical Economics* 144: 747–771.

Blanchard, Olivier Jean, and Stanley Fischer. 1989. *Lectures on Macroeconomics*. MIT Press.

Bolivia, Ministry of Planning. 1989. *Estrategia de Desarrollo Económico y Social, 1989–2000.* [Economic and Social Development Strategy, 1989–2000.] (In Spanish.)

Dornbusch, Rudiger. 1988. Notes on Credibility and Stabilization. NBER Working Paper no. 2790.

Dornbusch, Rudiger. 1989a. "Credibility, debt and unemployment: Ireland's failed stabilization." *Economic Policy* 8 (April): 174–201.

Dornbusch, Rudiger. 1989b. Short Term Macroeconomic Policies for Stabilization and Growth. Manuscript, MIT.

Drazen, Allan, and Elhanan Helpman. 1988. Inflationary Consequences of Anticipated Macroeconomic Policies. Manuscript, Tel Aviv University.

Helpman, Elhanan, and Leonardo Leiderman. 1988. "Stabilization in high inflation countries: Analytical foundations and recent experiences." *Carnegie-Rochester Series on Public Policy* 28: 9–84.

Kiguel, Miguel A., and Nissan Liviatan. 1988. "Inflationary rigidities and orthodox stabilization policies: Lessons from Latin America." *World Bank Economic Review* 2, no. 3: 273–298.

Makinen, Gail E. 1988. "Inflation stabilization in Bolivia: Comment." In *Inflation Stabilization: The Experience of Israel, Argentina, Brazil, Bolivia and Mexico*, M. Bruno, G. di Tella, R. Dornbusch, and S. Fisher, eds. (MIT Press).

Morales, Juan Antonio. 1988a. "Inflation stabilization in Bolivia." In *Inflation Stabilization: The Experience of Israel, Argentina, Brazil, Bolivia and Mexico*, M. Bruno, G. di Tella, R. Dornbusch, and S. Fisher, eds. (MIT Press).

Morales, Juan Antonio. 1988b. "The end of the Bolivian hyperinflation." *Vierteljahres Berichte* 114: 385–402.

Morales, Juan Antonio. 1989a. The Post-Stabilization Problems in Bolivia. Universidad Católica Boliviana, Instituto de Investigaciones Socio-económicas DT 89/06.

Morales, Juan Antonio. 1989b. Impacto de los ajustes estructurales en la agricultura campesina Boliviana [The impact of structural adjustments on the Bolivian peasant economy]. Manuscript, Oficina de la Cooperación Técnica Suiza, COTESU, La Paz.

Pastor, Manuel, Jr. 1988. Bolivia: Hyperinflation, Stabilization and Beyond. Manuscript, Occidental College.

Sachs, Jeffrey. 1986. The Bolivian Hyperinflation and Stabilization. NBER Working Paper no. 2073.

Sachs, Jeffrey. 1987. "The Bolivian hyperinflation and stabilization." *American Economic Review* 77, no. 2: 279–283.

Sargent, Thomas, and Neil Wallace. 1981. "Some unpleasant monetarist arithmetic." *Quarterly Review*, Federal Reserve Bank of Minneapolis.

Comments by Peter Bernholz

Morales has presented a comprehensive review of the problems faced by Bolivia after 1985. The analysis of the rather unsatisfactory growth performance is important from a theoretical and from an economic policy perspective. Only after understanding the reasons can successful additional measures be designed.

Given the complexity of the problems, my critique should not detract from the merits of the paper. The following points will be taken up. I will first discuss overvaluation and remonetization. Next, the reasons for the unsatisfactory real performance will be commented on. Finally, I turn to preconditions for sustained growth.

The Development of the Real Exchange Rate and Its Consequences

Morales believes (though he feels uncertain) that an overvaluation of the Bolivian currency has developed since 1985. By contrast, my impression is that the currency is still somewhat undervalued compared to the US$, although the selection of a base year and of adequate price indices is an issue. Anyhow, no further revaluation has occurred since the first quarter of 1987 (table 2.1). Moreover, the real value of the U.S. dollar has fallen substantially compared to the yen and the DM since 1985.

Morales is right that a tendency exists for the Boliviano to be overvalued compared to the currencies of Bolivia's neighbors since 1985. This is caused by the higher inflations in these countries, which leads to strong competition (Bernholz 1987), and it encourages smuggling. It is difficult to change this situation without monetary reforms in the neighboring countries.

It should be noted that the decrease of undervaluation from 1985–1986, together with the overvaluation compared to neighbors and the initial liberalization, can explain the pressures for more protection from industrialists and large agricultural producers.

Missing Institutional Safeguards Causing Bad Performance

We concluded that the credibility of the monetary and fiscal reforms of 1985 is still in doubt and may even be decreasing. The banking crisis of July and August 1989, following the elections, seems to confirm this impression. The lack of confidence in the permanency of the reforms is quite understandable, given the still high budget deficit financed by foreign credits and a reduction in foreign-exchange reserves (table 2.1).

According to Morales, credibility in the permanent nature of the reforms is secured by a consensus among political parties (first by the Pact for Democracy), by the debilitating effect of populism, and by the weakening of union power as a result of the experiences during the hyperinflation and the reform measures taken. I submit that these factors have not been sufficient to create the necessary level of credibility, as proved by the somewhat unsatisfactory results. Institutional safeguards, such as independence of the central bank, and statutory limitation of the budget deficit and the amount of credit which the central bank is allowed to extend to the government, are missing. This is reflected in the substantial budget deficit and its financing. More fundamentally, adequate institutional limitations of the discretionary powers of government would have to be protected against erosion, e.g., by stipulating in the constitution that simple majorities of parliament are not allowed to remove them, and by preventing a violation of such rules with the help of an independent constitutional court. Note that in the most successful currency reforms, institutional safeguards have been ingredients of the reforms. In Germany, for example, the new Rentenbank refused to grant additional credit demanded by the government one month after the reform. It could do so because it was forbidden by law to extend credit beyond a certain limit. This provision and the independence of the central bank saved the reform. It also stabilized expectations for the permanent nature of the reforms.

Morales rightly insists on the difference between confidence in monetary stability and securing property rights (including the safeguarding against exchange-rate manipulations, outright expropriation, varying regulations, and excessive taxes): "But the effect of credibility, not on stabilization, but on long-term developments, seems as important. Fears of a future reversal of policies still prevail in the private sector" (section 3). Excessive interest rates on dollar deposits and their short-term nature can—apart from inefficiencies and bad debtor risk in the banking sector—only be explained if creditors are afraid that they may once again be turned into deposits denominated in local currency, be blocked for some time, converted into low interest bonds, or be expropriated.

Low investment is caused not only by high interest rates, but also by the risk of expropriation or of not being able to repatriate dividends, interest earnings, and capital. These facts are rightly stressed by Morales, but they also extend to the credibility of the permanence of monetary and fiscal reforms. Thus, the fears of future exchange-rate manipulations (section 3) are not only detrimental to investment, but also to inflationary expectations. The same is true for "the persistent weakness of public finances" (section 3). Since no institutional safeguards exist against a return to deficit financing by money creation, concerns about public finances influence inflationary expectations.

Policies to Restore Growth

It would follow that the most important steps to restore growth should be directed at creating institutions, including a constitutional framework, at securing permanent monetary and fiscal stability, and at secure property rights.

I agree with Morales that it is necessary to reach "a generous inflow of foreign resources, full reassurances to domestic private investors that foreign aid will be forthcoming, the creation of a social infrastructure, and the strengthening of the judiciary to avoid uncertainties as to the full enjoyment of property rights" (section 3), if this statement was correctly understood. Monetary and fiscal stability and secure property rights are preconditions for a generous inflow of foreign resources. But the creation of a "social infrastructure" would rather harm growth if, instead of a better system of checks and balances in the government and a better educational system, this would mean the premature development of a welfare state.

To put it bluntly, the discretionary powers of the administration and of parliament have to be circumscribed, and this can only be achieved by constitutional and institutional reforms. An independent central bank that can refuse to extend credit to the government, constitutional limits on budget deficits and on maximum marginal tax rates, provisions against overt and hidden expropriation without adequate compensation, and an independent judiciary are some of the institutional requirements necessary. Any violation of these rules should be prosecuted in the courts, and changes in the corresponding constitutional rules should require, say, a two-thirds majority in parliament.

The changes required can only be reached with a broad political consensus, which may not emerge without a severe crisis. Also, given the lack of institutional stability, it may be difficult to develop an adequate tradition. But institutional instability lies at the heart of Latin American problems, and it engenders political and economic instability hindering economic growth. Since the latter bring about more institutional instability, only a breaking of this vicious self-reinforcing circle may lead countries like Bolivia out of their predicament.

Reference

Bernholz, Peter. 1987. "The political economy of revaluation—Induced protectionism under discretionary monetary regimes with flexible exchange rates." In *Free Trade in the World Economy*, Herbert Giersch, ed. (Tübingen: JCB Mohr).

Comments by Juan L. Cariaga

Upon reviewing the economic measures implemented in Bolivia between August 1985 and the second half of 1987, I feel it is fair to say that the Bolivian stabilization program was just that—a stabilization program. It was also accompanied by a structural adjustment reform, designed to transform the Bolivian economy into a market-oriented system. However, it did not claim to be a plan for economic recovery, let alone a strategy for economic and social development. It was designed to lay the groundwork for sound fiscal and monetary management and to establish the ground rules governing the actions of economic agents. Its ultimate objective was to restore economic credibility at home and abroad, which had been severely eroded during the years of hyperinflation. This objective was largely met, earning the recognition of international institutions and of the Bolivian people. The results of the 1989 elections demonstrated the widespread public support for continuing the stabilization and adjustment measures.

In his interesting and comprehensive study on the subject, Morales takes a critical look at the results of the Bolivian stabilization program during the transition from stability to sustained growth. He is gloomy, however, in his assessment of the level of unemployment and the low rate of growth recorded after the first two years of the program. In regard to this point it is important to reiterate that the program was essentially a stabilization effort and nothing more. It was conceived with the modest aim of reducing the country's soaring five-digit inflation rate to a manageable level. It did not attempt the (probably impossible) task of achieving extraordinary growth at the same time. One must bear in mind how much time is needed just to overcome the institutionalized uncertainty prevailing in a country such as Bolivia, with its past record of economic, political, and social instability. The program did succeed in reversing the hyperinflation and negative growth of the previous six years. It brought inflation down to a relatively low rate and restored a positive, albeit modest, rate of growth.

In his analysis of the impact of the stabilization program, Morales focuses on the post-stabilization macroeconomics and on a number of problems that have not yet been resolved. Although I agree with much of what is said in this section, I would like to raise just one point: In dealing with these problems, Morales gives the impression that they present major hurdles that are likely to dampen stabilization and growth in the short term, and possibly to place it in great danger in the long run.

Although these problems certainly do persist and pose a threat to the Bolivian economy, I believe they should not be viewed in isolation, but in the context of other factors and the program's overall success to date.

In considering the fiscal deficits reported in 1987 and 1988, for instance, it is important to determine to what extent they were attributable to external shocks, as opposed to a failure of the government's fiscal policy. It is also important to determine whether the tax reform had the effect—which Morales ascribes, without proof, to the Olivera-Tanzi effect working in reverse—of strengthening (or potentially strengthening) the tax base. In this context, it is important to assess the persistent effort, particularly at the national government level, to curb current expenditures in addressing the problem of the deficit. In the case of Bolivia, current expenditure in the nonfinancial public sector was pared from 34.4% of GDP in 1984 to 29.6% in 1986 and to 28.9% in 1987. This is perhaps one of the few recorded cases of a sustained effort to tackle a budget deficit simultaneously from both the revenue and the expenditure sides.

In pointing out the failure to correct the current-account deficit, one must also recognize exogenous factors contributing to the problem. Although Morales repeatedly notes the impact of external shocks on the stabilization program, he does not assess their real impact and the subsequent economic complications. On the other hand, a complete analysis must also examine the favorable impact of the net positive flows that resumed once credibility was restored abroad, and of the repatriation of substantial amounts of capital that served to sustain the stabilization efforts, especially during the first two years of the program. Morales mentions these developments, but fails to evaluate them in sufficient depth.

In the second part of his paper Morales touches upon aspects of political economy that concern credibility. As mentioned earlier, the main objective of the stabilization program was to restore economic credibility both at home and abroad, not simply to reestablish relations with official international creditors, as Morales states.

The government restored credibility at home by clearly expressing its political resolve to stay the course. Instrumental in bringing this about was the so-called Pact for Democracy, in which the main opposition party pledged to stand behind the government and to support the continuation of the stabilization plan.

The government restored credibility abroad by means of successive agreements with the International Monetary Fund that enabled the government to achieve three major objectives: Releasing multilateral credits immediately; setting an agenda for the bilateral rescheduling of debt within the Paris Club and releasing government credits; and opening up negotiations with private international banks, which concluded with the repurchase of 75% of the debt owed to these institutions.

The creation of the Social Emergency Fund (SEF) was of vital importance to the viability of the stabilization program at home. Morales does not dwell in depth on this point. The SEF provided temporary employment to thousands of workers who had been laid off because of the external shocks and the adjustment program. The SEF enabled the government to cushion the social pressures that were building up at the very difficult time when the program was implemented. The ethical assumptions underlying all economic systems in the late 20th century simply do not permit a stabilization program without an escape valve of this sort to alleviate social tensions. A number of international organizations are today helping to implement similar programs in several other countries in Latin America and in Africa.

Finally, let me say that I share the views expressed in section 3 of Morales' paper insofar as they concern the problems that arise from structural readjustment. I should add that I feel that control and stabilization measures must always go hand in hand with a change in the ground rules for economic agents. Bolivia used to be the typical case of a regulated economy, in which government control extended to prices, interest rates, wages, and labor agreements. A system of this sort inevitably commits major errors that give rise to subsidies of all kinds and the inefficient allocation of resources. In the Bolivian case, it was essential to give a clear signal to economic agents that they would be allowed to work without restrictions, to mobilize resources, and to receive positive interest on savings. It was also essential to end the inflexible labor legislation that gave employees ironclad security of tenure.

The ground rules issued in conjunction with the stabilization measures were intended not only to restore credibility inside and outside the country, but also to lay the foundations of future sustained economic growth and development. This was a necessary condition, although not in itself sufficient. In a country where economic, political, and social instability have been rampant for decades, four out of five years of stability are not enough to restore the confidence of an entire generation that has known only poor economic management. As Morales himself admits, "more important . . . are the credibility problems, not on stabilization, but on long-term developments. . . ."

General Discussion

Many participants were puzzled by the sizable real wage increase during Bolivia's post-stabilization period. Vittorio Corbo wondered why there had been a wage increase when the power of the unions had diminished and unemployment was high. Sebastian Edwards ascribed the increase in real wages to a probable large misalignment of the real exchange rate. Haim Barkai pointed out that such a development should be expected to erode the government's credibility. Such erosion is consistent, according to Peter Bernholz, with dollarization, in spite of the announcement of full backing by the government.

Juan Carlos de Pablo disagreed with the pessimistic view expressed in the paper with regard to growth. He pointed out that the Bolivian economy is growing and that the sharp decline in per capita GDP has stopped. Arie Hillman offered a different prognosis for growth, emphasizing the fact that the economy, being highly regulated by the government, should have less potential for growth.

3   Chile's Experience with Stabilization Revisited

Vittoria Corbo and Andrés Solimano

This paper evaluates Chile's stabilization policies since the early 1970s. Three episodes are examined: the orthodox stabilization program of 1975; the exchange-rate-based stabilization of February 1978–June 1982; and the post-1984 adjustment period, with a large real devaluation and low inflation. Finally, an overall evaluation of the experience with stabilization since 1975 is provided.

Chile has a long history of inflation. In the 1960s, when government policy was aimed at validating the inertial inflation that was resulting from the periodic increases in wages and in the exchange rate (Cauas 1970), inflation reached an average of 21.1% per year. In the early 1970s, under the socialist-populist policies of the Allende government, inflation accelerated, reaching 558% per year in August 1973, the month before the military coup that deposed Allende. The military government thus had to contend with an economy suffering from the worst inflation in Chile's history as well as from widespread distortions and major macroeconomic imbalances. With the public-sector deficit almost 30% of the GDP, financed mostly through the printing of money, real demand for money was shrinking and inflation accelerating despite extensive price controls.

In its initial years the military government attacked inflation by controlling the growth of the money supply through a drastic reduction in the public-sector deficit. Nonetheless, three-digit inflation continued well into early 1977. A key question is why inflation took so long to drop below the three-digit level, given the very significant reduction in the public-sector deficit. In February 1978, the government responded to the situation by introducing a preannounced devaluation schedule (*tablita*), with devaluations to proceed at decreasing rates much below the difference between domestic and foreign inflation. By June 1979, it fixed the exchange rate.

Three basic objectives underlay this new policy. First, in a small country such as Chile, which by then had lowered its trade tariffs substantially, such a policy was supposed to reduce the expected rate of inflation. Second, the new system was expected to exert downward pressure on the rate of increase in the price of tradable goods. Third, it was to lead to a further integration of the domestic and international capital markets, and to reduce domestic interest rates by lowering the expected rate of devaluation.

The authorities believed that the new policy was fully credible, given the fact that the fiscal deficit had been transformed into a surplus. Contrary to expectations, however, Chile's inflation remained higher than international inflation for over two years, and the resultant substantial real appreciation of the peso approached 30% by the end of 1981. The question then became: Why did it take so long for domestic to converge with international inflation? Furthermore, in spite of financial liberalization and the opening of the capital account, real interest rates averaged around 50% per year in 1976–1978 (see table 3.1). A key question here is: Why were real interest rates so high in this period?

On June 14, 1982, with Chile in the middle of a major crisis resulting from a large accumulated decline in competitiveness, from large losses in the terms of trade, and from significant increases in international and domestic interest rates, the government abandoned the fixed-exchange-rate policy. There ensued a couple of years of disorganized macroeconomic management, after which, in 1984, Chile achieved substantial real devaluation and started a sustained recovery at the time when a "solution" to a financial crisis was resulting in a large increase in central-bank liabilities. A key question is: How was that real devaluation achieved without an increase in inflation?

The paper is organized as follows. Section 1 presents an overview of Chile's macroeconomic policies, particularly in the 1970s and the 1980s. Section 2 examines the shock treatment of 1975. Section 3 looks at the exchange-rate-based stabilization of 1978–1982 and its impact on inflation. Section 4 examines the behavior of interest rates, and section 5 the post-1984 adjustment. Section 6 presents an overall evaluation of the post-1973 period, drawing the corresponding lessons from that stabilization experience.

1. Chile's Economic Policies: An Overview[1]

In September 1973 a military coup ousted Allende. The economic team of the new military government spent 1974 and 1975 trying to stabilize the economy. In 1974 it introduced a major tax reform, and in both 1974 and 1975 it lowered government expenditures significantly to reduce the major source of the public-sector deficit. It also sold government assets. In addition, good prices for copper in 1974 and a rollover of 30% of the outstanding debt service in 1973 and 1974 eased the adjustment to the first oil shock.

As to trade policy, the government lowered nominal tariffs to a maximum rate of at first 140% and then 120%. By June 1975 it had lifted all commodity price controls and removed the constraints on domestic interest rates. After a large devaluation late in 1973, the relative incentives for the production of exportable goods improved substantially, while those for home goods and highly protected import-competing goods fell.

By late 1974 and early 1975 the external environment was souring—copper prices dropped, oil prices stayed high. Because of severely restricted access to external financing, the government had to implement one of the most severe adjustment programs in Chile's economic history. The macroeconomic adjustment program of 1975 was followed by a comprehensive set of policy reforms. On the trade side, all remaining quantitative restrictions on trade were lifted, and tariffs were gradually reduced to a uniform 10% by July 1979. In 1976, when substantial real depreciation had been achieved, multiple exchange rates gave way to a unified exchange rate, and a crawling peg targeted to achieve a fairly stable real exchange rate was instituted (with two revaluations of 10%, the first in early June 1976 and the second in March 1977).

Liberalization was much slower in two areas. One was labor policy, although some qualifications are in order here. Suspension of collective bargaining and severe restrictions on labor-union activity until 1979,[2] and high unemployment through most of the period, weakened the bargaining power of labor, and in that sense it is hard to say that there was a very "protected" market in Chile during the military regime. However, with regard to wage policy, a serious mistake was made in mid-1979, from the viewpoint of consistency with the overall macroeconomic policy, at the time the Plan Laboral was launched: Compulsory 100%

Table 3.1
Annual macroeconomic indicators.

	GDP	Absorption[a]	GDP deflator (percent change)	CPI[b]	Unemployment rate[c] (percent)	Price of copper (cents per lb.)	Current account deficit	Public deficit[d]	Public capital formation[e] (% of GDP)	Total gross investment[f]	Terms of trade[g] (index)	Real interest rate (%)	Real wages (1960=100)
1960	—	—	—	11.6	7.4	30.8	-4.6	—	—	13.9	139.9	—	45.8
1961	4.8	6.1	6.5	7.7	6.7	28.7	-7.2	—	—	15.3	125.3	—	48.9
1962	4.7	2.5	13.4	13.9	5.3	29.3	-5.2	—	—	12.4	134.1	—	50.8
1963	6.3	5.8	43.6	44.3	5.1	29.3	-4.2	—	—	14.8	131.4	—	47.4
1964	2.2	2.9	47.3	46.0	5.3	44.1	-3.5	—	—	14.2	133.9	—	46.1
1965	0.8	0.4	39.3	28.8	5.4	58.7	-1.4	—	—	15.0	152.9	—	52.3
1966	11.2	16.5	28.5	22.9	5.4	69.5	-1.8	—	—	16.3	185.2	—	58.6
1967	3.2	0.6	25.6	18.1	6.1	51.1	-2.7	—	—	16.1	176.4	—	67.7
1968	3.6	4.8	33.9	26.6	5.1	56.1	-2.7	—	—	16.3	188.6	—	68.3
1969	3.7	5.8	39.9	30.7	6.2	66.6	-0.1	—	—	15.1	222.8	—	74.5
1970	2.1	1.8	40.5	32.5	7.1	64.2	-1.0	6.7	10.4	16.4	226.1	—	82.1
1971	9.0	9.7	18.4	22.1	5.5	49.3	-1.8	15.3	10.5	14.5	172.3	—	96.0
1972	-1.2	1.0	86.9	117.9	3.8	48.6	-3.1	24.5	9.6	12.2	166.2	—	86.3
1973	-5.6	-6.2	418.1	487.5	4.6	80.8	-2.8	30.5	8.4	7.9	187.2	—	58.6
1974	1.0	2.4	694.2	497.8	9.7	93.3	-1.9	5.4	12.5	21.2	197.8	—	55.5
1975	-12.9	-20.8	342.4	379.2	16.2	55.9	-6.8	2.0	9.2	13.1	118.5	16.0	53.9
1976	3.5	0.2	250.7	234.5	16.8	63.6	1.5	-3.9	6.1	12.8	127.8	64.3	59.8
1977	9.9	14.2	103.5	113.8	13.2	59.3	-4.1	-0.4	6.9	14.4	114.4	56.8	72.6
1978	8.2	9.7	56.6	49.8	14.0	61.9	-7.1	-1.5	6.7	17.8	111.0	42.2	83.0
1979	8.3	10.5	46.3	36.6	13.6	89.8	-5.7	-4.8	5.1	17.8	118.5	16.6 (22.9)	92.1
1980	7.8	9.3	29.2	35.1	11.8	99.2	-7.1	-5.4	5.2	21.0	100.0	11.9 (215.3)	100.0
1981	5.5	11.6	12.2	19.7	11.1	78.9	-14.5	-0.3	5.1	22.7	84.3	38.7 (14.5)	109.0
1982	-14.1	-24.1	13.3	9.9	22.1	67.1	-9.5	4.0 (8.9)	4.7	11.3	80.4	35.1 (16.9)	109.3
1983	-0.7	-4.6	26.6	27.3	22.2	72.2	-5.6	3.3 (7.2)	4.8	9.8	87.5	16.5 (10.0)	97.3

1984	6.3	8.5	14.3	19.9	19.2	62.4	-10.7	4.5	(9.0)	6.0	13.6	83.2	11.7	(9.0)	97.6
1985	2.4	-1.9	32.9	30.7	16.3	64.3	-8.3	2.9	(9.8)	7.1	14.6	78.5	10.5	(9.4)	93.2
1986	5.7	5.4	19.2	19.5	13.5	62.3	-6.9	1.6	(4.4)	7.6	14.7	82.0	7.7	(7.6)	94.9
1987	5.7	7.3	21.2	19.9	12.3	81.1	-4.3	-0.3	(0.4)	7.3	16.9	77.0	9.3	(7.3)	94.7
1988	7.4	8.9	21.2	14.7	11.2	117.9	0.7	3.6	(-3.0)	6.2	17.0		7.5	(7.6)	102.8

Sources: *Indicadores economicos y sociales 1960–1985*, and various issues of *Boletin Mensual*, Banco Central de Chile.

a. Includes private consumption, public consumption, and total investment.

b. From 1971 to 1979.

c. Greater Santiago, Universidad de Chile.

d. Until 1979—consists of general government and public enterprises, extracted from Larraín 1989; thereafter—from Marshall and Larrañaga 1989. The figures in parentheses include an estimate of the quasi-fiscal subsidies channeled through the central bank.

e. Until 1985—extracted from Larraín 1989; thereafter—from Fontaine 1989.

f. Constructed from fixed gross investment, change in stocks and GDP at current prices. Sources: *Indicadores Economicos y Sociales 1960*, 1985; Marshall and Larrañaga 1989.

g. Sources: *Cuadernos Estadiaticos de la Cepal. Indicadores Economicos y Sociales 1960*, 1985.

backward wage indexation (introduced in October 1974 for the public sector) was extended to workers under collective bargaining in the private sector.[3] This undesirable reform resulted in an unsustainable appreciation of the real exchange rate and a macroeconomic crisis. Liberalization of capital inflows also proceeded slowly, with important reforms introduced only in June 1979.[4]

With inflation continuing, a debate developed in early 1977 about the causes of inflation and the most appropriate way to deal with them. That debate led to two 10% revaluations, which were expected to lower inflation and sterilize part of the accumulation of reserves. Toward the end of 1977 the government targeted the rate of devaluation to exceed the rate of inflation, so as to compensate the import-competing sector for the announced tariff reductions. In February 1978 it established an active crawling peg with an explicit stabilization objective. For this purpose, the rate of crawl was established at well below the difference between domestic and foreign inflation.

Then, in June 1979, with monthly inflation about 2.5%, the government fixed the exchange rate at 39 pesos per dollar. Finally, toward the end of 1979 it introduced a new labor code that reestablished collective bargaining, albeit for just a fraction of the labor force, and mandated a formula for a wage floor that went well beyond the indexation instituted in late 1974.

The policy reforms from 1979 to 1982 emphasized improving the functioning of domestic commodity markets and further deregulating capital flows. However, pressure developed for more protective tariffs to sectors suffering the brunt of the emerging effects of the real appreciation. The government also modified its tariff policy to counteract foreign dumping.

Beginning in 1983, the government made several changes in the uniform tariff of 10%, citing fiscal reasons as justification. One such change was to raise the tariff level, first to 20% and then to 35%. However, as the anti-export bias of this policy became clear, the new minister of finance reduced the level of the uniform tariff gradually, until it reached 15% in January 1988.

On the financial side, after the large devaluation of 1982 and the sharp recession in that year (the GDP dropped 14.1% in 1982), a substantial financial crisis developed. To avoid widespread bankruptcy among financial institutions and productive enterprises, the government established a comprehensive policy to rescue financially distressed institutions, financed by a large expansion in the quasi-fiscal deficit of the central bank.[5] As a result, the overall public-sector deficit (including an estimate of the quasi-fiscal subsidies of the central bank) increased from a surplus of 0.3% of GDP in 1981 to a deficit of 9.8% of GDP in 1985 (see table 3.1). However, by 1988 it had turned into a surplus of 3% of GDP. The government financed the public-sector deficit through domestic and foreign borrowing by the central bank, thus avoiding—in the short run—monetization and inflation.

After 1984, the government designed a comprehensive adjustment aimed at restoring macroeconomic balances in a situation of restricted access to foreign borrowing. An aggressive nominal devaluation was combined with supportive fiscal and monetary policies to achieve a large real devaluation. Given the improved efficiency of the tradable sector, the real devaluation was designed to achieve a large expansion in import-competing and exportable activities, and in this way to start a sustained recovery. As mentioned before, a distinctive feature of the post-1984 adjustment process is that no major acceleration in inflation took place in spite of both a major real depreciation of the exchange rate—around 45% in 1984–1989—and the solution of a severe domestic financial crisis.

2. The Monetary Shock of 1975 and the Dynamics of Disinflation

Monetary Policy Revisited

The actual stance of monetary policy in the "shock treatment" of 1975, which entailed a drastic drop in the growth rate of money, has been the subject of controversy. The severe fiscal adjustment led to a further reduction (3.4%) of GDP in the consolidated non-financial public-sector deficit in 1975, in spite of a drastic recession that year (GDP dropped 12.9%). However, it is not clear if monetary policy was indeed tight. Some have even argued that there was no monetary shock in Chile in 1975; e.g., Harberger (1982) notes the high rates of money growth in that year.

We define the stance of monetary policy not just in terms of the supply side of the money market, but also by comparing the supply of money with the demand for money. As is well known, a stabilization plan—if credible—is expected to reduce the velocity of money, i.e., to increase the demand for money. To determine the degree of excess demand or supply in the money market, we estimate a demand-for-money equation using a semi-logarithmic demand-for-money equation with a partial adjustment mechanism, and quarterly data for 1976/I–1989/I:[6]

$$\ln(M/P) = -1.45 - 0.005i + 0.326\ln Y + 0.645\ln(M/P)_{-1}$$
$$\quad\quad (-1.92)\ (-1.85)\ \ (2.06)\quad\quad (7.69)$$

$R^2 = 0.88$

D.W. = 1.91

F-stat = 121.68

N = 53

Log likelihood = 57.19.

As table 3.2 shows, there was *excess demand* for money in the money market in 1975 and in the first two quarters of 1976.[7] That is, monetary policy, as measured by the degree of excess demand in the money market, was particularly tight in the second quarter of 1975—and the "Cauas Plan" was launched in April of that year.[8] It is also interesting to note that monetary policy was tightened in the second quarter of 1976 as the rate of inflation regained the pace of early 1976.

Having established that monetary policy was indeed tight under the orthodox stabilization plan of 1975 (fiscal policy was undoubtedly restrictive as well, since the fiscal deficit dropped from 10.5% of GDP in 1974 to 2.6% in 1975), it remains an open question why it took so long for the rate of inflation to fall below the three-digit level, a drop that only took place in 1977.

Table 3.2
Excess supply of money in 1975 and early 1976 (money supply *minus* money demand, as a share of money demand, percentages).

1975	I	7.9
	II	−12.3
	III	−1.5
	IV	−1.8
1976	I	−1.1
	II	−11.3

Why Inflation Took So Long to Come Down

To address the question asked in the preceding section, we examine the role of two factors that may have retarded the deceleration of inflation:

· The inflationary effect of the exchange-rate policy (and fiscal restraint), which was aimed at achieving a further real depreciation of the peso in 1975. That real depreciation was, in turn, a response to the large (45%) drop in the real price of copper between 1974 and 1975 and the planned reductions in tariffs. A real depreciation was accomplished by following a very aggressive policy of nominal devaluations.

· The persistency effect that resulted from the wage indexation rule geared to the previous periods rate of inflation.

We also will examine the speed of disinflation and the output cost of a counterfactual path for money growth during the stabilization shock of 1975.

A simple model of inflation determination, along the lines of Bruno and Fischer 1986 and Fischer 1988, is set up to deal empirically with the issue of velocity and the cost of disinflation needed to explain the difficulty in lowering inflation in Chile after 1975.

This aggregative, open economy model comprises aggregate demand, aggregate supply, and wage equations. Aggregate demand in the goods market, Y^d, is made a function of the stock of real balances, M/P; a vector of fiscal variables, Z, including real spending and taxes; and the real exchange rate, EP^*/P. A shift factor, q, is introduced to reflect demand shocks. The equation is

$$Y^d = f(M/P, Z, EP^*/P, q) . \tag{1}$$

Aggregate supply, Y^s, is made an inverse function of the real wage, W/P; the real price of imported inputs, which is made equal to the real exchange rate for the sake of simplicity, EP^*/P; and a factor, u, that reflects the effects of supply shocks:

$$Y^s = h(W/P, EP^*/P, u) . \tag{2}$$

If we let the price level, P, equilibrate aggregate demand with aggregate supply, we get

$$P = P(M, EP^*, W, Z, q, u) . \tag{3}$$

Expressing equation 3 in terms of rates of change, where g_x is the rate of change in the variable x, $g_x = \delta x / x$, and denoting the rate of inflation by π, we have

$$\pi = \pi(g_m, g_w, g_e, \pi^*, \varepsilon) , \tag{4}$$

where g_m is the rate of growth of the money supply, g_w is the rate of growth of nominal wages, g_e is the rate of devaluation, π^* is the rate of foreign inflation, and ε represents changes in aggregate supply and aggregate demand.

Solving for the rate of growth of demand, we have

$$g_Y = f(g_{M/P}, g_{ep^*/p}, k) , \tag{5}$$

where $g_{M/P}$ is the rate of growth of real balances, $g_{ep^*/p}$ is the rate of change in the real exchange rate, and k is a vector representing changes in the fiscal parameters and the terms of trade.

The growth rate of nominal wages in the model, g_w, is made a function of the rate of expected inflation, π^e, the deviation of current output from potential output, Y/Y^p, and the rate of growth of labor productivity, g_{yl}. Given that wages are indexed to past inflation, we use the last period's inflation—instead of expected inflation—in the wage equation (although the *degree* of indexation has changed during the period).[9] Thus,

$$g_w = s(\pi^e, Y/Y^p, g_{yl}) . \tag{6}$$

The econometric estimation of the inflation, GDP growth, and wage equations is carried out, equation by equation, using the two-stage least-squares (2SLS) method, in order to get consistent estimates of the parameters. The equations are estimated using quarterly data for the period 1974/I–1989/I. The 2SLS estimate of the inflation equation yields[10]

$$\pi = -0.0045 + 0.358 g_w + 0.197(g_e + \pi^*) + 0.210[g_{e(-1)} + \pi^*_{-1}]$$
$$\quad (-0.62) \quad (3.68) \quad\quad (2.19) \quad\quad\quad\quad (6.96)$$

$$\quad + 0.155 g_{M1(-3)} + 0.029 DUMP$$
$$\quad\quad (3.95) \quad\quad\quad (1.19)$$

$R^2 = 0.94$

$D.W = 2.11$

F-stat = 197.79

N = 61

Log likelihood = 116.71,

where the numbers in parentheses are t-statistics; π^* is measured as the implicit rate of foreign inflation in the imported component of the wholesale price index, g_{M1} is the rate of change in M1; and the variable DUMP is a dummy whose value is 1 in 1979/II, 1982/II–III, and 1984/III, when discrete devaluations took place. An interesting result of the estimation is the time lag with which the rate of money growth affects the rate of inflation *significantly*: three quarters (the value of the coefficient is rather low). This result is evidence of a lack of sensitivity of inflation to decelerations in the rate of growth of nominal spending in the short run, a well-recognized feature of inflationary processes with an inertial component.

The 2SLS estimation of the GDP equation in rate-of-growth form for the same sample period is[11]

$$g_Y = 0.023 + 0.211[g_{M1(-1)} - \pi_{-1}] - 0.051[g_{e(-2)} + \pi^*_{-2} - \pi_{-2}]$$
$$\quad (4.28) \quad (4.85) \qquad\qquad (-1.60)$$

$$\quad - 0.517 g_{Y(-1)} - 0.071 DUMMY$$
$$\quad (-4.36) \qquad (-5.06)$$

$R^2 = 0.49$

D.W. = 2.57

F-stat = 13.57

N = 60

Log likelihood = 116.44.

It appears, here, that the growth rate of real money is significant with one lag. A real depreciation affects the rate of change in GDP with two lags, as was expected (following the dynamics of the export response to changes in the real exchange rate). The sign of the coefficients suggests the possibility of a contractionary devaluation in the short run in Chile, a feature that confirms the findings of other empirical studies of devaluation in Chile and other developing countries.[12] Finally, the dummy variable takes the value of 1 in 1975/I–IV and in 1981/IV–1983/I, corresponding to the two large recessions that took place during the sample period.

Finally, the 2SLS estimation of the wage equation for the same sample period yields[13]

$$g_w = 0.011 + 0.912\pi_{-1} + 0.636[g_{y(-1)} - g_{l(-1)}]$$
$$\quad\ (1.044)\ \ (14.76) \quad\ \ (1.11)$$

$R^2 = 0.86$

D.W. = 2.22

F-stat = 184.59

N = 60

Log likelihood = 85.97.

The coefficients of the contemporaneous rate of inflation and the output gap in the current period were excluded from the regression because they were found to be statistically nonsignificant. As expected, the rate of inflation in the last period turned out to be highly significant, with a value close to unity, reflecting the lagged wage indexation in Chile during most of the sample period. Moreover, the coefficient for the rate of change in labor productivity with a one-period lag, $g_{y(-1)} - g_{l(-1)}$, is 0.636.

Figures 3.1, 3.2, and 3.3 show how the model performs, by comparing a (dynamic) base simulation using the observed values of the exogenous variables with the actual values of inflation, GDP growth, and rate of change in nominal wages.

Using the estimates of the model reported above, we perform some counterfactual simulations to shed light on the factors underlying the slow pace of disinflation observed after the orthodox shock treatment was implemented in Chile in 1975. The counterfactual simulations involve (a) an exchange-rate rule whereby PPP is maintained by devaluing the nominal exchange rate at a rate equal to the difference between domestic and foreign inflation in 1975 (as mentioned, the actual rule in that year was to devalue at a rate higher than the difference between the rates of domestic and foreign inflation), (b) a change in the wage rule from lagged wage indexation to indexation based on contemporaneous inflation, and (c) a combination of (a) and (b). For each simulation we examine the associated path of inflation, output, and nominal wages, which we compare against the simulated values (see tables 3.3–3.6). We are not advocating that a PPP rule should have been followed for the exchange rate, as the fundamentals also were changing during this period. Rather, we use this alternative rule for the purpose of designing a counterfactual.

The counterfactual simulations show that to some extent the exchange-rate and wage rules pursued during the disinflation of 1975 tended to postpone the reduction of inflation in Chile. Table 3.3 (column 1) shows that the anti-inflationary gains from the slower pace of devaluation are larger in the short run. However, the implicit acceleration of inflation associated with the exchange-rate rule actually implemented in 1975 tended to disappear toward 1977.

On the other hand, the alternative wage rule—the one geared to current rather than to lagged wage indexation—has a more lasting disinflationary effect over time (see table 3.3, column 2). Furthermore, the counterfactual simulation combining both a change in the exchange rate and the wage rule (simulation 3) shows that the magnitude of disinflation under those two counterfactual policy rules are non-negligible. With the benefit of hindsight we observe that adverse external shocks—such as a drop in real copper prices—are likely to have retarded disinflation in 1975. At the same time, the practice of lagged wage indexation and aggressive devaluation also contributed to the inertial inflation, rendering the restrictive fiscal and monetary policies less effective in reducing inflation.

Chile's experience of 1975 illustrates the common tradeoff between more rapid disinflation and the need to adjust the real exchange rate (a move that often results in a temporary acceleration of inflation) so as to restore external balance in the wake of adverse external shocks.

The slow pace of disinflation in Chile, in spite of the fiscal adjustment and the tight monetary policy put in place in 1975, suggests two different views of the dynamics of disinflation and the appropriate policies for attacking it. One view questions the degree to which it was efficient to rely *solely* on tight money and fiscal policies to reduce inflation in 1975 in a country with a history of four decades of inflation and one in which the indexation mechanisms and the record of failed stabilization would likely make people skeptical of the possibility of quick disinflationary results. In fact, recent experience with a combination of restrictive fiscal and income policies in chronic-inflation countries shows that the speed at which inflation is slowed and the output cost of disinflation can be reduced in comparison with what is possible using a purely orthodox package (e.g., Israel and Mexico).[14] The other view argues that disinflation was slow because monetary policy was too accommodating,

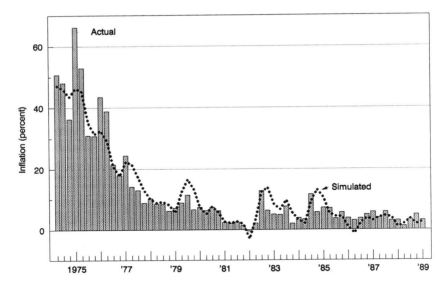

Figure 3.1
Inflation (actual and base-simulated values).

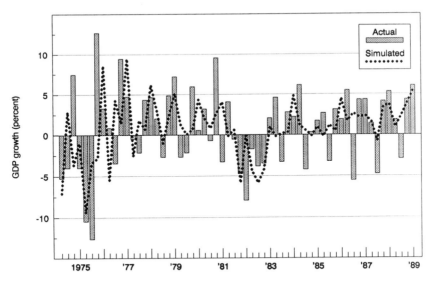

Figure 3.2
GDP growth (actual and base-simulated values).

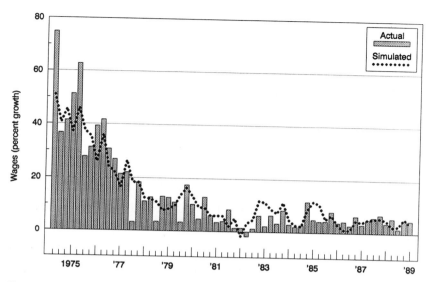

Figure 3.3
Wage growth (actual and base-simulated values).

Table 3.3
Rate of inflation—counterfactual simulations (difference between the counterfactual simulations and the base simulation, percentages).

		Exchange-rate policy of maintaining PPP in 1975 (simulation 1) (1)	Change in the wage rule to contemporaneous indexation (simulation 2) (2)	Simulation 3 (simulations 1 and 2) (3)
1975	I	−5.52	2.78	−5.96
	II	−11.52	1.11	−15.39
	III	−5.30	−4.38	−8.85
	IV	−4.16	−0.92	−6.32
1976	I	−8.76	1.84	−11.69
	II	−2.77	−1.13	−1.32
	III	4.93	−4.05	6.13
	IV	3.39	−1.17	0.68
1977	I	−4.80	3.01	−9.12
	II	−4.37	−0.17	−6.81
	III	2.69	−2.19	4.37
	IV	5.06	−2.10	4.74

a situation that validated inflationary expectations in spite of the sharp fiscal adjustment.

The following counterfactual simulation examines the anti-inflationary gains and the cost of disinflation on output growth that might have resulted had a tighter monetary policy been followed. In this simulation we reduced the rate of growth of M1 gradually, starting in 1975.[15] The exercise shows (table 3.4) that a tighter monetary policy would have produced little extra anti-inflationary gain in the short run—say, in the first year—compared with the actual monetary policy. Instead, the larger anti-inflationary gains would have become manifest in the second and third years. On the real side, the tighter monetary package carries with it an extra cost to the stabilization package, as it is accompanied by additional deceleration in the growth of GDP—mainly (but not only) in the short run. That is, the cost of quicker disinflation is slower growth in the short run. This result is basically a consequence of the stickiness of inflation to decelerations in money growth (a goods-market phenomenon) and of the fact that lagged wage indexation acts like a static expectations mechanism that slows the adjustment of wages and prices over time.

Table 3.4
Counterfactual simulation: tighter monetary policy 1975–1977 (difference with control simulation, percentages) (Simulation 4).

		Rate of inflation	Rate of GDP growth
1975	I	0.00	0.00
	II	0.00	−1.97
	III	−0.45	−1.85
	IV	−0.57	−2.82
1976	I	−0.83	−4.62
	II	−1.33	−0.16
	III	−0.47	−2.83
	IV	−0.80	−1.50
1977	I	−0.60	−7.65
	II	−1.94	−0.20
	III	−0.68	−1.68
	IV	−0.61	−0.24

3. Exchange-Rate-Based Stabilization: 1978–1982

An important shift in the approach to stabilization took place in 1978. Closed-economy monetarism gave way to strong emphasis on using the exchange rate as the chief tool for disinflation. This change in approach was the result of the popularization at the time, in Southern Cone countries, of the monetary approach to the balance of payments. It was also due to the fact that as the trade liberalization initiated in 1974 was approaching a uniform, across-the-board tariff of 10% (except for small cars) in 1978, international prices in domestic currency started to play a major role in domestic price formation.[16] Viewed in this context, the nominal exchange rate was thought to be a key determinant of domestic inflation. Thus, in February 1978 the government instituted a system of preannounced rates of devaluation that culminated in a rate of 39 pesos per dollar, a level that was maintained until June 1982.

The result of the new stabilization plan was disinflation at a lower pace than expected and a lack of convergence between domestic and foreign inflation within a reasonable period. These results, in turn, led to overvaluation of the currency, an unsustainable expansion in domestic expenditures, and unsustainable high current-account deficits—close to 14% of GDP in 1981. In addition, unfavorable external conditions in 1982 (the drop in terms of trade and the increase in international interest rates) resulted in high real domestic interest rates and a cut in expenditures. With a fixed nominal exchange rate and inflexible prices for nontradables, a major recession developed. Faced with a sharp increase in unemployment and an emerging recession in June 1982, the government abandoned the fixed exchange rate. Then, just as Chile was initiating the adjustment, it was hit by another external shock—a sharp reduction in capital inflows that followed the difficulties encountered by Mexico in serving its debt. On top of the sharp recession, a financial crisis was emerging.

One popular explanation for the appreciation of the peso was that a system of complete wage linkage to the CPI of the previous period—the system instituted by law—was, in the context of declining inflation, bound to result in substantial inertial inflation and appreciation. Furthermore, the large and unsustainable capital inflows of the late 1970s and the early 1980s provided temporary support for the much-appreciated real exchange rate and permitted an unsustainable level of domestic expenditures. At the same time, real wages rose at the rate of the reduction in inflation, with real wages in dollars rising even more because the fixed nominal exchange rate led to increasing overvaluation.[17]

To explore the role of alternative wages rules in disinflation under an exchange-rate-based stabilization effort such as the one tried in Chile between 1978 and mid-1982, we perform two counterfactual simulations: a change in the wage indexation rule, from full lagged indexation (the rule followed after June 1979) to full contemporaneous indexation, and the indexation of nominal wages to the exchange rate.

Table 3.5 shows that indexing wages to the exchange rate produces larger and quicker disinflation. In turn, the rule of contemporaneous wage indexation tends to dominate the rule of lagged indexation in terms of disinflationary gains.

We now examine the path of GDP growth and the behavior of real wages and the real exchange rate under these two alternative wage rules. As table 3.6 reveals, replacing lagged for current inflation or the exchange

Table 3.5
Effects on inflation of alternative wage rules in 1978–1982—counterfactual simulations (difference with respect to base simulation; percentages).

		Full contemporaneous wage indexation (Simulation 5)	Wage indexation to exchange rate (Simulation 6)
1978	I	−4.28	−6.18
	II	−2.29	−5.37
	III	0.17	−6.52
	IV	−2.14	−6.12
1979	I	−4.81	−4.38
	II	9.62	1.87
	III	6.58	−12.24
	IV	−5.41	−16.40
1980	I	−9.13	−12.33
	II	−3.86	−7.49
	III	2.95	−5.75
	IV	−3.85	−8.17
1981	I	−6.20	−6.30
	II	−1.62	−3.48
	III	−0.67	−2.95
	IV	−2.72	−3.82
1982	I	−9.02	−3.09
	II	7.86	21.68
	III	13.23	40.29

Table 3.6
Real wages and the real exchange rate under alternative nominal wages rules (differences in rates of growth with respect to the base simulation; percentages).

		Real wages		Real exchange rate	
		Contemporaneous indexation rule (simulation 5)	Indexation to exchange rate (simulation 6)	Contemporaneous indexation rule (simulation 5)	Indexation to exchange rate (simulation 6)
1978	I	−2.74	−3.97	1.53	2.22
	II	−1.47	−3.44	0.82	1.92
	III	0.11	−4.18	−0.06	2.34
	IV	−1.37	−3.93	0.77	2.20
1979	I	−3.09	−2.81	1.73	1.57
	II	6.17	1.20	−3.45	−0.67
	III	4.22	−7.85	−2.36	4.39
	IV	−3.47	−10.52	1.94	5.88
1980	I	−5.85	−7.91	3.27	4.42
	II	−2.47	−4.80	1.38	2.69
	III	1.89	−3.69	−1.06	2.06
	IV	−2.47	−5.24	1.38	2.93
1981	I	−3.98	−4.04	2.22	2.26
	II	−1.04	−2.23	0.58	1.25
	III	−0.43	−1.89	0.24	1.06
	IV	−1.74	−2.45	0.97	1.37
1982	I	−5.78	−1.98	3.23	1.11
	II	5.04	13.90	−2.82	−7.78
	III	8.49	25.84	−4.74	−14.45

rate as the indexer of wages to speed up disinflation produces slower growth in real wages. In fact, the rate of growth of real wages under both the contemporaneous-inflation indexation rule and the exchange-rate-linked rule is slower than in the base simulation (where the wage indexation rule is according to lagged inflation). Furthermore, indexation to the exchange rate reduces the rate of growth of real wages more than does indexation to contemporaneous inflation. The reason is the deceleration in the rate of devaluation after February 1978 (the rate was fixed in June 1979). This result would have been reversed had the exchange-rate policy accelerated devaluation.

The counterfactual simulation indicates that the real exchange rate depreciates at a higher pace under the exchange-rate-linked indexation rule for nominal wages than under the rule of indexation to current inflation. This result mirrors the slower growth of real wages under this rule. Nominal wages grow less than do prices because the exchange rate is devalued at a lower rate in order to speed the reduction in inflation.

4. Financial Openness and Interest Rates: Why Were Real Interest Rates So High?

In an economy where controls on the movement of private capital are not completely effective, the observed domestic interest rate (i) can be expressed as a weighted average of the interest rate had the country been completely open (i^*) and the domestic interest rate that would have been observed if the private capital account were completely closed (i') (see Edwards and Khan 1985 and Haque and Montiel 1989). That is,

$$i = \Psi i^* + (1 - \Psi)i', \quad 0 \le \Psi \le 1 \tag{7}$$

where Ψ measures the degree of capital mobility. If $\Psi = 1$, capital mobility would be perfect and the observed domestic interest rate would be equal to sum of the world interest rate and the expected rate of depreciation. If, on the other hand, $\Psi = 0$, the capital account would be closed and the observed domestic interest rate would be equal to a hypothetical closed-economy interest rate. As the capital account is liberalized, Ψ should increase.

Starting with the demand for money,

$$\ln(M^D/P) = \alpha_0 + \alpha_1 i + \alpha_2 \ln(y) + \alpha_3 \ln(M/P)_{-1}, \quad \alpha_1 < 0; \alpha_2, \alpha_3 > 0 \tag{8}$$

where y is real output, P is the domestic price level, and M^D is the demand for money. Assuming equilibrium in the money market,

$$\ln(M^D/P) = \ln(M^s/P) = \ln(M/P) ,$$

an expression for the observed domestic interest rate can be derived:

$$i = -(\alpha_0/\alpha_1) - (\alpha_1/\alpha_1)\ln(y) - (\alpha_3/\alpha_1)\ln(M/P)_{-1} + (1/\alpha_1)\ln(M/P) . \qquad (9)$$

If the private capital account is closed, this expression can be used to derive the hypothetical closed-economy interest rate,

$$i' = -(\alpha_0/\alpha_1) - (\alpha_2/\alpha_1)\ln(y) - (\alpha_3/\alpha_1)\ln(M/P)_{-1} + (1/\alpha_1)\ln(M'/P) , \qquad (10)$$

where M' is the money supply given a closed private capital account ($M' = M$ *minus* Private Capital Account). Replacing this hypothetical closed-economy interest rate in equation 7, we obtain

$$i - i' = \Psi(i^* - i') . \qquad (11)$$

That is, the deviation of the observed interest rate from the hypothetical closed-economy interest rate is proportional to the divergence of the closed-economy interest rate from the completely open-economy interest case.

Edwards and Khan (1985) use a similar equation to derive fixed estimates of the degree of capital mobility,[18] but a major problem with their approach is that Ψ is not constant for countries where the degree of capital mobility is changing. In what follows we conclude that Ψ is a variable coefficient whose value varies with the degree of openness in the capital account. A similar idea was used by Corbo and McNelis (1989) for the estimation of price equations in economies where the degree of openness of the trade account is changing during the period of estimation.

To obtain a measure of the effective degree of capital mobility for Chile, equation 11′ is used to estimate Ψ with quarterly data from 1975 to 1983:

$$(i - i')_t = \Psi(i^* - i')_t + \varepsilon_t . \qquad (11')$$

Equation 11′ is estimated using a time-varying coefficient and using a constant coefficient. Under the time-varying-coefficient method, the coefficient is assumed to follow the process

$$\Psi_t = A\Psi_{t-1} + \nu_t . \qquad (12)$$

The constant-coefficient method may be viewed as a special case of the time-varying method, where $A = 1$ and var(v_t) $= 0$. In this paper, the time-varying parameter estimation is done using the Kalman filter.[19]

The significance of the variability in capital mobility can be seen in figures 3.4 and 3.5, where the time-varying coefficient estimates, the ordinary least-squares estimate, and upper and lower bounds for the OLS estimate (calculated at 90% confidence intervals, based on the estimated standard error and the critical t-statistic) are plotted. If the Kalman-filter estimate falls outside the upper or lower bounds, then the variation is significantly different from the variation one may tolerate under the constant-coefficient assumption. The pattern that Ψ follows is directly related to the relaxation of restrictions on capital inflows (Corbo 1985a). The large drop in the value of Ψ after the second quarter of 1982 coincides with a period in which capital inflows all but disappeared after the domestic crisis and the international debt crisis.

The observed and estimated domestic interest rates obtained from the two methods are shown in figures 3.6 and 3.7. As can be seen, the time-varying model tracks the behavior of the observed domestic interest rate quite well during this period. In contrast, the OLS estimates overpredict interest rates for most of the period. As expected, the fit is much better using the black market exchange rate of devaluation. The large overestimation after the first quarter of 1981 coincides with a period when the central bank began to suggest an interest rate to the financial system.

From these results, we conclude that up to early 1978 domestic interest rates were driven mostly by domestic monetary policy; only in the second half of 1978 did the interest rate act in a way similar to the way it would in an open economy.

5. The Post-1984 Adjustment: Real Devaluation without Inflation Acceleration[20]

For 1984–1988 Chile engineered a large real devaluation that approached 50%. In the same period the public-sector deficit, including an estimate for the quasi-fiscal deficit of the central bank, was reduced from 9% of GDP in 1984 to a surplus of 3% of GDP in 1988 (see Marshall and Larrañaga 1989). After the large devaluation of 1984, inflation increased in 1985, reaching 30% per year, but then came down to a level close to 20% per year. GDP growth slowed down in 1985 but then averaged 6.3% per year in 1986–1988, and the rate for 1989 was around 10% (table 3.1). This growth was pulled by non-copper exports, which grew at an average rate of 13% per year in 1986–1988.

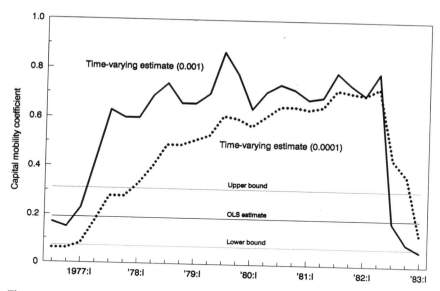

Figure 3.4
Capital mobility coefficients (using the black-market exchange rate).

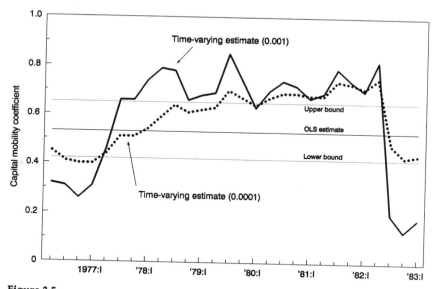

Figure 3.5
Capital mobility coefficients (using the official exchange rate).

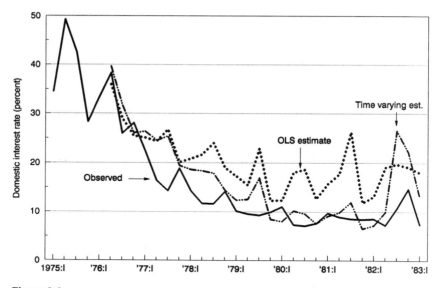

Figure 3.6
Domestic interest rates (black-market base).

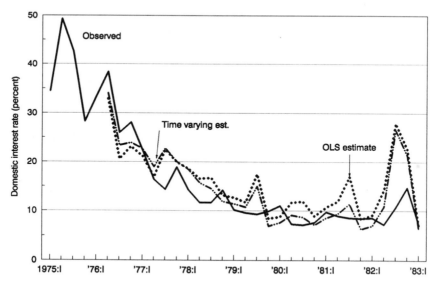

Figure 3.7
Domestic interest rates (official base).

Real Depreciation and Inflation

We are interested in analyzing how this real devaluation and this turnaround of the Chilean economy were achieved. Different factors are important here. First there is the central bank's access to foreign markets—part of the renegotiations on the private-sector debt. The large deficits associated with bailing out afflicted financial institutions (stemming from the financial crises of 1983) were financed not by printing money but by issuing foreign and domestic interest-bearing liabilities of the central bank. As the initial debt of the public sector was very small and monetary policy was quite activist, the domestic real interest rate did not increase much. External financing was obtained from commercial banks as part of new money packages, and from multilateral financial institutions. Further reduction in government expenditures and quasi-fiscal subsidies stemming from the programs of subsidies to debtors and preferential exchange rates by the central bank (ended by 1986) contributed to a drastic cut in the nonfinancial public-sector deficit, turning it into a surplus of around 3% in 1988. The large fiscal adjustment made it possible to achieve a significant real devaluation without a permanent acceleration in inflation in spite of the burden imposed on the central bank by the solution of the financial crises of 1983.[21]

A second factor that contributed to Chile's noninflationary adjustment in relative prices, in spite of a major real depreciation, was the combination of wage de-indexation, engineered in 1982, and the persistence of considerable unemployment, at least until 1987. In fact, in contrast with some other Latin American countries, in Chile the authorities did not have to use inflationary acceleration to erode real wages in order to make them consistent with a higher real exchange rate.

A third element that contributed to the avoidance of an inflationary spurt from an adjustment of the real exchange rate and the external accounts was the relatively "low" level of inflationary expectations as the public internalized a rather tough fiscal stance by the authorities designed to prevent a return to higher levels of inflation in spite of fiscal difficulties. In other words, a reluctance to use the inflation tax (and the willingness and political ability to cut current public spending even in socially sensitive areas) was perceived by the public, giving rise to an anti-inflationary bias in the system.

The above discussion can be supported econometrically with a simple accelerationist specification of inflation run for both a pre-1982 and a post-1982 sample using quarterly data. The 2SLS estimate for the sample 1976/I–1982/II[22] yields the following result (t-statistics appear in parentheses):

$$\pi = 0.007 + 0.805(g_{e(-1)} + \pi^*_{-1} - \pi_{-1}) + 1.11\pi_{-1}$$
$$\quad\ (0.47)\quad (3.87) \qquad\qquad\qquad\ (9.89)$$

$R^2 = 0.79$

D.W. = 1.58

N = 26

F-stat = 45.27

Log likelihood= 42.47.

The 2SLS estimates for 1982/III–1989/I yield

$$\pi = 0.027 + 0.178(g_e + \pi^* - \pi) + 0.368\pi_{-1}$$
$$\quad\ (2.07)\quad (0.99) \qquad\qquad (1.47)$$

$R^2 = 0.13$

D.W. = 2.43

N = 27

F-stat = 1.94

Log likelihood = 62.69.

It is apparent that a significant change occurred in the structure of the inflation equation in the post-1982 period. On the one hand, the degree of persistence or inertia in the process of inflation is reduced significantly in the post-1982 period in comparison with the pre-1982 period; in fact, the coefficient of π_{-1} is reduced from larger-than-unity in 1976/I–1982/II to 0.368 in 1982/I–1989/I. Undoubtedly, the elimination of the clause specifying full lagged wage indexation since the third quarter of 1982 goes a long way to explain this reduction in price. Another major result, and very important for our discussion, is the sharp reduction in the coefficient of the rate of depreciation of the real exchange rate in the inflation equation. In fact, the elasticity of the inflation rate with respect to the rate of depreciation of the real exchange rate falls from 0.80 in 1976/I–1982/II to 0.17 in 1982/II–1989/I. Indeed, the equation captures well the large reduction in the inflationary impact of real depreciation observed after mid-1982 in the Chilean economy.

Real Depreciation and Growth

Real depreciation has been one of the factors behind the recovery and growth record of the post-1984 period. In particular, we find that non-copper exports and efficient import-competing activities responded rapidly to the new higher real exchange rate and to a modest increase in tariffs that took place after 1983.[23] Concerning the new configuration of relative prices, it is also worth mentioning that the policy of maintaining a real interest rate compatible with a reasonable rate of return for physical investment was another important element behind the recovery of private investment and the resumption of growth after 1984.[24]

These other factors were also behind the recovery-*cum*-growth process of the Chilean economy after 1984:

the large availability of labor and some unused capacity until 1987,

the fact that the economy had very few distortions,

very favorable copper prices in 1988-89, providing a cushion for the external sector and improved public finances, and

the support provided by an increase in the share of public investment in GDP after 1985 coupled with a recovery in private investment starting more forcefully since 1987 (see Solimano 1989b).

Inflation and Real Wages

An important question in the adjustment process followed by the Chilean economy after 1984 is the impact of the real depreciation of the exchange rate on real wages. A tradeoff between external competitiveness and the standard of living is often present in the course of an adjustment process. To gain further insight on the relationship between real wages, the real exchange rate, and other variables (such as labor productivity, terms of trade, and spending), we set up a simple model of the determination of the real exchange rate (see Corbo 1985b).

The following equations constitute the model. First, the real exchange rate, R, is defined as the ratio between the domestic currency price of foreign goods, eP^*, and the price of domestic goods, P. Say,

$$R = eP^*/P .$$

$$(13)$$

The price of domestic goods is a linear homogeneous function of the price of exportable goods, P_x, the price of importable goods, P_m, and the price of non-traded goods, P_n:

$$P = P(P_x, P_m, P_n) . \tag{14}$$

The price of export goods, in turn, is assumed to be a function of the wage rate adjusted by labor productivity, w/a_x, and the price of imported intermediate goods in domestic currency, P_m:

$$P_x = f(w/a_x, P_m) . \tag{15}$$

The economy is assumed to be a price taker for the goods it imports:

$$P_m = eP . \tag{16}$$

The price of home goods is determined by wages adjusted by labor productivity in the home goods sector, w/a_n, the price of imported inputs in domestic currency, P_m, and the ratio of expenditure over real output, E/y:

$$P_n = h(w/a_n, P_m, E/y) . \tag{17}$$

Replacing equations 15–17 in equation 14 and inserting in the definition of the real exchange rate (equation 13), we get

$$R = eP^*/P[f(w/a_x, eP), eP, h(w/a_n, eP, E/y)] . \tag{18}$$

Rearranging terms, equation 18 can be written as

$$R = R(e/w, P^*/P, a_x, a_n, E/y) . \tag{19}$$

Equation 19 indicates that the real exchange rate depreciates (R rises) with a cut in real wages in dollars (an increase in e/w), a deterioration in the external terms of trade, and an increase in labor productivity in export activities and import-competing activities. In turn, the real exchange rate appreciates (R falls) when there is an increase in domestic spending relative to output.

The semi-reduced-form solution of the model, equation 19, is estimated econometrically with quarterly data for the 1980s.[25] The results for the log-linear estimation with quarterly data for 1980/I–1989/I yields[26]

$$\ln(R) = -1.153 + 0.237\ln(e/w) + 0.129\ln(a_x) + 0.449\ln(a_{nc})$$
$$\quad (-0.96) \quad (2.77) \qquad\quad (1.20) \qquad\quad (1.62)$$

$$\quad + 0.117\ln(p^*_{-1}/p^*_{m(-1)}) - 0.506\ln(E_{-1}/y_{-1}) + 0.916\ln(R_{-1}) - 0.337\ln(R_{-2})$$
$$\qquad (1.20) \qquad\qquad (-1.50) \qquad\qquad (4.96) \qquad\quad (-2.15)$$

$R^2 = 0.93$

D.W. = 1.95

N = 37

F-stat = 62.07

Log likelihood = 57.29.

The estimate of the equation for the real exchange rate in Chile in the 1980s reveals some interesting results. First, the elasticity of the real exchange rate with respect to the real wage in dollars, w/e, is –0.23, a rather low number. This finding is consistent with the fact that, especially after 1984, the initial drop in real wages (even in dollar terms) associated with a large real depreciation was not too large—given the magnitude of the real depreciation, around 45% in 1984–1989. Second, the ratio of absorption to output seems to have had a considerable quantitative impact on the real exchange rate: the elasticity is –0.506. That, in turn, is consistent with the casual observation that the implementation of expenditure-changing fiscal and monetary policies to support the real depreciation of the peso after mid-1982 played an important role in achieving such a real depreciation in Chile in the post-1982 period. Third, the size and significance of the coefficient of the lagged real exchange rates in the equation supports the notion of a gradual approach of the real exchange rate to "equilibrium" or, at least, sustainable levels after changes in fundamentals take place.

6. Conclusions and Lessons from the Chilean Experience: An Overall Assessment

The past 15 years of Chile's economic history provide some important lessons on stabilization. First, the experience of 1975–1977 shows that the elimination of the fiscal deficit is a necessary but not sufficient condition for controlling inflation. In economies with a long history of inflation, where credibility problems are at stake and indexation schemes—introduced *de facto* or *de jure*—are pervasive, a strong inertia is likely to exist, which makes inflation stabilization very costly without some sort of incomes policy that solves the coordination problem implicit in guiding individual wage and price setters to reach a low-inflation equilibrium.

In addition, if the exchange rate is used as an anchor in a stabilization program, then other nominal prices should be free or fixed with reference to the exchange rate; otherwise, key relative prices such as the real exchange rate, the real wage rate, and the real interest rate could move onto unsustainable paths, making the macroeconomic situation unsustainable.

In sum, both the fiscal shock therapy of 1975–1977 and the experiment with exchange-rate-based stabilization of 1978–1982 show that the convergence to a low-inflation equilibrium may be a slow process. Hence, the dynamics of disinflation matters a great deal in the design of a stabilization plan.

The two stabilization episodes just mentioned neatly highlight the potential tradeoffs between meeting the inflation target and achieving a real exchange rate consistent with the fundamentals in the course of disinflation. In 1975–1977 a real depreciation of the exchange rate was required to accommodate lower real copper prices and a reform of the trade regime. However, the exchange-rate policy designed to produce a real depreciation conspired against rapid disinflation, making the tradeoff between achieving a real devaluation and attaining the inflationary target more evident. A similar problem arose during the exchange-rate-based stabilization experiment of 1978–1982, when the use of the exchange rate for stabilization purposes after February 1978, in the context of backward wage indexation and declining inflation, led to an overvaluation of the real exchange rate, a large increase in expenditures and an unsustainable current-account deficit. When lack of foreign financing forced a reduction in the current-account deficit, expenditure-reducing policies resulted in a sharp increase in unemployment. Again, the low-inflation target had to be temporarily suspended and the exchange rate had to be devalued in 1982 in order to correct the unemployment that was generated from the expenditure-reducing policies.

Another important issue is the cost of stabilization. The cost of stabilization in the 1975 program, in terms of cuts in real wages and output and employment losses, was certainly high, and the strategy was apparently to pay the costs up front at the beginning of the program (a recently installed authoritarian regime provided some of the background for that). In the exchange-rate-based stabilization program, the costs of stabilization seemed at first to be zero, as a boom in economic activity developed. However, the crisis of 1982–83, largely associated with the need to correct an unsustainable current-account deficit that had resulted from the exchange-rate policy followed in the preceding period of exchange-rate-based stabilization, showed that the costs of stabilization did not disappear; rather, they were merely put off until the final phase of the exchange-rate-based stabilization plan. Moreover, the size of these costs (in the form of a correction of the current-account deficit) was considerable. This different intertemporal distribution of the costs of stabilization across different programs (fiscal shock versus exchange-rate-based stabilization) is another important lesson of the Chilean experience.

Finally, the post-1984 experience illustrates the importance of well-functioning goods markets (although the existence of high unemployment, even if it was dropping fairly rapidly, shows that adjustment in the labor market is often more sluggish), a competitive real exchange rate, and the restoration of the basic macroeconomic balances. All of these—complemented with favorable terms of trade—were the basic conditions for restoring non-inflationary growth.

Acknowledgments

Comments made by Sebastian Edwards, Leo Leiderman, Nissan Liviatan, and participants in the conference are acknowledged. We thank Larry Bouton and Fernando Quevedo for research assistance, Raquel Luz for word processing, and Whitney Watriss for editorial help.

Notes

1. Much has been written on the Chilean economic experience. See in particular Corbo 1985a, Edwards and Edwards 1987, Foxley 1981, Harberger 1982, Zahler 1983, Fontaine 1989, and Solimano 1990.

2. The 1979 *Plan Laboral* sanctioned the flexibilization of labor practices in a new labor code.

3. For a review of the indexation, see Edwards 1985. For a review of wage and labor policies in the past 25 years in Chile, see Solimano 1988.

4. See Corbo 1985a, appendix.

5. On the innovative plan to deal with the financial crisis, see Larraín 1989.

6. In estimating the quantity of money demanded in 1975/I–1976/II we control for the 12.9% drop in GDP that year. We do so by using the level of GDP that would have been observed if the growth target of 6%, set by economic policy for 1975, had been achieved (Cauas 1975). On the specification and estimation of demand for money in Chile, see Corbo 1982.

7. Sjaastad and Cortes 1978 and Lagos and Galetovic 1989 arrived at a similar conclusion for 1975.

8. The decision to reduce inflation through tight fiscal policies seemed to have been very firm, as the following quotation from Cauas (1975, p. 155) indicates:

The budgets and programs in force for the purchase of goods and services in public institutions and state enterprises will be reduced between 15 and 25%. These reductions will be implemented at any cost, including the dismissal of any functionaries who are unable to understand that the reduction of inflation receives top priority in the economic policy . . . their particular interests as institutions or individuals, although very respectable, are totally without importance in comparison with the principal preoccupation of all Chileans, namely inflation.

9. See Cortázar 1983, Corbo 1985b, and Solimano 1988 for an analysis of wage policy in Chile.

10. The instruments used in the estimation of the inflation equation are the constant, $g_{w(-1)}$, $g_{e(-1)}$, π^*_{-1}, $g_{e(-2)}$, π^*_{-1}, $g_{M1(-3)}$, π_{-1}, and $DUMP$.

11. The instruments used in the estimation are the constant term, $g_{M1(-1)} - \pi_{-1}$, $g_{e(-3)} + \pi^*_{-3} - \pi_{-3}$, $DUMMY$, $g_{y(-1)}$, and the rate of change of GDP in mining.

12. See Solimano 1986 for the effect of a devaluation on output, employment, and the trade balance in the case of Chile. See Edwards 1986 for a sample of developing countries.

13. The instruments used in the estimation are the constant term, π_{-1}, $g_{y(-2)} - g_{f(-2)}$, and π^*_{-1}.

14. For reviews of different stabilization experiences, see Bruno et al. 1988, Kiguel and Liviatan 1988, and Solimano 1989a.

15. The counterfactual quarterly rates of money growth under this (tighter) money alternative are 20% per quarter for 1975, 10% per quarter for 1976, and 5% per quarter for 1977. The actual average quarterly rates of growth of M1 were 37.6% in 1975, 30.6% in 1976, and 20.3% in 1977. The average rate of growth of M1 in 1974 was 37.9%.

16. There is a vast literature on that period, including Corbo 1985a,b and Edwards and Edwards 1987. Corbo and McNelis (1989) used time-variant parameter-estimation techniques to detect structural changes in the rules of price formation in manufacturing during the period of trade liberalization in the 1970s in Chile.

17. There was domestic deflation in Chile in February 1982. However, what was needed to correct the cumulative overvaluation *and maintain the fixed nominal parity with the dollar* was a protracted period of domestic *deflation*. Obviously, the real cost of such a path of deflation-induced real depreciation was enormous.

18. Haque and Montiel (1989) modify their specification in a way that permits them to apply it to countries where interest rates are controlled and thus there are no data on the domestic market clearing interest rate.

19. In order to proceed with time-varying estimation, the Kalman filter must be initialized. In the absence of *a priori* knowledge, OLS estimates of Ψ, var(Ψ), and

var(ε) are used as initial estimates of Ψ_0, var(Ψ_0), and var(ε_0). Some *a priori* assumption must be made about the initial variation of the innovation to the coefficients var(v_0). The time-varying coefficients are very sensitive to the initial value of this innovation. By theory, Ψ is bounded by 1 and 0. The restrictions placed on these innovation should be such that this restriction is met. The initial value of the innovation to the coefficients is assumed to be some fraction of the innovation to the observation equation. For estimation purposes we have chosen two values for this fraction, 0.001 and 0.0001; higher values result in estimates of Ψ that violate the above-mentioned theoretical bounds.

20. On policies during this period, see Arellano 1988, Fontaine 1989, and Marshall and Larrañaga 1989.

21. It could be argued, however, that the large internal debt accumulated by the central bank in Chile constitutes "latent" inflationary pressure that can be triggered if other (than printing money) sources of revenues of the central bank—e.g., returns from holdings of international reserves, transfers from the treasury, or earnings from assets it acquired during the intervention of financial institutions in 1983—deteriorate (see Solimano 1990).

22. The instruments used in the estimation are the constant term, the rate of nominal devaluation lagged one period, the rate of foreign inflation lagged one period, and the rate of domestic inflation lagged two periods.

23. On the response of exports to the real exchange rate see Caballero and Corbo 1989.

24. The interest-rate policy represents a departure from the extravagant levels of the real interest rates observed in the Chilean economy in the mid and late 1970s and in the early 1980s (particularly in 1981). For a further discussion of the sources of growth after 1984 in Chile see Solimano 1990.

25. The equation is estimated by OLS with the ratio absorption to output lagged one period to avoid a simultaneity problem with the contemporaneous real exchange rate.

26. The variables were constructed as follows: the real exchange rate, R, is the ratio of the index of foreign goods in the wholesale price index *multiplied by* the nominal exchange rate and *divided by* the consumer price index. The ratio e/w was constructed by *dividing* the nominal exchange rate by average nominal wages. The average productivity of labor in exportables, a_x, is the ratio between total output in mining, manufacturing, and agriculture *divided by* total employment in the three sectors. Average labor productivity in the home goods sector, a_n, is the ratio of output in services and other nontraded activities to total employment in that sector. The terms-of-trade index, p^*/p, is approximated by the ratio between the international price of copper *divided by* the price index of prices of the OECD countries. The ratio of absorption to GDP, E/y, was constructed as 1 *minus* the ratio of the trade surplus to GDP.

References

Arellano, J. P. 1988. "Crisis and economic recovery in Chile in the 1980s." *Colección Estudios.* Cieplan. June. (In Spanish.)

Banco Central de Chile. 1985. "Economic and Social Indicators 1960–1985." *Boletin Mensual.* Various issues. (In Spanish.)

Bruno, M., et al. 1988. *Inflation and Stabilization: The Experience of Israel, Argentina, Brazil, Bolivia and Mexico.* MIT Press.

Bruno, M., and S. Fischer. 1986. "The inflationary process: Shocks and accommodations." In *The Israeli Economy: Maturing Through Crises,* Y. Ben-Porath, ed. (Harvard University Press).

Caballero, R., and V. Corbo. 1989. "Real exchange rate uncertainty and exports: Multi-country empirical evidence." *World Bank Economic Review* (May): 263–278.

Cauas, J. 1970. "Stabilization policy: The Chilean case." *Journal of Political Economy* 78 (no. 4): 815–825.

Cauas, J. 1975. "The government economic recovery program." Reprinted in J. C. Mendez, *Chilean Economic Policy* (Santiago, 1979).

Corbo, V. 1982. "Monetary policy with an overrestricted demand for money equation: Chile in the 60s." *Journal of Development Economics* 10 (February): 119–126.

Corbo, V. 1985a. "Reforms and macroeconomic adjustments in Chile during 1974–84." *World Development* 13 (no. 8): 893–916.

Corbo, V. 1985b. "International prices, wages and inflation in an open economy: A Chilean model." *Review of Economics and Statistics* 67 (November): 564–573.

Corbo, V., and P. McNelis. 1989. "The pricing of manufactured goods during trade liberalization: Evidence from Chile, Israel and Korea." *Review of Economics and Statistics* 71 (August): 491–499.

Cortázar, R. 1983. "Políticas de reajustes y salarios en Chile: 1974–82." *Estudios Cieplan* (June): 10.

ECLAC. 1983. Balance preliminar de la economia de America Latina y el Caribe. 1984 [Preliminary Balance of the Economy of Latin American and the Caribbean. 1984]. Santiago.

Edwards, A. 1985. Wage Indexation and Real Wages: Chile 1974–1980. Unpublished paper, World Bank.

Edwards, S. 1986. "Are devaluations contractionary?" *Review of Economics and Statistics* 68 (August): 501–508.

Edwards, S., and A. Edwards. 1987. *Monetarism and Liberalization: The Chilean Experiment.* Ballinger.

Edwards, S., and M. Khan. 1985. "Interest rate determination in developing countries." *IMF Staff Papers* 32 (September): 377–403.

Fischer, S. 1988. "Real balances, the exchange rate and indexation: Real variables in disinflation." *Quarterly Journal of Economics* 103 (February): 27–49.

Fontaine, J. A. 1989. "The Chilean economy in the 1980s: Adjustment and recovery." In *Debt Adjustment and Recovery*, S. Edwards and F. Larraín, eds. (Blackwell).

Foxley, A. 1981. "Stabilization policies and their effects in employment and income distribution: A Latin American perspective." In *Economic Stabilization in Developing Countries*, W. R. Cline and S. Weintraub, eds. (Brookings Institution).

Haque, N. Ul., and P. Montiel. 1989. Capital Mobility in Developing Countries—Some Empirical Tests. Mimeograph.

Harberger, A. C. 1982. "The Chilean economy in the 1970s: Crisis, stabilization, liberalization, reform." In *Economic Policy in a World of Change*, K. Brunner and A. M. Meltzer, eds. (Carnegie-Rochester Conference Series on Public Policy, vol. 17).

Kiguel, M., and N. Liviatan. 1988. "Inflationary rigidities and stabilization policies." *World Bank Economic Review* 2 (no. 3): 273–298.

Larraín, M. 1989. How the 1981–1983 Chilean Banking Crisis was Handled. PPR Working Paper 300. World Bank.

Lagos, F., and A. Galetovic. 1989. Inflación e indexación en la economia Chilena [Inflation and Indexation in the Chilean Economy]. Paper presented at IX Congreso Latinoamericano Sociedad Econometrica, Santiago.

Marshall, J., and O. Larrañaga. 1989. Política fiscal y ajuste en Chile [Fiscal Policy and Adjustment in Chile]. Mimeograph, ECLAC.

Sjaastad, L., and H. Cortes. 1978. "The monetary approach to the balance of payments and real interest rates in Chile." *Estudios de Economia* 11.

Solimano, A. 1986. "Contractionary devaluation in the Southern Cone. The case of Chile." *Journal of Development Economics* 23 (September): 135–151.

Solimano, A. 1988. "Políticas de remuneraciones en Chile: Experiencia pasada, instrumentos y opciones a futuro [Wage Policies in Chile: Experience, Instruments and Future Options]." *Colección Estudios Cieplan.*

Solimano, A. 1989a. Inflation and the Costs of Stabilization: Country Experiences, Conceptual Issues and Policy Lessons. PPR Working Paper 226, World Bank.

Solimano, A. 1989b. How Private Investment Reacts to Changing Macroeconomic Conditions. The Case of Chile in the 1980s. PPR Working Paper 212, World Bank.

Solimano, A. 1990. Economic Growth, Social Equity and Macroeconomic Stability. Looking at the Challenges for the Chilean Economy in the 1990s. Paper presented at UNU/WIDER conference on Medium Term Growth Strategies, Stockholm.

Zahler, R. 1983. "Recent Southern Cone liberalization reforms and stabilization policies: The Chilean case, 1974–82." *Journal of Interamerican Studies and World Affairs* 25 (no. 4).

Comments by Sebastian Edwards

Corbo and Solimano have presented us with an important and ambitious paper on the 1975–1989 Chilean experience with inflation and stabilization. What is particularly interesting about this paper is that, contrary to most previous work on the subject, the authors have attempted to tackle the issue by following a formal econometric approach. They have identified a number of key questions and puzzles and used counterfactual simulations to ask what would have happened if alternative policies had been pursued.

Generally speaking, I am very sympathetic toward the authors' approach. It makes sense from a methodological point of view, and, in principle, one can learn important lessons from it. This paper is, in fact, a good complement to some of the previous work on Chile—some of it by Corbo himself—which was analytic and more historical in nature. It seems to me, however, that in the current study the authors have gone a bit too far in emphasizing the econometrics and the simulations. By focusing on the regression results, they tend to lose the global perspective, and end up presenting—at least to the uninformed reader—a somewhat misleading picture of what happened and the possible alternatives. Moreover, the authors do not provide an overall evaluation of the program, and are circumspect about the way in which adjustment was achieved after 1985.

I will divide my comments into three interrelated parts. First I will deal with some specific issues addressed by the authors in the paper and, more specifically, in their simulation analysis. In the second part I will discuss the post-1985 adjustment, a period covered only briefly by the authors. Finally, I will extend their analysis to the "aftermath" of the stabilization program—an issue that forms part of the title of this conference—briefly discussing future economic developments in Chile.

Inflation and Stabilization in Chile: 1975–1985

The main conclusion drawn by the authors from their counterfactual simulation analysis for 1975–1978 is that Chile erred in its wage and exchange-rate policies. More specifically, the authors argue that the combination of the exchange-rate policy of devaluing the nominal rate by more than the inflation differential (followed until 1978) and the wage-indexation policy that linked wage increases to past inflation conspired to generate a very slow reduction of inflation in 1975–1978. In addition, the authors argue that for the period 1979–1982 the policy of indexing wages to past inflation was responsible for the slow speed at which domestic inflation converged toward world inflation. From this analysis the authors conclude that alternative wage-adjustment and exchange-rate policies in 1975–1982 would have been more appropriate. In particular, they advocate incomes policies, suggesting that wage guidelines of the type used in other Latin American countries (in the heterodox programs) would have helped the anti-inflationary process in Chile.

I have some quarrels with these conclusions and with the methodology used to reach them. The core of the analysis consists of three equations—for output, inflation, and wages—which are first estimated by ordinary least squares and then used to analyze, through counterfactual simulations, the role played by changes in velocity and by wage inertia in the Chilean stabilization process. I have four specific issues to raise regarding this approach.

The first has to do with the three-equation model used in the empirical analysis. It is not clear to me how these equations are obtained, or whether they are in any way derived from an optimization process by economic agents. Moreover, the authors do not explain their choice of a particular lag structure. Possibly the most important limitation of this analysis is that the authors have made no effort to account for the profound structural changes that affected the Chilean economy during this period. For instance, there are no tests of the stability through time of the estimated parameters, nor is there an attempt to use interactive dummy variables to capture some of these structural changes. This contrasts with the elegant approach the authors take in section 4, where they use a time-varying coefficient method to estimate an interest-rate equation for Chile.

The second issue has to do with the role of forward-looking variables. Nowhere in the estimation process can we find these variables; in fact, expectations of future inflation have been replaced by past inflation rates. This, of course, introduces serious limitations to a model that tries to assess how stabilization policy affects velocity. Moreover, it is rather difficult to discuss credibility aspects without formally incorporating forward-looking variables into the analysis.

The third issue is a factual one. The authors develop their discussion under the assumption that throughout the whole period wages were adjusted according to *past* inflation. This is not so. In fact, until July 1975 an effort was made to adjust wages by less than past inflation. Between January 1, 1974, and July 1, 1975, there were seven mandated wage adjustments, for an accumulated total of 1,141%. In the same period, accumulated (past) inflation was 2,567%.[1] Consequently, during this period the wage-rate policy resulted in a very significant *decline* in real wages: in May 1975, blue-collar wages were 44% lower than in May 1971, and 37% lower than their 1970 level.

Ignoring the historical evolution of wage rates during the initial years of the military regime is, in my opinion, an important limitation of the analysis. All the "preferred" simulations, including the ones on which the authors base their conclusion that wage guidelines would have been useful, imply a reduction in real wages (in some cases a fairly substantial one). An obvious question here is: Would this "preferred" policy have indeed been socially and politically possible in an economy where real wages were already about half of what they were in 1971?

The fourth issue is related to the authors' remarks regarding the exchange-rate policy followed in Chile between 1975 and 1978. Corbo and Solimano argue that the practice of devaluing the nominal rate by more than the inflation differential conspired against a more rapid reduction of inflation. Moreover, based on their simulation results, they conclude that if a strict PPP exchange-rate rule had been followed— whereby the exchange rate would have been devalued in magnitudes equal to inflation differentials—inflation would have been reduced at a faster pace. The problem with this assertion is that it ignores the relationship between equilibrium and actual real exchange rates. That is, the authors do not incorporate into their analysis the crucial question of real-exchange-rate overvaluation. During 1975–1978 Chile was subject to a number of structural changes that greatly affected the level of the equilibrium real exchange rate. First, the trade-liberalization process eliminated all quantitative restrictions and reduced import tariffs from an average of over 100% to a uniform 10%. Second, during this period Chile suffered very dramatic negative terms-of-trade shocks. For example, the price of copper—Chile's main export—went from approximately $1 per pound in 1974 to 59¢ in 1977.[2] Of course, as a consequence of all of this, the real exchange rate "required" to maintain external equilibrium in 1977–78 was significantly higher (that is, more depreciated) than in 1974. Thus, the policy of devaluing in excess of the inflation differentials was indeed motivated by these considerations and was aimed at avoiding a situation of real-exchange-rate overvaluation. Had the authorities followed a strict PPP rule, as suggested by the authors, a serious situation of real-exchange-rate misalignment would have evolved, placing the success of the structural reform in serious jeopardy.

Real Devaluation and Export Boom: 1985–1989

Between 1985 and 1989 Chile was, in many respects, a model of adjustment. Output grew rapidly, exports boomed, unemployment was reduced dramatically, and inflation remained at a relatively low level by Latin American standards. This adjustment was accomplished by the combination of two forces. First, the authorities pursued a very active macroeconomic policy, including an aggressive policy of nominal devaluations aimed at generating a large depreciation in the real exchange rate. Second, the structural reforms of the 1970s resulted in a major modernization of the Chilean economy, allowing it to respond very quickly to the new macroeconomic policy and, in particular, to the incentives generated by a competitive real exchange rate. Unfortunately, the authors are very circumspect regarding this period. Little is said about the policies followed; the authors do not tell us what, in their opinion, were the forces that allowed Chile to engineer a real-exchange-rate depreciation of 75% between 1982 and 1987.[3]

After a period of hesitation in 1982–1985, fiscal policy in 1985 became very active, focusing on redirecting public resources away from current expenditures and toward public investment. As a result, public investment increased by more than 7 percentage points of GDP between 1985 and 1989. In addition, fiscal policy in this period was geared toward encouraging private savings via a reduction in taxation. For example, the tax rate on corporate earnings was reduced from 46% to 10%, providing special encouragement to corporate savings. As a result, between 1985 and 1988 investment grew at a rate of 11% per year. What was crucially important, however, was that these measures were taken while maintaining an overall fiscal balance and avoiding unsustainable pressures on the real exchange rate.[4]

In terms of monetary policy, the post-1985 period was characterized by an *active* manipulation of the stock of domestic credit, mainly geared at targeting interest rates. Indeed, an overriding concern of the authorities in this period was to avoid a repetition of the "high real interest rates" of the late 1970s. In this regard it is important to contrast the attitude of Finance Minister Hernan Buchi's team after 1985 with that of the "Chicago boys" of the 1970s. While the former had a clearly pragmatic view regarding the role of active macroeconomic, and especially monetary, policy in achieving stability, the latter group firmly believed that the only way to tackle macroeconomic problems was by letting the economy adjust on its own. In fact, a number of observers have argued that the "automatic adjustment" approach to macroeconomic policy, followed between 1979 and 1982, was one of the most important policy mistakes made by the early "Chicago boys."

The active macroeconomic policy allowed the Chilean government to greatly increase the real quantity of money without generating unsustainable inflationary pressures. For example, taking 1979 as the base year, the index of M1 increased from 94 to 135 between 1985 and 1988, while real interest rates remained in the range of 4–5% per year.

On the other hand, there is little doubt that the exchange-rate policy based on periodic devaluations was one of the most important policies of the post-1982 period. Between 1982 and 1988 the *real* exchange rate was devalued by approximately 90%. This not only allowed the country to improve its level of competitiveness, thus greatly helping the boom in nontraditional exports; it also contributed to the maintainance of reasonable interest rates levels and to avoiding capital flight.

Contrary to the fiscal and monetary policies, the active exchange-rate policy began in 1982. In fact, starting that year, when the fixed exchange rate was abandoned, and continuing until 1985, the various authorities made a point of devaluing the peso by amounts that significantly exceeded the domestic rate of inflation (see table 3.C1). Starting in 1986, after a substantial real depreciation had been achieved, the government implemented a more sophisticated devaluation policy that took into account the evolution of the real exchange rate, domestic inflation, and

Table 3.C1
Rate of inflation and rate of devaluation of the peso, 1982–1988 (%).

	Average rate of increase of CPI	Average rate of devaluation of the official US$ exchange rate
1982	9.9	30.5
1983	27.3	54.8
1984	19.8	24.9
1985	30.7	63.3
1986	19.5	19.9
1987	19.9	13.7
1988	14.6	11.9

Source: Banco Central de Chile.

other domestic and international macroeconomic developments. As a result, the rate of nominal devaluation with respect to the U.S. dollar declined somewhat in 1986–1988.

Chile's successful experience with exchange-rate management in this period has generated a number of valuable lessons for other countries. Perhaps the most important one is that by devaluing the nominal exchange rate it is possible to engineer substantial real devaluations without generating very high inflation. In that regard, Chile can be put together with Colombia and Korea as a (very) successful case of active exchange-rate management. In Chile the main keys to this result were the maintenance of fiscal discipline and the recognition that changes in real-exchange-rate "fundamentals" are very important in determining the extent to which the real exchange rate can be altered. The Chilean authorities have followed a particularly pragmatic approach in which the classification of shocks as permanent or transitory, the evolution of terms of trade, and the availability of foreign funds have played crucial roles in determining the pace at which the nominal exchange rate should be devalued. Finally, it should be pointed out that the nature of labor relations in Chile during the military period helped the adjustment process, particularly the achievement of the depreciated real exchange rate. After the military coup the labor movement was restricted and unions' ability to engage in serious bargaining was greatly curtailed. Indeed, an important feature of the 1982–1989 adjustment process is the significant decline in real wages (table 3.C2).

The Aftermath

An important characteristic of the Chilean adjustment process is that it was achieved under an authoritarian military regime.[5] In December 1989 free presidential elections were held, and the centrist opposition candidate, Patricio Aylwin, was elected president. After almost 17 years Chile is returning to democracy. What can we expect in the next few years in terms of economic policy? Is it likely that the new government will reverse the market-based policies of the military regime?

Table 3.C2
Average real wages in Chile, 1980–1989 (1980 = 100).

1980	1981	1982	1983	1984	1985	1986	1987	1988	1989
100.0	109.9	108.6	97.1	97.2	93.5	95.1	94.7	101.0	102.9

Source: ECLA.

Surprisingly, Aylwin's economic program exhibits a remarkable degree of continuity. In fact, the democratic forces have pointed out that they want to maintain the high degree of openness of the economy, the reliance on market forces, and the outward orientation of the development process. At the same time they have presented a detailed program for social plans which they intend to finance fully through taxes and not through debt or monetization.

Perhaps the most remarkable aspect of the transition process toward democracy is that the incoming government backed a new law that transformed the central bank into a completely independent institution that will not respond to political pressures from the executive or other sources. In this way Chilean politicians of all persuasions have shown a sophisticated understanding of what it takes to generate credibility. Words and promises are not sufficient; institutional reform may indeed help.

Acknowledgments

I am indebted to the National Science Foundation and to the University of California Pacific Rim Studies program for financial support.

Notes

1. See Edwards and Edwards 1987, chapter 6.

2. The index of terms of trade was 106 in 1974 and 67 in 1977.

3. Since 1987 there has been a slight appreciation in the real exchange rate. On the post-1982 adjustment see Fontaine 1989.

4. It should be noted, however, that the form of the social security system makes it difficult to compare the fiscal finances before and after 1983. See the discussion in Fontaine 1989.

5. Indeed, a number of critics have argued that the structural reforms and the adjustment program were made possible by the dictatorial nature of the regime.

References

Edwards, S., and A. C. Edwards. 1987. *Monetarism and Liberalization: The Chilean Experiment.* Ballinger.

Fontaine, J. A. 1989. "The Chilean economy in the 1980s: Adjustment and recovery." In S. Edwards and F. Larraín, eds., *Debt, Adjustment and Recovery* (Blackwell).

Comments by Leonardo Leiderman

Corbo and Solimano analyze important aspects of Chile's process of inflation and disinflation since the early 1970s. They concentrate on the high inflation of October 1973 and of 1974–1975, the orthodox stabilization program of 1975, the exchange-rate-based program of 1978–1982, and the post-1984 period of large real devaluation and low inflation. For each of these episodes the authors advance a hypothesis (or a set of hypotheses) about which empirical evidence is provided.

In my view, the paper is clearly written and interesting, and it represents an important contribution to the study of Chile's experience with stabilization. Since the analysis proceeds by focusing separately on each episode, it is hard to summarize the main results in terms of a single conclusion. In what follows I briefly elaborate on some of the limitations of the analysis, which could be overcome in future work.

My first comment is that it would have been useful had the authors provided an overall assessment of the Chilean stabilization strategy. Of all the disinflation attempts analyzed in this volume, Chile's is perhaps the strongest one to date in terms of reaching what appears to be a firm and sustainable position with low inflation. At the same time, it is clear that during the transition to this position there were many periods characterized by marked increases in the rate of unemployment and by substantial cuts in the standard of living. What was the "sacrifice ratio" associated with the Chilean disinflation? How does this ratio compare with that of heterodox programs such as Israel's and Mexico's? Obviously, these are difficult questions to answer, but it is necessary to deal with them before we can reach some general conclusions on the pros and cons of orthodox and heterodox stabilization programs.

Another important limitation of the analysis has to do with the methodology. The authors use coefficients that were estimated under one policy regime in order to quantitatively assess phenomena that can be attributed to another regime. In so doing, they abstract from the implications of the well-known Lucas Critique, in that they assume that key building blocks of the macroeconomic structure are invariant with respect to the policy regime. To the extent that this invariance property does not hold in the data, the authors' calculations and simulations may be biased.

An example of abstraction from the Lucas Critique appears when the authors examine why it took so long for inflation to slow down after the orthodox stabilization program of 1975. The main hypothesis advanced by Corbo and Solimano is that the aggressive policy of nominal devaluations and the inertial effects of backward-looking wage indexation played key roles in accounting for the slow disinflation. To examine this hypothesis, they estimate a three-equation model for the following dependent variables: the rate of inflation, the growth rate of output, and the growth rate of the nominal wage. Exchange-rate depreciation is assumed to be exogenous and appears as one of the explanatory variables in the equations. After the model's parameters for 1974/I–1989/I are estimated, they are used in "counterfactual" simulations of the effects of adopting a PPP rule for exchange-rate depreciation and of shifting from lagged to contemporaneous wage indexation to inflation. A main result derived by the authors is that exchange-rate and wage rules contributed to the postponement of disinflation during this period.

A key assumption made in deriving this result is that most of the coefficients in the macroeconomic model are invariant with respect to the simulated changes in the wage and exchange-rate rules. Yet much of the research on rational-expectations macroeconomic models provides clear examples of cases in which shifts in these rules affect the model's reduced-form coefficients. For example, changes in the exchange-rate depreciation rule are likely to affect the frequency and magnitude of price adjustments by business firms and of wage adjustments demanded by trade unions. Similarly, changes in the wage rule are likely to affect the parameters describing the stochastic process of prices and output. Although in some circumstances Lucas Critique arguments may have only second-order effects, it is precisely in the context of high inflation and volatile economies such as Chile that their quantitative implications may well be sizable. Thus, caution is advised in regarding the authors' results as final and decisive.

Last, the period 1984–1988 has shown remarkable results for Chile's macroeconomy. The public-sector deficit dropped from 9% of GDP in 1984 to a surplus of 3% of GDP in 1988, inflation remained below 20% per year, and at the same time a real devaluation of about 50% was achieved. While the authors point to four main sets of factors that contributed to this outcome, the paper does not provide a quantitative assessment of their relative importance. It would be interesting, in future work, to determine whether, e.g., the impact of the fiscal contraction on macroeconomic performance was stronger or weaker than the impact of labor-market factors such as wage deindexation, and to have an expanded analysis of this interesting episode.

General Discussion

The most striking feature of the Chilean economy is the successful transition from stabilization to growth. This issue was addressed by some participants who agreed that the paper should have elaborated on it in greater detail. A favorable condition was the real devaluation, which did not cause acceleration in inflation. According to Peter Bernholz, this was due to the budgetary policy's being "proper," i.e., consistent with low inflationary expectations (similar to the German case in 1923). Nadav Halevi emphasized the importance of the successful liberalization of trade and capital, and of its correct sequencing, and thought that more should have been said about it. Jacob Frenkel wondered why the debt issue was not raised, as its overhang might have consequences for the performance of Chile's economy, much as it had in other countries.

4

From Sharp Disinflation to Hyperinflation, Twice: The Argentine Experience, 1985–1989

Daniel Heymann

In recent years, Argentina has added new episodes to its history of high inflation and attempts at stabilization. This paper reviews the experience of the period 1985–1989. The Austral plan and its aftermath have been widely analyzed in the literature[1]; for the sake of completeness, the first section briefly describes the early effects of the program and the growing instability that developed as they were not sustained. Section 2 discusses the disinflation and the reasons for its fragility in more general terms, focusing particularly on fiscal policies. In 1989, Argentina underwent an extremely rapid inflation, unusual even by the country's own standards: at its peak, the rate of increase of the CPI reached almost 200% per month. Section 3 describes the process that resulted in that inflationary explosion, the new shock disinflation program that started in July 1989 and the program's failure.

1. From Austral to Primavera: 1985–1988

The Austral plan was formulated as a shock against an inflation running at a rate over 25% per month. The plan was announced in June 1985, although preparations had started some months before with measures to raise the real exchange rate and public-sector prices. The program had three main components. First, there was to be a drastic fall in the fiscal deficit to cut the monetary financing of the government. Second, the program fixed the exchange rate and public-sector prices and froze most prices and private-sector wages. Third, to ease the transition and to avoid large wealth redistributions due to the fall of inflation, a currency reform was announced to correct the nominal value of pre-contracted payments.

The program induced a noticeable change in expectations. The inflation rate dropped sharply (see table 4.1) without significant product shortages. At the same time, a quite rapid remonetization took place. This allowed the government to collect large seigniorage revenues (see table 4.2).[2] Given the fall in the fiscal deficit, these revenues had a counterpart in the growth of rediscounts and in the accumulation of foreign reserves. However, the domestic debt also increased, as the central bank raised (interest-bearing) reserve requirements to prevent a too-rapid growth in the money supply. This policy took its toll, given the large differential remaining between the domestic interest rate and the yield on central-bank assets.

Despite its initial success, the program faced several problems. The "residual inflation" was not generally interpreted as transitory, but set a floor to expectations, and it triggered a drift in wages beginning in the last months of 1985. In addition, fiscal policies were not based on solid instruments, and the central bank did not show much strength in resisting demands for rediscounts.

The government was not prepared to face the conflicts that may have ensued from the proposal of a definite reform in fiscal policies, and (despite the recovery in production that had been taking place) it was quite sensitive to the criticism that its policies had lowered output and real wages. Thus, it was unable to try for a clear-cut stabilization program. Also, the freeze had to end in any case, and a large fall in the real value of the main anchoring variables had to be avoided. The measures taken in April 1986 were consistent with this logic: the government announced that it would periodically adjust the exchange rate and public-sector prices, controls over industrial prices were relaxed, and firms and unions were allowed to set wages through direct negotiations.

Contrary to many fears at the time, prices did not jump at the end of the freeze. However, inflation did accelerate. The authorities first reacted by making steeper increases in the exchange rate and in public-sector prices; then, in August 1986, they announced a policy of adjustments at declining rates. The sequence of compression and decompression phases in the management of the anchors was to become a recurrent feature in the following two years.

The fiscal deficit increased noticeably in the latter part of 1986 and in 1987, a year when policies were much influenced by political events (an abortive military coup at Easter and elections to Congress and provincial governorships in September, which were lost by the ruling party) and by a marked fall in external terms of trade. High interest on bank reserves and rediscounts with poor repayment prospects contributed to raise the actual deficit. As time went by, the lack of ready sources of financing became apparent[3]; compounded by the fall in real money holdings, this meant that the fiscal deficit could be financed only at a very high inflation rate.

Under these conditions, incomes policies were used several times in an effort to stop the rising inflation, but without much effect. Two short freezes (in February and October 1987) were followed by rapid increases in the inflation rate, which reached over 20% per month on average in the third quarter of 1988. The announcement of the Primavera program in August 1988 was widely perceived as a final attempt to moderate inflation before the 1989 presidential elections.[4] One of the main elements of this plan was a new foreign-exchange regime: a "free exchange rate"— a dirty float—would apply to financial transactions and imports; proceeds from agricultural exports would sell at an "official," pegged exchange rate. This established an implicit export tax, given by the spread between the two rates. In addition, guidelines for industrial prices were negotiated with large industrial firms; as part of the agreement, the rate of the value-added tax was lowered from 18% to 15%. It was also announced that transfers from the treasury to public enterprises would be cut and that fewer rediscounts would be issued by the central bank.

These were not well-rounded measures; moreover, they were taken when confidence was at a low ebb. However, foreign reserves initially increased, and only small sales in the free market were needed to keep the spread between the exchange rates in the targeted 20–25% range. The inflation rate dropped to a low of 6% in November, while a (modest) increase in real money demand suggested that short-run expectations had calmed down.

But the program was still very fragile. There had been no definite reduction in the public deficit, and the government had few tools available to tighten fiscal policies. Interest rates were high: since the domestic debt had been increasing, this put a heavy burden on government finances and fed back into expectations. There was a growing mass of funds ready to be transformed into foreign exchange, especially as elections drew nearer. Although the trade surplus was still high, the future supply of foreign exchange depended on the financial decisions of exporters. Despite the moratorium, payments on the foreign debt were quite large (Machinea 1989), while substantial arrears had been accumulated. Thus, the volume of disposable reserves was uncertain, and, in any case, neither its size nor the general outlook of economic policy was such as to discourage a potential run.

Table 4.1
Main nominal variables (monthly growth rates).[a]

	SPI[b]	WPI[b]	Exchange rates Average trade[c]	Parallel[d]	Hourly wages[b]	Public-sector prices[e]	M1[f]	M4[g]
1984	*18.8*	*17.4*	*18.1*	*18.0*	*20.1*	*20.2*	*16.8*	*18.5*
I	16.5	12.5	13.1	26.6	16.4	14.8	21.6	18.5
II	17.8	18.1	15.2	11.4	22.0	23.0	15.1	15.8
III	22.8	21.5	20.8	17.8	22.7	23.6	14.5	19.8
IV	18.0	17.7	23.7	16.9	19.4	19.7	16.1	19.7
1985	*14.1*	*13.6*	*14.3*	*13.8*	*11.9*	*14.1*	*17.8*	*14.2*
I	24.1	22.2	24.8	30.6	19.1	20.1	18.5	19.3
II	28.4	34.9	32.6	25.6	28.4	37.9	24.6	22.5
III	3.7	0.4	2.6	5.6	−0.6	2.3	21.5	9.4
IV	2.5	0.8	0.7	−3.1	3.1	0.0	7.3	6.3
1986	*5.1*	*3.9*	*3.9*	*5.2*	*5.0*	*3.9*	*5.2*	*6.6*
I	3.1	0.7	0.6	2.0	2.5	0.1	6.4	6.0
II	4.4	3.4	3.0	−0.5	5.6	4.8	5.1	5.5
III	7.6	7.1	6.8	10.9	5.8	5.7	3.8	5.4
IV	5.4	4.4	5.4	8.6	6.0	4.9	5.4	9.4
1987	*8.8*	*9.0*	*9.5*	*9.3*	*8.2*	*8.6*	*7.0*	*7.8*
I	7.4	6.7	8.9	6.3	4.5	6.8	8.0	6.5
II	5.2	4.5	3.4	3.4	6.5	4.2	4.5	6.6
III	11.8	13.5	13.0	18.5	11.2	10.4	3.5	8.1
IV	10.9	11.7	13.3	9.5	10.7	13.3	12.1	10.2
1988	*14.1*	*14.9*	*12.8*	*11.0*	*14.5*	*14.6*	*12.6*	*15.1*
I	11.4	13.9	12.5	12.1	10.5	13.8	7.7	11.1
II	17.0	21.3	17.8	17.4	16.1	22.1	11.8	14.8
III	21.4	20.6	18.4	11.9	20.0	18.6	17.6	20.6
IV	7.2	4.7	3.2	3.2	11.6	4.6	13.5	14.0
1989	*38.6*	*39.6*	*42.0*	*44.6*	*37.3*	*38.0*	*37.5*	*37.0*
I	11.8	11.3	10.7	37.2	9.1	7.4	12.2	13.4
II	72.2	96.1	108.7	113.8	62.2	46.3	48.3	53.8
III	64.8	50.9	45.6	17.5	55.9	106.7	71.0	58.6
IV	16.4	15.4	21.0	26.7	28.9	12.9	24.7	23.6

a. Monthly growth rates between the end months of each quarter. Annual figures are December-to-December growth rates on a monthly basis.
b. CPI, WPI, and hourly wages are based on data published by the National Institute of Statistics (INDEC). Hourly wages are measured implicitly by dividing the wage bill paid by a sample of large manufacturing firms to blue-collar workers (including overtime, but excluding items such as paid vacations and mid-year and end-of-year bonuses) by the number of man-hours worked.
c. The average exchange rate for trade transactions is calculated by CEPAL Buenos Aires on the basis of data from the central bank, the Secretariat of Agriculture, and other sources; it is an average of the exchange rate applying to imports and the effective exchange rate for exports, which takes into account the effect of multiple exchange rates (when applicable) and of taxes or tax rebates on exports.

d. The parallel exchange rate (or the free exchange rate, when applicable) is based on quotations published in the local press.

e. Public-sector prices are an aggregate of prices charged by public enterprises, including taxes. (Source of basic data: Controller of Public Enterprises—SIGEP.)

f. M1 defined as currency outside banks *plus* demand deposits held by private units (seasonally adjusted).

g. M4 includes savings and time deposits (except those held by government agencies), with accrued interest, and bank acceptances; the basic data are from the central bank.

Table 4.2
Fiscal deficit, seigniorage, and inflation tax (percentages of GDP).

	Primary deficit[a] (1)	Interest[b] (2)	Operational deficit (1)+(2) (3)	Redis-counts[c] (4)	Deficit including rediscounts (3)+(4) (5)	Seignior-age[d] (6)	Infla-tion tax[d] (7)
1984							
I	5.8	5.2	11.0	0.7	11.7	10.2	7.9
II	3.4	5.9	9.3	0.4	9.7	7.2	8.5
III	2.1	4.8	6.9	0.1	7.0	5.2	9.6
IV	3.7	5.6	9.3	0.1	9.4	5.8	6.4
1985							
I	3.6	6.5	10.1	0.2	10.3	6.0	7.8
II	0.1	6.4	6.5	1.0	7.5	6.8	7.9
III	−3.5	6.5	3.0	0.6	3.9	8.9	1.5
IV	−4.8	6.8	2.0	0.4	2.4	4.1	1.4
1986							
I	−1.1	5.8	4.7	0.8	5.5	4.1	2.0
II	−3.5	5.7	2.2	0.1	2.3	3.3	2.8
III	−1.3	2.8	1.5	0.3	1.8	2.4	4.6
IV	3.0	5.7	8.7	0.5	9.2	3.1	3.1
1987							
I	1.0	4.1	5.1	1.3	6.4	4.5	4.2
II	0.4	6.3	5.7	1.8	8.5	2.7	3.1
III	1.4	6.7	8.1	1.9	10.0	1.7	5.8
IV	1.6	4.3	5.9	1.6	7.5	5.0	4.4
1988							
I	0.3	9.0	9.3	1.1	10.4	3.3	4.9
II	−0.7	5.8	5.1	0.6	5.7	4.2	6.0
III	2.6	0.9	3.5	0.5	3.8	5.3	6.5
IV	2.1	4.0	6.1	0.2	6.3	5.0	2.6
1989							
I	—	—	—	—	—	4.9	4.7
II	—	—	—	—	—	10.5	16.2
III	—	—	—	—	—	10.8	9.5
IV	—	—	—	—	—	8.8	6.0

Source: Machinea 1989, tables II.3, II.6, and II.9.

a. Primary deficit on a cash basis of the non-financial public sector.

b. Foreign and domestic. Interest is measured at the moment it falls due. Interest on the domestic debt is measured in real terms. Includes the central government, public enterprises, and the central bank. Figures on the domestic interest of the central bank for 1984 are estimates.

Table 4.2 (continued)

c. Flow of rediscounts of doubtful recovery. Includes rediscounts to banks under central-bank intervention and to the Mortgage Bank.

d. Seignioriage and the inflation tax are ratios to the seasonally adjusted GDP, in constant prices, of quarterly sums of monthly quantities $\Delta M1/p$ and $m1^*\pi/(1 + \pi)$ (respectively), where $\Delta M1$ is the nominal increase in M1 (currency *plus* private checking deposits), seasonally adjusted; p is the CPI; m1 is the (CPI-deflated) real value of M1 (seasonally adjusted) in the previous month; π the rate of increase of the CPI in a given month.

2. Some Policy Issues

Disinflation Policies and Stabilization Strategies

Stabilization implies reaching a state in which decisions incorporate the expectation of a low and reasonably predictable inflation over a relatively long time horizon and in which policies can validate such expectations under a variety of contingencies. This is quite different from a transitory disinflation, which does not, in itself, guarantee such a durable change.

In these terms, a shock stabilization would be an extremely demanding task. In practice, a program can hardly pre-specify a complete set of present and future policies with an implied certainty that they will be carried out in due time and form; it is also unlikely that individuals would immediately change behavior patterns that they had developed in periods of high inflation. From this perspective, it is to be expected that a stabilization attempt will start with some transitory measures and that later moves will not be precisely determined from the beginning, and also that, even if inflation is low for a while, the economy will still remember the inflationary period, which will influence its performance and constrain policies. After a high inflation, the propagation of upward price shocks would probably be much stronger than in a traditionally stable economy, and policies would have less room for "error correction."

In any case, disinflation is much harder to achieve, and more easily reversible, if there is no clear-cut change in short-run expectations. Credibility is an elusive concept: reasonable reactions to given policy actions or announcements can vary according to the particular perceptions different individuals have of the authorities' objectives and opportunities, and of the possible effects of specific measures. Making the complete transition from high inflation to stability will generally require redefining the set of policy instruments (i.e., in the process, the government will have to gain control over some variables, while others will be left to be determined endogenously); often, it may imply changes in the procedures that generate the values of the instruments. Implementing a transition is clearly a test of a government's willingness and ability to design and enforce policies; the resulting uncertainty is likely to be reflected in people's behavior. Still, an incipient stabilization program would have little chance of success if it did not provide information about the actions that the authorities plan in the future and about the means they have available to execute them. That is, policies must find the right sequence of actual measures and announcements: identifying the nature and the timing of the actions, and the appropriate combination of commitment and flexibility (to guide expectations without causing costly disappointments while leaving open the possibility of solving the problems that appear along the way), is far from a trivial matter.

The collapse of the Austral plan poses the question: Was the failure already implicit in the design of the program, or did the plan provide a reasonably useful starting point but fail when certain necessary actions were not taken? In retrospect, it would still seem that, although the Austral plan was insufficient for a durable stabilization, it managed the disinflation phase at a relatively low cost, and it did open up new opportunities.

Different types of inflation need different treatments. The general features of the Austral plan were adapted to the conditions of the Argentine inflation at the time—which was high enough for a shock to seem advisable, both because of the costs of maintaining a high and prolonged price instability and because economic policies could thus be helped by a probable shift in expectations. Also, as has often been remarked about this and other programs, inertial effects were still active in financial contracts and in the setting of prices and wages. There was a risk that inflation would be perpetuated (or its fall heavily dampened) by index-like mechanisms, and that price setters would not modify their pricing behavior if they did not actually observe others doing the same. Since rapid disinflation had high priority, there were reasons to hedge against this possibility, even at the cost of using initially overdetermined instruments. On the other hand, inflation had been sufficiently steady in the first part of 1985 so that it was possible to measure approximately the rate of inflation incorporated in contracts and to deal with it through the conversion system (Leijonhufvud 1984; Heymann and Leijonhufvud 1989).

The arguments for multiple anchors have been widely discussed.[5] In fact, most disinflation programs use several anchors by pegging the exchange rate, fixing public-sector prices and government salaries, and (sometimes) intervening more or less directly in private wages and prices. With its obvious costs, a measure like a freeze can, in some circumstances, be a way of providing a definite signal for a sharp disinflation, if it is part of a comprehensive program and if it is used as a transitional instrument.

Whatever the particular variables that are fixed, or pre-announced for some time, their nominal values must somehow be determined. This decision implies a tradeoff: to create confidence in the anchors' stability, their real values should probably be high at the beginning of the program. But this can mean that the initial set of relative prices is not sustainable, or, at least, that to avoid a sizable "residual inflation," other instruments have to be tightened more than would otherwise be required. In particular, a real exchange rate that is initially "too low" may disturb expectations; a high real price of foreign currency will induce a balance-of-payments surplus. In this case, if fiscal policies are not restrictive enough, the central bank will have to either allow the money supply to rise or sterilize by borrowing at a high interest rate; since such policies cannot be maintained indefinitely, the price of non-tradables would eventually increase.[6]

In any case, even when fiscal and monetary policies are kept tight (and especially if they are not) it is likely that relative price movements will make the price level drift upward in the first disinflation period. Coming from a high inflation, this opens the possibility of an early re-indexing at an initially lower but still sizable inflation rate, which can quickly erode the real value of the anchors. The consequent policy dilemma is whether to accept the residual inflation as a floor or to try reducing it further. The first option (as the Argentine experience suggests) implies the risk of going back to rapid inflation. The alternative choice puts strong demands on policies: inflationary pressures have to be dealt with while the transitory features that the initial program may have included, in the form of emergency fiscal measures, government borrowing (directly or through the central bank) at high interest rates, and "overdetermined" anchors, are replaced by more permanent policies. It would follow that fiscal management is particularly critical in this stage and that, while the first disinflation phase need not be contractionary, at this point the government should be willing to put price stability ahead of other objectives.

Outside shocks did contribute to the return of high inflation in Argentina. However, the Austral plan did not have an outline of what was to be done once the initial measures wore out. The plan concentrated on the problems of the disinflation transition; the following steps were left undefined. There was probably an underestimation of the effort that would be required after the first effect was achieved and, also, an overestimation of the capacity of short-run policies to manage the economy. Thus, the momentum generated by the program was not used to consolidate the disinflation. Whether or not a sufficiently solid coalition could have been built to back a durable reform of fiscal policies is an open question. But in retrospect it seems clear that the remaining inflationary pressures were too strong to be handled by a policy of "muddling through."

It has become apparent that in Argentina there is not much room to finance public deficits of a significant size at tolerable levels of inflation. The government can only borrow abroad to cover part of the interest on its foreign debt, and this through long and difficult negotiations. The domestic market for public debt is very small, and will only absorb government paper at high yields, for short terms and in limited doses.[7] This means that the "monetarist arithmetic" works unpleasantly and swiftly; it is also incorporated in the public's expectations. The experience after the Austral plan shows that under these conditions the central bank can only delay the monetization of deficits for a short time, and at a high cost.

In addition, money demand has fallen over the years. The changes in real money holdings (M1/GDP) in the recent inflationary cycles are plotted in figure 4.1. What this figure shows is that increases in real balances during disinflations have typically followed a lower path than the declines in the previous price acceleration. This does not, of course, ous evidence of "hysteresis" (Piterman 1988; Ahumada 1989); it does suggest, however, that the shifts away from money as inflation accelerates are becoming more and more pronounced, and may not be fully reversible. The consequences on the inflation tax can be seen in figure 4.2. The curve of the inflation tax yield has become lower and flatter in recent years. The difference compared with, say, the early 1970s is quite plain: a revenue that could then be generated at an inflation rate of around 5% per month could now only be achieved at a very high rate of inflation. Also, given the response of money demand in the later period, it is likely that the "steady-state" inflation would have a large swing with relatively small increases in the monetized deficit.[8] If this is considered together

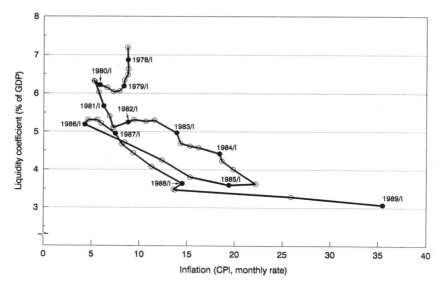

Figure 4.1
Money demand and inflation, 1977–1989. The graph shows five-quarter moving averages of the quantities π and $m1/GDP$, where π is the rate of growth of the CPI in each quarter, $m1$ is the real money stock ($M1$ seasonally adjusted deflated by the CPI; quarterly averages of monthly data), and GDP is measured at constant prices and is seasonally adjusted. The basic data are from the central bank and the National Institute of Statistics (INDEC).

with the fiscal lag effect, it would indicate that the economy has evolved mechanisms that strongly amplify the effects of deviations in policies.

Accordingly, the government has to operate under very tight financial constraints. In the period after the Austral plan, fiscal instruments were not improved to satisfy these restrictions. This caused frequent dilemmas in the management of public-sector prices. The authorities had the recurrent choice between allowing the deficit to rise and trying to overindex these prices, with the risk of an immediate inflationary impulse. A similar tradeoff was faced with regard to exchange-rate policies.

Economic policies thus went through several cycles, according to whether the authorities perceived a strong urgency to correct relative prices or whether they reacted to the possibility of a rapid inflationary spiral. The amplitude of the resulting movements in the short-run inflation rate grew over time. Eventually, such oscillations came to be expected; this accelerated the upswings (especially because industrial firms raised their prices in anticipation of tighter controls) and made the

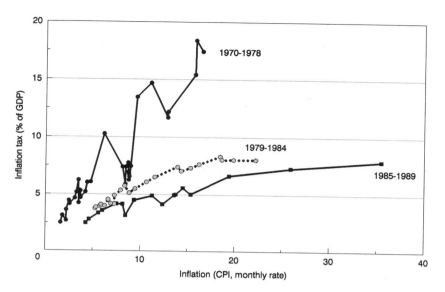

Figure 4.2
Inflation and the inflation tax. The graph shows five quarter moving averages of the
CPI inflation rate (monthly equivalent growth rates between final months of each
quarter) and the inflation tax in three selected periods. The inflation tax in each
quarter is measured as the ratio to the GDP at constant prices (seasonally adjusted) of
the sum of monthly values of $m1[\pi/(1 + \pi)]$, where $m1$ is the real money stock (M1
seasonally adjusted, deflated by the CPI) in the previous month and π is the growth
rate of the CPI in a given month. The basic data are from the central bank and the
National Institute of Statistics (INDEC).

decelerations shorter and less clear-cut. Until 1988, however, the public
generally felt that the government was able to prevent a runaway
inflation. But this remaining confidence was gradually eroded as repeated attempts to anchor nominal variables proved only a transitory
expedient against rising inflation.

Fiscal Policies

Independent of particular views on the detailed behavior of price dynamics, it is generally agreed that the crucial reason why inflation
accelerated again after the Austral plan was the lack of a sustainable fiscal
correction. This cannot be attributed to deliberate neglect: the link
between government deficits and inflation was recognized, and the
authorities had every incentive to stabilize, but although the deficit fell

from the extremely high values of the early 1980s the fiscal problem remained unsolved.[9]

In 1983 Argentina emerged from a long period of military rule with its fiscal policies in a state of disorder and without a tradition of negotiating and enforcing a well-defined budget. Erratic inflation would, in itself, have made it difficult to run a pre-defined budget. Moreover, fiscal institutions were not adapted to operate under a constitutional political system. In recent years, the budget did not serve its intended purposes of allowing an *ex ante* discussion of alternative measures and of providing a legal framework for spending; rather, since it was always approved late in the year, it validated actions that had already been taken. Accordingly, the deficit resulted, in fact, not from an overall discussion, but as a "residual" of decisions made along the way; in addition, vested-interest groups confronted the government on a "one on one" basis instead of having to deal with one another in comprehensive negotiations. In other words, while such groups had ample scope for voicing their demands, there was no readily available mechanism that could reconcile their claims to produce a consistent outcome.

It is always possible that political obstacles prevent an agreement on a low-deficit budget. However, a situation in which specific groups conduct "bilateral" negotiations with the government may have an inherent inflationary bias.[10] Not being restricted by a budget, the government can allocate funds at will, but it also exposes itself to "unwanted" demands, which (if they are solidly backed) it may be forced to accommodate. Each bargaining group has reason to bring all its power to bear so as to maximize its interests, and is usually much less concerned with contesting specific concessions to others. Inflation can be deplored in general, but the institutional means of organizing a coalition that would back a concrete and enforceable policy of lowering the deficit have failed to materialize.[11] The government pays the price, in terms of popularity, of allowing inflation to continue, but cannot bear the costs of resisting the various demands made of it.

Soft budgets (Kornai 1986) have been a common feature in Argentina. In particular, transfers from the central government to the provinces, the financial relations between the treasury and public enterprises, state assistance to private firms (either through direct subsidies or through indirect mechanisms administered by the central bank), and the relative earnings of different groups of public employees have changed over the years, often in response to pressures of one type or another. In the process of resolving the use of public funds, large amounts of time, skill, and clout are expended on lobbying. The resulting allocation seems to depend more on the amount of pressure that various groups can exert than on considerations of economic performance or overall equity.

In addition, the tax system suffers from obvious weaknesses: there are many taxes, some with high legislated rates but low actual revenues (see table 4.3). A striking indication is that in 1988 the value-added tax (18%, lowered to 15% in the last part of the year) and the income tax (with a marginal rate of 45% on the highest bracket), taken together, generated around 4.5% of the GDP. The general picture is that of a system without a clear design, with a complicated legislation that is not enforced, which cannot collect broad-based taxes and has to rely on a diversity of rather primitive taxes. The low yield of "basic" taxes like those on income and the VAT was due not only to evasion but also to a variety of authorized exemptions, particularly those established through industrial promotion subsidies (Artana 1987; Azpiazu 1988). In turn, the existence of these gaps in legislation further complicated the administration of taxes.

Reference to the foreign-debt problem has become a routine feature in discussions of inflation in countries like Argentina, and there is no doubt

Table 4.3
National tax revenues (percentages of GDP).[a]

		Taxes on income and wealth		Excise taxes		Taxes on foreign trade	Social security	Total[c]
	VAT	Income	Other[b]	On fuels	Other			
1980	4.0	1.5	1.1	1.3	1.6	1.8	5.5	17.9
1981	4.9	1.6	1.1	2.1	1.7	1.9	3.4	17.5
1982	4.2	1.6	1.6	2.5	1.8	1.8	3.0	17.1
1983	3.7	1.2	1.7	2.8	1.5	3.0	3.1	17.8
1984	3.1	0.6	1.3	3.5	1.3	2.5	3.3	16.6
1985	3.2	1.0	1.9	3.1	1.5	3.4	4.6	19.8
1986	3.7	1.3	1.8	2.5	1.7	2.7	5.6	20.7
1987	3.8	1.6	1.4	1.7	1.7	2.1	5.6	19.2
1988	3.0	1.5	2.4	2.3	1.5	1.8	4.9	19.3
1989	2.3	1.2	3.6	2.0	1.2	3.1	3.8	18.1

a. Taxes collected by national agencies. Each figure results from deflating (by the CPI) monthly nominal values of tax collection; annual aggregates of these deflated values are expressed as percentages of the annual GDP at constant prices.
b. Includes revenues from the compulsory loan (linked to income tax) that was levied between 1985 and 1989.
c. Includes miscellaneous taxes collected by the national tax administration.

that the debt severely limits the chances of stabilization. The government has a large (though hard-to-measure) liability; the servicing of this debt is determined one period at a time in a game whose outcome is very difficult to predict, played by parties differing in skill and luck. From the point of view of the country's fiscal policy, foreign creditors behave like a large interest group—and not the weakest one. In any case, spending and taxation have to adjust to allow the public sector to service its debt (or to "buy" the trade surplus) if the inflation tax is to be avoided. But a policy of "belt tightening" to pay the foreign debt usually fails to command widespread support, especially when it is not known if (or to what extent) that would draw a comparable response by creditors in reducing their demands. Thus, the debt has made it more difficult to reach a sustainable fiscal agreement.

In an economy without a systematic budget process, with an ineffective tax system and very low demand for domestic money, and whose foreign debt is priced far below its face value, it is to be expected that the supply of new loans to the government will be small and quite inelastic. The domestic public debt can grow sporadically in relatively tranquil times, when the government's creditworthiness improves somewhat or, more dangerously, by offering high real yields. As there are no ready sources of funds to guarantee repayment, the perceived default risk probably rises steeply with the volume of the outstanding debt and may also vary sharply with news that reaches the market: rolling over a short-run debt under these conditions can be quite costly and imply a high risk of "confidence crises" (Alesina et al. 1989). This means that, in practice, the government is liquidity constrained.

If the public does not lend to the government and knows how to operate with low real cash balances, the short-run deficit has to be cut. This was clear in Argentina, at least as a general proposition. Fiscal policies did try to control spending and increase receipts, but in some instances (as in 1987) the government seemed less willing to sustain that attempt, and there was a delay in realizing that the available instruments were insufficient. In order to reduce its immediate financing requirements, the government had to use costly means in its fiscal policies. Investment fell and the provision of basic government services deteriorated further. While some goods or activities were heavily taxed in an effort to raise revenues, others escaped taxation. Thus, part of the adjustment was done in a way that created a future burden for fiscal policy.

Still, there was growing recognition of the depth of the fiscal problem. Although the attempts to improve the tax administration did not have much effect, the government took several measures to tighten budget constraints. In 1988, a new law was passed to regulate the division of taxes between the central government and the provinces; it spelled out the revenues of local governments, and was meant to limit the size of discretionary transfers.[12] Changes were made in industrial promotion regimes, stipulating their fiscal cost and limiting subsidies to be granted in the future. In the same vein, it was proposed that central-bank rediscounts be subject to Congress's approval. Also, the government tried to clarify the financial relations between the treasury and public enterprises by taking over the foreign debt of those enterprises in exchange for a cut in transfers.

These initiatives were aimed at making fiscal policies more systematic and closing the "windows" through which pressures that led to high deficits were channeled (see note 11). However, they were insufficient to balance public finances. Moreover, although most groups seemed to agree on the need to cut the deficit, there was no definite consensus on how to do so in practice. Also, when the government started to stress the need for reforms, the economy was once again in a state of high inflation. Whatever effects such measures may have had if they had been the beginning of a perceptibly reliable trend, they were drowned in the "noise" generated by instability. That is, while the disinflation induced by the Austral plan could not be sustained without concomitant changes in fiscal policy, the renewed macroeconomic volatility made it more difficult to implement such changes and to maintain them until their effects could begin to be felt. Short-run stability seems a condition for effective reform.

3. Runaway Inflation and a New Shock Program: 1989

By the end of 1988 the weakness of the Primavera program was becoming apparent (see section 1). Participants in the financial markets were keenly aware of the growing internal public debt and closely followed the news of difficult negotiations between the government and foreign creditors. Opinions differed as to how long the program would last, but its eventual breakdown seemed inevitable to many asset holders. In January 1989, a tight monetary policy failed to stop the rise in the demand for foreign currencies; in the first week of February, the central bank lost reserves of around US$500 million. Given this indication that the run was irreversible, the authorities decided to float the exchange rate in the free market, and created a new pegged exchange rate for imports. It soon became clear that the pressure on the free market would not moderate and that official reserves would continue to diminish.

The dramatic balance-of-payments crisis in the first half of 1989 was of a particular type. Most noticeably, the trade surplus had been relatively large in the previous months, and kept growing during this period. However, this was swamped by a massive portfolio shift toward foreign assets.[13] Thus, the market equilibrated (in a fashion) at real prices that had no historical precedents. In June, the real exchange rate for financial transactions was 3.5 times higher than six months earlier, while the average exchange rate for trade in goods had increased almost 80%.

In the turbulence triggered by the rapid exchange depreciations, economic policy lost its capacity to take the initiative; it reacted after the fact and encountered an almost complete lack of confidence.[14] The fiscal deficit increased noticeably as the government allowed public-sector prices to fall and real tax revenues declined faster than spending.[15] At times the government tried to curb the demand for foreign exchange by offering bonds with extremely high returns; in other cases it reversed course for fear of further rises in interest rates. In any case, money growth accelerated.[16] And the very high (and rising) inflation did not reduce the real value of the internal public debt by much until July, since a good part of the outstanding debt was linked to the dollar.[17]

The political situation contributed in no small measure to the extreme economic instability. Many people were apprehensive about the policies that the Peronist party might apply in the likely event of its winning the May elections; of course, the chances of a victory for the opposition increased as the economic performance deteriorated. The incumbent regime felt that the lack of precision in the Peronist statements about their program was making the economy unmanageable. From the opposition's point of view, the government had followed policies (especially regarding the growth of the internal debt) that would bequeath a heavy burden to its successor. These conditions could easily raise anxieties that the new government would not abide by promises made by the outgoing one; this increased the risk of holding assets that could be taxed or whose real value could be "diluted" (in one way or another) in the political transition.[18]

The switch from "mere" high inflation to a runaway process seems to have happened in April. The CPI growth rate doubled to 33%, and the real money demand took a definite downward trend. The inertial effects that had held inflation back for some time could not continue operating. Thus, wages were no longer based on the inflation of the previous month, and prices were adjusted with increasing frequency. In May, the inflation rate more than doubled, reaching almost 80%. The elections held on the 14th of that month gave, as expected, a large victory to the Peronist party. Finally, it was agreed that the new president would take office on July 8 (instead of seven months later, as established originally). The rate of inflation rose to over 100% in June. However, for the first time since February, the real exchange rate declined. In time, it became apparent that the president-elect was forging an alliance with conservative political and business groups and that a disinflation program was on the way; it is possible that the (perhaps diffuse) perception that the new government had sufficient backing to try to disinflate helped prevent a further collapse of the currency.

The very rapid inflation between April and July was associated with visible changes in behavior. Pricing obviously became a very difficult problem. Prices of some assets (such as real estate) were already dollarized; now, there was apparently an incipient movement to link the prices of commonly traded goods to the exchange rate. However, this did not

Table 4.4
Exchange rate of the U.S. dollar, 1989[a] (daily rate of change).

From	To	Average	Standard deviation
January 2	February 3	0.3	0.8
February 7	February 10	10.9	18.2
February 13	April 7	1.8	4.4
April 10	July 7	4.7	9.4
July 10	July 21	1.9	4.9
July 24	September 29	−0.1	1.1
October 2	November 7	0.5	1.2
November 8	December 7	1.6	4.8
December 12	December 27	8.8	15.1

a. Until May 19 and from December 20 on, the data correspond to the price of the dollar in the official free market; between May 30 and December 20 the data correspond to the quotation in the parallel market, according to figures published in the press. (The exchange markets were closed between May 19 and May 30.)

spread generally to the retail level.[19] Broadly, it would seem that there was no well-defined standard by which to set prices, and that different pricing rules were applied depending on the firm and the market. This created a great noise in relative prices. Under these conditions, trade credit practically vanished; also, most firms probably tried to build large precautionary margins and, in certain cases, simply refused to sell.[20] This suggests a downward shift in the supply of goods, which contributed to the steep drop in real activity in the second quarter. Labor demand consequently declined. Unemployment increased, and the acceleration of nominal wages (sometimes adjusted more than once a month) did not prevent a serious drop in their purchasing power. Lower real earnings, and uncertainty about prices and even about whether goods would be available at all, generated intense social tensions.

The program announced by the new government in July (the BB program) thus met an urgent need. Without going into detail, we note that this program had two distinguishing features: the role of a group of large firms as one of its main supports[21] and the emphasis of the authorities on their intention to reform fiscal policies. The government announced that it would privatize a number of public enterprises, starting with the telephone company, and that subsidies would be cut. A "law of economic emergency" halved industrial promotion subsidies for six months (but firms were promised a government bond in compensation). Also, after some loud discussions, a tax package was tabled in Congress; the new system would rely on a uniform-rate VAT with fewer exemptions and on a simplified income tax with lower rates. The disinflation strategy consisted of a short-run fiscal adjustment (with more permanent measures proposed in the near future), a freeze on the exchange rate and on public-sector prices after a sharp initial rise, and guidelines for private prices and wages.

Financial markets responded quickly: the nominal interest rate fell immediately, the gap between the exchange rates in the official and the parallel market came down to almost zero, and the central bank started to accumulate reserves. However, prices increased more than 60% in the second week of July, after rising around 50% in the previous week. This was due in part to the jump in the exchange rate and in public-sector prices, and in part to a strong reaction of industrial prices, possibly because firms tried to increase their markups in anticipation of the price agreement. Although prices showed a marked deceleration after the initial shock, the residual inflation was sizable. Whereas the 38% increase (measured by the CPI) in August was due in part to a carryover of past increases, the rates of near 10% in September and 5% in October suggested that convergence to very low inflation would be hard to achieve.

There was, indeed, a reduction in the fiscal deficit, but the primary surplus of the treasury still did not cover the real interest on the domestic debt and on purchases of foreign currencies from the private sector. The expectation that the official price of the dollar would stay constant in the short run led to an excess supply in the exchange market, and the central bank faced the typical dilemma of whether or not to sterilize such flows. At first, the authorities did not offset the increase in reserves, so as to encourage a fall in interest rates and reduce the quasi-fiscal deficit. Soon, however, they started to increase the domestic debt again. At the same time, the money stock increased rapidly: M1 multiplied almost by 5 between July and October. Real money demand recovered, although it remained lower than at the beginning of the year.

In August and September, the drop of interest rates (to a minimum of around 5% per month) with a practically constant parallel exchange rate could be interpreted as an indication that expectations had calmed down in the very short run. However, the disinflation was not solidly based. In the immediate future, the treasury was to gain from the suspension of subsidies but, on the other hand, the government had announced a gradual reduction in export taxes, and wages in the public sector were to increase. The tax reform was resisted by business groups, and, if approved as it stood, its effectiveness in increasing revenues would still have to be tested. The quasi-fiscal deficit remained high, and the domestic debt was rising. In addition, while the government had proposed that the private sector negotiate wages for six months with a one-off adjustment of around 15%, the demands of the unions were much higher. Real wages were low, and it remained to be seen how strong the pressure for a recovery would be and whether firms were prepared to lower their markups. In addition, although an agreement was reached with the IMF, negotiations with foreign creditors were yet undefined.

The authorities tried to deter inflationary expectations by announcing that the official exchange rate and public-sector prices would stay constant until March 1990. However, as time went by, financial markets started to reflect increasing doubts about the evolution of the program. By mid-November the spread between the official and the parallel exchange rate had increased to around 30% and exporters reduced their sales of foreign exchange to the central bank. It looked as if wealth holders, after earning high returns for some months, were again ready to shift back to foreign currencies, and that confidence in the government's ability to stabilize was quickly wearing out. Official statements indicating that the fiscal deficit had been much reduced and that stronger measures were on the way had little effect; higher interest rates only reinforced the impression that a devaluation was imminent. This situation was similar to that of the beginning of the year; this time, however, the response of the asset and goods markets was even more rapid: in a few weeks the economy moved from a monthly inflation rate of 6% into outright hyperinflation.

Faced with a sharp decline in reserves, the government decided on a 50% rise in the exchange rate early in December; public-sector prices were increased by around 70%. Also, in a very controversial move, the maturity of domestic public bonds was unilaterally rescheduled. Although the authorities tried to present these measures as a one-shot adjustment to a going program, they were widely interpreted as the end of the BB plan, and as a signal that policy had once again lost control over events. Both interest rates and the price of foreign currencies in the financial market kept increasing; after several days, the spread between the commercial and the free exchange rate was as high as before the devaluation. The reaction of goods prices was very quick: according to some estimates, the CPI rose more than 25% in one week. After the resignation of the Minister of Economy, new economic authorities announced the removal of all remaining price and exchange controls and the end of the central bank's intervention in the foreign-exchange market. For some days, the now floating exchange rate dropped sharply, but interest rates grew to over 100% per month. On December 26, the price of foreign currencies suddenly jumped more than 30%; this increase in one day was even larger than the one that had marked the end of the Primavera program in February.

The extreme volatility in the foreign-exchange market was transmitted at once to goods prices: all residual stickiness practically disappeared. Naturally, the prices of tradable goods oscillated with the exchange rate (which had wide swings even within a single day); in addition, many firms apparently decided to dollarize the prices of domestically produced goods. As had happened in the mid-year inflationary explosion, but perhaps with greater intensity, supplies were restricted. A generalized uncertainty, and probably also the perception that prices were being dollarized, strengthened the demand for foreign exchange. Although there was no panic withdrawal of funds from the banks, many people refused to renew their deposits even when offered extremely high yields. Since this behavior opened up the possibility of an almost complete repudiation of the domestic money by the public, it was clear that the government would soon resort to new measures.

4. Summary and Conclusions

High inflation has been a feature of the Argentine economy for a long period and has resisted a variety of treatments. In the past few years the cycle of failed disinflation attempts followed by sharp accelerations has grown dramatically in amplitude. These oscillations have had lasting effects, and have probably made stabilization more difficult.

With this accumulated experience, agents have learned to reduce their money holdings and to quickly shift away from cash when they fear that inflation may rise. The government has little or no credit: new debt can be issued for only very short maturities and must offer extremely high returns. More generally, keeping assets in the country (for people who have a choice, which excludes low-income groups) is seen as a risky proposition: wealth holders demand flexibility and high yields, and are both willing and able to switch to foreign currencies on short notice. The instability of portfolio decisions is replicated in the goods markets, as price setters have developed a precautionary behavior pattern that rapidly propagates inflationary impulses.

Confidence in the effectiveness of economic policies has also been severely eroded. This means that policy declarations are received with increasing skepticism: agents (especially in financial markets) now require stronger and stronger signals from the government before expecting stabilization to be feasible. This can mean that the pace and the intensity of policy actions may end up being guided by the urgency the authorities ascribe to influencing short-run expectations, sometimes leading to hasty moves or to untenable commitments.

Behind the Argentine inflation there is clearly a crisis in government finances that has found no solution. Governments of various types have been unable to deal with claims on fiscal policies so as to arrive at a more or less consistent outcome; basic tools such as the budget have not functioned. As a result, while the authorities have often bowed to the demands of powerful interest groups, the supply of public goods has deteriorated, and there is scarce administrative capacity to cut spending without further reducing the quality of basic services. The tax system is obviously deficient in enforcing collection and in its very design. The foreign debt has contributed much to the fiscal problem, not only because of the direct burden it has put on the treasury but also because it has created strong doubts about the government's solvency. The relatively small domestic debt has also been a very major source of instability, given the terms of yield and the maturities demanded by markets.

Stabilizing an economy like that of Argentina is not a simple matter. However, there is no argument that high inflation has extremely high costs, particularly after an episode like that of mid-1989, which showed that even day-to-day transactions can be visibly disrupted. Stabilization seems to weigh heavily in people's preferences (and, apparently, also in their votes); it would be hard to attribute Argentina's high inflation to a simple-minded neglect of the problem.

The Austral plan managed to produce a rapid and relatively smooth disinflation; it served a useful purpose. On the negative side, the experience of the Austral plan highlights in retrospect the limitations of short-run policies lacking sufficiently rapid steps to strengthen fiscal instruments. It also suggests that after an inflation of the Argentine type, while strict price stability may be out of reach, it can be difficult to maintain inflation in an "intermediate" range of, say, 100% per year without risking a rapid acceleration in the event of a shock or an (even potentially transitory) deviation in policy.

Stabilization requires non-trivial choices regarding the sequencing of decisions and the selection of instruments. The public sector should program its expenditures and receipts while acknowledging that it will have to operate initially, and maybe for quite a long time, under tight liquidity restrictions. This has clearly discernible costs, regardless of whether aggregate output falls or not: a cash-constrained government raises revenue and cuts spending without much freedom to consider the consequences on resource allocation and income distribution. By the same token, some reforms that can reduce the "permanent" deficit (and which may be desirable in themselves) need not have the same effect in the short run. Since reforms are not likely to succeed in a situation of instability, it seems crucial to maintain macroeconomic balances on a period-by-period basis until a sustainable state is reached. This places a heavy burden on policies: stabilizing without credit is no easy task.

The tension between the stated goals of reforming public finances and the short-run management of a potentially very unstable economy was apparent in the July 1989 program. The sudden collapse of the BB plan was probably more than a response to the shortcomings of a specific program. The capital flight in the early 1980s had already shown that people were reluctant to hold assets in the country. After a decade in which varying policies (implemented by governments of very different characteristics) were unable to stop this flight, confidence in any government's words or promises had sunk very low. By the end of 1989 the very survival of the domestic currency was being questioned.

The monetary and the financial systems will certainly undergo important changes after this episode. It is also clear that urgent measures are needed to allow at least a recovery of everyday transactions. In Argentina macroeconomic stability is commonly referred to as a public good. The analogy is apt, especially in discussing the fiscal conditions for stabilization. There is a large demand for stability, but there must be ways of revealing this demand so as to identify a concrete willingness to pay for, and then secure the financing of, such an endeavor. How to accomplish this remains open to debate.

Acknowledgments

Comments by F. Navajas, J. L. Machinea, S. Teitel, and two anonymous referees are acknowledged. Thanks are due to the members of the Macro team at CEPAL Buenos Aires (A. Aller, M. Fernández Mouján, R. Martínez, P. Nicholson, and S. Scheimberg) for their help.

Notes

1. See, for example, Blejer and Liviatan 1987, Canavese and Di Tella 1988, Dornbusch and De Pablo 1988, Frenkel and Fanelli 1987, Gerchunoff and Bozalla 1987, Helpman and Leiderman 1988, Heymann 1986 and 1987, Kiguel 1988, Machinea and Fanelli 1988, and Rodríguez 1988.

2. Given that reserve requirements on demand deposits have been very high, it is customary in Argentina to measure seigniorage as the real value of the increase in M1 (and the inflation tax as the real depreciation of the M1 stock). This practice has also been followed here. The central bank pays interest on the reserves held by banks on time deposits; the resulting flow of real interest is part of the "quasi-fiscal deficit," and appears in table 4.2 (column 2).

3. In April 1988, the country entered into a *de facto* moratorium on the foreign debt. Also, when a large volume of internal bonds fell due, the treasury found no ready takers for new issues; this led the central bank to raise (interest-bearing) reserve requirements.

4. The program was popularly called *Primavera* (spring), after the time of year in which it started. The name itself already suggested that the plan was not expected to last very long.

5. Bruno (1985) and Bruno and Fischer (1986) model the transition out of a "high inflation trap"; Simonsen (1988) and Dornbusch and Simonsen (1987) stress the coordination problem of disinflation; Heymann (1989) discusses the arguments for using "redundant" instruments in the case of "model uncertainty." See Lopes 1984 and Frenkel 1984 for discussions of the inertia caused by indexation.

6. The connection between the trade balance (and, implicitly, the real exchange rate) and domestic inflation has recently been widely discussed in several Latin American countries (see, for example, Cardoso 1988).

7. The stock of treasury bonds and interest-bearing liabilities of the central bank, denominated in domestic currency, stood at around 8.5% of GDP at the beginning of 1986 and reached a peak of 15% of GDP in the second quarter of 1989. In this period, the volume of bonds in the open market never exceeded 4% of GDP (even though they sometimes offered high interest premiums and a variety of indexing clauses); most of the debt consisted of reserve requirements on bank deposits.

8. The figures are based on five-quarter moving averages of the liquidity coefficient, the inflation rate, and the inflation tax [defined as $m1\pi/(1+\pi)$, where $m1$ is the stock of real balances in the previous month and π is the inflation rate in a given month]. Although the evidence is suggestive, the points depicted need not, of course, represent steady states. It is also clear that in periods of high unexpected inflation (as probably was the case in 1989) the revenue from the inflation tax can temporarily be quite large (see table 4.2).

9. The Argentine fiscal system is analyzed from different perspectives in Carciofi 1989, FIEL 1987, and Gerchunoff and Vicens 1989.

10. This argument is developed in Heymann, Navajas, and Warnes 1988 and in Heymann and Navajas 1989; see also Fraga and Werlang 1983. Kiguel and Liviatan (1989) have studied other types of games in high-inflation contexts. Cukierman et al. (1989) discuss the link between political instability and the effectiveness of the tax system.

11. Put differently: Given the institutional setting, there are high "transaction costs" for negotiating away the externalities that groups impose on one another by forcing transfers that result in inflation. Clearly, an inflationary outcome is more likely if an agreement is not made binding, or if sizable funds can be transferred off-budget, since this reopens the "windows" to which groups have access individually.

12. According to a law that expired in 1984, the national government administered the collection of a number of taxes (including the VAT and the income tax) and distributed a given proportion of the proceeds to each province, after deducting a share that went to the treasury. A similar system was established in

1988. Between 1984 and 1988 the national government received all the tax revenue and assisted the provinces through direct transfers, which were determined in an *ad hoc* fashion.

13. And beyond the reach of the central bank. Most dollar deposits in local banks (which initially totaled around US$1 billion) were turned into cash; this caused a large fall in official reserves, since those deposits had a 100% reserve requirement.

14. An indication of this loss of control was the succession of measures on the exchange-rate system. Two weeks after floating the exchange rate in the free market, the government authorized the sale of 20% of export proceeds in that market, and announced a schedule of future exchange-rate "mixes" with increasing proportions of exports going through the free market. In the beginning of April the "special" exchange rate for imports was eliminated; commercial transactions were to be canceled—50% at the "official" rate and 50% at the free rate. Ten days later, imports were fully transferred to the free market, while exports proceeds were sold at a pegged "reference" rate. This reference rate was abolished in the beginning of May. Until May 19 there was a single floating exchange rate, with higher export taxes. Between May 19 and the end of the month, the exchange market was shut down. After this, the free exchange market was eliminated (and again became a "parallel" market); authorized transactions were to be carried out at an exchange rate fixed daily by the central bank.

15. However, in an obvious emergency, the government was allowed to take some measures that it could not have envisaged before, such as an increase in export taxes and a suspension of subsidies granted under the industrial promotion regimes. But these actions, strong as they may have been, had no immediate effect in improving the fiscal situation or in calming expectations.

16. In May, fearing large-scale withdrawals of deposits and possible shortages in the physical supply of currency, the central bank decided to ration the funds that could be withdrawn from the banks (although money could still be shifted between deposits). For an analysis of some aspects of this episode see Almansi 1989.

17. In periods of extremely rapid inflation like this one, deflation of nominal data often produces unreliable indicators. When the value of the nominal debt (measured at the end of each month) is deflated by the price index of the month, the series grows until June. However, a deflation by the estimate of the end-of-month CPI (the average of the CPI in one month and the following one) suggests a slight decrease in the real debt in the first half of 1989. Also, given that relative prices varied rapidly during the period, results differ according to the price index used in the deflation.

18. Milder cases of the time-inconsistency problems derived from the alternation of parties in power are analyzed in Persson and Tabellini 1989. See also Calvo 1988.

19. Dollarization could be very inconvenient for the consumer, particularly when the exchange rate varied erratically even within the day; some residual "price stickiness" is valuable not only for menu cost reasons but also because it facilitates programming purchases (at least for a very short period). There is some anecdotal evidence that retailers resisted dollarization by their suppliers, since they had difficulties in pricing their merchandise accordingly.

20. A link between price instability and higher markups has been suggested in other episodes (see Frenkel 1979). By mid-1989, one could find shops bearing signs reading "Closed for lack of prices," vividly revealing how extreme price volatility can lead to the suspension of trade. In the Argentine experience of the recent years, market-induced shortages at times of great uncertainty have been more significant than those provoked by price controls.

21. The program was popularly known as *Plan BB* after the Bunge y Born company, whose executives were placed in top positions on the economic team.

References

Ahumada, H. 1989. Real Money Balances and Inflation: Tests for Asymmetric Effects Using Co-integration Techniques (Argentina, 1971–1988). CEMYB-BCRA working paper. (In Spanish.)

Alesina, A., A. Prati and G. Tabellini. 1989. Public Confidence and Debt Management: A Model and a Case Study of Italy. Mimeograph.

Almansi, A. 1989. 'Bi-paperism' and Inflation in Argentina. Working paper, Instituto Torcuato Di Tella, Buenos Aires. (In Spanish.)

Artana, D. 1987. Fiscal Incentives to Industrial Investment. Working paper, Instituto Torcuato Di Tella, Buenos Aires. (In Spanish.)

Azpiazu, D. 1988. Industrial Promotion and Investment in Argentina. Working paper, CEPAL, Buenos Aires. (In Spanish.)

Blejer, M., and N. Liviatan. 1987. Fighting Hyperinflation: Stabilization Strategies in Argentina and Israel: 1985–86. Working paper, IMF, Washington, D.C.

Bruno, M. 1985. Stabilization of the Israeli Economy: The Emergency Program in Its Early Stage. Mimeograph.

Bruno, M., and S. Fischer. 1986. "The inflation process: Shocks and accommodation." In *The Israeli Economy: Maturing through Crises*, Yoram Ben-Porath, ed. (Harvard University Press).

Calvo, G. 1988. "Servicing the public debt: The role of expectations." *American Economic Review* 78 (no. 4): 647–661.

Canavese, A., and G. Di Tella. 1988. "Inflation stabilization or hyperinflation avoidance? The case of the Austral plan in Argentina, 1985–87." In *Inflation Stabilization: The Experience of Israel, Argentina, Brazil, Bolivia, and Mexico*, M. Bruno, G. Di Tella, R. Dornbusch, and S. Fischer, eds. (MIT Press).

Carciofi, R. 1989. The Breakdown of the Fiscal Pact. An Interpretation of the Evolution of the Argentine Public Sector in the Last Two Decades. Working paper, CEPAL, Buenos Aires. (In Spanish.)

Cardoso, E. 1988. "Seigniorage and repression: monetary rhythms in Latin America." *Revista Brasileira de Economia*, October–December. (In Portuguese.)

Cukierman, A., S. Edwards, and G. Tabellini. 1989. Seigniorage and Political Instability. Mimeograph.

Dornbusch, R., and J. C. De Pablo. 1988. *Foreign Debt and Macroeconomic Instability in Argentina.* Ed Sudamericana. (In Spanish.)

Dornbusch, R., and M. Simonsen. 1987. Inflation Stabilization with Income Policy Support. Working paper, NBER, Washington, D.C.

FIEL. 1987. *Public Spending in Argentina.* Buenos Aires: FIEL. (In Spanish.)

Fraga, A., and C. Werlang. 1983. "A vision of inflation as a distributive conflict." *Revista Brasileira de Economia* 37 (no. 3): 361–368. (In Portuguese.)

Frenkel, R. 1979. "Price decisions in high inflation." *Desarrollo Económico* 19 (no. 75): 291–330. (In Spanish.)

Frenkel, R. 1984. "Industrial wages and inflation. The period 1976–82." *Desarrollo Económico* 24 (no. 95): 387–414. (In Spanish.)

Frenkel, R., and J. M. Fannelli. 1987. "The Austral plan one year and a half later." *El Trimestre Económico* 54: 55–118. (In Spanish.)

Gerchunoff, P. and C. Bozalla. 1987. Possibilities and Limitations of a Heterodox Stabilization Plan: The Case of Argentina. Working paper, Instituto Torcuato Di Tella, Buenos Aires. (In Spanish.)

Gerchunoff, P., and M. Vicens. 1989. Public Spending and Financing in an Economy in Crisis: The Argentine Case. Working paper, Instituto Torcuato Di Tella, Buenos Aires. (In Spanish.)

Helpman, E., and L. Leiderman. 1988. "Stabilization in high inflation countries: Analytical foundations and recent experiences." *Carnegie-Rochester Conference Series in Public Policy,* 28.

Heymann, D. 1986. *Three Essays on Inflation and Stabilization.* Santiago, Chile: CEPAL. (In Spanish.)

Heymann, D. 1987. "The Austral plan," *American Economic Review* 77 (no. 2): 284–288.

Heymann, D. 1989. Decisions With Limited Knowledge. Mimeograph. (In Spanish.)

Heymann, D., and A. Leijonhufvud. 1989. On the Use of Currency Reform in Inflation Stabilization. Working paper, European University Institute.

Heymann, D., and F. Navajas. 1989. "Fiscal policies in high inflation economies." Paper presented at conference of the International Institute of Public Finance, Buenos Aires.

Heymann, D., F. Navajas, and I. Warnes. 1988. Distributive Conflict and the Fiscal Deficit: Some Inflationary Games. Working paper, Instituto Torcuato Di Tella, Buenos Aires. (In Spanish.)

Kiguel, M. 1988. Ups and Downs in Inflation: Argentina Since the Austral Plan. Working paper, World Bank, Washington, D.C.

Kiguel, M., and N. Liviatan. 1989. Implications of Policy Games for Issues of High Inflation Economies. Mimeograph.

Kornai, J. 1986. "The soft budget constraint." *Kyklos* 39 (Fasc. 1): 3–30.

Leijonhufvud, A. 1984. "Inflation and economic performance." In *Money in Crisis*, B. Siegel, ed. (Ballinger).

Lopes, F. 1984. "Inertial inflation, hyperinflation and disinflation: notes and conjectures." *Revista Da Anpec* 9 (December). (In Portuguese.)

Machinea, J. L. 1989. Stabilization Under the Alfonsín Government: A Frustrated Attempt. Mimeograph.

Machinea, J. L., and J. M. Fanelli. 1988. "Stopping hyperinflation: the case of the Austral plan in Argentina, 1985–1987." In *Inflation Stabilization: The Experience of Israel, Argentina, Brazil, Bolivia, and Mexico*, M. Bruno, G. Di Tella, R. Dornbusch, and S. Fischer, eds. (MIT Press).

Persson, T., and G. Tabellini. 1989. Macroeconomic Policy, Credibility and Politics. Mimeograph.

Piterman, S. 1988. "The irreversibility of the relationships between inflation and real money balances." *Bank of Israel Economic Review* 60.

Rodríguez, C. 1988. "Comment." In *Inflation Stabilization: The Experience of Israel, Argentina, Brazil, Bolivia, and Mexico*, M. Bruno, G. Di Tella, R. Dornbusch, and S. Fischer, eds. (MIT Press).

Secretaría de Hacienda, Buenos Aires. 1989. Message to Congress with the 1989 Budget. (In Spanish.)

Simonsen, M. 1988. "Price stabilization and income policies: Theory and the Brazilian case study." In *Inflation Stabilization: The Experience of Israel, Argentina, Brazil, Bolivia, and Mexico*, M. Bruno, G. Di Tella, R. Dornbusch, and S. Fischer, eds. (MIT Press).

Comments by José Luis Machinea

Daniel Heymann presents an interesting analysis of economic events in Argentina since the Austral plan and up to the end of 1989. My comments will focus on some issues of the Alfonsín period, adding a brief discussion of the economic policy strategy of the newly elected government.

I wholly agree with the author's idea that the Austral plan was a good vantage point—perhaps the only possible one—from which to tackle the issue of a high and chronic inflation such as Argentina was experiencing at the time. I also agree that stabilizing the economy permanently would have required a more lasting adjustment of fiscal accounts. But to state that the fiscal deficit was the main (though not the only) issue behind the stabilization failures in Argentina does not help much. The crucial question is: Why was this so?

In addressing this issue Heymann mentions three main problems: the lack of a discussion about the national budget as a way to organize a coalition to back a concrete and enforceable policy with a view to reducing the deficit and hence the pressure that different groups were putting on the government, a deficient tax system and tax administration, and the impact of the external debt on fiscal accounts.

I agree that these were the main problems. However, let me say that making the budget the pivot of the discussion about the level of expenditures, subsidies, and revenues requires a more consolidated political system than the one Argentina had after so many years of military rule. It is true that the government sent the budget to Congress with delays, but it is no less true that the main comments of the opposition (especially in 1985–1987) were that the government was overly concerned with the level of public deficit and that public expenditures should be increased. Thus, while I agree with the importance of the budget as the focus of the discussion on the demands made on the public sector, for this instrument to be useful one needs a political system in which a low rate of inflation is a "superior good" to be left out of the political dispute. That was not the case during Alfonsín's government. In other words, in a democratic society the key issue is how to achieve a minimum political and/or social agreement in order to implement a stabilization program. That was the case with Israel in 1985 and Mexico in 1987; even Bolivia reached a political agreement in 1985. This was impossible under Alfonsín's government for several reasons, which I am not going to discuss here for the sake of brevity. Let me just say that although the authorities bore some of the responsibility for that failure, the main obstacle was the total opposition of the Peronists to any government initiative (the Peronists controlled the Senate, most provinces, and to some extent the General Confederation of Labor).

As time went by, the lack of social and political support resulted in a generalized feeling that a power vacuum existed in the decision-making process: several initiatives were never even put forward, as it was assumed beforehand that they were going to be rejected. Therefore, the spreading awareness of the need for structural reforms was accompanied by a growing understanding of the limited political resources on which the government could count. Some initiatives did come through, but they sometimes lacked the required depth and strength, or were blocked by the opposition parties.

I would like to mention two other issues regarding Alfonsín's government. The first one concerns incomes policy, a subject that Heymann does not discuss in detail. In the management of imbalances, incomes policy was used most of the time. Although price controls were effective in breaking inertial forces as the economy moved to a low rate of inflation, one gets the impression—when the period is considered as a whole—that the authorities made excessive use of this instrument. Moreover, as the author mentions, some freezes were introduced more in response to adverse inflation news than as part of a well-thought-out program. However, in an economy with a large fiscal deficit from the fourth quarter of 1986 on, closed to international trade, and with powerful labor unions, the lack of an incomes policy could have led to hyperinflation before the second quarter of 1989—the main reason being, again, that in a highly indexed economy any shock can accelerate inflation in the short run beyond the level that fiscal and monetary variables may account for. This rise in inflation tends to increase the fiscal deficit, thus perpetuating a higher inflation rate or, in an extreme case, making inflation explosive. The freeze and the guidelines tend to reduce the impact of full indexation, at least for a short while.[1]

The above could explain why incomes policy was used most of the time, but it should be stressed that its permanent use in Argentina was basically a sign of the lack of adjustment of the fiscal sector. Hence, throughout the period considered (except for the first months of the Austral plan), resorting to incomes policy was mainly a defensive mechanism.

The last comment I want to make regarding the Alfonsín administration is linked to the hyperinflation that developed in the second quarter of 1989. Heymann cites three reasons for the February crisis in the exchange market and the subsequent events: the fragility of the "Primavera program," the lack of external support, and the strong apprehensions about the policies that the Peronist party would pursue in the likely event of its winning the May elections.

Although I agree with Heymann's discussion of these points, I would like to emphasize that what happened in Argentina was more than a reduction in money demand: people ran away from any financial assets—including government bonds and deposits in dollars. This can only be explained by the prevailing political crisis and by the expectation that the promises made by Alfonsín's government in relation to financial assets (especially the domestic debt) would not be upheld by the new administration. In such an environment it was almost impossible to avoid the hyperinflation.[2] The portfolio shift produced an increase in the free exchange rate that led, from the very beginning, to the acceleration of the inflation rate.

Let me now comment very briefly on the economic policies implemented by the Peronist government. Assuming that the situation in 1989 was not very different from that prevailing in 1985, the new economic team launched a program that attempted to be similar to the Austral plan, but added the announcement of several major structural reforms. Evidently, after so many failed stabilization attempts, something else was needed than the mere announcement of structural reforms, which by their very nature take time to be implemented and even more time to bear fruit. Besides that, an incorrect set of relative prices was established at the beginning of the stabilization program. But the main mistake of the authorities was the rescheduling of the maturity of government bonds, announced on December 10.[3] What is even worse, no additional measure was taken to support this action and to secure that public accounts would be balanced.

As Heymann reports, by the end of the year the economy was again on the verge of hyperinflation. There were some leakages of confidential information, and the press reported that the government was working on a scheme of full convertibility with 100% backing by international reserves.[4] Prices rose more than 100% in three days, although most transactions were halted. The need for a new program was evident; however, on January 1 the Minister of Economy announced only a single measure: all time deposits, which had an average maturity of less than 10 days, were going to be exchanged for External Bonds ("Bonex") with an average maturity of 10 years. The domestic debt would also be exchanged for external bonds. The basic aim of this move was to avoid the flight from australes, which would have enabled the price hikes of the previous days. Although this extreme measure eliminated the threat of hyperinflation in the short run, it will have lasting effects on the financial system and on the saving ratio of Argentina in years to come. Moreover, the Peronist government does not seem prepared to take the additional measures needed to stabilize the economy. After the experience of the past four years we know that this is not an easy task, but we also know that unless such measures are taken in the next few weeks the country will soon slip into another hyperinflation. The hyperinflation of 1989 resulted in the resignation of President Alfonsín; the one that developed in the last days of December ended in the confiscation of half the financial assets. Another hyperinflation will not only mean the disappearance of the domestic currency; it could also lead to a severe crisis in the political system.

Notes

1. In order to show the relation between inflation and the fiscal deficit, the Olivera-Tanzi effect for different rates of inflation has been estimated. Taking into account the level and structure of revenues of the national and provincial governments and of public enterprises in the year that followed the launching of the Austral plan (July 1985 to June 1986), it can be seen that at a monthly inflation rate higher than 10 percent the marginal loss produced by the Olivera-Tanzi effect is larger than the marginal revenue produced by the inflation tax. Hence, the inflation rate that maximizes total revenues (around 10%) is substantially lower than the one that maximizes the inflation tax (around 22%). Therefore, ignoring other effects of the inflation rate on the fiscal deficit, at a monthly rate of inflation higher than 10 percent the fiscal deficit and the inflation can get out of control, depending on (among other things) the level of expenditures and the way expectations are formed.

2. The key question here is: Would hyperinflation still have developed if, in January 1989, Menem had announced the economic policy he was going to follow, as well as the composition of his economic team?

3. It is difficult to determine the rationale for this measure. These bonds represented less than 4% of GDP and were to fall due in a proportional manner over the next two years. Moreover, they had already been rescheduled by the new administration, and the measure included the bonds sold by the government one month earlier.

4. As the level of reserves was no more than $1.9 billion (including a possible loan of $1.0 billion with gold guarantees), and M3 amounted to around $8.7 billion, this would have implied an exchange rate of around 4,600 australes per dollar. On the last business day the dollar was quoted at 1,800 australes.

Comments by Simón Teitel

Argentina is a troubled country, and it has recently experienced very difficult times. Daniel Heymann has produced a detailed review of the collapse of the Austral and Primavera plans undertaken during the Alfonsín government, and of the initial measures taken by the Menem government.

Heymann has produced a comprehensive description of the recent stabilization programs in Argentina and provided abundant supportive statistical material. He does a particularly good job of describing the steps taken in the micromanagement of the stabilization programs, but he is not equally convincing in providing the big picture. However, this may not be his fault; it may be intrinsic to the chaotic nature of Argentine economic behavior. As is noted in a recent book, "the microscopic pieces were perfectly clear; the macroscopic behavior remained a mystery," and "phase transitions involve a kind of macroscopic behavior that seems hard to predict by looking at the microscopic details" (Gleick 1988, pp. 44, 127).

In my comments I will address the fiscal problem, investment and growth, and the nature of the programs implemented.

The Fiscal Problem

Is it really because there is no budget process that fiscal deficits are so difficult to control in Argentina? Heymann makes too much, I believe, of the advantages of confrontation among groups in an open process of budgetary review instead of each group's trying to influence the government. For example, a well-defined budgetary and appropriation process exists in the United States, and yet lobbies generally find ways, within this process, to further the interests they represent. In addition, the executive branch and the Congress both follow their own political mandates in allocating funds and in deciding how to raise the necessary resources through taxation. Although the U.S. deficit has been large and persistent in recent times, it is met without greater inflation because of foreign investors' willingness to bring their capital to the United States. Another key difference lies in the role of taxation and how it is perceived by the citizens. There is a clear consensus to pay taxes in the United States, and this is backed up by the enforcement mechanisms of the IRS.

Argentina's tax revenue structure is lopsided. A comparison with data for other countries and groups of countries (see table 4.C1) shows that Argentina has one of the lowest proportions (if not the lowest) of tax revenue accounted for by taxes on income, profits, and capital gains, has a higher than average reliance on taxes on the domestic consumption of goods and services, and has a higher than average proportion of revenue originating in taxes on international trade. This reliance on indirect and trade taxes makes the tax system regressive and primitive.

The fact that the government cannot finance substantial fiscal deficits without inflation (as is now done in the United States) should constitute a compelling reason to find a permanent solution to the fiscal deficit. It remains a puzzle why it has been so difficult to attain a coalition to produce durable fiscal reform and put the public revenue machinery back to work, as was done in the not too distant past (Díaz Alejandro 1970, p. 386).

Investment and Growth

At the Toledo seminar only perfunctory attention was paid to the reestablishment of growth after stabilization. Similarly, the Austral plan overlooked the need to stimulate the economy along a path of long-term investment and growth. Thus, not only was the program not used to consolidate the disinflation in the long run, but there was a failure to seriously consider how to activate the economy, i.e., to generate the necessary investment.

I remember meeting a distinguished member of the Austral economic team in Washington and asking him where the investment required for future growth would come from. Basking in the glory of their then recent achievement in reducing inflation, he answered: "from the investors!" Leaving humor aside, he was obviously relying on automatic reactivation as a result of price stability. We know, however, that no such automatic stimulus-response mechanism is at work, and consequently, early in the game, the government must decide how to promote growth without rekindling the fires of inflation.

In the Argentine case (and also, as has been suggested, more recently in Bolivia), the promotion of manufactured exports was the obvious choice. Such a program would have increased industrial capacity utilization at times of reduced domestic demand, generated badly needed

Table 4.C1
Central government revenue of Argentina and other selected countries, circa 1986 (proportions of total tax revenue; %).

	Taxes on income, profit, and capital gains	Domestic taxes on goods and services	Taxes on international trade
Middle Income Economies			
Latin America			
Argentina	4.9	37.4	14.7
Bolivia	6.5	14.3	28.6
Brazil	17.7	16.4	2.4
Chile	11.7	43.6	8.8
Costa Rica	10.8	28.2	21.1
Mexico	24.3	67.0	4.0
Nicaragua	14.4	48.5	7.1
Peru	22.0	46.6	22.6
Uruguay	8.2	43.6	13.7
Venezuela	58.4	5.4	15.4
Other			
Israel	36.9	29.0	4.8
Malaysia	43.0	17.6	16.6
Rep. of Korea	25.2	42.7	14.9
All	*25.7*	*25.5*	*8.3*
Industrial Market Economies			
Australia	60.0	23.5	5.2
Canada	49.3	18.5	4.7
France	17.5	29.9	0.1
Ireland	33.6	32.1	7.2
Italy	38.5	23.5	0.0
Japan	67.4	18.9	1.7
New Zealand	61.8	17.5	3.5
Fed. Rep. of Germany	17.5	21.8	0.0
Spain	22.9	15.8	4.5
U.S.A.	50.1	3.9	1.7
All industrial market economies	*40.0*	*17.3*	*12.2*

Source: World Bank (1988), table 24.

foreign exchange, and contributed to maintaining a higher level of employment. Argentina had the potential for substantially increasing such exports as a result of investments made during prior import-substitution stages (Teitel and Thoumi 1986).

Nature of the Programs

Given the use of a nominal foreign-exchange anchor for extended periods of time, an ample stock of international reserves seems to be a precondition for success. It is also needed to cushion the economy against possible adverse terms-of-trade shocks. Consequently, why was the government so dependent on the decision of exporters as to whether they would sell their dollars? Given that the structure of the Argentine economy has for many years required taxing agricultural exports (or having a dual rate of foreign exchange), why has this problem not been addressed one way or another? A propos, I remember the sad complaint by Minister Pugliese after a sharp run on the Austral: "While I spoke to them [the exporters] with a hand on my heart, they answered me with their hands in their pockets." The problem is that Argentine governments have placed themselves in situations of such extreme vulnerability as a result of their own self-defeating rules.

There seems to be a resignation to inflation in the country and an acceptance of residual inflation at quite a high level (more than 100% per annum). This has been a feature common to both the Martínez de Hoz program and the Austral plan. If, as Heymann says, after the initial stage one must get serious with the fiscal policies and contract the economy if necessary, those are things Argentine politicians—irrespective of their affiliation and power base—apparently feel they are not able to do. Not only was the Alfonsín government sensitive to criticisms about low real wages and a low level of economic activity; the military government had also exhibited similar sensitivity, which precluded the generation of substantial unemployment.

Thus, the adoption of an incomes-policy approach seemed to be politically required in Argentina. But once it had been learned that price and wage controls have only an ephemeral life and are discounted by the public, why did the Argentine programs continue to rely on price and wage controls? Why was there not more reliance on devaluations and fiscal and monetary policies? Central-bank independence has been attained in other developing countries. Why is it that the central bank cannot resist rediscount demands in Argentina, and what can be done about it?

Paraphrasing Kornai: The results achieved in Argentina were really based on a "soft" approach to stabilization, one in which all sorts of taboos and political compromises made it impossible to adopt the fiscal and monetary measures required to attain significant and durable results.

Note

1. Mathematically, chaotic behavior may be described as being induced by small differences in the intial conditions of nonlinear dynamic systems.

References

Díaz Alejandro, C. F. 1970. *Essays on the Economic History of the Argentine Republic*. Yale University Press.

Gleick, J. 1988. *Chaos—Making a New Science*. Penguin.

Teitel, S., and Thoumi, F. E. 1986. "From import substitution to exports: The manufacturing exports experience of Argentina and Brazil." *Economic Development and Cultural Change* 34(3): 455–490.

World Bank. 1988. *World Development Report, 1988*.

General Discussion

A number of participants addressed the Argentine tax system. They pointed out that Argentina relies heavily on trade taxes and seigniorage whereas its income tax and its value-added tax are relatively small. They all agreed that a reform in this area is needed, and that the question is why policy makers did not take such measures. Sebastian Edwards attributed it to a political system that causes decentralized decision making. According to Mario Blejer, the tax system deteriorated (compared with the 1950s); he questioned whether this development had anything to do with the strengthening of the lobbying power of various interest groups.

Not all the participants shared the view expressed in the paper regarding the importance of the mechanism in which the budget is formed, although it was agreed that it did contribute to the size of the deficit. Juan Antonio Morales pointed out that the official figures do not reveal a larger deficit that can account for the failure of the Austral program, and he suggested that the deficit is much higher since there is a quasi-fiscal deficit which is omitted from the official figures. Arie Hilman went further, suggesting that democracies tend to have higher inflation rates since they provide fertile ground for lobbyists of all kinds.

5

From Inertia to Megainflation: Brazil in the 1980s

Eliana Cardoso

Brazil's inflation rate reached 40% per month during the last quarter of 1989. Once again policy makers discussed the possibility of imposing price controls, despite the failure of three previous attempts (in 1986, 1987, and 1989) to beat inflation by freezes. Figure 5.1 shows inflation rates before and after the Cruzado Plan, the Bresser Plan, and the Summer Plan.

This paper discusses the acceleration of inflation in Brazil in the 1980s. Section 1 presents an overview of the recent Brazilian macroeconomic performance. In the early 1980s the Brazilian inflation rate increased largely because of the balance-of-payments crisis and because of large depreciations of the cruzeiro. The Cruzado Plan failed to stop inflation because of an extremely loose monetary policy coupled with a lack of fiscal austerity. Repeated price controls have increased the variability of inflation. More recently, the decline in tax collections and the growth of interest payments on a ballooning domestic debt have been building up a massive fiscal problem. Flight from money has further aggravated Brazilian inflation.

Two approaches are particularly useful in explaining the Brazilian inflationary process: an analysis of price freezes in the context of sustained fiscal imbalance, and research on the consequences of financing the fiscal deficit (sections 2 and 3). Section 2 presents a simple model introducing financial markets and interest rates in the traditional (Cagan-style) model of inflationary finance with rational expectations. It assumes inflation inertia. This means that inflation in the current period reproduces inflation in the previous period. Inertia occurs through the existence of formal or informal indexation interacting with a staggered setting of wages, prices, and financial contracts. Inflation fluctuation relative to previous periods depends on the behavior of interest rates. After characterizing steady states, we use the model to simulate the paths of

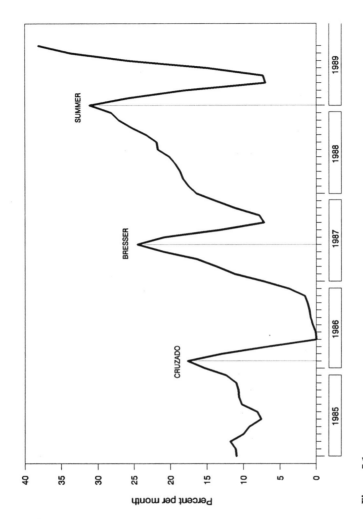

Figure 5.1
Brazilian inflation rate (3-month moving average).

inflation and real cash balances in response to different shocks. The focus is on the effects of controls that impose a temporary reduction of the inflation rate under different choices for monetary and fiscal policies. Section 3 examines the central relationship of budget deficits, external finance, and inflation. It extends the model of section 2 to an open economy where agents can hold money, domestic bonds, and inventories of goods. Our contribution clarifies the link between Brazil's growing inability to finance the public-sector deficit externally after 1982 and the acceleration of inflation. The suddenly limited access to external finance and the inadequacy of the government's savings effort profoundly affected the domestic macroeconomic structure. Applying the model developed in section 3 to the analysis of inflation in Brazil after 1982, we discuss fiscal imbalances and balance-of-payments crises as causes of accelerating inflation.

1. Overview

Brazil has a tradition of high inflation rates. Between 1960 and 1964, increasingly populist administrations carried inflation from 2% to 6% per month. By 1968, inflation was down to 1.5%, a level that persisted until the first oil shock. Then it doubled to 3% per month, and it doubled again to 6% in 1980–1982. Between 1983 and 1985 inflation increased to 10.5% per month. With the Cruzado Plan it fell to an average of 5% per month. From then on it increased every year, reaching more than 50% per month in December 1989 (see table 5.1).

Debt Strategy and Inflation

The foreign-debt strategy of the 1970s and the balance-of-payments crisis of the early 1980s play an important role in the history of Brazilian inflation. After 1968, the government embarked on a deliberate program of tapping private capital markets to underwrite rapid expansion. Brazil relied extensively on this external capital market, implementing a debt-led model of development to help finance mounting imports of capital and intermediate goods associated with average growth rates of about 10% between 1968 and 1973. In 1968, another component of the strategy was the explicit adaptation to inflation through indexation of exchange rates. This came in addition to the indexation of wages, rents, and financial assets since 1964.

Table 5.1
Inflation rates.[a]

	Average inflation during the year (percent per month)	Coefficient of variation (percent)	Price freeze
1976	3	22	
1977	3	34	
1978	3	18	
1979	5	32	
1980	6	17	
1981	6	52	
1982	6	19	
1983	10	24	
1984	10	11	
1985	11	24	
1986	5	162	March 1986
1987	15	45	August 1987
1988	23	17	
1989[b]	27	54	March 1989

Source: Conjuntura Economica.
a. Indice Geral de Precos [Wholesale Price Index], from Fundacao Getulio Vargas.
b. Preliminary.

When the oil shock struck in late 1973, Brazil was the largest oil importer among the developing countries. Already faced with the prospect of weakening growth from internal cyclical causes, the government chose not to risk a significant decline in real income from the adverse terms-of-trade shock. It increased external borrowing, thus postponing the contractionary effects of the petroleum "tax" and permitting domestic expansion to proceed. Brazil opted for adjustment through an ambitious program of generalized import substitution rather than through export promotion or domestic recession.

An elastic supply of debt responded to Brazilian requirements. External borrowing and brief episodes of slower domestic activity kept the balance of payments under control until the late 1970s. Higher prices for coffee and other commodities also contributed by reversing the decline in the terms of trade. Brazil's economic performance after the first oil-price shock remained above its trend level of growth of 7% per year: petrodollar recycling transferred considerable resources to Brazil, translating them into high rates of investment and economic growth.

On the eve of the second oil shock, Brazil had the largest external debt in the world. Whereas the first stage of debt accumulation saw a large transfer of real resources, in later stages more and more borrowing went simply to cover interest obligations on earlier loans. The dynamics of debt-led debt had become part of the Brazilian story, a process magnified by rising interest rates.

The Debt Crisis

In 1980, facing rising oil prices and interest rates, Brazil found additional finance available. But terms became more expensive as spreads widened. The country was forced to adopt a more austere set of policies and domestic adjustment in 1981. For the first time in the postwar period, income declined. Discipline was rewarded with new capital flows.

During the generalized debt crisis in 1982 the government insisted that Brazil's situation was distinct and susceptible to a simple remedy. With congressional elections in November, politics precluded any appeal to the IMF until after the votes had been counted. Only then did Brazil join the rapidly lengthening queue of problem cases. But it did so with the disadvantage of having its own inadequate stabilization program on the table beforehand.

Brazil managed best on its external accounts. A greater export recovery in 1984 distinguished it from other large Latin American debtors (see table 5.2). The current account was quickly restored to balance, and the foreign-exchange constraint became less pressing. Although the recession was worse than the Great Depression of the 1930s, the intervening decline in per capita income was smaller than for other problem debtors. Output in 1984 was already on the way up, led by export growth.

External Adjustment

To judge from trade performance, adjustment to the debt crisis was nothing short of phenomenal. The combination of export growth and import substitution have produced large export surpluses in recent years. The trade deficits of the 1970s turned into large surpluses after 1983. Merchandise exports increased from $13 billion per year in 1977–1979 to $34 billion in 1988. At the same time, Brazil restrained imports by continuing to expand alternative domestic supply sources. Imports in 1983–1988 were lower than in 1977–1982, despite the increase in output.

Table 5.2
Trade balance and real exchange rates.

	(Billions of US$)			Index of the real effective exchange rate[a]	Terms of trade
	Exports	Imports	Trade balance		
1977–79[b]	13.3	14.6	−1.3	104.0	100
1980–82[b]	21.2	21.5	−0.3	100.0	66
1983	21.9	15.4	6.5	86.4	61
1984	27.0	13.9	13.1	85.7	63
1985	25.6	13.2	12.5	85.2	62
1986	22.3	14.0	8.3	74.4	67
1987	26.2	15.0	11.2	73.6	60
1988	33.8	14.7	19.1	80.9	63[c]

Sources: Conjuntura Economica, Morgan Guaranty, Banco Central, and IDB.
a. Appreciation up.
b. Yearly average.
c. Preliminary.

In 1988, real GDP was 29% higher than in 1979, but the volume of imports was 23% lower (see table 5.2).

In part, trade flows responded to the real depreciation of the 1980s. In 1983–1988 the real effective exchange rate was 20% lower than in 1977–1982. But since the late 1960s Brazil has also been exceptional among the Latin American countries in its successful combination of import substitution and growth and in its diversification of exports. Four factors have played a role: the size and efficiency of the industrial sector, a crawling-peg exchange-rate policy (which averted long periods of overvaluation), an active promotion of manufactured exports through incentives and subsidies, and import restrictions that relied not merely on controls but also on the active policy of investment directed toward import substitution in the late 1970s.

The recent large trade surpluses tend to create an illusory optimism about the ease with which large external transfers of resources can be realized. A broader perspective is necessary, incorporating the debt as an integral part of the Brazilian development problem. Soaring debt service is an important component of fiscal deterioration in Brazil, and it has been financed by growing trade surpluses. (Section 3 explores the important link between trade surpluses and inflation.) In Brazil, trade surpluses were used to pay interest on government debt while the government financed the purchase of foreign exchange from the private sector by issuing debt and printing money. As a consequence, inflation increased.

The Brazilian experience also led to the understanding that improvement of the balance of payments and domestic equilibrium were not tightly linked. Indeed, as will be discussed in section 3, trade surpluses might create new problems for macroeconomic policy.

Internal Adjustment

Progress on the external account was not matched internally. The large positive government savings of the first half of the 1970s had shrunk and turned negative in the second half of the 1980s (table 5.3). Government savings are not a measure of the budget surplus, because they exclude public enterprises. They do, however, show that public finance in Brazil has been deteriorating. Two factors explain the sharp decline in government savings. One is the growing interest payments on domestic debt. The other is the reduction in revenues from indirect taxes. The latter results from less-than-perfect fiscal indexation, from evasion, and from a growing underground economy. The Instituto Brasileiro de Geografia e Estatistica (IBGE) estimates the size of the underground economy at some 15% of GDP. The decline in revenue from indirect taxes was in part counterbalanced by an increase in direct taxation in 1986, but the overall trend remains one of declining tax revenues.

In 1983, successive letters of intent under IMF programs had no sooner been dispatched than they were made obsolete by accelerating inflation, which crippled attempts to observe the monetary targets. That experience led to the development of a new deficit concept, adjusted for the indexation of government debt, which is now widely applied in other countries.

Budget Concepts

Table 5.4 shows alternative measures for the budget. When inflation rises or abruptly falls, different budget concepts are strongly affected. Inflation in Brazil accelerated sharply in the 1980s, as did the public-sector borrowing requirements (PSBR). The PSBR move dramatically with inflation because of the inflationary component of interest payments. If inflation were to cease, the PSBR would shrink to the size of the budget deficit corrected for inflation.

Table 5.3
Government revenues, expenditures, and savings as shares of GDP, all levels of government (percent).

	Direct taxes (1)	Indirect taxes (2)	Revenues (1)+(2)+ others[b] (3)	Interest on internal debt[c] (4)	Transfers and consumption expenditures [incl. (4)] (5)	Taxes (6)
1970–77[a]	10.6	14.8	25.0	0.5	19.4	5.6
1978–80[a]	12.0	13.0	24.0	0.8	21.2	2.8
1981	11.7	12.9	23.5	1.1	21.2	2.3
1982	12.6	12.5	23.8	1.1	22.0	1.8
1983	12.1	12.6	23.2	1.6	22.0	1.2
1984	11.2	10.2	20.7	2.4	19.7	1.0
1985	11.7	10.3	21.2	3.3	21.6	−0.4
1986	13.0	11.6	22.2	3.5	23.7	−1.5
1987d	10.2	11.3	19.3	2.4	23.4	−4.1
1988[d]	9.7	10.2	17.2	2.7	24.0	−6.8

Source: Resende et al. 1989.
a. Yearly average.
b. "Others" include other revenues *minus* external debt service.
c. Excludes monetary correction.
d. Preliminary.

Table 5.4
Different measures of the budget deficit as shares of GDP and real depreciation rates (percent).

	PSBR[a]	Operational deficit[b]	Deficit corrected for inflation[c]	Real depreciation rate[d]
1981	12.5	5.9		
1982	15.8	6.6	9.1	−3
1983	19.9	3.0	22.1	43
1984	23.3	2.7	9.0	0
1985	27.5	4.3	5.0	−2
1986	11.2	3.6	2.1	−8
1987	31.4	5.5	3.3	−6

Source: Banco Central.
a. Public Sector Borrowing Requirements, as defined by the IMF.
b. Subtracts monetary correction from PSBR.
c. Calculation shown in tables 5.A2 and 5.A3.
d. [(1 + depreciation rate)/(1 + inflation rate)] − 1; December to December.

The operational deficit (table 5.4, column 2) captures the behavior of the budget deficit better than the PSBR. It is calculated by subtracting the monetary correction payments from the PSBR. Nonetheless, because the monetary correction index is not always equal to the inflation rate, the operational deficit still is not a proper measure of the budget deficit corrected for inflation. The difference between the two represents capital gains or losses for the public sector. Moreover, like the PSBR, it excludes the deficit of the monetary authorities (which distribute large credit subsidies), and thus it may substantially underestimate the actual borrowing needs of the public sector.

One can try to overcome the shortcomings of the operational deficit by calculating the budget deficit corrected for inflation from the consolidated debt of the public sector (table 5.4, column 3). Its calculation is shown in the appendix. This measure underestimates the deficit when prices are rising. In this definition, payments and revenues are deflated by the December price index. If inflation is high and the excess of expenditures over revenues occurs throughout the year, deflating the deficit of each month by the December price index grossly underestimates the budget deficit of the year. Thus, while this measure shows the behavior of the consolidated real debt, it does not show the deficit according to the conventional definition, i.e., it does not measure the difference between revenues and expenditures. Moreover, this calculation is very sensitive to real depreciations when the share of external debt in total debt is large. Thus, in a year of large real depreciation, the debt/GDP ratio will show a large increase. After 1985 this measure underestimates the deficit because the rate of depreciation has been smaller than that of inflation.

In 1983 the budget deficit as a percentage of GDP, corrected for inflation, was unusually large. There are at least three major causes for this large deficit:

• In contrast with historically large and positive growth rates, output fell 3.4% during 1983.

• The domestic cost (corrected for inflation) of servicing the external debt increased greatly during 1983 because of the real devaluation.

• Interest on government bonds included compensation for the 30% devaluation of February, because the return on these bonds had been linked to the rate of exchange depreciation.[1]

In the following year the budget deficit, corrected for inflation, declined. But in 1985 the budget deficit was still as large as 5% of GDP. The Cruzado Plan grossly miscalculated the size of the fiscal deficit, assuming a budget close to equilibrium when the Cruzado Plan was launched in February 1986.

The Cruzado Plan

Relations with the IMF deteriorated, and previous plans for a multiyear rescheduling agreement with the banks were scrapped after a new civilian government took office in March 1985. Although interest on the external debt was paid in full, there were no new inflows of capital. Recovery was then based on internal demand, with a limited increase in imports. Despite strong output growth, worrisome signs came from increasing government internal debt service, low investment rates, and accelerating inflation. New and bold measures were called for.

The Cruzado Plan, implemented in February 1986 as a substitute for a conventional recession-based strategy of stabilization, rested on the premise that the high rates of inflation were driven by the inertial, self-replicating force of indexation.[2] Accordingly, the Cruzado Plan enforced a sophisticated short-term standstill that maintained real income positions and abolished future indexation. The key steps of the Cruzado Plan were these:

1. Wages, rents and installment payments were readjusted and frozen, as were all prices and the exchange rate.

2. A *tablita* was devised to compensate for the expected inflation built into extant contracts and thus avoid arbitrary redistribution between debtors and creditors. A new currency was introduced to help facilitate the readjustment.

3. Indexation was virtually eliminated. An *escala movel*, with a 20% threshold, was substituted for wages. In financial markets, indexation was maintained only for instruments of more than one year's maturity.

Inflation was to be zero. For a few months it seemed true, and general euphoria set in. But signs of disequilibrium from excess demand mounted without eliciting an adequate compensatory response. Another election loomed, and, in the best Brazilian political tradition, corrective actions were placed on hold.

This time the new measures were announced immediately after the elections. They proved much too late, and much too little. The ice of controls had thawed, and there was no opportunity to restore an orderly process of readjustment of prices and wages. Events rapidly moved out of control as inflation rates mounted. Policy seemed to be impotent. The deterioration in the balance of payments became as significant as the mounting internal problem. Suddenly, Brazil's comfortable cushion of reserves, which could lend credibility to the maintenance of a fixed exchange rate, had vanished.

There is no controversy about the reasons why the Cruzado Plan failed. The most prominent factor was the overheating of the economy through loose fiscal and monetary policies, as well as through the overly generous wage policy. On the fiscal side, tax revenues disappointingly rose only a little, revenues of state-owned companies were hurt by the price freeze, spending ran higher than anticipated, and subsidies—cut during 1983–84—staged a comeback in 1986. The public-sector wage bill also increased, in line with the economy-wide trend. There was a sharp initial monetization of the economy: in the first three months following stabilization the monetary base doubled. Loose monetary policy produced very low interest rates that permitted firms lacking confidence in the program to build up speculative stocks. Furthermore, the increase in real wages promoted by the Cruzado Plan and the fast-growing economy rapidly expanded wages and sustained a consumer boom.

New attempts at controlling inflation were made in mid-1987 (the Bresser Plan) and in January 1989 (the Summer Plan). Once again the government froze prices and cut zeros off the face value of the currency. Promises to eliminate the budget deficit were made but not kept. President José Sarney lacked the political will to implement measures of fiscal consolidation. He also lacked credibility, determination, and allies in the Congress. With the budget deficit left unscathed and trade surpluses growing, all three plans amounted to attempts to stop inflation by decree.

Institutional Adaptation

In designing the Cruzado Plan, policy makers believed that past inflationary shocks were being perpetuated in a vicious circle created by indexation. Freezing prices, exchange rates, and wages would create a rupture with the past, thus permitting the economy to rid itself of inertial inflation.

The main obstacle to the price and wage freeze was the absence of synchronization in price readjustments. Simply freezing wages and prices on a given day would greatly favor wage earners and entrepreneurs who had readjusted their prices immediately before the freeze. In like manner, such a step would drastically penalize those who were to have received their new settlements the following day.

Incomes policy, rather than playing the role of a coordinating device, became the major objective of the Cruzado Plan. All attention was concentrated on deriving formulas that would permit a "neutral" price freeze. Nonetheless, the objective of "neutrality" in income distribution remains elusive because the choice of a reference point remains arbitrary.

The initial price freeze will not produce excessive windfall profits or losses only if there is little dispersion of relative prices. The dispersion of relative prices in the context of a staggered price setting introduces a serious problem for the use of freezes in the coordination of expectations during a stabilization program. It is sometimes asserted that dispersion of relative prices will be smaller when inflation is higher, because adjustments take place at shorter intervals. The Brazilian experience does not support this view. When inflation rises, adjustments take place at shorter intervals but are also bigger. Rising inflation does not contribute to reducing the dispersion of relative prices, but it can exacerbate the problem. In Brazil, during the last week of December 1989, a Chevette cost the same as 42 standard-size brassieres, and a refrigerator the same as a linen shirt. The same bottle of wine cost 50 cruzados in one supermarket and 15 cruzados in another.

Institutional adaptation to rising inflation has become pervasive as buyers and sellers, borrowers and lenders, and government and taxpayers have engaged in a self-defeating race to shorten the lags on pricing and indexation. Since 1988 supermarkets in Rio have closed each Monday morning to re-mark prices; by the end of 1989 firms were discussing weekly adjustments for wage earners. By November 1989 the sales of electronic calculators and the number of credit cards had doubled in relation to their numbers in 1988. To avoid delayed reimbursement, many merchants were offering shoppers a 30% discount for instant payment in cash or checks. By the end of 1989 most restaurants and hotels had stopped accepting credit cards, because the 20-day billing period had eroded the value of payments. Contracts were made not in cruzados, but in terms of BTNs (a national treasury bond, corrected daily for inflation and used as unit of account).

Figure 5.2 shows the daily inflation rate between April 4, 1988 and August 31, 1989. On average, inflation picked up at regular weekly intervals. At the beginning of 1989 there was an extraordinary jump in the daily index as merchants increased prices in response to an expected price freeze that did, indeed, materialize with the Summer Plan. Controls were soon lifted, and once again inflation was on the rise.

2. Inflationary Finance

This section presents a model of inflationary finance and explores the role of price controls on inflation behavior.

Consider an economy where government expenditures, G, are financed by money creation, $H_t - H_{t-1}$:

$$G = H_t - H_{t-1} . \tag{1}$$

Dividing both sides of equation 1 by nominal income, assuming zero real growth, and using the definition of the inflation rate, we obtain[3]

$$h_t = g + h_{t-1}[1/(1 + \pi_t)] , \tag{2}$$

where g is the share of the real budget deficit in real income and h is the ratio between real cash balances and real income.

Our next question concerns the dynamics of inflation. The inflation rate accelerates whenever aggregate demand exceeds the full-employment output level. For a given fiscal stance and real exchange rate, there is a unique real interest rate at which aggregate demand equals full-employment output. Accordingly, equation 3 shows that inflation increases whenever the actual real interest rate, $i - \pi$, is below the full-employment real interest rate, ρ:

$$\pi_t - \pi_{t-1} = \phi \{\rho(g) - [i_t(h_t) - \pi_t]\} , \tag{3}$$

where ρ is a function of the share of government expenditures in GDP. We also assume that the nominal interest rate moves in order to clear the money market all the time. The demand for real cash balances is inversely related to the nominal interest rate. Thus, we can write the actual interest rate, i_t, as a function of real cash balances in the equation above. Note that equation 3 implies the existence of both inflation inertia and a scope for monetary policy to affect inflation.

Figure 5.3 illustrates steady-state equilibria. In steady state, the inflation rate is constant. We represent the steady-state inflation rate in figure 5.3 as the curve[4] showing $\pi_t = \pi_{t-1}$:

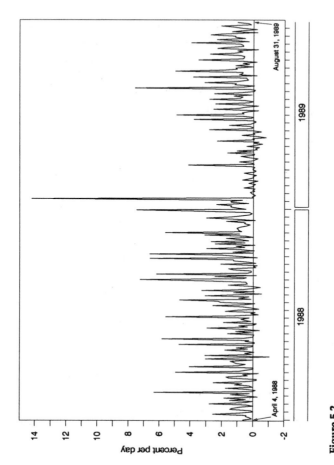

Figure 5.2
Daily inflation rate, Brazil: April 4, 1989 to August 31, 1989.

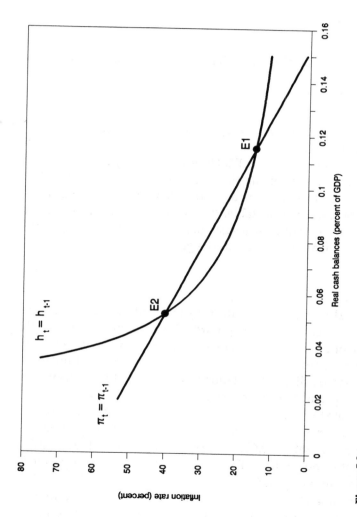

Figure 5.3

$$\rho = i(h) - \pi .\qquad (4)$$

In steady state, the ratio of real cash balances and real income is also constant:

$$h\pi = g(1 + \pi) .\qquad (5)$$

We represent the steady-state budget constraint in figure 5.3 by the curve showing $h_t = h_{t-1}$.

There are two equilibria: E1 and E2. The low-inflation equilibrium, E1, can be stable. The nature of the time path around the low-inflation equilibrium is one of oscillations as in the cobweb model. The high-inflation equilibrium, E2, is unstable.[5] This model exhibits the essential property that, in the transition to a sustained increase in money growth, the inflation rate, on average, exceeds the growth rate of money.

Price Controls

In the context of a budget deficit financed by the printing of money, price controls would reduce inflation temporarily. Continuous money growth in the presence of price controls increases real cash balances, reducing interest rates. As a consequence, once price controls are removed, inflation picks up. Through oscillations, inflation would then return to its initial level, if the initial equilibrium were stable.

We can simulate the path of inflation by assuming specific functional forms for money demand and values for the parameters in equations 1–3. We make $i_t = j - vh_t$, with $j = 0.62$ and $v = 4$. We also assume that $\phi = 0.05$, $\rho = 1\%$ per month, and $g = 1.5\%$. Thus, in the initial stable steady state $\pi = 15\%$ per month and $h = 0.115$.

Figure 5.4 compares two situations. In the first, the government freezes prices during one period. In the second, it uses guideposts rather than a price freeze. Once controls are removed, the price freeze leads to a bigger overshooting of the inflation rate than in the case of loose controls. Under both circumstances, the inflation rate finally returns to the 15% steady-state level. In this model, price controls can lead to an explosive inflation rate only under two circumstances. The first situation corresponds to one with an unstable initial equilibrium; the second corresponds to one in which the inflation rate, in response to the price freeze, moves out of the stability region.

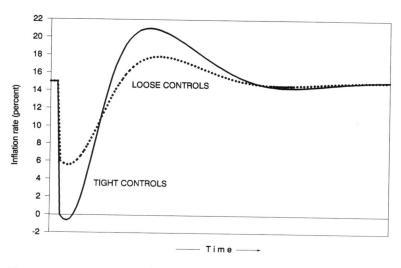

Figure 5.4
Inflation path after price controls.

Cutting the Budget Deficit

Figure 5.5 compares equilibria for different fiscal deficits. A cut in government expenditures shifts the steady-state budget constraint downward. It also reduces the full-employment real interest rate, thus shifting $\pi_t = \pi_{t-1}$ to the right.

Assume that, consistent with a zero real interest rate per month, the reduced budget deficit's share in output, g, is 1%. In the new stable steady state, the inflation rate will be 8% per month and the share of real cash balances in income will be 0.135.

How does the economy move from the initial 15% inflation to the new 8% final equilibrium? If policy makers could precisely determine both the new steady-state inflation rate and the size of the desired real cash balances consistent with it, they could cut the deficit and at the same time increase money by the right amount and choose adequate price controls. Under these very special circumstances, they could immediately bring the economy to the new steady state.[6] Unfortunately, perfect information and synchronization do not exist. Thus, we must compare less perfect but more realistic policies. We compare the inflation path that follows the adoption of a budget-deficit cut with and without price controls and a budget-deficit cut with and without a change in the money stock.

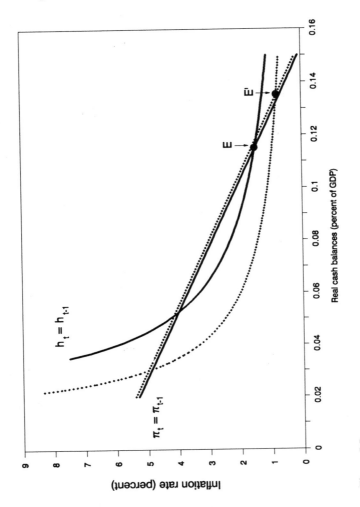

Figure 5.5

Price Controls in the Presence of a Fiscal Contraction

Figure 5.6 compares the inflation path in response to a cut in the budget deficit in three different situations: no controls, loose controls during five periods, and a price freeze during five periods. This figure shows that loose controls produce a deceleration of inflation sooner than would have taken place in its absence, and also reduce the size of the cycles around the new steady state. By contrast, when the inflation rate is not zero in the new steady state, the price freeze exaggerates the size of the cycles.

This exercise helps to understand the success of loose controls in the 1965–1968 stabilization in Brazil.

Combining Fiscal and Monetary Austerity

Figure 5.7 shows that a cut in the budget, combined with a monetary squeeze, is overkill. The inflation rate declines faster, but the recession and the following cycles are more acute.

Monetizing Public Debt

Fiscal and monetary austerity were not part of the economic package adopted in Brazil with the Cruzado Plan. On the contrary, fiscal policy was left untouched in the immediate aftermath of the Cruzado Plan, and monetary policy was expansionary.

Figure 5.8 shows the path of real cash balances in response to an increase in the money stock with and without price controls. This figure can be compared with figure 5.9, which shows the actual behavior of real M1 in Brazil. The acceleration of inflation in Brazil once price controls were removed after the Cruzado Plan does not need a very elaborate explanation.

3. The Causes of Inflation

Section 2 clarified two processes. The model showed how price controls, in the presence of a sustained budget deficit, ultimately increase inflation instability. We also argued that a monetary expansion combined with a price freeze clearly was one of the factors in the acceleration of inflation

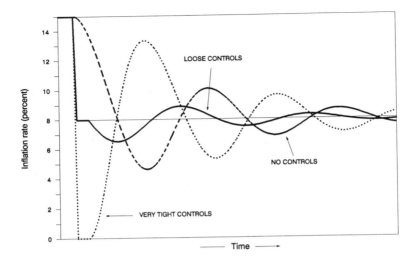

Figure 5.6
Inflation path after fiscal contraction, with and without price controls.

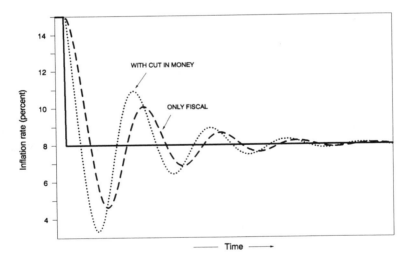

Figure 5.7
Inflation path after a cut in the budget deficit.

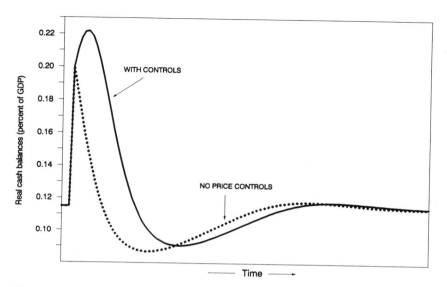

Figure 5.8
Path of real cash balances after an increase in the money stock.

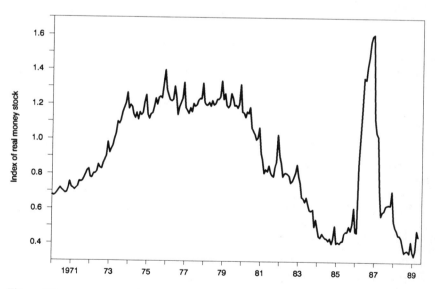

Figure 5.9
Real money (M1), Brazil: January 1970 to May 1989.

after the Cruzado Plan. Questions concerning the link between domestic and external debts with inflation have to be answered in the context of a more complex model than the one described in section 2. We now develop a model to study the inflationary impact of financing the budget deficit in different ways and of depreciating the exchange rate.

Montiel (1989) divides recent analyses of inflation into a "fiscal" view and a "balance of payments" view. Followers of the "fiscal" persuasion point to movements in the budget deficit as the fundamental source of monetary emission that moves the economy to higher inflation rates. Supporters of the "balance of payments" theory link inflation to exchange-rate depreciation triggered by balance-of-payments crises. Computing historical decompositions of the Brazilian inflation rate based on vector autoregressions, Montiel concluded that movements in base money and the nominal exchange rate played an important role in determining the time path of the rate of inflation in Brazil between 1983/I and 1985/IV. Brazilian inflation for most of that period resulted in good part from inertia; it increased because of new shocks from exchange-rate depreciation. Monetary shocks had an important role only in the last two quarters of 1985.

Rodriguez (1978) offered a starting point for the discussion of the devaluation-inflation spiral in a model where the government finances the budget deficit through the creation of credit by the central bank.[7] He showed that under these circumstances, while casual observation would indicate that inflation is preceded by devaluation and monetization of the resulting balance-of-payments surpluses, the conclusion that the external sector is the cause of inflation would be inappropriate:

Although it is correct that over a short period following the devaluation external sector developments lead the movement in domestic prices, over the entire typical cycle the price level follows the path of the money supply, which is determined entirely by domestic credit creation to finance the fiscal deficit . . . . Both the price level and the exchange rate [are] led by developments in the monetary sector, which are in turn determined by the monetization of the internal fiscal deficit. (Rodriguez 1978, p. 78)

The situation described by Rodriguez can be complicated if external credit rationing follows a period of external borrowing by the government. Consider, for example, a situation where a government has a large external debt. Suddenly, deprived of foreign capital inflows needed to finance interest payments and non-interest deficits, it will have to foster trade surpluses to produce the exchange resources needed to service the external debt. In order to produce these trade surpluses, the exchange rate is greatly depreciated in real terms. The government now has to finance domestically the purchase of the foreign exchange it needs to service the external debt. In the absence of a cut in the budget, there will be more government credit creation. Moreover, depreciation has an important impact on the domestic cost of servicing the external debt. Debt service measured in domestic currency increases, and thus the budget deficit measured in that currency also increases. This, in turn, increases money creation and, hence, inflation.

Observe that the inflationary impact of the trade surpluses does not necessarily come from an increase in foreign reserves, as in Rodriguez 1978. If the trade surplus is used to pay interest on government debt and is not counterbalanced by an increase in taxes, it will increase money creation even if reserves remain unchanged.

Under these circumstances, what "caused" inflation to rise? The disappearance of the external source of finance? The exchange-rate depreciation? The deterioration of the budget that resulted from the depreciation? The monetization of budget deficits that were previously financed by external borrowing and counterbalanced by trade deficits?

The answer, of course, is all of the factors mentioned above. In the absence of a budget deficit, neither external credit rationing nor exchange depreciation would cause a persistently higher inflation rate. On the other hand, without credit rationing and depreciation the inflation rate would not increase.

We now explore this situation formally. Our first question concerns the fiscal budget and its financing. The government finances the budget deficit by borrowing abroad, by issuing domestic debt, and by creating money. We assume that the current account is financed either by commercial loans or by changes in foreign reserves. All external borrowing is done by the public sector. The appendix shows how we can combine the equations for the budget constraint and the balance of payments to obtain[8]

$$g + \psi + ib = h\mu + bv, \tag{6}$$

where g is the share in output of the primary budget deficit, y is the share in output of net exports, i is the nominal interest rate, b is the ratio between domestic debt and income, h is the ratio between the monetary base and income, m is the growth rate of the monetary base, and n is the growth rate of domestic debt.

Net exports are equal to the interest payments on the public external debt in the special case where, after a decade of external borrowing by the government, there is external credit rationing and no change in foreign reserves.[9]

Domestic agents hold money, domestic bonds, and inventories of goods. Demand for real cash balances is inversely related to the interest rate, i, and inversely related to the inflation rate, π:

$$h = \gamma_0 - \gamma_1 i - \gamma_2 \pi \,. \tag{7}$$

The demand for domestic bonds depends positively on the interest rate and inversely on the inflation rate:

$$b = \beta_0 + \beta_1 i - \beta_2 \pi \,. \tag{8}$$

The government follows a "passive" monetary rule, letting money growth match the inflation rate when inflation is stable but reducing the money growth rate when the inflation rate increases:

$$\mu = \pi - \alpha \dot{\pi}. \tag{9}$$

The growth rate of domestic debt is endogenous. Substituting equations 7–9 in equation 6, we obtain the equation that describes the behavior of the real domestic debt through time:

$$v - \pi = i - \pi + (1/b)[(g + \psi) - (\gamma_0 - \gamma_1 i - \gamma_2 \pi)(\pi - \alpha \dot{\pi})] \,, \tag{10}$$

where $i = (b - \beta_0 + \beta_2 \pi)/\beta_1$.

Our next step is to reinterpret equation 3, which describes the dynamics of inflation. As before, the equilibrium nominal interest rate is part of the real interest rate that influences inflation dynamics. In the goods market, inflation increases whenever the actual real interest rate, $i - \pi$, is below the full-employment real interest rate, ρ, which is now a function of both the share of government expenditures and the share of net exports in income:

$$\pi = \phi[\rho(g, \psi) - (i - \pi)] \,, \tag{11}$$

where

$$i = (b - b_0 + b_2 \pi)/b_1.$$

We can represent the model as in figure 5.10. $v = \pi$ shows the budget constraint in steady state[10]:

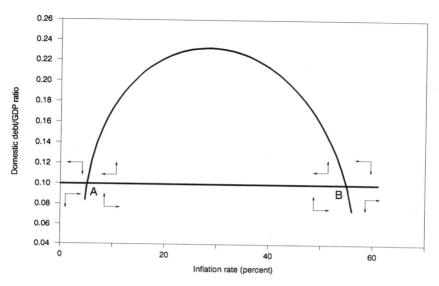

Figure 5.10
$\phi = 0.5$, $\alpha = 0.5$, $\gamma = 0.5$, $\beta = 1$, $m = 0.3$, $b = 0.06$, $g = 0.01$, $\rho = 0.04$.

$$v - \pi = 0 = (1/b_1)[b^2 - b_0 b - (b_1 - b_2)b\pi] + (g + y)$$
$$- \{\gamma_0 - \gamma_1[(b - \beta_0 + \beta_2\pi)/\beta_1] - \gamma_2\pi\}$$
$$\times \{\pi - \alpha\phi[\rho + \pi - (b - \beta_0 + \beta_2\pi)/\beta_1]\} . \tag{12}$$

The $\pi = 0$ curve shows the steady-state inflation rate, under the assumption that $\beta_1 = \beta_2$:[11]

$$\rho + \pi = (b - \beta_0 + \beta_2\pi)/\beta_1 . \tag{13}$$

There are two steady-state equilibria.[12] The high-inflation equilibrium, point B in figure 5.10, is unstable—any disturbance will move inflation onto an explosive path. The low-inflation equilibrium in figure 5.10, point A, can be stable. The nature of the time path around the low-inflation equilibrium is one of oscillations as in the cobweb model.

Comparative Dynamics: External Credit Rationing Changes the Source of Finance of the Budget Deficit

If external finance dries up and the government responds by depreciating the exchange rate, there is an increase in the trade surplus, ψ. The increase in the trade surplus shifts the schedule representing the steady-state budget constraint downward as shown in figure 5.11. On the other hand, the increased trade surplus requires a higher full-employment real interest rate, i.e., a higher domestic debt/income ratio. Thus, the schedule that represents steady-state inflation shifts upward.

The economy moves from the initial equilibrium, A, to a new, higher one, A´. With the increase in the trade surplus, the economy moves, with oscillations, to the higher-inflation equilibrium. Initially, the inflation rate increases ahead of the nominal interest rate and the real interest rate falls, stimulating activity and pushing up the inflation rate. Gradually, the interest rates exceed inflation rates, increasing the real interest rate and the domestic debt.

An increase in the budget deficit generates results exactly the same as those described above. A reduction of the external finance of the budget, requiring a devaluation and an increase in the trade surplus, is thus equivalent to an increase in the budget deficit.

Because there is a limit to the budget deficit that can be financed by seigniorage, or to the trade surplus that can be monetized, further increases in the budget deficit or in the trade surplus might rule out any intersections of the two curves, thereby denying the existence of an equilibrium solution to the model.

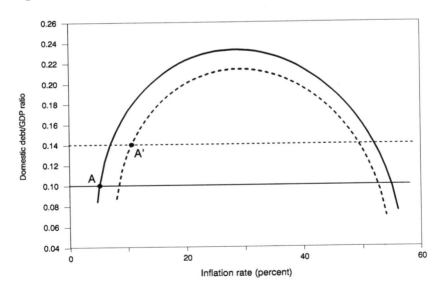

Figure 5.11
$\phi = 0.5, \alpha = 0.5, \gamma = 0.5, \beta = 1, m = 0.3, b = 0.06, \Delta g = 0.005, \Delta \rho = 0.04.$

We also observe that in response to an increase in the budget deficit, or to a reduction in the external finance of the budget deficit, both the inflation rate and the ratio of domestic debt to income increase. The debt crisis in Brazil manifests itself not only in rising inflation but also in the rapid growth of domestic debt (see table 5.5). The rapid domestic debt growth results in part from the financing of the primary deficit and from the financing of debt service. In 1989, the problems were made more acute by the high real interest rates, shown in figure 5.12.

During the last two quarters of 1989, the goal was to maintain a restrictive monetary policy; in practice, this was translated into very high real interest rates. Nonetheless, the public could effectively write checks on their overnight deposits which were backed by the government debt. This implied that open market operations traded non-interest-bearing money for interest-bearing money and thus did not affect liquidity. The high interest rate avoided the flight into dollars and real assets, and the government continued to enjoy financing for the deficit. But without debt relief, fighting current inflation with tight monetary policy must eventually lead to higher future inflation or to debt repudiation of some kind. In the case of Brazil, the situation is more serious because of the extremely short maturity of the debt.

4. Conclusions

Several factors explain inflation in Brazil. Between 1979 and 1983 its acceleration resulted from supply shocks and large real depreciations in the context of an indexed economy.[13] Because of a large external debt, the fiscal imbalance also increased in this period, with real depreciations and an increase in foreign real interest rates. After 1984, when the government could no longer finance the deficits externally, monetization of deficits and acceleration of money growth became important inflationary factors. Despite the decline of inflation-corrected budget deficits, the disappearance of external sources of finance made the fiscal deficits more inflationary because they had to be financed domestically.[14] Moreover, the perception of unsustainable fiscal imbalances led to financial adaptation and flight from money, further aggravating the inflation problem.[15]

Table 5.6 summarizes the stylized facts that our model has tried to replicate. In the two years that followed the Cruzado Plan, the average monthly inflation rate was about the same as it had been in the two years

Table 5.5
Domestic debt held by private
investors (billions of US$).

1987	December	33.8
1988	March	32.4
	June	42.2
	September	43.3
	December	44.7
1989	January	40.9
	February	51.1
	March	62.0
	April	68.0
	May	63.0
	June	58.0

Source: Banco Central.

Figure 5.12
Real interest rates (accumulated past 12 months).

Table 5.6
Before and after the Cruzado Plan (percent).

	2 preceding years Jan. 1984 to Feb. 1986	2 following years March–April 1988	May 1988 to May 1989
Average monthly inflation rate	11	10	20
Coefficient of variation of inflation rate	3	8	4
Real annual interest rate[a]	2	3	20
Black dollar premium[b]	21	45	68
Coefficient of variation of real Ibovespa[c]	48	75	40

Source: Conjuntura Economica and Banco Icatu.
a. $[\Pi_i(1 + r_{1-i})] - 1$, $i = 1, \ldots, 12$, and $(1 + r) = (1 + i)/(1 + \pi)$.
b. (Black-market rate)/(Official rate) − 1.
c. São Paolo Stock Market Index.

that preceded the Cruzado Plan. Instability nonetheless increased, as measured by the coefficient of variation of inflation, by the premium in the black market for dollars, and by the coefficient of variation of the index of the São Paolo stock market.

The very fast acceleration of inflation after 1988 and the recent sharp increase in real interest rates cannot be directly attributed to the failure of the Cruzado Plan alone. The culprits are several attempts to control inflation through price freezes and, more recently, by tight monetary policy alone, all the while avoiding the necessary fiscal adjustment.

There are four important lessons to be learned from the Brazilian experience.

The first lesson derives from the inadequacy of the public-sector savings effort. What occurred in the 1980s can be characterized as an "accommodation" to the disappearance of external sources of finance rather than as a structural adjustment. External debt reduction through different types of swaps, coupled with large budget deficits financed by expensive domestic debt, have evolved into a massive fiscal problem.

Inflation stabilization now requires a major fiscal effort. In the Brazilian case it requires action on three fronts. First and foremost, the position of the public sector in Brazil continues to be badly compromised by the need to extract resources from the private sector for the service of the external debt. To obtain fiscal consolidation without a major recession,

Brazil need to reduce the transfer of resources abroad. Today this means debt reduction and postponement of debt service.

Domestic debt has also grown to finance the budget deficit, as well as to pay for large subsidies granted to public enterprises and the private sector itself. The maturity of this debt is explosively short. Budget equilibrium requires the consolidation of the domestic debt. This could be achieved by privatization, with the proceeds used to retire debt, and by a forced lengthening of the maturity of the remaining instruments. Moreover, solving the two debt problems will not be enough to restore stability. Fiscal consolidation requires major cuts in subsidies and better tax administration.

The second lesson concerns the use of price controls. In the absence of fiscal consolidation, price controls increase inflation instability. They stimulate demonetization and increase the financial vulnerability of the economy. These effects are not easily reversed after stabilization.

Here one should also notice the difficulty of managing neutral disinflation. In 1986 real wages were increasing at the expense of profit margins, helping to provoke shortages, black markets, and disorderly growth.

Third, even if fiscal and monetary policies are just right for stabilization, the problem of the transition from a situation with high inflation to one with low inflation still has to be dealt with. In that case, a price freeze should be avoided, but price guideposts will help to smooth the transition.

Finally, it is too easily asserted that getting rid of indexation is essential to achieve inflation stabilization. This is wrong, as is demonstrated by the excessive boldness of the Cruzado Plan in aiming for zero inflation and abolishing indexation. While indexation contributes to the propagation of inflation, it also protects against the kind of volatile inflationary acceleration that occurred at the end of 1986 and the beginning of 1987. Indexation establishes inertia at a lower inflation rate, locking in disinflation gains. A good example are the years of low and stable inflation rates in Brazil between 1968 and 1974. Indexation also facilitates political acceptance of a stabilization program, an attribute whose importance cannot be overestimated.

Appendix

Macroeconomic statistics are given in tables 5.A1–5.A3. The remainder of this appendix shows how to obtain equation 6.

Table 5.A1
Financial indicators.

	Velocity[a]	External debt GDP[b]	Consolidated debt of the public sector GDP[c]	Real effective exchange rate[d]
1970–73	6.6	13.3	130.5	
1974–77	7.8	17.3	116.9	
1978–80	10.0	31.1	93.9	
1981	13.7	25.6	103.2	
1982	15.4	28.0	29.6	112.9
1983	19.4	42.6	48.9	86.4
1984	26.4	45.5	54.5	85.7
1985	26.8	45.4	55.8	85.2
1986	12.2	39.8	44.9	74.4
1987	21.6	38.3	55.0	73.6
1988[e]	36.9	33.0	68.0	80.9
1989[e]	42.0			

Source: Banco Central and Morgan Guaranty.
a. GDP/M1.
b. External debt calculated as the average between the debt outstanding in December of current and of previous year times the average exchange rate during the year.
c. Consolidated debt calculated as the average between the debt outstanding in December of current and of previous year.
d. Morgan Guaranty.
e. Preliminary.

Table 5.A2
Budget deficit corrected for inflation (percent).

	Change in real debt[a] GDP (1)	Inflation tax GDP (2)	Deficit corrected for inflation GDP (3) = (1) + (2)
1982	7.1	2.0	9.1
1983	20.0	2.1	22.1
1984	7.5	1.5	9.0
1985	3.7	1.3	5.0
1986	1.4	0.7	2.1
1987	−0.5	3.8	3.3

Source: Banco Central, *Brazil Economic Program*, various issues.
a. See table 5.A3.

Chapter 5

Table 5.A3
Consolidated public-sector debt and share in GDP of the real debt change.

	Debt stock (December) (millions of NCZ) (1)	Price index December (2)	Change in real debt Δ[(1)/(2)] (3)	Nominal GDP (millions of NCZ) (4)	GDP deflator (5)	Change in real debt Real GDP (percent) (3) (4)/(5) (6)
1981	8.524	1.01		24.6	0.8	
1982	21.743	2.05	222	51.0	1.6	7.1
1983	94.745	5.68	604	118.9	3.9	20.0
1984	334.120	17.54	237	393.7	12.4	7.5
1985	1,242.335	61.16	127	1,413.8	41.0	3.7
1986	2,084.175	100.00	53	3,708.2	100.0	1.4
1987	10,988.000	532.52	−20	11,884.7	309.3	−0.5

Source: Banco Central, *Brazil Economic Program*, various issues.

The government budget constraint is

$$(G - T) + i^*ED + iB = E\dot{D} + \dot{B} + \dot{C},$$ (A.1)

where $G - T$ is the primary budget deficit, i^*ED stands for interest payments on the external debt (E is the exchange rate), iB stands for interest payments on the domestic debt, D represents external borrowing, B represents domestic borrowing, and C represents domestic credit creation. C is equal to the change in the monetary base, H, *minus* the change in foreign reserves,

$$F: \dot{C} = \dot{H} - E\dot{F}.$$ (A.2)

Consider now the balance of payments in dollars under the assumption that only the government borrows abroad:

$$\dot{F} = NX - i^*D + \dot{D},$$ (A.3)

where NX denotes net exports. Substitute equations A.2 and A.3 in equation A.1, to obtain

$$(G - T) + E(NX) + iB = \dot{H} + \dot{B}.$$ (A.4)

Dividing both sides of equation A.4 by income, Y, and defining

$$(G - T)/Y = g, \quad E(NX)/Y, \quad H/Y = h, \quad B/Y = b, \quad H/H = \mu, \quad /B = v$$

we obtain

$$g + \psi + ib = h\mu + bv.$$ (A.5)

Acknowledgments

I thank Rudi Dornbusch, Eustaquio Reis, Elhanan Helpman, and one anonymous referee for comments and suggestions. I also thank Daniel Dantas, who kindly made the data available.

Notes

1. Surprisingly, the deficit corrected for inflation in 1983 is practically the same as the PSBR. Here the reason might well be large subsidies given through the monetary authorities and excluded from PSBR but not from the deficit corrected for inflation.

2. For detailed analyses of the Cruzado Plan see, e.g., Arida and Resende 1985, Barbosa and Simonsen 1989, Cardoso and Dornbusch 1987, Cardoso and Fishlow 1990, Modiano 1988, and Simonsen 1988.

3. We divide equation 1 by P_tY to obtain

$$(G/P_tY) = (H_t/P_tY) - (H_{t-1}/P_{t-1}Y)(P_{t-1}/P_t),$$

where we substitute $\pi_t = (P_t/P_{t-1}) - 1$. We assume that government can choose g. And, of course, ΔH is endogenous.

4. The slope of the steady-state inflation curve is given by $d\pi/dh = \delta i/\delta h < 0$. In drawing figure 5.2 we assumed a linear relationship between i and h, i.e., $i_t = j - vh_t$, with $j = 0.62$ and $v = 4$.

5. For stability, $h_t = h_{t-1}$ should intersect $\pi_t = \pi_{t-1}$ from below, i.e., $-(\delta i/\delta h) > \pi/(h-g)$.

6. This policy mix entails a credibility problem. Increasing money by the right amount may be interpreted by the public as a phase of expansionary monetary policy despite the cut in the budget deficit.

7. See also Dornbusch 1987 and Ize and Ortiz 1987.

8. For simplicity, we use continuous time.

9. We assume that policy makers determine expenditures and taxes, and thus choose g. We also assume that they set the nominal exchange rate and its devaluation rate. Given inflation inertia, they actually set the rate of real devaluation, and thus can choose ψ.

10. The slope of $v = \pi$ is

$$\frac{db}{d\pi} = \frac{(\beta_1\gamma_0 + \beta_0\gamma_1) + b(\beta_1 - \beta_2 - \gamma_1) - 2\pi(\beta_2\gamma_1 + \beta_1\gamma_2)}{\beta_0 + \beta_1 i + \beta_1 \rho + \gamma_1 \pi}.$$

Observe that $db/d\pi > 0$ for small π and $db/d\pi < 0$ for large π.

11. The slope of $\dot{\pi} = 0$ is $db/d\pi = -(\beta_2 - \beta_1)$.

12. The necessary condition for stability, as shown by the arrows in figure 5.10, is that the curve representing the steady-state budget constraint intersect the curve representing the steady-state inflation rate from below.

13. Table 5.2 shows a sharp real depreciation at the end of the 1970s and another in 1983.

14. Between 1982 and 1988, the ratio of the consolidated debt of the public sector to GDP more than doubled. The ratio of external debt to GDP increased sharply in the mid-1980s and declined in recent years (see table 5.A1).

15. Velocity shows a growing demonetization of the economy between 1970 and 1985, a remonetization in 1986, and a rapid demonetization since 1987.

References

Arida, Persio, and Andre Lara-Resende. 1985. "Inertial inflation and monetary reform." In *Inflation and Indexation: Argentina, Brazil, and Israel*, J. Williamson, ed. (MIT Press).

Barbosa, Fernando de Holanda, and Mario Simonsen. 1989. *Plano Cruzado: Inercia versus Inepcia*. Rio de Janeiro: Editora Globo.

Cardoso, Eliana, and Rudiger Dornbusch. 1987. "Brazil's Tropical Plan." *American Economic Review* 77: 288–292.

Cardoso, Eliana, and Albert Fishlow. 1990. "The macroeconomics of the Brazilian external debt." In *Developing Country Debt and Economic Performance*, J. Sachs, ed. (University of Chicago Press).

Dornbusch, Rudiger. 1987. "Stopping hyperinflation: Lessons from the German experience in the 1920s." In *Essays in Honor of Franco Modigliani*, Stanley Fischer, ed. (MIT Press).

Ize, Alain, and Guillermo Ortiz. 1987. "Fiscal rigidities, public debt, and capital flight." *IMF Staff Papers* (June): 311–332.

Modiano, Eduardo. 1988. "The Cruzado first attempt: Theory and the Brazilian case study." In *Inflation Stabilization*, M. Bruno et al., eds. (MIT Press).

Montiel, Peter. 1989. "Empirical analysis of high-inflation episodes in Argentina, Brazil and Israel." *IMF Staff Papers* 36(3): 527–549.

Resende, Fernando et al. 1989. "A Questao Fiscal." In *Perspectivas da Economia Brasileira* (Rio de Janeiro: INPES/IPEA).

Rodriguez, Carlos. 1978. "A stylized model of the devaluation-inflation spiral." *IMF Staff Papers* 25(1): 76–89.

Simonsen, Mario Henrique. 1988. "Price stabilization and incomes policy." In *Inflation Stabilization*, M. Bruno et al., eds. (MIT Press).

Comments by Persio Arida

I share Cardoso's analysis of Brazilian inflation in its basic lines. Instead of emphasizing the common ground, I will concentrate on some aspects that deserve further reflection. Two models are offered to support the analysis and the policy prescriptions. The following comments are organized around the issues posed by the models, starting with the second one.

The first model is set to explain some features of the Cruzado Plan as well as to support policy recommendations on how to build up a successful stabilization program.

The model shows that a price freeze without a deficit cut will not alter steady-state inflation; it will simply increase its variability. Cardoso claims that the model reflects the Cruzado experience on the grounds that the average inflation in the two years preceding the Cruzado Plan of February 1986 was roughly equal to the average in the two subsequent years. This interpretation of empirical evidence, however, is doubtful. The two-year comparison period is arbitrary. Moreover, the comparison overlooks the Bresser Plan, a general price freeze launched in July 1987, which brought inflation to an abrupt halt and which was followed by rapid acceleration when controls were lifted. Since the Bresser Plan has no equivalent in the years preceding the Cruzado Plan, the similarity in average inflation rates is misleading; however, the increase in variability is hardly surprising. In fact, the inflation rate between the first round of lifting price controls of the Cruzado Plan (December 1986) and the launching of the Bresser Plan (July 1987) was 17.3%, *higher* than the 10% average observed before the Cruzado Plan. The evidence of the similarity between inflation before and after the Cruzado Plan results from an artificial construct.

Inflation was also higher after each of two subsequent plans than before it. This cannot be explained by saying that fiscal policy was always looser after stabilization than before stabilization. Cardoso's first model, in which equilibrium inflation depends on the budget disequilibrium, does not, therefore, account for the evidence. The explanation lies in the endogenous shortening of indexation lags.

As in Argentina, restoring political liberties made Brazilian society less tolerant toward inflation. Democratization in Brazil took place in 1985; starting in 1986 stabilization plans were launched periodically in an attempt to curb inflation by price freezes.[1] The intolerance of society to inflation derives largely from its concentration in the income effect. In an open society, departures from what is socially perceived as a "fair" income distribution generate strong political pressures for immediate policy action. The stabilization program is apprehended by the general public as an attempt to restore the "fair" distribution. When inflation comes back, a new indexation regime, based on more frequent wage readjustments, is put in place in a vain effort to maintain unaltered the "fair" distribution. Inflation after the plan is higher than before, for the same deficit, because the indexation regime after the plan requires a higher inflation rate to replicate the same real variables.[2] When it became clear that the supposedly better indexation arrangement cannot reverse income concentration, agents anticipate the launching of another stabilization program. A further inflationary jump occurs as firms attempt to enter the next round of price controls in a favorable position.

Again as in Argentina, democratization did not render society more conscious of the need to achieve fiscal equilibrium.[3] In particular, the connection between the quest for better income distribution and external credit rationing has hardly been realized. Lacking external finance, the government resorts to domestic credit markets to finance its budget deficits. The increase in domestic debt requires, in turn, a larger excess of private savings over investment, even abstracting from any increase in the private demand for foreign assets. Higher inflation rates stimulate savings by transferring income from workers to recipients of capital incomes, as the propensity to save of the former is smaller than that of the latter. External credit rationing unmatched by larger primary budget surpluses concentrates income distribution. Instead of more frequent indexing arrangements, the proper routes to a more egalitarian distribution of opportunities are fiscal austerity, external debt restructuring, and structural reforms such as deregulation and privatization.

As for policy prescriptions, the model is supposed to support the conclusion that loose price controls are better than tight price controls. It does not. In the model, the optimal tightness of price controls depends only on the size of the fiscal effort. If the fiscal contraction supports an inflation of 8% (as in figure 5.6), it stands to reason that loose price controls aiming at 8% inflation perform better than no controls or tight price controls aiming at zero inflation. However, the same model implies that if fiscal contraction is enough to ensure price stability, then tight price controls will perform better than loose price controls or no price controls. Cardoso is probably right in condemning price freezes, not on the grounds offered by the model but rather because the credibility of this particular form of incomes policy was eroded by its repeated utilization.

Another misinterpretation of the model relates to monetary policy. It refers to a closed economy in which the deficit is financed by printing money, nominal rates of interest are endogenous, and the only policy variable is fiscal policy. Monetization is identified with a helicopter money experiment. Contrary to Cardoso's interpretation, the actual issue of how fast and to what extent the replacement of domestic debt by money should occur under stabilization cannot be addressed in such a model.

Cardoso's identification of loose money as one of the main factors accounting for the failure of the Cruzado Plan and subsequent plans is nonetheless correct. Owing to the existence of a variety of institutional mechanisms not mentioned in the paper, money supply is endogenous to a considerable degree, casting doubt on the identification of tight money with high interest rates.[4] Institutional reform of the monetary authorities is a *sine qua non* condition of stabilization in Brazil, overlooked in Brazilian literature because of a monochromatic concern with fiscal equilibrium.[5]

The second model addresses the inflationary effect of external credit rationing when the government has a large external debt. Deprived of foreign capital inflows, the government depreciates the exchange rate in order to obtain higher trade surpluses. The Brazilian literature since the early 1980s has explained the inflationary effect through the interaction of a supply shock and comprehensive 100% (and above) backward indexation schemes.[6] In contrast, Cardoso focuses on the budget constraint. By construction, a larger trade surplus increases the need for domestic finance and raise the natural interest rate exactly like an equivalent decrease in the primary surplus. Since inflation depends on the extent of domestic finance, an external credit cut matched by the trade balance is proved to be inflationary.

Cardoso concludes that achieving stabilization in Brazil without a major recession requires a reduction of debt transfers. The policy conclusion is undisputable; yet the exact equivalence between an increase in the trade surplus and a decrease in the primary budget surplus needs qualification. If debt finances public investment carrying a long-run rate of return equal to interest on loans, the cut in external credit imposes just a transitory increase in domestic debt. In this extreme case, the debt burden is fully compensated over time as investments mature. The exact equivalence applies only when debt finances government consumption or zero-return public investments.[7]

Cardoso does not take her result as a guide to the thorny search for the best concept of fiscal deficit in an indexed economy. In trying to overcome well-known deficiencies of the operational deficit, Cardoso builds up a new series derived from the sum of the variation of *total* public-sector debt *plus* the inflation tax (column 3 of table 5.1). Adding the inflation tax gives a measure of the distance from the deficit that would exist under price stability. Yet the lesson of the second model is precisely that the inflationary impact of a deficit depends on the availability of external finance. A preferable measure is given by the real variation of *domestic* public-sector debt in all its forms *plus* the inflation tax. This measure directly reflects the pressure on domestic financial markets, be it derived from a reduced primary surplus or from a cut in external finance. It is worth pointing out, in passing, that conventional measures of inflation tax based on primary money, as Cardoso's is, tend to underestimate overall seigniorage. Because of the size of public commercial banking, an important source of treasury revenues derives from floating receipts, which evaporate under price stability.[8]

Finally, I would like to comment on two briefly stated policy prescriptions. Cardoso argues that deindexation is to be avoided and that a forced lengthening of the maturity of domestic bonds is needed. Although not grounded on the models, these prescriptions address critical aspects of stabilization that will come to center stage with the Collor Plan.

As to deindexation, it is useful to separate out two senses of the concept. The first refers to deindexation as the breaking down of inertial mechanisms when a stabilization program is launched. In this context, deindexation means a policy act designed to change the indexing laws that prevailed before the program in order to ensure that nominal variables after the program do not reflect pre-program inflation rates. The second sense refers to after-program deindexation. Keeping indexation in this sense means that nominal variables enjoy automatic escalation clauses according to after-program inflation.

Deindexation in the first sense is difficult. The distortions caused by price freezes hardly need elaboration. Tight controls were set in Brazilian stabilization plans not in order to multiply the number of nominal anchors but because they seemed to provide the only politically feasible way to persuade workers to accept the initial cut with past inflation. Cardoso's criticisms against neutrality conversion rules miss the point;

they are nothing but an attempt to minimize relative price distortions caused by controls.[9] Alternative deindexation techniques are called for to dispense with price controls.[10]

In criticizing deindexation, Cardoso probably refers to the second sense of the concept. The three Brazilian plans handled after-plan indexation in different ways.[11] Cardoso is obviously right in asserting that indexation clauses facilitate the acceptance of the program. The demand for indexing rules is stronger the smaller the initial credibility of the program. It is also true that in any sensible stabilization program long-term government bonds are to keep indexing clauses; the same applies to long-term supply contracts depending on specific baskets of goods and services. The real issue is posed by short-term wage indexation. Residual inflation is likely to occur even when the fundamentals are right. If the exchange rate is the nominal anchor, for instance, it becomes of paramount importance to avoid transferring back to wages the impact of any devaluation. The advantages of generous automatic wage-indexation clauses conceded at the outset of the program exact a price on its performance at later stages.

Cardoso interprets the Brazilian experience as supporting the conclusion that getting rid of indexation is not essential to stabilization. In Brazilian experience, however, the fundamentals were wrong. Lifting price controls led to a violent inflationary outburst that made the resumption of indexation unavoidable. The tradeoff between easy initial acceptance and later poor performance appears only when the fundamentals are set properly.

As for domestic debt consolidation, Cardoso recommends forced lengthening of the maturity of debt instruments on the grounds that current maturity is explosively short. To the extent that the preference for short maturities reflects prudence on the part of wealth-holders in an extremely uncertain environment, it tends to reverse itself if stabilization is achieved.

Two arguments can be given in favor of Cardoso's suggestion. The first is fiscal. The decision to launch a stabilization program tends to be determined by politics, disregarding underlying fiscal conditions. Building up credibility in the government's commitment to a sustainable fiscal adjustment requires time. Since short-term maturities impart high liquidity to private-sector net financial wealth, potential speculative attacks against nominal anchors become serious threats. As individuals assign a positive (possibly high) probability to the collapse of the program, high nominal interest rates are necessary to avoid a flight into assets. Fiscal-policy lags reinforce the need to keep interest rates at high levels, as demand tends to be transitorily strong even if the fundamentals are properly tackled. Forced lengthening will then alleviate the interest burden on domestic debt, provided that the interest paid on compulsorily lengthened assets is smaller than the short-term rate.

The second argument pertains to the allocation of wealth between indexed bonds and assets. Transaction costs make it difficult to diversify portfolios of real assets. Indexed bonds, in turn, refer to a large basket of goods in set proportions. Relative price variability increases with inflation. For risk-averse portfolio decision makers, the demand for indexed bonds becomes an increasing function of inflation. Under a price freeze the relative variability of asset prices goes to zero, making the holding of financial assets less attractive than the holding of less risky assets. The adverse portfolio change is obviously mitigated by dispensing with price controls, but it will nonetheless occur if relative price variability decreases with stabilization. Indexation from the viewpoint of stock equilibrium mitigates inflationary pressures at the cost of making stabilization more difficult (see Arida 1990).

The two arguments describe relevant processes that take place during stabilization. Compulsory lengthening schemes are simple and enjoy popular appeal; the danger lies in the extent to which they may undermine the confidence of the general public in contracts, thus precipitating what Keynes aptly called "the real degringolade" (1971, p. xix). Taxation penalizing short-term maturities and money substitutes seems preferable to forced lengthening as an instrument for depriving financial assets of liquidity. Giving a premium to holding long-term instruments is preferable to locking in wealth-holders by fiat. Taxation on liquidity is to be revised as credibility builds up or as debt stock is reduced to a level compatible with stability by fiscal surpluses or a capital levy.

Notes

1. It took 12 months from the Dornelles partial freeze to the Cruzado Plan, 16 months from the Cruzado Plan to the Bresser Plan, 18 months from the Bresser Plan to the Summer Plan, and 14 months from the Summer Plan to the Collor Plan.

2. The Cruzado Plan is a case in point. Before this plan, wages were readjusted every six months. After the plan, a threshold rule imposed monthly readjustments up to 20%. In December 1986, accumulated inflation since the launching

of the plan reached 22.3%, surpassing the critical 20% limit. The rule then led to a 20% general wage increase, which fueled further price increases. It is not surprising that from January 1987 to June 1987, the period in which the trigger rule was in operation, average inflation was about 19% monthly. The decline in real wages took place because of the initial jump of 22.3%. Similar patterns of change occurred in subsequent plans.

3. As a matter of historical record, it is to be observed that in each of the Brazilian stabilization plans the economic team was conscious of the need to promote fiscal adjustment side by side with incomes policy. Strategies, however, differed. During the Cruzado Plan, fiscal imbalances were not openly emphasized, in an effort to maintain credibility. The price freeze was presented as a first step that would be followed by the needed adjustments. The economic team expected that the political support enjoyed by the plan would suffice to make fiscal adjustments viable. In contrast, open recognition of fiscal imbalances occurred at the launching of the Summer Plan. The practical results, however, were similar. The Cruzado fiscal adjustment was backed by the president, desirous of holding back unpopular measures until the elections scheduled to be held 10 months after launching the plan. The Summer Plan's fiscal adjustment was blocked by the Congress because it had a great mistrust of Administration proposals. In retrospect it seems clear that the Sarney period (March 1985 to March 1990) was one of a painful social learning process. It is unfair to infer from the poor fiscal performance that the economic teams designing stabilization programs in Brazil were oblivious to the budget constraint.

4. As examples, consider the drawing facilities held at the central bank by banks holding passbook savings liabilities, deposits denominated in foreign currency by exporters and creditor banks, and automatic rediscounting mechanisms for public financial institutions.

5. I am not suggesting, of course, that fiscal equilibrium is within reach. Achieving fiscal equilibrium, however, will not suffice. To the extent to which the money supply is to work as the nominal anchor of stabilization, it becomes crucial to cut the deposit facilities of the treasury in public financial institutions, to suppress multiple compulsory requirements in favor of a single rate, to separate out short-run monetary control bonds from long-run indexing bonds financing treasury deficits, etc. Policy debates in Brazil have given much more emphasis to fiscal than to monetary policy control. Cardoso's paper is no exception.

6. The argument runs as follows: Backward indexation differentiates between the frequency of wage adjustments and the frequency of exchange readjustments. Wages are altered every two quarters, and the exchange rate daily. Because of the greater frequency of readjustments of the crawling peg, a higher inflation rate reduces real wages but has a negligible effect on the real exchange rate. The trade surplus is a function of the ratio of wages over traded goods. The devaluation reduces the wage/exchange ratio in two ways. The direct effect comes through the jump in nominal exchange rate, the roundabout effect

through higher inflation as the initial jump propagates over the cost structure. Monetary policy is accommodating.

7. The qualification in no diminishes the model. In all likelihood, the long-run rate of return on debt-financed assets in Brazil falls short of the external rates of interest. An external credit cut unmatched by fiscal effort then provokes a permanently higher long-run inflation rate with overshooting in the short run.

8. During the first months of the Cruzado Plan, private commercial banks dismissed around 130,000 employees in an effort to compensate for the loss of floating receipts; it is debatable whether this effort would have sufficed had the plan succeeded. The effect on public commercial banks was enormous, as they refused to fire employees. Drawings on central-bank reserves by the Rio de Janeiro state bank, for instance, amounted to 0.25% of GDP.

9. It stands to reason that stabilization programs cannot be neutral, because inflation molds the shape of real activities, the foremost example of which is provided by commercial banking. As a guiding principle for converting contracts in monetary reforms, however, neutrality means that deindexation in the first sense should be handled in such a way as to minimize arbitrary gains and losses in contractual incomes. It contributes enormously to the acceptance of the program. There is no reason, for instance, to modify rental contracts in a monetary reform to the benefit of tenants or landlords. The example of the Summer Plan is revealing in this connection. Large transfers of financial wealth took place in an almost random fashion. Public confidence in financial assets was eroded. The price paid for the careless conversion of contracts was high: a consumption boom took place despite extraordinarily high rates of interest. Last but not least, the principle of neutrality does not rule out deliberate exceptions. As an example, the Cruzado Plan treated claims of the government against the private sector more generously than intra-private-sector claims.

10. Some suggestions on how best to cut the link with the past at the launching of a stabilization program are the Larida proposal (Arida and Lara-Resende 1985; Dornbusch 1985), the Real Plan (Lopes 1989), and changing backward indexation into falling-forward indexation (a recurrent theme in Brazilian policy debates).

11. Both the Cruzado Plan and the Bresser Plan kept indexation. The Cruzado Plan set a 20%-trigger-point indexing scheme for wages; the Bresser Plan set the URP, a lagged monthly readjustment scheme based on average quarterly inflation. Both also kept indexation for passbook savings and long-term bonds. The Cruzado Plan was more radical in forcing short-term contracts to be readjusted by floating exchange rates instead of price indexes. In contrast, the Summer Plan was the prototype of deindexation in the second sense. Wages were left to labor-market bargaining, financial indexation was prohibited, and for the first time in 20 years the OTN (the very index that served as a basis for readjustment of contracts) was abolished. As a historical record, Cardoso's description is not accurate, since it is the Summer Plan and not the Cruzado Plan that stands for the bold attempt to eliminate indexation.

References

Arida, P. 1990. Heterodox Shocks and Stock Equilibrium. Unpublished.

Arida, P., and A. Lara-Resende. 1985. "Inertial inflation and monetary reform: Brazil." In *Inflation and Indexation: Argentina, Brazil and Israel*, J. Williamson, ed. (Washington, D.C.: Institute for International Economics).

Dornbusch, R. 1985. "Comments." In *Inflation and Indexation: Argentina, Brazil and Israel*, J. Williamson, ed. (Washington, D.C.: Institute for International Economics).

Keynes, J. M. 1971. "A tract on monetary reform." In *Collected Writings*, vol. IV (Macmillan).

Lopes, F. L. 1989. *O Desafio da Hiperinflacão—em Busca da Moeda Real* [The Challenge of Hyperinflation—In Search of Real Currency]. São Paolo: Campus.

Comments by Juan Carlos de Pablo

Most Latin American countries display a tradeoff between inflation and growth—for example, Chile and Columbia, with growth and low or moderate inflation, versus Argentina and Peru, with very high (even hyper-) inflation and stagnation. Brazil, however, does not fit neatly into this pattern, having both very high inflation and a growing economy.

I have three comments on Cardoso's penetrating analysis of the performance of Brazil in the turbulent 1980s.

The Deficit and Its Financing

Inflation in Brazil rose steadily in the course of the 1980s, but if the author's figures are correct, the fiscal deficit as a percentage of GDP did not peak at the end of the decade. How could this be so? The answer is that some sources of finance dried up, especially the option of obtaining genuinely "fresh" money from abroad and from the domestic capital market. The essential distinction to be made is not one between countries that have fiscal deficits and those that have surpluses, but one between countries that can finance their imbalances and those that cannot.

The Balance of Payments and Fiscal Effects of Servicing the Foreign Debt

Brazil's experience in the 1980s, like that of Argentina, shows that it is easier to generate the trade surplus required to pay the interest due on foreign debt than it is to generate a fiscal surplus sufficient to service the public sector's foreign debt. In my opinion, this is clearly associated with capital flight that constricts the tax base in debtor countries. This, coupled with the fact that some debtor countries nationalized part of the foreign debt (i.e., transferred it to the public sector), complicates the *fiscal* aspect of the debt problem considerably.

On paper it seems fairly easy to declare "Let's generate a fiscal surplus of, say, 8% of GDP so as to make public-sector foreign debt servicing compatible with price stability." In practice, however, this is no easy task. Unable to tax wealth held abroad by residents, should debtor governments tax wage earners or slash pensions in order to meet their foreign debt obligations?

The Transition to Democracy

When President Sarney started the transition to democracy in 1985, inflation in Brazil stood at 7% per month. In the beginning of 1990, with a democratically elected government about to take the reins, inflation is *ten times higher*. In its 20-year reign, the military government placed three brilliant civilians in charge of economic affairs: Roberto de Oliveira Campos, Antonio Delfim Netto, and Enrique Mario Simonsen. In spite of oil and debt shocks, they worked a miracle, demonstrating the benefits of systematically applying rational rules of the game (particularly in connection with exchange rates). The transition that began in 1985— difficult enough in its own right—was impeded by the untimely death of President Neves. The economy today is in deep trouble (as, indeed, it was in 1964), but this time, I submit, the reason is largely the excessive prolongation of the transition to democracy, a point that was perhaps understated in the author's analysis.

General Discussion

The major issue raised was the fiscal deficit and its financing. Several participants pointed out that the small deficits, if measured correctly, can hardly explain the high inflation in Brazil. Peter Bernholz observed that the deficit calculated should be the one generated by both the government and the central bank; this procedure yields larger deficits. Persio Arida noted that there are multiple concepts of deficit in Brazil. In the 1970s and the early 1980s, the measurement of the deficit was in bad shape, but it has improved since then. Even when the necessary changes are taken into account, the deficit is still pretty small relative to such high inflation.

Mario Blejer emphasized that the current operating deficit is not a good indicator of public-sector borrowing requirements when refinancing of the outstanding debt is not done on the same terms as before. Since inflation increased and the government's credibility deteriorated, refinancing became much costlier. Daniel Heymann agreed, adding that Brazil differed from Argentina because the latter's internal debt could not grow as needed—instead, the external debt grew. In Brazil, no such limit on internal debt was observed. Don Patinkin suggested that although the deficit was small, its finance mix changed from borrowing to seigniorage. Persio Arida agreed, stating that monetary policy was loose and therefore largely responsible for inflation.

6 The Inflation-Stabilization Cycles in Argentina and Brazil

Miguel A. Kiguel and Nissan Liviatan

The Austral plan in Argentina and the Cruzado plan in Brazil were major stabilization attempts with lasting effects on the inflation process in both countries. They differed from previous stabilization efforts in at least two respects: first, they were the first programs that succeeded, albeit temporarily, in reducing inflation drastically in the short run; second, they had a lasting effect in the sense that they changed the pattern of inflation in both countries.

Inflationary developments in the two countries became surprisingly similar after the failure of the heterodox shocks (see figure 6.1). This stands in contrast to the differences in the characteristics of the inflation process in previous years in the two countries. Before these programs inflation was higher, more unstable, and had a clearer fiscal nature in Argentina than in Brazil. These differences all but disappeared in the aftermath of the Austral and Cruzado programs as both countries underwent similar inflation-stabilization cycles.

There is a systematic pattern in the cycles. Inflation falls dramatically in response to a stabilization program based on price and wage controls, and remains low for a number of months. Inflation then starts to accelerate as controls are removed, and eventually becomes explosive, often reaching hyper levels. This explosion is stopped through a new round of controls, which sets the stage for the new cycle. The system becomes more unstable over time, inflation reaching new record high levels in each successive cycle and the periods of low inflation following the imposition of controls becoming shorter.

The purpose of this paper is to understand the reasons that led to the large instability in inflation in both countries during this period, and to explain why neither country succeeded in sustaining a high but *stable* rate of inflation. This instability was not accompanied by a noticeable increase

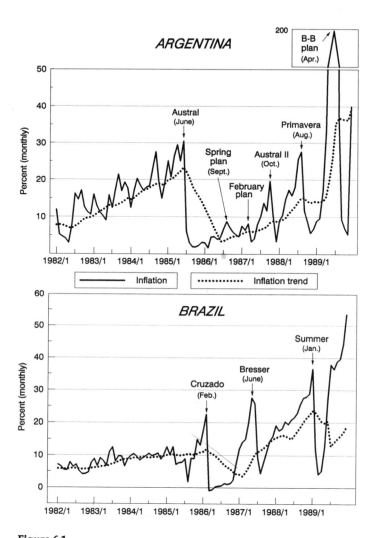

Figure 6.1
CPI inflation and inflation trend. Sources: Argentina—Indicadores de Coyuntura;
Brazil—Conjuntura Economica. Note: Inflation trend = $CPI/(CPI_{t-12})^{1/12-1}$.

in the *average* rate of inflation. In Argentina inflation was in fact lower on average during the first three years after the Austral plan than in the three preceding years, and in Brazil the increase in the average rate of inflation after the Cruzado plan was not dramatic.

In our view, the type of instability that emerged after the failure of the heterodox shocks was a consequence of the large reliance on income policies to stop inflation in the Austral and Cruzado plans and in the follow-up programs. It was the repeated use of controls accompanied by expectations and anticipations about government actions by firms and workers that introduced the observed instability during this period.

The current cycles are difficult to explain using the fiscal approach. Of course, it could be argued that the fiscal imbalance made low inflation an unreachable target, and that lack of fiscal discipline was the most important factor in the eventual collapse of the Austral and Cruzado plans. But this does not mean that inflationary developments in this period can be easily linked to the government budget. The fiscal approach does not help us to understand why inflation was so unstable during a regime of recurrent cycles. In addition, it fails to explain why we do not observe a high but *stable* inflation level during the period, or why the hyperinflation explosions were not accompanied by massive budget deficits or extremely high seigniorage levels, as was the case in most European hyperinflations.

Likewise, it is difficult to link the instability of inflation to the foreign debt overhang in both countries. The debt overhang became apparent in 1982 and may have been a major cause of the increase in inflation before the cycle period. But the external debt situation did not deteriorate significantly during the cycles.[1] Lack of external financing might explain why inflation was high, but not why it was so volatile.

The paper is organized as follows. In section 1 we present a brief summary of the process of inflation in both countries before the heterodox shocks, and the basic features of the new regime that emerged after their failure. In section 2 we examine the difficulties encountered when one uses the "fiscal" view and the "inertial inflation" view to explain the increasing instability of inflation during this period. We provide an alternative explanation for these cycles, placing more emphasis on expectations and on the repetitive use of controls as an anti-inflation device. We argue in this section that both countries are experiencing a new type of inertia: inertia in processes. A more in-depth analysis of the cycles is presented in section 3, including a discussion of the reasons that led to the freeze, those that forced the authorities to flexibilize controls, and the eventual explosion of inflation. We conclude in section 4 with some thoughts about the sustainability of the regime and about the implications of these developments for the design of stabilization plans in both countries.

1. Inflation Before and After the Heterodox Shocks

Inflation Before

The inflation processes in these two high-chronic-inflation countries were very different before the heterodox shocks (HSs) of the 1980s. As seen in figures 6.2a and 6.2b, which show the evolution of annual inflation and seigniorage[2] since the early 1970s, inflation was more unstable in Argentina than in Brazil during this period, while its fiscal nature was more apparent in the former country than in the latter.

Argentina
Changes in inflation in Argentina were closely related to changes in the budget deficit and seigniorage in the same direction. As shown in figure 6.2a, the 1973–1975 and 1983–1985 explosions in inflation occurred in periods of extremely high budget deficits, in which seigniorage reached unsustainable levels (exceeding 7% of GDP). Although the fiscal view explains a significant part of the behavior of inflation, non-fiscal factors also had a bearing on the inflation process. The long tradition of failed stabilization attempts, for example, implied that each new anti-inflation program had to confront severe credibility problems that added to the downward rigidities of the inflation process.

In practice this meant that stabilization attempts based on orthodox programs did not succeed in achieving rapid reductions in inflation. The slow pace of the reduction in inflation during the Martinez de Hoz period can be explained by lack of credibility in the ability of the government to enlarge and sustain the fiscal adjustment, but perhaps as important was the lack of credibility in the maintenance of the nominal anchors. Doubts about whether the government would stick to the preannounced exchange-rate rule (the *tablita*) when faced with an overvalued currency certainly added to the downward rigidity of inflation, which eventually led to the failure of the attempt. Indeed, there is an important difference

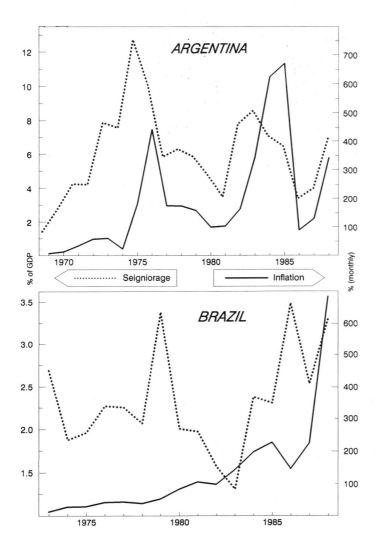

Figure 6.2
Seigniorage and CPI Inflation. Sources: Argentina—Indicadores de Coyuntura;
Brazil—Conjuntura Economica. Notes: Argentina—Seigniorage = $(M1_t - M1_{t-1})/GDP_t$,
where GDP_t is current GDP; Brazil—Seigniorage = $(MB_t - MB_{t-1})/GDP_t$, where MB =
money base.

between credibility in the commitment to the fiscal adjustment and credibility in the adherence to the nominal anchor.[3]

Brazil

The inflation process in Brazil is more difficult to explain, since jumps to higher inflation plateaus over the years were not associated with conspicuous increases in seigniorage, which has remained fairly stable over the years (ranging between 1.5% and 3.5% of GDP). Instead, those jumps resulted from the adoption of a set of policies that induced an asymmetric behavior of inflation: inflation moved up in response to adverse (external) shocks, but did not come down as a result of favorable developments. The use of accommodating monetary and exchange-rate policies and the widespread resort to indexation in the labor and financial markets were instrumental factors for inflation to stabilize at higher plateaus, but equally important was the perception that the government preferred to validate inflation rather than fight it and sacrifice growth. In practice, this view can explain why inflation roughly doubled and stabilized at new, higher plateaus after the large devaluations in response to the two oil crises (in 1974 and 1979), and again in the 1980s in response to the debt crisis (in 1983), rather than generating a temporary inflationary outburst as in other countries.

   It is useful in this respect to analyze the macroeconomic developments after the 1982–83 debt crisis. The adjustment to the new situation was based on a policy of sharp fiscal contraction, stepping up the rate of devaluation, and reducing the real wage. In a non-indexed economy this last objective can be achieved by a one-time devaluation. However, with full backward wage indexation and downward rigidity in the real base wage, the real wage can be brought down only by an increase in the inflation plateau. We thus observe the somewhat paradoxical conjunction of a reduction in the fiscal deficit and an increase in the inflation plateau in 1983–1985 (these developments are described more fully in Kiguel and Liviatan 1989).

The Change in Regime after the HSs

The failure of the HSs marked the beginning of a new era in the inflation processes in Brazil and Argentina. This can readily be seen in figures 6.1a and 6.1b, which show monthly inflation rates and the overall trend in inflation from 1982 onward. The striking element in these figures is the increased inflation instability and the similar pattern of inflation-and-stabilization cycles that emerged after the failure of the Austral and Cruzado plans.[4] Two countries with different causes and characteristics of inflation are now undergoing similar patterns of it.

The common element in the Austral and Cruzado plans was the use of income policies as a stabilization instrument. In both countries, the motivation for using controls was the perception that non-fundamental forces (expectations, indexation, etc.) were important in explaining the short-run dynamics of inflation. The Austral plan was better designed, paid more attention to the fiscal imbalance, and followed more prudent monetary and wage policies at the outset, but that was not enough to prevent a similar outcome. The use of controls in both countries became more apparent in the follow-up programs. The main features of the various stabilization attempts are summarized in tables 6.1 and 6.2.[5] Note the systematic use of controls, while little attention was devoted to the correction of the fundamentals.

The pattern of the cycles was similar in both countries. Typically, we observe drastic accelerations of inflation, sometimes possibly positioning the economy on a unstable hyperinflationary path, always halted abruptly by a program based on price and wage controls. Price stability was usually short-lived, and was followed by a rekindling of inflation which very quickly exploded into a new inflationary outburst, generally stronger than the previous one.

It would be inaccurate to say that there was no attempt to use nominal anchors in the follow-up programs. Tighter monetary policy was used in Argentina in the spring plans of 1986 and 1988. In Brazil, tight money was one of the main policy tools used in the Summer Plan of 1989. However, these policies were not pursued persistently, because of their recessionary effects and because they were not supported by appropriate adjustments on the fiscal side.

It is easy to cite the inconsistency between price freezes and continuing fiscal deficits in describing the failure of the various stabilization attempts. It is more difficult to explain why a relatively high, but *stable*, level of inflation could not be maintained in the post-Austral-Cruzado period. For example, after Argentina's flexibilization of the exchange rate (April 1986) and of prices (May), the objective was not a freeze but rather a stable crawl. This was also the case in the Primavera II plan of August 1988. Similarly, Brazil's policy in 1988 was to stabilize inflation, even at extremely high rates. Thus, toward the end of 1988, a social pact was

Table 6.1
Heterodox stabilization in Argentina (percentages).

	Austral I June '85	Spring Plan I August '86	February Plan February '87	Austral II October '87	Plan Primavera II August 1988
Reduction in inflation					
From	30.5 (June)	8.8 (Aug.)	6.5 (Feb.)	19.5 (Oct.)	27.6 (Aug.)
To	3.1 (Aug.)	6.1 (Oct.)	3.4 (April)	3.4 (Dec.)	9.0 (Oct.)
Acceleration of inflation before program	29.5 (April) 30.5 (June)	4.5 (June) 8.8 (Aug.)	4.5 (Dec. '86) 6.5 (Feb. '87)	13.7 (Aug.) 19.5 (Oct.)	18 (June) 27.6 (Aug.)
Duration of low (under 5%) inflation	11 months	2 months	1 month	1 month	—
Type of income policy	Freeze	CAP on increases	Freeze	Freeze	CAP on increases
Wage policy	Freeze	CAP on increases	Freeze	Freeze	Guideline
Monetary policy					
Interest rates	31 to 5	8 to 4	No change	15 to 9	22 to 9
Money growth	Accommodating	Tight	Tight	Tight, then accomodating	Tight
Fiscal policy	Large fiscal adjustment	No adjustment	No adjustment	Announced adjustment, not effected	Minor and temporary adjustment in the deficit

Table 6.2
Heterodox stabilization in Brazil (percentages).

	Cruzado Plan February 1986	Bresser Plan June 1987	Gradualist Plan April 1988	Summer Plan January 1989
Reduction in inflation				
From	22 (February)	25.8 (June)	No change	36.5 (January)
To	−0.5 (April)	4.5 (August)		4.3 (March)
Acceleration before program	13.2 (December) 22.4 (Feb. '86)	20.1 (April) 23.8 (June)	17.6 (February) 20.3 (April)	27.9 (Dec. '88)
Type of income policy	Freeze	Freeze	CAP on increases	Freeze
Duration of low inflation	9 months	1 month	—	1 month
Monetary policy				
Interest rate	13 (February) 0.7 (March)	24 (May) 0.9 (July)	20 (April) 18.6 (May)	18.9 (February) 11.5 (April)
Money growth	Expansionary	Accommodating	Accommodating	Accommodating
Fiscal policy	Expansionary	Unchanged	Unchanged	Unchanged

invoked in order to stabilize inflation at 26.5% per month. Although there was a readiness to accommodate a high but stable inflationary path, the realities of the situation did not make this possible.

There was an important difference in the manner in which the two countries entered the unstable regime. In the case of Argentina, the Austral I was already a reaction to a possible hyperinflationary trajectory, which may have had its origins in the extremely high levels of seigniorage in 1982–1984. On the whole, the repeated use of controls in the post-Austral period aggravated an existing instability problem. By contrast, the inflationary process in Brazil before the Cruzado plan (since 1984) was quite stable (excluding the few months immediately preceding the plan, when the freeze may have been anticipated). Therefore, in the case of Brazil the connection between overreliance on income policies and inflationary instability stands out more clearly.

Process Inertia

The recurrent pattern of the cycles indicates that both countries experienced a new type of inertia: inertia in the inflation process. Traditionally, the concept of inflation inertia has been used to describe a situation in which past inflation rates set the norm for current inflation; past developments tend to repeat themselves. This notion is not useful in explaining a process of continuously accelerating inflation. Nevertheless, a reinterpretation of this concept can still be appropriate. The current cycles have established a pattern: stabilization is short-lived, and is followed by an acceleration in inflation that comes to an abrupt end after an income-policies-based stabilization program. This "inertia" in the process, observed during the cycles regime, is a new feature that emerged from the failure of the HSs.

The systematic pattern in this regime is reflected in the use of anchors and in expectations. The anchors were multiple and very strong during the freeze, and lax (almost nonexistent) after flexibilization. Indeed, the exchange rate, wages, and public- and private-sector prices all served as nominal anchors during the freeze. However, the economies were left without any effective nominal anchor once flexibilization started. Prices and wages were freely determined, while the exchange rate and the prices of public-sector enterprises were indexed to past inflation. On the whole, the freeze, even though it lasted for a relatively short period, proved to be the nominal anchor during this regime, providing some stability to the system. The usefulness of this anchor decreased over time as the duration of controls and periods of low inflation became shorter, in effect resulting in a protracted increase in inflation.

As the new regime became better understood by private agents, it was incorporated in the way in which they formed their expectations. This added to the instability observed in the period. Any new shock that resulted in an increase in inflation rapidly gave rise to a new acceleration in inflation that eventually was expected to end through a new round of controls.

2. Alternative Explanations for the Inflation-and-Stabilization Cycles

The pattern of inflation in this period raises a number of interesting questions. Why did both countries experience similar patterns of cyclical inflation despite a history of very different inflationary policies? Why did inflation in both countries fail to stabilize at a constant (possibly high) level, compatible with the fundamentals? Were the explosive parts of the cycles due to repressed inflation during the period of controls? Were these economies on an overall hyperinflationary path, or was it once again chronic high inflation? Were the causes the same in both countries? The last question is especially interesting because the underlying causes of the chronic inflation in the two countries were, as already noted, very different.

Traditional approaches can at best provide a partial answer to these questions. Neither the fiscal approach (which was instrumental in understanding inflationary developments in Argentina before the Austral plan) nor the "inertia"/indexation view (usually employed to understand Brazilian inflation) provides a satisfactory and comprehensive explanation of the inflationary processes after the HSs.

The Fiscal View

There are basically two alternative ways to rationalize the drastic and rapid acceleration in each cycle using the fiscal view. First, it could be argued that the underlying fiscal situation was characterized by massive budget deficits which the government was unable to control and which would eventually result in a full-blown, "traditional" hyperinflation. The role of controls was to repress this outcome and to provide a temporary boost to taxes through a reverse Tanzi Effect. However, since this did not correct the basic fiscal disequilibrium, it was not possible to sustain the freeze for long. The removal of controls paved the way for the inevitable explosion of inflation. An alternative way to use the fiscal approach is to argue that there was a *stable* level of inflation consistent with the needs to finance the deficit through money creation. Controls repressed inflation temporarily below this "fiscal" equilibrium, but then inflation overshot during the flexibilization period to compensate for the lost revenues during the period of controls, after exhausting the short-term benefits of the Tanzi Effect. This framework implicitly assumes that the acceleration of inflation was a temporary phenomenon that would be reversed at a later stage as inflation stabilized at a level consistent with the needs of financing the deficit through money creation. Neither of these possibilities, however, appears to "fit" the stylized facts of the period.

We first consider the plausibility of the hyperinflation view. In our opinion, for most of the period the level of seigniorage did not warrant a hyperinflation. Two features have characterized traditional hyperinflations: extremely high budget deficits and seigniorage levels, and a relentless acceleration of the rate of inflation. In Brazil, seigniorage never exceeded 3.5% of GDP, and the average operational deficit was lower than in the pre-Cruzado period. Likewise, in Argentina the deficit was much lower than during the pre-Austral period, while seigniorage remained below pre-Austral-plan levels in 1986 and 1987; although there was an increase in seigniorage in 1988, this took place toward the end of the year, and by then two large accelerations in inflation had already taken place. Neither case resembled the fiscal situation in Bolivia, where hyperinflation developed because of deficits in excess of 15% of GDP and seigniorage levels continuously exceeding 12% of GDP.

This view is consistent with the overall trend in inflation in the two countries. A continuous increase in average inflation in the post-HS period, after the initial fall in inflation, was not accompanied by a clear increase in average seigniorage. This is confirmed by figure 6.3, which shows monthly real revenues from money creation (RMC).[6] This figure indicates that in Brazil, and to a lesser extent in Argentina, there was no clear upward trend in RMC over the period, except for the recent hyperinflation in Argentina. Further evidence can be obtained from table 6.3, which shows that the coefficient of the inflation trend (line 1) in Argentina and Brazil in the post-HS period was only about one-third of

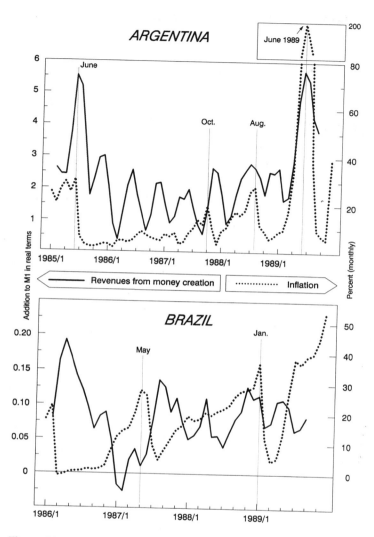

Figure 6.3
Revenues from money creation and inflation. Sources: Argentina—Carta Economica;
Brazil—Conjuntura Economica. Note (Brazil): Revenues—3-month moving average of
seigniorage, $(M_t - M_{t-1})/CPI$.

Table 6.3
Auto-regression of inflation in Argentina, Brazil, and Bolivia.

Period	Equation[a]	Constant	Independent variables			Adjusted R^2	D.W.
			$CPINF_{t-1}$	Time			
1. Argentina before and after Austral							
1981/1	(1)	−0.7404		0.3770		0.7508	1.21
		(−0.59)		(12.56)		[157.66]	
to	(2)	−0.3353	0.3953	0.2292		0.7854	1.81
1985/5		(−0.29)	(3.04)	(4.09)		[96.15]	
	(3)	2.3429	0.8568			0.7193	2.10
		(2.10)	(11.59)			[134.18]	
1986/6	(1)	−44.8594		0.6103		0.5453	0.83
		(−4.56)		(5.67)		[32.18]	
to	(2)	−21.3554	0.6291	0.2843		0.6769	1.82
1988/8		(−1.97)	(3.34)	(2.13)		[28.23]	
	(3)	1.6280	0.9231			0.6309	2.04
		(1.06)	(6.74)			[45.45]	
1986/6	(1)	−141.554		1.6797		0.2558	0.97
		(−3.24)		(3.75)		[14.06]	
to	(2)	−70.3082	0.5137	0.8380		0.4382	1.75
1989/8		(−1.64)	(3.61)	(1.85)		[15.82]	
	(3)	8.4197	0.6245			0.3732	1.70
		(1.62)	(4.86)			[23.63]	

2. Brazil before and after Cruzado

Period	Eq.	C	$CPINF_{t-1}$	a	R^2 [F]	D-W
1980/2 to 1985/12	(1)	4.5829 (9.84)		0.0832 (7.51)	0.438 [56.33]	1.24
	(2)	2.8617 (4.14)		0.0532 (3.79)	0.4988 [35.83]	2.04
	(3)	2.7086 (3.59)	0.3755 (6.93)		0.4019 [48.05]	2.27
1987/1 to 1989/12	(1)	9.7948 (3.03)		0.6622	0.3379 (4.34)	0.55 [18.86]
	(2)	2.0479 (0.77)	0.7681 (5.82)	0.2187 (1.65)	0.6635 [35.51]	1.31
	(3)	3.5029 (1.36)	0.8928 (8.06)		0.6465 [65.02]	1.35

3. Bolivia, hyperinflation

Period	Eq.	C	$CPINF_{t-1}$	a	R^2 [F]	D-W
1983/1 to 1985/8	(1)	−81.7774 (−2.71)		2.1944 (3.88)	0.3121 [15.06]	1.84
	(2)	−75.3915 (−2.22)		2.0252 (2.91)	0.2928 [7.42]	1.96
	(3)	21.2929 (2.67)	0.0791 (0.43) 0.3842 (2.26)		0.1171 [5.11]	2.01

Figures in parentheses are t-statistics.
Figures in square brackets are F-statistics.
a. Equation 1: $CPINF_t = C + at$
   Equation 2: $CPINF_t = C + CPINF_{t-1} + at$
   Equation 3: $CPINF_t = C + CPINF_{t-1}$.
Notations: CPINF = CPI inflation, t = time in months.

that for Bolivia. Only if we include the 1989 acceleration in Argentina do we approach the Bolivian coefficient.

The autoregression coefficients in table 6.3 (lines 2 and 3) may shed additional light on the nature of the inflationary instability. We note that in Bolivia, which represents a classical hyperinflation, the coefficients indicate a very weak inertia, or a low persistence of inflationary shocks (which include also stabilization attempts). By contrast, persistence remained at high levels in Argentina and Brazil in the post-HS period, suggesting a different process—presumably not a fiscal hyperinflation.

There are also difficulties in using the alternative fiscal view, i.e., that the underlying fiscal imbalance required a high but stable level of inflation toward which the cycles tend to converge. A pattern of inflation consistent with this approach would start with an acceleration coinciding with the removal of controls, after which inflation would tend to stabilize at a level consistent with the fundamentals. An initial overshooting of inflation in the flexibilization stage is consistent with the basic arguments of the approach, but this increase should be reversed at a later stage as inflation stabilizes, so that the inflation tax revenue stays in line with the need to finance the deficit through money creation.

This view that inflation was converging to a stable level is not supported by the available evidence. Table 6.4 shows the results of the autoregressive equations for the individual cycles. In both countries the large size of the coefficient of the trend in equation 1 shows that inflation was not converging to a stable level. Moreover, they indicate that within each cycle the dynamics of inflation were akin to inflation explosions characteristic of hyperinflations, as opposed to the "inertia" observed in these two countries before the HSs. In fact, the coefficients of CPINF(−1) in Argentina bear a striking resemblance to those of the Bolivian hyperinflation. The only non-explosive cycle corresponds to the period between the Bresser and Summer plans in Brazil when, as a result of a gradual stabilization attempt between March and August 1988, there was a hiatus in the increase in inflation.

It could be argued that, although the fiscal view cannot explain the pattern of inflation during the cycles, it can still be useful in understanding the overall increasing trend in inflation in the post-HS period. Tables 6.5 and 6.6 suggest that although this argument could still be made for Argentina, where the reduction in average inflation was accompanied by a reduction in average fiscal deficits, the increase in average inflation in Brazil in these years was accompanied by relatively stable (and, according to some estimates, falling) budget deficits and seigniorage levels.

Table 6.4
Individual inflation cycles in Argentina and Brazil. (See equation 1 below.)

Period	Constant	Coefficient of independent variable time	Adjusted R^2	D.W.
1. Argentina				
1985/9–1986/8	0.6656	0.5091	0.7216	1.36
	(0.96)	(5.43)	[29.50]	
1987/4–1987/10	0.1893	2.4745	0.8844	3.03
	(0.12)	(6.85)	[46.91]	
1987/12–1988/8	2.2123	2.7098	0.9238	1.80
	(1.44)	(9.90)	[97.96]	
1988/11–1989/7	−51.7816	20.8247	0.7087	0.66
	(−2.0)	(4.52)	[20.46]	
2. Brazil				
1986/4–1987/5	−7.1441	1.9385	0.8103	0.42
	(−3.25)	(7.52)	[56.51]	
1986/10–1987/5	−3.3267	3.5226	0.9534	1.69
	(−2.25)	(12.01)	[144.18]	
1987/8–1989/1	6.6856	1.4063	0.9179	0.91
	(6.07)	(13.83)	[191.15]	
1989/3–1989/12	0.795	5.2552	0.8805	0.99
	(0.20)	(8.20)	[67.30]	

Figures in parentheses are t-statistics.
Figures in square brackets are F-statistics.
Equation 1: $CPINF_t = C + at$.
Notation: CPINF = CPI Inflation, t = time in months.

The Inertia-Indexation Approach

The recent events are also difficult to explain using the inertia-backward indexation view, formalized by Bacha and Lopez (1983) and Modiano (1988) among others. Broadly speaking, this approach argues that because of wage indexation there is significant short-term inertia (or persistence) in inflation, and that increases in inflation are usually associated with attempts to erode the average real wage. Two features observed during the cycles cast doubts on the validity of this approach. First, inflation was accelerating during the upward part of the cycle rather than staying stable at past inflation levels. Second, in contrast to the predictions of this approach, in some of the cycles (especially in Brazil) the accelerations in inflation coincided with increases in real wages.

The relative ineffectiveness of this approach in explaining inflation does not mean that inertial inflation disappeared in the post-HS period.

Table 6.5
Pre- and post-stabilization macroeconomic indicators—Argentina.

	Pre-Austral				Post-Austral			
	1982	1983	1984	Average 1982–84	1986	1987	1988	Average 1986–88
1. Percentage change in prices (in annual terms)								
CPI inflation	164.8	343.8	626.7	378.4	90.1	131.3	343.0	188.1
CPI inflation (Dec. to Dec.)	209.7	433.7	688.0	443.8	81.9	174.8	387.7	214.8
Official devaluation	488.8	306.2	542.4	445.8	56.7	227.6	308.0	197.4
Official devaluation (Dec. to Dec.)	484.8	364.6	652.3	500.6	51.4	190.4	271.3	171.0
Nominal interest rate (overnight)	213.8	682.4	748.0	548.1	117.8	227.8	407.8	251.1
Real interest rate[a] (overnight)	1.3	46.6	7.6	18.5	19.7	19.3	4.1	14.4
2. Money (percent of GDP)								
M1	4.7	3.8	3.4	4.0	4.9	5.2	3.8	4.6
Seigniorage[b] (M1)	7.8	8.6	7.1	7.8	3.4	4.0	7.1	4.8
3. Aggregate demand (percent of GDP)								
Total consumption	80.3	81.0	83.7	81.7	83.8	83.1	80.6	82.5
Investment	16.4	14.3	12.4	14.4	11.6	13.2	12.5	12.4
GDP growth (percent)	-4.6	2.8	2.6	0.3	5.7	4.1	-5.2	1.5
4. Relative prices (1980 = 100)								
Real exchange rate	208.4	246.4	229.4	228.1	252.8	260.5	265.5	259.6
Real wage	115.9	175.4	180.7	157.3	153.0	143.1	136.2	144.1
5. External sector (billions of US$)								
Trade balance	2.3	3.3	3.5	3.1	2.1	0.6	3.6	2.1
Current account (percent of GDP)	-4.1	-3.8	-3.2	-3.7	-3.6	-2.5	-2.2	-2.8

6. Public sector (percent of GDP)

Operational deficit[c]	n.a.	-8.8	-8.0	-5.6	-2.0	-4.3	-4.9	-3.7
Total deficit	n.a.	-19.8	-16.6	-12.1	-5.2	-9.3	-9.9	-8.1
External debt	83.8	77.3	67.5	76.2	66.8	69.7	61.3	65.9
Internal debt	n.a.	n.a.	n.a.	n.a.	7.5	9.0	10.4	9.0

Source: Machinea 1989.
a. Real interest rate = $[(1 + i)/(1 + \pi)] - 1$; π = inflation.
b. Seigniorage = $M1_t - M1_{t-1}/GDP_t$.
c. Operational deficit = Revenue *minus* Expenditure; Total deficit = Operational deficit + Central bank deficit.

Table 6.6
Pre- and post-stabilization macroeconomic indicators—Brazil.

	Pre-Cruzado				Post-Cruzado			
	1983	1984	1985	Average 1984–85	1986	1987	1988	Average 1986–88
1. Percentage change in prices (in annual terms)								
CPI inflation	142.1	197.0	226.9	188.7	145.2	224.8	684.6	351.6
CPI inflation (Dec. to Dec.)	177.9	208.7	248.6	211.7	63.5	432.3	1,037.6	511.1
Official devaluation	221.4	220.3	235.5	225.7	120.2	187.9	568.7	292.3
Official devaluation (Dec. to Dec.)	126.7	119.0	117.8	121.2	32.3	385.1	889.4	435.6
Nominal interest rate (overnight)	179.4	231.0	250.2	220.2	76.7	398.8	1,061.1	512.2
Real interest rate[a] (overnight)	0.5	7.2	0.5	2.7	8.1	-6.3	2.1	1.3
2. Money (percent of GDP)								
M1	4.8	3.5	3.5	3.9	7.4	3.8	2.2	4.5
Seigniorage[b] – M1	1.3	2.4	2.3	2.0	3.5	2.5	3.3	3.1
3. Aggregate demand (percent of GDP)								
Private consumption	72.3	69.7	67.2	69.7	66.2	65.1	n.a.	65.7
Public consumption	9.6	8.2	9.7	9.2	10.2	12.2	n.a.	11.2
Investment	15.4	16.5	18.0	16.6	20.5	19.5	17.0	19.0
GDP growth (percent)	-2.5	5.7	8.3	3.8	8.2	3.6	-0.3	3.8
4. Relative prices (1980 = 100)								
Real exchange rate	116.4	118.1	135.0	123.2	154.6	143.4	153.6	150.5
Real wage	102.4	114.3	117.4	111.4	107.1	95.8	112.2	105.0

5. External sector (billions of US$)								
Trade balance	−6.9	0.05	−0.2	−2.3	−5.3	−1.4	4.5	−0.7
Current account (percent of GDP)	−3.3	0.0	−0.1	−1.1	−2.0	−0.5	1.3	−0.4
6. Public sector (percent of GDP)								
Operational deficit	4.8	2.7	4.3	3.9	3.6	5.5	4.3	4.5
Total deficit	n.a.	n.a.	n.a.	n.a.	n.a.	n.a.	n.a.	n.a.
External debt	45.7	48.6	46.4	46.9	40.8	37.9	33.8	37.5
Internal debt	20.2	19.5	21.1	20.3	21.1	32.6	n.a.	26.9

Sources: *Conjuntura Economica*; Central Bank of Brazil; IMF Report; CEM 1988.
a. Real interest rate $= [(1 + i)/(1 + \pi)] - 1$; π = inflation.
b. Seigniorage $= MB_t - MB_{t-1}/GDP_t$, where MB is monetary base.

As the regressions discussed earlier indicate, the inflation process persisted. The degree of price synchronization observed in Bolivia is not apparent in either economy.

An Alternative View: Anticipations of Recurrent Controls

In our view the main explanation for the regime of explosive inflationary cycles that emerged in both countries after the failure of the Austral and Cruzado plans lies in the nature of the policies adopted to fight inflation during this period. Specifically, it was the repeated use of price controls in stabilization programs, which were not accompanied by appropriate supporting policies, that generated the new regime. The very use of price controls undermined credibility in the government's resolve to implement and sustain a fiscal adjustment and to use more traditional nominal anchors such as the money supply, nominal bank credit, or the exchange rate. In addition, anticipations by private agents of the use of controls created a perverse mechanism that exacerbated the instability of inflation.

The various price freezes during the cycles attempted to stop inflation by synchronizing wages, prices, and the exchange rate, thus putting an end to the spiral. However, these attempts were frustrated time and again by inflationary acceleration getting out of hand. In the post-HS period the lack of credibility in stabilization seems to have generated expectations that accelerations are most likely to be stopped by the reimposition of controls. The realization that this would be the stabilization strategy induced a corresponding behavior pattern on the part of the private sector.

Suppose that firms know that once inflation exceeds a certain level, price controls (in the form of a freeze) are likely to be introduced, but there is uncertainty regarding the rate of inflation that would trigger their imposition. Firms will attempt to enter the freeze in a favorable position.[7] They would need to balance the forgone profits they could incur by setting their prices "too high" against the potential losses resulting from setting their prices "too low." Once inflation exceeds a critical level, the probability that the government will attempt to stop inflation through controls increases. Firms will then increase prices further, in an attempt to anticipate the government's action. If monetary and exchange-rate policies are basically accommodating, inflation will thus continue to increase and firms will raise prices further, resulting in an acceleration of inflation of the type observed in Argentina and Brazil before the freeze.

3. Analysis of the Cycles

Phases of the Cycles

There are typically three phases in the cycles. The first corresponds to the imposition of the freeze, which results in a rapid reduction in inflation. In the second phase, when controls are removed, inflation usually accelerates rapidly and quickly reaches the level of inflation that prevailed before the last stabilization effort. After the initial acceleration there is usually a brief pause in the rate of acceleration of inflation, followed by a drastic explosion in the third and last phase.

The best example of these phases is the period from the Bresser plan to the Summer plan in Brazil (see figure 6.1b). Inflation accelerated very rapidly during the flexibilization stage between September and December 1987, but there was a sharp drop in the rate of increase of inflation once it reached 20% per month. Inflation then crept up slowly for almost 8 months, but exploded toward the end of the year. A similar pattern is observed in Argentina between the Austral II and the Plan Primavera.

The Fall in Inflation

The price-wage-exchange rate freeze was usually implemented once inflation was on an explosive hyperinflationary path (as argued in Canavese and Di Tella 1988). Before Australs I and II, and Plan Primavera in Argentina, and the Cruzado, Bresser, and Summer plans in Brazil, hyperinflation was all but unavoidable in the absence of a heterodox shock. In most cycles, the rapid acceleration of inflation immediately before the introduction of controls was largely induced by anticipations about the use of controls.[8]

Since controls had been anticipated, it is not surprising that inflation fell so quickly in all instances after the introduction of controls, even when there was no adjustment in the fundamentals.[9] Firms were willing to abide by the freeze, since their prices had already been increased in anticipation of the freeze. Figure 6.4 tends to support the view that the freezes were indeed anticipated by the private sector. Controls were applied mainly in the industrial sector, usually at the wholesale level. We can readily observe that in both countries the ratio of industrial prices to consumer prices increased substantially before the freezes.

Before the freeze there had been a deterioration on the fiscal side due to the deterioration in tax revenues from the Olivera-Tanzi effect (see

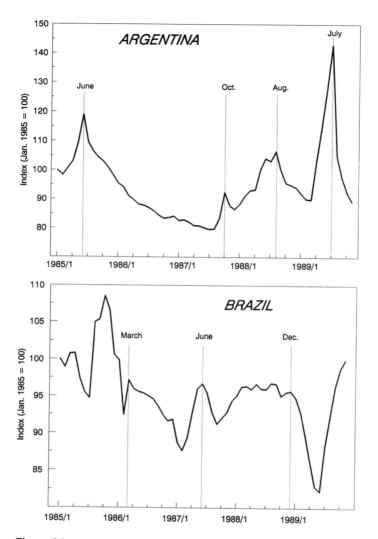

Figure 6.4
Ratio of non-agricultural WPI to CPI. Sources: Argentina — Indicadores de Coyuntura; Brazil—Conjuntura Economica.

figure 6.5), and a drastic deterioration in the prices of public-sector enterprises (see figure 6.6 for Argentina). This fiscal deterioration was partly offset by the reduction in real interest rates, because nominal rates did not catch up with the rapid increase in inflation. Holdings of international reserves and the trade balance were usually at a relatively comfortable level (due, in part, to a flexible exchange policy before the freeze), thus adding credibility to the ability of the central bank to fix the exchange rate in the short run.

The short-run sustainability of the stabilization effort was made possible by an initial, transitory improvement in the fiscal accounts. In the recent heterodox programs, at least in Argentina, the prices of public-sector enterprises were increased significantly at the beginning of each program, while tax revenues rose from the Olivera-Tanzi Effect working in reverse. In addition, the acceleration of inflation before the stabilization package eroded the real value of the internal debt.[10] The only problem on the fiscal side was caused by the higher real interest rates usually observed at the beginning of each stabilization effort (this phenomenon is discussed below). However, these pressures were not necessarily inflationary in the short run, because they were usually financed by issuing domestic interest-bearing debt, even if the strategy was unsustainable in the medium term.

Why were the freezes introduced at higher rates of inflation in each subsequent cycle? This is probably related to an increasing reluctance on the part of the authorities to use controls as a stabilization instrument. Thus, the trigger point for the introduction of controls was higher after each failure. But since firms thought that inflation would be eventually stopped through a new round of controls, rather than by orthodox measures, they continued to engage in anticipatory pricing. The authorities finally gave up and imposed controls, confirming the firms' forecasts, but only after experiencing a higher rate of inflation.

The Rise in Inflation during the Flexibilization Stage

It was easy to bring inflation down during the freeze, but it was difficult to maintain it at this low level for a prolonged period. A common reason for flexibilization is the misalignment of relative prices and wages, often combined with a deterioration in the fiscal and external accounts, high real interest rates, a buildup of domestic debt, and a large premium for the parallel exchange rate. The flexibilization stage generally marked the beginning of an inflationary outburst.

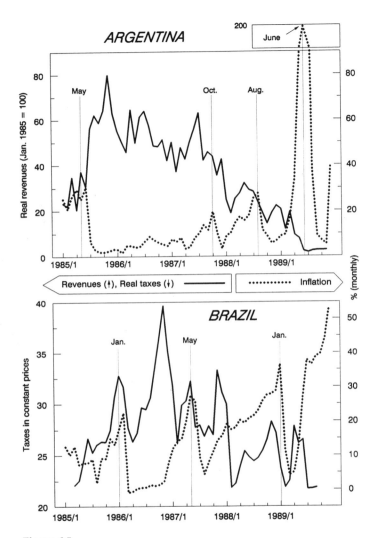

Figure 6.5
Real taxes and CPI inflation. Sources: Argentina—Indicadores de Coyuntura; Brazil—
Conjuntura Economica. Note (Brazil): Real taxes—3-month moving average.

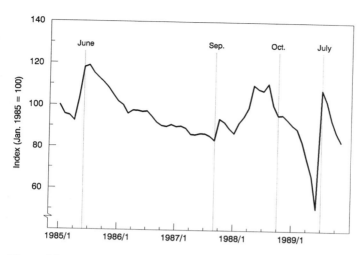

Figure 6.6
Real public utility prices: Argentina. Source: Indicadores de Coyuntura.

The deterioration of the fiscal accounts over time was due primarily to the transitory nature of the initial fiscal adjustment. On the revenue side, there was a slow but steady erosion in real prices of public-sector enterprises (one of the key anchors of the programs) because inflation was not fully eliminated.[11] On the expenditure side the main problem was that high real interest rates were rapidly leading to a buildup of domestic debt. This issue was particularly acute in the Plan Primavera in Argentina and the Summer plan in Brazil.

The increase in real interest rates and the related buildup of domestic debt during the freeze were critical factors in some of the cycles for the abandonment of the freeze. As can be seen from figures 6.7 and 6.8, there was a noticeable cyclical pattern: high real interest rates and debt accumulation are characteristic of the early stage, with the pattern reversed at the end of the cycle. These cycles were marked in Brazil, and milder in Argentina. It can be seen that the accelerations of inflation in Brazil before the Bresser and Summer plans generated negative real interest rates, thus eroding the buildup of domestic debt in the previous part of the cycle. However, this was a temporary phenomenon, as the stock of debt increased rapidly in the first stage of the HS programs, quickly exceeding previous stocks, and real interest rates turned strongly positive. A similar story is observed in the data for Argentina. The debt cycle is more apparent for central-bank debt, with a small buildup after

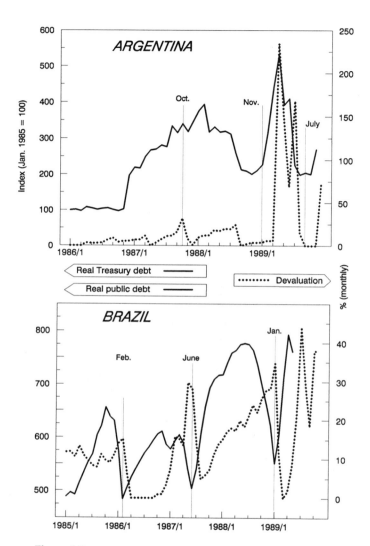

Figure 6.7
Real public debt and official devaluation. Sources: Argentina—Central Bank of
Argentina; Brazil—Conjuntura Economica and The World Bank.

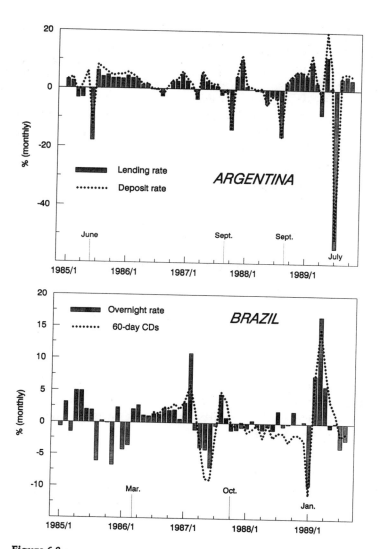

Figure 6.8
Real interest rates. Sources: Argentina—Indicadores de Coyuntura; Brazil—
Conjuntura Economica. Note (Argentina): Interest rate = $(1 + i)/(1 + \pi) - 1$, where i =
nominal interest rate, π = WPI inflation.

Austral II and a large one during the first phase of Plan Primavera. One remarkable feature of these episodes is that neither in Argentina nor in Brazil were hyperinflationary outbursts effective in eroding the debt in the medium term.

The initial rise in real interest rates was endogenous to the program.[12] It was due primarily to lack of credibility in the sustainability of the program. The high nominal interest rates embodied a risk premium to compensate for the possible collapse of the program. If the program succeeded in keeping inflation low for some time, the high nominal rates would result in high real *ex post* interest rates, although real rates were not high on an *ex ante* basis. The high real interest rates complicated the fiscal balance in Argentina and Brazil (especially in the more recent period) because they occurred in association with a high level of domestic debt.

Flexibilization was often also prompted by difficulties on the external side, though more conspicuously so in Argentina. The maintenance of the fixed exchange rate led to an appreciation of the real exchange rate, although in most cases it did not reach significant proportions because controls were also maintained on domestic prices and wages. Nevertheless, as the end of the freeze was becoming apparent there was typically a large deterioration in the reserves position of the central bank, resulting from short-term speculation against the currency and an increase in the premium for the black-market exchange rate. In some instances, as in the Plan Primavera, the run on the central bank's reserves was the trigger for the final collapse of the program.

The Importance of the Flexibilization Stage
The flexibilization stage is the key period in a heterodox shock. Ideally, the fiscal situation should remain sound during this stage as prices are gradually liberalized, supported by a strong nominal anchor (either the exchange rate or money). The lack of fiscal effort in both countries ruled out the possibility of sustaining low inflation as prices were liberalized, but it was still possible to stabilize inflation at a level consistent with the fundamentals. One surprising feature in both countries is that inflation failed to stabilize on a long-term basis once controls were removed. Though some initial overshooting of inflation could be a natural response to price liberalization, a well-planned flexibilization stage should have succeeded in stabilizing inflation, perhaps at high rates. This required, in addition to the maintenance of the fiscal stance, a clear signal regarding

the choice of nominal anchor and the target for nominal changes (e.g., the rate of devaluation or monetary growth). The inability to adhere to a nominal anchor during the flexibilization stage set the stage for the hyperinflationary outbursts that were to follow.

In none of the efforts in Argentina and Brazil was there a clear strategy for getting out of the freeze. This stage was not well planned, and in most instances it involved the simultaneous abandonment of all the nominal anchors. This problem was apparent in the aftermath of the Cruzado plan and the Plan Primavera: forced by the large existing imbalances, all the nominal anchors (wages, public-sector and private-sector prices, and the exchange rate) were released at once, resulting in a rapid acceleration in inflation. But this pattern was also observed, though it was in a milder, during the flexibilization phase in the Bresser and Austral II plans.

Despite the lack of strong anchors, there was usually a pause in the increases in inflation once it reached the previous plateau. Inflation then temporarily stabilized at that level (around 20% in Brazil and 15% in Argentina), perhaps because there was a perception that the economy could function with a rate of inflation around that level and hence that the government would not take bold steps to fight it. Since a stabilization program based on controls was not likely to be implemented, there was no reason to engage in anticipatory pricing. However, rates of inflation in this range can easily be destabilized by real or nominal shocks. Since the inflation process was basically asymmetric, the response to shocks almost always involved an increase in inflation. This increase rapidly gained momentum as agents perceived that inflation was accelerating once again and that the imposition of controls had become more likely. At this stage the acceleration becomes almost unstoppable in the absence of a stabilization shock.

The Erosion of Credibility and Inflation Instability over Time

The available evidence indicates that the Austral and Cruzado plans, the first of their type in each country, enjoyed more credibility than the programs that followed them. One reason for this is that these two programs were the first major attempts at stopping inflation since the beginning of the debt crisis. Moreover, they were the first anti-inflation efforts in many years that succeeded in bringing down inflation in a significant way and keeping it down, even if this stability lasted only a few months. The programs that followed the Austral and Cruzado plans were less comprehensive: it was clearer that the use of controls was largely a substitute for the adjustment of the fundamentals.

The lesser credibility enjoyed by each subsequent program made the sustainability of low inflation during the period of controls more difficult and the explosions that followed more dramatic. The greater credibility attached to the first program was due partly to the fact that it was the first stabilization attempt to be based on incomes policy. As the same stabilization tactic was used over and over again, it became apparent that the approach would not succeed in maintaining low inflation for long, and the private sector became better at anticipating behavior in the public sector.

The erosion of credibility over time was accompanied by a shorter duration of low inflation at the beginning of each cycle and a stronger explosion toward its end. These events were certainly not unrelated. Since the programs were less credible, it was more difficult for the government to maintain low inflation in the period of controls. The combination of events that made it possible to maintain low inflation in the initial programs (such as relatively large seigniorage and low interest rates) were less favorable in the subsequent ones.

The difference between the credibility of the initial program and that of the follow-up programs is apparent from the behavior of money demand during the various stabilization attempts. Figure 6.9 shows the ratio of M1 to M4 in Argentina and Brazil. This ratio increased significantly in both countries during the Austral and Cruzado plans, but did not change much after the implementation of the follow-up programs. In Argentina we observe only a small, brief increase in this ratio during the Austral II program, but no change in the downward-sloping trend during Plan Primavera. A more significant reversal is observed after the BB plan in 1989, but the remonetization did not even come close to the early levels of the Austral plan. Likewise in Brazil, this ratio increased during the Bresser plan, but the increase was relatively small and short-lived.

Macroeconomic Performance in the Cycle Regime

One striking feature of the macroeconomic performance during the period of the cycles is that despite the large fluctuations in nominal variables, average inflation did not increase significantly in this period. Tables 6.7 and 6.8 show that in Argentina for the period 1986–1988 inflation, budget deficits, and seigniorage were on average lower than in

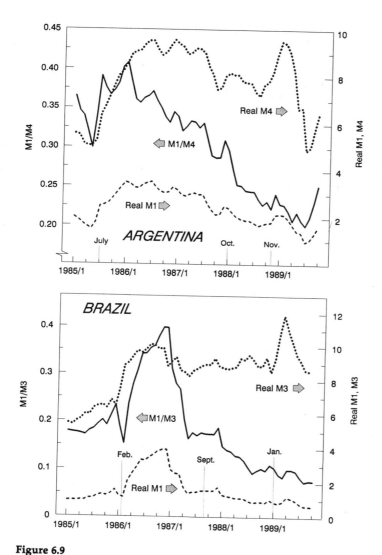

Figure 6.9
Composition of money: M1, M3, and M4. Sources: Argentina—Carta Economica;
Brazil—Conjuntura Economica.

Table 6.7
Indicators of macroeconomic performance—Argentina.

Variables	Pre-Austral (1982/1–1985/5)			Excluding hyperinflation (1985/7–1989/2)			Including hyperinflation (1985/7–1989/9)		
	Mean	S.D.	$\frac{\text{S.D.}}{\text{Mean}}$	Mean	S.D.	$\frac{\text{S.D.}}{\text{Mean}}$	Mean	S.D.	$\frac{\text{S.D.}}{\text{Mean}}$
CPI inflation	15.9	6.3	39.6	8.6	6.0	69.8	16.5	31.4	190.3
Non-agriculture WPI/CPI	105.0	6.2	5.9	91.5	8.4	9.2	94.2	12.3	13.1
Deposit interest	14.5	7.1	49.0	9.4	4.8	51.1	15.6	24.7	158.3
Lending interest	17.8	7.5	42.1	10.1	4.8	47.5	17.2	27.9	162.2
Real exchange rate	83.6	9.2	11.0	89.7	6.9	7.7	95.3	21.3	22.3
Real wage	113.0	12.3	10.9	99.9	6.1	6.1	98.5	8.1	8.2
Real taxes	99.2	21.4	21.6	162.6	63.4	39.0	149.0	67.5	45.3
Industrial production[a]	84.4	6.4	7.6	95.1	6.8	7.2	93.3	8.2	8.8
GDP growth[a]	−0.1	3.2	n.a.	0.4	2.5	n.a.	0.0	3.0	n.a.

a. Based on quarterly data.

Table 6.8
Indicators of macroeconomic performance—Brazil.

Variables	Pre-Cruzado (1983/1–1986/2)			Post-Cruzado (1986/3–1989/8)		
	Mean	S.D.	S.D. Mean	Mean	S.D.	S.D. Mean
CPI inflation	10.0	3.3	33.0	17.6	13.5	76.7
Industrial WPI/CPI	97.5	3.9	4.0	93.2	3.7	4.0
Overnight interest	10.4	1.8	17.3	15.4	9.4	61.0
Real exchange rate	87.9	18.8	21.4	96.8	10.6	11.0
Real wage	96.0	10.9	11.4	118.1	7.2	6.1
Real taxes	122.2	36.2	29.6	135.1	28.9	21.4
Industrial production	104.0	10.6	10.2	121.6	10.5	8.6

the pre-Austral period, while growth and the external performance remained at similar levels. In part this is because inflation in Argentina was already very high before the Austral plan, and the performance during that period had been affected by the high, unstable inflation rates prevailing at the time. Nevertheless, a similar pattern is observed in Brazil, where there was no indication of any significant deterioration in macroeconomic indicators during the cycles. True, inflation on average almost doubled in the post-Cruzado period, but increases of this size were not unusual in Brazil and had already happened in 1975, 1980, and 1983.

Neither did the increased variability in nominal variables result in larger variability in real variables. Tables 6.7 and 6.8 show the mean and standard deviation of inflation, interest rates, some key relative prices, real taxes, and indices of real activity. If we exclude the hyperinflation period in Argentina, the data indicate that the greater variability of inflation in the post-HS period did not lead to larger variations in relative prices, in production, or (in Argentina) nominal interest rates. Quite surprisingly, in both countries the real exchange rate was more stable in the post-HS period.

Although performance was on average similar in both periods, there was a continuous deterioration in the overall situation in the post-HS period over time. For example, whereas growth in Argentina did not change on average very much before and after the HS, there has been a downward trend over the more recent period. Likewise, inflation has been rising in both countries over time. More dramatic results are obtained if one includes the recent Argentine hyperinflation in the analysis. Growth, slightly negative in 1988, became more so in 1989, and the increase in inflation was accompanied by increased variability in real variables.

4. Implications of this Regime and Puzzles

The relatively short experience with the inflation-and-stabilization cycles analyzed in the previous sections does not allow a thorough evaluation of the regime. We can nevertheless draw some preliminary implications regarding the nature of the inflation process during the period, the likely developments in the absence of a change in regime, and the features of the existing regime that are relevant for the design and implementation of a successful stabilization program.

Is Hyperinflation Avoidable?

It is difficult to tell whether the system could have continued functioning in this manner without facing hyperinflation. The average rate of inflation has been increasing constantly over time in both countries. In addition, the cycles have tended to become shorter, and inflation tends to peak at higher levels in each new round. All the evidence indicates that it is difficult to avoid hyperinflation while the economy remains in this regime. Argentina faced a full-blown hyperinflation after the collapse of Plan Primavera, and another in the aftermath of the BB plan; now Brazil is going in the same direction.

The Argentine hyperinflation did not follow the pattern observed in other experiences of this type. There seems to be a consensus that the drastic acceleration that started in February 1989 was triggered by a run out of domestic money. This run was driven by the interaction of two factors: first, there was an unsustainable buildup of domestic public debt, resulting from very high interest rates to support the exchange rate, that raised fears that a maxi-devaluation was imminent; second, there was an increasing likelihood that the Peronist party would be elected in May and that it would follow populist policies, including a further increase in the budget deficit.

Under other circumstances, the run out of domestic currency would have led to a depreciation of the domestic currency, but not necessarily to an acceleration in inflation of the type observed at that time. The main reason why the run led to hyperinflation was that it took place in an already unstable environment, with very weak nominal anchors. It is difficult to rule out the possibility that if the economy had continued under this regime for a sufficiently long period, hyperinflation would have developed anyway. In fact, the way things are developing in Brazil, where inflation is relentlessly increasing (it exceeded Cagan's "critical" level of 50% in January), hyperinflation appears to be all but unavoidable.

The Alternative Scenarios to Price Controls

The failure of the Austral and Cruzado programs set the stage for the cycles that were to follow. As noted, the main destabilizing factor in Argentina and Brazil was the repeated use of price controls. Was there any other feasible way of dealing with inflation in the initial and the follow-up programs?

One option would have been to refrain from using price and wage controls or price guidelines, maintaining the same fiscal stance. In Brazil this may have prevented the increased instability observed after the Cruzado plan. However, this does not mean that the upward trend in inflation could have been prevented. It is unrealistic to assume that inflation can be stabilized in the long run at an annual rate of 200%, as is often claimed by the authorities. If inflation persists at this rate, the government loses credibility in its ability to reduce inflation, and reactions to inflationary shocks become *asymmetrical*, eventually leading to change only in the upward direction.

In Argentina, one plausible option would have been to apply a one-time heterodox shock (of the type used in Austral I) but to refrain from applying price controls in subsequent stabilizations. With the reduction in the fiscal deficit to a level financeable by the inflation tax it might have been possible to have a much more stable development than the actual one.

A different option would have been to announce a target for the nominal anchors and maintain them at a level consistent with the reduced fiscal deficit. We know from recent developments in policy game theory that if the government can establish greater credibility in its rule on monetary (or exchange-rate) policy, inflation will come down even in the same fiscal setting. Thus the "monetary arithmetic" of Sargent and Wallace is not applicable when credibility issues are involved.

At present it is difficult to evaluate the July 1989 stabilization program in Argentina in terms of a possible change of regime. Although, as in the previous cycles, the program contained freezes of the exchange rate and public-sector prices, the official freeze was not extended to wages and prices in the private sector. In addition, the program had the "benefit" of taking place in the wake of a hyperinflationary experience in the second quarter of 1989, which may have created a more favorable setting for breaking with the past. Finally, a fiscal reform (and more announcements about privatizations) came on top of the benefits from the reverse Tanzi-Olivera Effect. Nevertheless, last December inflation erupted again, driven by a depreciation of the free-market exchange rate, thus reinforcing the perception that the latest stabilization efforts were not strong enough to break with the old regime.

We have already mentioned that tight monetary policies were put into effect in Argentina toward the end of 1986, 1987, and 1988, and in the Summer Plan of 1988-89 in Brazil. However, the governments were unwilling to persist with these policies in view of sharp increases in real interest rates. Consequently, these policies were abandoned, and eventually a new round of income policies was put into effect. Therefore the tightening of monetary rules seems to have been an option for which the authorities were not ready. Until there is sufficient resolve to deal with inflation (and bear the cost of disinflation) there is no way in which the inflationary trend could be reversed in either country. However, much of the excessive instability could have been prevented by avoiding the repeated use of income policies.

Implications for a Successful Stabilization Program

One of the main problems that will confront any stabilization in these countries is the establishment of a minimum degree of credibility in government's disinflationary policies.

In the fiscal area it will be necessary to establish credibility in the *sustainability* of the fiscal adjustment, a property which was lacking not only in the Austral Plan but also in all the stabilization programs over the past 30   years in Argentina. Presumably this will require the implementation of basic fiscal reforms aimed at convincing the public of the sustainability of the adjustments. The mere reliance on the Olivera-Tanzi Effect (in reverse), high public-sector prices, and a fall in real wages during the freeze will not suffice, because these measures are not immune to inflationary shocks.

In addition, it is necessary to restore credibility in the governments' commitment to stand behind the nominal anchors in spite of the costs that this may entail. This is a different dimension of the credibility issue, which is not identical with the fiscal aspect. This aspect is important because it is well known that governments can use inflation (or devaluation) to achieve non-fiscal objectives, such as a reduction in the real wage or a real depreciation. Since inflation has been used to fulfill these functions in the past (especially in Brazil, to erode the real wage), the fiscal adjustment will not be enough to overcome these difficulties. The critical aspect here is whether the government is willing to maintain the announced exchange rate or monetary targets even when faced with overvaluation or high real interest rates due to adverse expectations. Given the recurrent failures during the cycles period, there is no possibility in the present situation of avoiding the confrontation between pessimistic expectations and the effort to set nominal anchors. This confrontation will result in a monetary crunch or in overvaluation of the currency, depending on whether the money supply or the exchange rate is used as an anchor. In either case, the growth of the economy will have to suffer in the short or intermediate run.

The foregoing remarks imply that stabilization programs should undergo a shift of orientation in the orthodox direction. Further use of price controls should be avoided in order to restore credibility in conventional anchors. There are, of course, well-known arguments for government intervention in nominal contracts in labor and capital markets in order to alleviate the surprise effect of stabilization. In practice, this took the form of constructing "conversion tables" for loans contracted before the stabilization and of temporary suspension of lagged wage indexation, combined with a realignment of the base wage. It was especially the latter element that entailed the introduction of price controls as a form of insurance against real wage erosion. However, since it is essential at the present stage to redress the erosion of credibility in both countries as a result of the use of controls, the imposition of a wage-and-price freeze in the private sector should be avoided.

Acknowledgments

We are grateful to Mario Blejer, Michael Bruno, Stanley Fischer, Elhanan Helpman, José Luis Machinea, and Assaf Razin for comments on an earlier version, and to Jariya Charoenwattana for research assistance.

Notes

1. In fact, Argentina and Brazil have recently suspended service on their external debt.

2. Seigniorage is measured as the change in the central bank's non-interest-bearing liabilities (typically the monetary base) as a percentage of GDP. Given the type of remuneration on bank reserves in Argentina, M1 is the basis of seigniorage and inflation tax. The level of seigniorage is an indicator of the amount of resources the government extracts from the private sector thanks to its monopoly on printing money. The figures of budget deficit and inflation, available from the authors upon request, present a similar pattern.

3. In the last section of this paper we present a more thorough discussion of this issue.

4. The problems with the design of the Austral and Cruzado plans and the reasons for their failure are discussed by Bruno et al. (1988), Heymann (1987, 1990), Kiguel (1989), Machinea (1989), and Cardoso and Dornbusch (1987), among others.

5. See also Heymann 1990 and Cardoso 1990.

6. RMC is defined here as the three-month moving average of $\Delta H/\text{CPI}$, where H denotes the non-interest-bearing liabilities of the central bank. For Argentina the relevant monetary aggregate is M1; for Brazil it is the monetary base. This concept is basically similar to seigniorage (just discussed), except that the latter is defined as a percentage of GDP.

7. Since the freeze involves a maximum price, each firm has an incentive to set its price high to gain a safety margin and then provide a discount if necessary. This margin can allow for possible increases in wages during the price freeze.

8. The one exception is the BB plan in Argentina, which addressed a full-blown hyperinflation.

9. In almost all cases, controls did not result in widespread shortages. The Cruzado plan was the only exception in this respect: after a short span in which the above-mentioned pattern occurred, a generalized situation of excess demand led to the emergence of shortages and black markets.

10. In most instances, however, this gain was transitory and domestic debt increased rapidly during the freeze. As opposed to other hyperinflationary outbursts, domestic debt was not fully eroded in the process.

11. It might be puzzling that, even during the freeze, inflation was not fully eliminated. There are two reasons for this. First, due to the way the in which price indices are computed, current inflation rates usually reflect past inflation with one or two months' lag. Second, and probably more important, controls were usually not applied drastically so as to completely avoid all price increases; exceptions were made if justified by increases in costs of imported inputs or if prices were markedly out of line at the time of the freeze. In addition, prices of

agricultural products subject to seasonal fluctuations were, by and large, not subject to controls.

12. The reasons for the high *ex post* real interest rates are discussed in the existing literature (see, for example, Dornbusch 1986; Dornbusch and Fischer 1986; Sachs 1986).

References

Bacha, Edmar, and Francisco Lopez. 1983. "Inflation, growth and wage policy." *Journal of Development Economics* 13: 1–20.

Bruno, M., G. Di Tella, R. Dornbusch, and S. Fischer, eds. 1988. *Inflation Stabilization: The Experience of Israel, Argentina, Brazil, Bolivia, and Mexico*. MIT Press.

Canavese, Alfredo, and Guido Di Tella. 1988. "Inflation stabilization or hyperinflation avoidance: The case of the Austral Plan in Argentina, 1985–87." In *Inflation Stabilization*, Bruno et al., eds. (MIT Press).

Cardoso, Eliana. 1990. From Inertia to Megaflation: Brazil in the 1980s. Mimeograph, Tufts University.

Cardoso, Eliana, and Rudiger Dornbusch. 1987. "Brazil's Tropical Plan." *American Economic Review Papers and Proceedings*, May.

Dornbusch, Rudiger. 1986. "Money, interest rates and stabilization." *Review of Economic Conditions in Italy* 3: 439–453.

Dornbusch, R., and S. Fischer. 1986. "Stopping hyperinflations past and present." *Weltwirstchaftliches Archiv* (January): 122.

Dornbusch, R., and M. Simonsen. 1987. Inflation Stabilization with Incomes Policy Support, a Review of the Experience of Argentina, Brazil and Israel. Group of Thirty, New York.

Heymann, Daniel. 1987. "The Austral Plan." *American Economic Review* 77 (no. 2): 284–287.

Heymann, Daniel. 1990. "From Sharp Disinflation to Hyper and Back: The Argentine Experience 1985–89." Mimeograph, CEPAL, Buenos Aires.

Kiguel, Miguel A. 1989. Inflation in Argentina: Stop and Go Since the Austral Plan. PPR Working Paper no. 162, World Bank.

Kiguel, Miguel A., and Nissan Liviatan. 1989. The Old and the New in Heterodox Stabilization Programs: Lessons from the Sixties and the Eighties." Mimeograph, World Bank, CECMG.

Machinea, José Luis. 1989. Stabilization under the Alfonsín Government: A Frustrated attempt. Mimeograph.

Modiano, Eduardo M. 1988. "The Cruzado first attempt: The Brazilian stabilization program of February 1986." In *Inflation Stabilization*, Bruno et al., eds. (MIT Press).

Sachs, J. 1986. The Bolivian Hyperinflation and Stabilization. NBER Discussion Paper no. 2073.

Simonsen, Mario Henrique. 1988. "Price stabilization and income policies: Theory and the Brazilian case study." In *Inflation Stabilization*, Bruno et al., eds. (MIT Press).

Comments by Mario I. Blejer

I have no quarrel with the basic claims made by Kiguel and Liviatan: that the overutilization of price controls can backfire; that for future stabilization attempts to succeed, income policies should be de-emphasized in favor of more fundamental reforms; and that it is essential to rebuild confidence and credibility. However, I believe that the absence of a number of elements and the very marginal treatment of others reduce the generality of Kiguel and Liviatan's explanation.

Strengthening the authors' argument, but to some extent disregarded in their paper, is the fact that price controls are not neutral with respect to the fundamentals. Price controls whose sustainability is dubious tend to worsen the fiscal deficit, not only because of lags in the adjustment of public utility prices but also because of what can be called "fiscal hedging." When people expect price controls to be eliminated, they tend to put off tax payments because the real value of these taxes is bound to fall. In addition, since the price controls are not expected to last very long, expected inflation in the short run remains high, with consequent high nominal interest rates on public debt. In these circumstances, fiscal hedging is profitable. People withhold paying taxes and acquire government debt: if inflation rises, the value of taxes falls; if inflation is controlled, the real *ex post* return on the debt is very high. In either case, people profit to the detriment of the budget.

In addition to the cycles described by the authors, there is another type of cycle (more important in the current context of Argentina): the portfolio-financial cycle based on runs against the currency. In order to continue financing the debt and sustaining the exchange-rate freeze, the government had to offer very high rates of return, inducing people to move to domestic assets: at some point, as in bank-run crises, they switched back to foreign exchange. At this point the run could no longer be contained, no matter at what rate of domestic interest (as in the case of Argentina in December 1989). This mechanism could be much more important than the one cited by the authors (advance overpricing in anticipation of price controls) in explaining the stop-go process of inflation.

It is claimed that credibility and confidence are central to the issue at hand and should be restored. But what is credibility? There are, in fact, two concepts of credibility: (a) honesty and time consistency—the belief that governments will keep their promises—and (b) faith in the ability of governments to actually implement their plans. People will clearly evaluate the political-institutional capability to perform an adjustment even if they believe in the government's intentions. Credibility of type b is endogenous to both the nature of the adjustment and the strength of vested interests.

The lesson to be learned from the cycles is that to foster credibility the sequence should be reversed: in Argentina and Brazil it was claimed that stabilization (including incomes policies) should precede the structural reform of the public sector. In fact, until serious measures to reform the public sector are undertaken, there will be no credibility in the government's ability to sustain stabilization.

Note

The views expressed here are those of the author and do not necessarily represent those of the IMF.

Comments by Assaf Razin

In the book on the rise and fall of heterodox policies (if one is ever written) the paper by Miguel A. Kiguel and Nissan Liviatan will probably be one of the last chapters. The authors are well versed in the details of the policy developments without being emotionally attached to a specific policy episode. Thus, they retain their objective judgment of major events.

The paper describes the unstable nature of inflation under a regime of heterodox shocks in the form of discrete changes in wages, prices, and the exchange rate following periods of freeze. Low inflation is not sustainable, since the freeze in wages, prices, and the exchange rate is inconsistent with fundamental underlying factors. In such a regime firms tend to engage in anticipatory pricing. Whenever the controls are lifted, firms price their products excessively in order to be in a favorable position for the next round of price controls. The main theme of the paper is that Argentina and Brazil behaved remarkably similarly during the regime of heterodox shocks, even though in the past—under different regimes—the growth-and-inflation patterns were markedly different.

It is noteworthy that such convergence of inflation patterns under heterodox shocks is not unique to Argentina and Brazil. In table 6.C1 (constructed similarly to table 6.1 in the paper) I describe the policies implemented in Israel from 1981 to 1985. The table describes the "synchronization policies" of finance minister Yoram Aridor and the "package deals" implemented by the National Unity government between the second half of 1984 and the first half of 1985. (A short policy episode with Yigal Cohen-Orgad as the finance minister between the second half of 1983 and the first half of 1984 is of a different nature.) During most of that period, a high and volatile inflation prevailed. A key policy instrument that was used extensively was ceilings on price increases of a significant segment of the CPI (with a weight of about 1/3 in the cost-of-living index), through subsidies. Thus, the ratio between controlled prices and free prices was relatively low in 1983 and 1984. In July 1985 the policy regime changed markedly when the government launched a comprehensive stabilization policy based on both orthodox measures (such as a sharp cut in the government budget deficit, about 13 GNP percentage points) and heterodox measures (such as wage and price freezes together with a tight monetary policy). The July 1985 policy package put a successful end to four years of unsuccessful stabilization policies.

Table 6.C1
Stabilization policies, Israel, 1981–1985.

	Aridor I (1981)	Aridor II	Cohen-Orgad	Package deal I	Package deal II	Package deal III
Inflation reduction From:	6% in Dec. 1980	7.6% in Sep. 1982	11.6% in Dec. 1983	21.3% in July 1984	5.5% in Nov. 1984	19.3% in Feb. 1985
To:	3.3% in May 1981	5.6% in Nov 1982	10.6% in Feb. 1984	16.5% in Aug. 1984	3.2% in Dec. 1984	12.0% in March 1985
Acceleration in inflation prior to program	7.6% in Sep. 1982	11.6% in Dec. 1983	16.5% in Aug. 1984	21.4% in Sep. 1984	19.3% in Feb. 1985	24.9% in June 1985
Duration of low inflation (under 6% monthly)	5 months	5 months	—	—	2 months	—
Type of income and synchronization policy	Tax decrease, rise in subsidies	5% Cap on exchange rate depreciation + 5% Cap on controlled prices inflation	—	Freeze on wages, prices and exchange rate	Freeze on wages, prices and exchange rate	Guidelines
Fiscal policy	Expansionary	Expansionary	Tight	Expansionary	Expansionary	Expansionary
Monetary policy	Easy	Easy	Tight-easy	Easy	Easy	Easy

The detailed and original account of heterodox shocks in Argentina and Brazil by Kiguel and Liviatan, which is extremely important as a description of the mechanism of such policies, does not, however, address some questions concerning the more fundamental economic mechanisms underlying such inflationary regimes. In the following discussion I elaborate on three key points.

The Upward Inflation Trend

The see-saw type of inflation under cycles of price controls does not, as such, necessarily set an upward trend for inflation. In principle, three economic mechanisms that could account for such a trend are thresholds in the wage-indexation scheme; costs of price changes; and a deterioration of fiscal and monetary discipline, especially when subsidies to government enterprises are used in order to keep their prices below market prices. Identifying which one of these economic mechanisms is mainly responsible for the acceleration of inflation under heterodox shocks will, however, require more structured econometric work.

Real Costs

The paper does not analyze the real costs and the kinds of wedges between demand and supply prices that are associated with heterodox policies. To what extent do these policies bring about a deterioration of the external position, a reduction in output growth, or a rise in unemployment?

Motivation for Heterodox Shocks

Given the authors' description of how weak the performance of the economy is under a regime of heterodox shocks, what motivated the authorities to engage in a policy exercise of this kind? A possible hypothesis is that the policy reflects a defensive strategy. That is, if the authorities believe either that the costs of inflation are not high or that the government is not held responsible for the inflation, they may want to pursue heterodox policies. Under these circumstances the "hetero" part of the "heterodox" policies may help to "shift the blame" for the inflation from the government to the private sector, and especially to violators of the price and wage controls. It seems that when the public realizes how significant the costs are and begins to understand the role of government in the inflationary process, such heterodox shocks are no longer useful as a policy strategy on the part of the government. This may be the turning point, as in the case of Israel.

General Discussion

The paper uses the term "heterodox shocks" as opposed to "heterodox policies." The former consist of policies to control wages and prices—with no orthodox components—whereas "heterodox policies" in the more widely used terminology also incorporate orthodox components. Stan Fischer emphasized the fact that the second part of the word "heterodox" (the dox) was from "orthodox," that policies consisting simply of wage and price controls were not heterodox policies, and that it was well known that they could never work. The usage that crept into the discussion that wage and price controls are heterodox policies certainly did not seem useful.

Kiguel and Liviatan considered heterodox shocks as a new "regime." Leonardo Leiderman opposed the concept of "regime," believing that it should be viewed simply as a sequence of failed programs.

A number of participants pointed out various elements in the heterodox packages that played an important role in the collapse of the sequence of programs in Argentina and Brazil. Persio Arida mentioned the role of the price freezes in countries where indexation exists, and the danger embodied in wage increases when the freeze is abandoned. Nadav Halevi mentioned the government's probable fear of increasing unemployment, which could have caused it to abandon the program. Jacob Frenkel questioned the need for a nominal anchor in an orthodox program.

The credibility issue was also raised. Amos Rubin drew a distinction between two types of this concept—broad and narrow. When there is a lack of credibility in the broad sense, the public does not trust the government and will not lend to it even if interest rates on government bonds are very high; credibility in the narrow sense has to do with the public's expectations regarding short-term matters such as abiding by the pegging of the exchange rate. He stated that in the course of the Austral program there was only a problem with credibility in the narrower sense, and that therefore a better heterodox program could have dealt with it. Reuben Gronau suggested using signals to restore credibility: in the Israeli case, cutting the defense budget was a signal showing that the government was determined and serious about cutting inflation. No such signals were apparent in Argentina's and Brazil's stabilization programs.

7 The Costly Transition from Stabilization to Sustainable Growth: Israel's Case

Michael Bruno and
Leora (Rubin) Meridor

1. Introduction and Overview, 1987–1989

By mid-1987, two years after the start of the July 1985 stabilization program, Israel seemed to have extricated itself—at minimal cost—from the worst economic crisis in its history. Not only did inflation drop from 500% to 16–20% per annum. The government deficit came down from an average of around 15% of GNP in the preceding decade to a complete balance and even a slight surplus in 1986, and the external financial position of the country improved dramatically (as shown by the fall in the foreign debt). After a short initial recession with higher unemployment in the second half of 1985 (phase I of the program), output in the business sector went up 6% on average in 1985–1987 and unemployment quickly fell to below its pre-July 1985 rate of 6% (see table 7.1). Although many obvious adjustment problems remained, the second phase (1986–87) seemed at the time to herald the almost complete success of the program, not only in enabling the economy to stabilize, at relatively low real transition costs, but also in laying the foundations for sustainable growth.[1]

In the second half of 1987 a recession developed; it deepened into a real slump in economic activity in 1988 and 1989, with GDP growth falling to around 1% per annum, unemployment gradually rising to 9.5% by the second half of 1989, and inflation persisting at around 15–20% annually.

Given the excessive private-consumption boom of 1986–87 (an average annual growth rate of over 11%), it was only natural to anticipate a subsequent slowdown, which in itself was expected to lead to a lower growth rate for 1988. Two other factors played roles here. One was the beginning of the uprising in the administered territories (the "Intifada"), in December 1987, which temporarily reduced international tourism and disrupted trade in goods and labor services with the territories. The other had to do with the policy disruptions and uncertainties of an election year

Table 7.1
Major economic indicators, 1980–1989.

	1980–1984 average	1985	1986	1987	1988	1989
Rate of growth (percent) in:						
1. Business sector GDP	2.8	5.3	5.8	7.2	1.8	1.5
2. Private consumption	5.5	0.5	14.2	8.4	3.0	−1.0
3. Gross domestic investment	2.7	−10.6	10.4	2.9	−1.9	−2.7
4. Exports	4.4	8.7	5.6	10.8	−2.1	4.6
Other indicators						
5. Consumer prices (percent rate of change)	189.2	304.6	48.1	19.9	16.3	21.0
6. Unemployment (percent)	5.1	6.7	7.1	6.1	6.4	8.9
7. Real interest rate[a]	23.0	100.0	33.0	39.0	26.0	11.0
8. Unit labor costs[b] (index, 1984 = 100)	100.2	99.0	104.5	109.1	109.1	105.2
9. Current account surplus (billions of $)	−1.7	1.1	1.6	−0.9	−0.6	1.2
Percent of GNP						
10. Total public sector deficit	10.9	−1.1	−3.5	−0.1	1.9	6.1
11. Deficit corrected for cyclical downturn					0.7	1.1
12. Tax revenue	43.2	44.9	48.0	47.2	45.9	41.5
13. Internal debt	128.8	129.5	116.8	109.6	103.7	111.7
14. External debt	65.2	80.0	63.3	53.2	45.1	38.4

a. Average short-term rate.
b. In the business sector.

(national elections were held in November 1988, and municipal elections 4 months later), one of whose major manifestations was the postponement of a decision to adjust the exchange rate. The last adjustment had been made in January 1987, and growth in unit labor costs continued to erode the profitability of exports. A series of speculative foreign-exchange outflows ensued, peaking after the elections, in December 1988.

Shortly after a new government was sworn in, two consecutive devaluations (5% and 8%) were made, in December 1988 and January 1989, as part of a new policy package that accompanied the 1989 budget, also involving further reform steps in the money and capital markets. An agreement with the trade unions was signed in February 1989; like the 1985 and 1987 devaluations, it temporarily suspended the existing COLA agreement to partly neutralize the inflationary consequences of the devaluations. A new agreement, to cover the period April 1989 to April 1990, was signed, whereby 85% compensation would be paid twice a year and only for price increases exceeding a monthly threshold of 0.5% (6% annual inflation).

The fall in revenues from tourism and the delayed adjustment of the exchange rate contributed to a real fall in total export receipts of 2% in 1988 (versus an 11% increase the year before—see table 7.1). Together with the fall in investment and private-consumption expenditures, total expenditures dropped and GNP growth slowed down substantially. This slowdown, as well as the moderation in wage adjustments accompanying the devaluation, contributed to the fact that 1989, for the first time since 1985, showed substantial real wage restraint and a fall in unit labor costs—especially in manufacturing (see line 8 of table 7.1 and line 1 of table 7.2).

The recession caused a fall in tax revenues, which explains the opening up of a government deficit in 1988–89. If one applies a cyclical correction for the deficit (table 7.1, lines 10 and 11), fiscal policy seems to have kept a restrained stance through 1989. Monetary restraint could accordingly be relaxed. This tendency was further strengthened by mid-1988 as the depth of the domestic recession became apparent. Only toward the end of 1988, when speculative foreign-exchange purchases heightened, did domestic interest rates start rising again, though only briefly. From January 1989 onward the Bank of Israel resumed its downward pressure on interest rates (and on the commercial banks),[2] which finally dropped almost to international levels by the second half of 1989. A similar pattern can be observed for long-term credit rates, which followed the sharp fall in yields on indexed government bonds. The private mortgage market, in particular, which was largely liberalized, exhibited a dramatic fall in real interest rates (from 11–12% in the previous two years to 5–6% by October 1989).

The effect of a fall in real interest rates and in unit labor costs on outputs tends to be felt only after a considerably lag. Only in the second half of 1989 (after another 4% devaluation in June 1989, making for a cumulative 18% exchange-rate adjustment since December 1988) did exports start growing again. There has been no evidence, however, of a recovery on the domestic demand front. The year 1989, as a whole, was a second low-growth year.

The protracted recession, a process of restructuring, and an unprecedented increase in labor-force participation rates led to a steep rise in

Table 7.2
Indicators of business-sector profitability,[a] 1982–1989.

	1982–1984 annual average	1985	1986	1987	1988	1989
Indexes, 1986 = 100						
1. Labor cost per man-hour in the business sector, product prices	91.0	88.5	100.0	104.7	108.7	105.1
Thereof: Manufacturing	87.5	89.2	100.0	106.3	110.0	108.2
2. Labor cost per unit of business sector product	95.0	90.3	100.0	101.6	105.3	101.8
Thereof: Manufacturing	92.1	89.2	100.0	102.3	106.5	101.2
Percent						
3. Rate of return to gross capital in business sector[b]	12.8	13.6	10.3	10.9	9.8	10.9
Thereof: Manufacturing	13.2	12.7	8.6	8.7	7.9	8.9
4. Real interest rate on short-term credit in business sector[c]	—	17.5	6.9	16.0	12.1	10.6
Thereof: Manufacturing	—	11.7	1.4	10.0	6.7	10.5
5. Real marginal interest rate on overdraft facilities	25.1	94.7	34.7	39.4	25.6	11.3
6. Real yield to maturity of 10-year bonds	2.4	6.3	6.4	5.3	4.5	2.5
7. Taxation rate on non-wage income	24.9	27.5	33.3	31.0	30.0	26.0
8. Net rate[d] of taxation on non-wage income	10.9	19.5	26.5	24.0	23.8	20.8

Source: 1982–1989 Bank of Israel, *Annual Reports.*
a. The share of labor in GDP is 2.4 times that of capital, and has tended to rise in recent years.
b. Includes imputed labor input of self-employed in each sector, at hourly wages equal to those of wage earners in the same industry.
c. The differences between interest rates reflect the differences in the shares of the various kinds of credit in the same industry.
d. After deduction of credit subsidies and capital transfers to business firms; includes taxes on salaries of managers, which are classified as non-wage income.

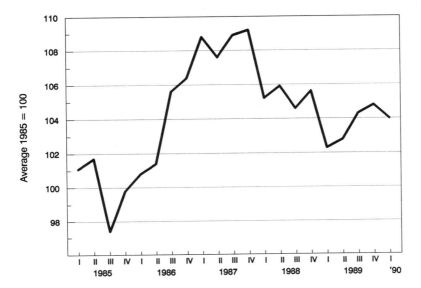

Figure 7.1
Industrial production.

unemployment from an average of 6% in 1987 to over 9% in the third quarter of 1989 (see figure 7.2). This development alone temporarily shifted the focus in the political arena to short-term employment issues.

The fall in imports due to the drop in the rate of economic activity and the recovery in exports in 1989 produced a sharp fall in the trade deficit. For the first time since 1986, the year 1989 showed a surplus in the current account (of $1 billion, after inclusion of foreign-exchange transfers). Thus the foreign debt, both in absolute terms and relative to GDP (see line 14 of table 7.1), has declined steadily since 1985.

The protracted slump may have had structural explanations, which will be discussed in the next section. The cumulative experience of stabilization in Latin American countries, as well as a closer look at the hyperinflation experience of Germany and Central Europe in the 1920s, points to an almost universally observed post-stabilization cycle with similar attributes. In the case of Israel, at any rate, this third phase is a manifestation of slow structural adjustments, in large part endogenous to the post-stabilization process, in which the business sector has to recuperate not only from the distortive effects of a 12-year crisis but also from the effect of rising real labor costs, high initial real interest rates, and a heavier taxation burden.

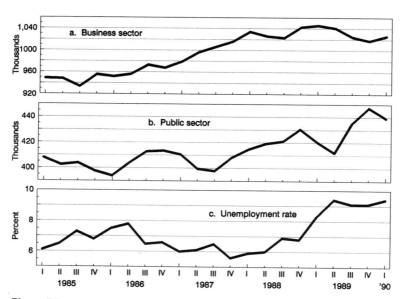

Figure 7.2
Employment and unemployment. a. Business sector employment. b. Public sector employment. c. Unemployment rate.

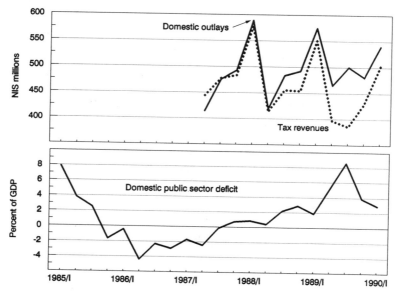

Figure 7.3
Public sector cash flows.

The next section will attempt to disentangle the exogenous and endogenous components of the 1988–89 slump. It will also address the rise in open unemployment, part of which replaced the previously disguised unemployment. Evidence will be given of the restructuring process going on in some major sectors of the economy. Section 3 takes up the main developments in the capital and financial markets. Section 4 returns to a key macro-problem which also characterized earlier stabilization phases: the size and the timing of step-wise adjustments in the exchange rate in the face of rising, though gradually decelerating, loss of export competitiveness due to real wage overshooting. Another key question is taken up in section 4—why the inflation rate failed to decline in spite of the sharp recession. The last section will try to assess where the economy is heading in the near future.

2. Explaining the 1987–1989 Recession: Unanticipated Shock, or Inherent Adjustment and Restructuring Process?

The recession that started in mid-1987 marks the beginning of a new (third) phase in the stabilization process. Until that point, economists considered the stabilization to be a very successful one, both in substantially reducing inflation and in creating only a temporary and slight rise in unemployment.[3] Only when the first figures on economic development in 1988 were revealed did it become evident that a real slack was developing. The recession deepened, reaching its nadir in mid-1989. Output decreased and unemployment surged to a post-1985 record of 9.4% in the second quarter of 1989. The question that emerges is this: Was the recession caused by exogenous factors that have nothing to do with the stabilization of inflation, or was it an inherent outcome of the process of stabilization?

We argue that both types of factors were active in producing the slump in the economy. On the one hand, there existed exogenous factors of a short-term nature, particularly the consequences of the events in the administered territories; these factors led to a temporary slowdown in growth. On the other hand, one can detect factors that are connected to stabilization and to the way it was implemented. Such factors can be deduced from theoretical, *ex ante* considerations, and some of them can be found in other countries that underwent similar disinflation processes.

The uprising in the territories that began in December 1987 affected the Israeli economy through its contractionary effects on the supply of labor to the business sector (mainly in the construction industry) and on the output demand side (mainly a decline in tourism and in Israel's exports to the territories). The 1988 annual report of the Bank of Israel estimates these contributions to the business sector's product loss at 1.5% in 1988; the further, much smaller, effect of the aggravation of the Intifada in 1989 is estimated at 0.3%.

The Intifada, with its implications for future developments, may have had a greater impact through its effect on firms' expectations and investment plans. At least part of the pessimistic perception of firms (as evidenced in the Bank of Israel Company Surveys) and the low investment, especially in 1989, can be attributed to the uncertainty generated by the political situation. Estimating the effects of expectations on investment is, of course, a very hard task. A likely order of magnitude may be obtained by comparing actual investment with the estimated demand for aggregate net investment in the business sector, based on an investment function that involves output levels and increments as well as changes in profitability and in the real interest rate (Lavi 1989).[4] Such a comparison yields an investment shortfall which could have caused an output-demand loss of 0.2% and 0.8% in 1988 and 1989 respectively.

In 1988, when inflation stood at 16%, the public had built up expectations for inflation that affected wages and prices (see section 4 for a detailed discussion). The gap between the prices of traded and non-traded goods was not sustainable, and a devaluation became necessary. We believe that such a devaluation sometime in the first half of 1988 would have prevented relative prices from deteriorating further and thus would have prevented part of the decline in exports. Around 4% of the erosion of the real exchange rate in the second half of 1988 can be attributed to the postponement of the devaluation. By using standard elasticities (see Litvin and Meridor 1977) we arrive at a 4% loss in exports, or, given the time lag, an annual equivalent of 2% for that year. This, in turn, can account for a 0.5% shortfall in business-sector product in 1988.[5] Table 7.3 sums up the exogenous part of output contraction.

The actual shortfall (comparing actual business-sector growth rates in table 7.2 with a hypothetical 5% growth rate each year) amounted to 3.2 (5 – 1.8) and 3.5 (5 – 1.5) in 1988 and 1989, respectively, leaving a 1.0% and a 2.4% (or a cumulative 3.4-percentage-point) gap attributable to the other, presumably "endogenous" structural factors. Let us turn to these now.

Table 7.3
Contributions to output loss[a] (percentage of GDP).

	1988	1989	1988–89
Direct effect of Intifada	1.5	0.3	1.8
Investment shortfall	0.2	0.8	1.0
Delayed devaluation	0.5	—	0.5
Subtotal	*2.2*	*1.1*	*3.3*
Difference between actual and hypothetical (5%) growth	3.2	3.5	6.7
Unexplained residual	1.0	2.4	3.4

a. Ignored here are the mutliplier effects of aggregate demand which, given the openness of the economy, are very small. Likewise we ignore the effect of the postponement of the devaluation on imports, since the elasticity of imports with respect to relative prices is very small.

Experience from other stabilization programs reveals two possible patterns of adjustment from high to low inflation rates. The first involves an initial cost in terms of output loss because of rigidities in wage and price adjustment stemming from initial lack of credibility and/or backward linkages in wage contracts and the like (Fischer 1977; Taylor 1979). When credibility is built up and expectations adjust, the economy should move to a sustainable growth path, provided, of course, that the fundamentals have been taken care of.[6]

The second pattern involves a period of expansion in both output and consumption after the first small loss due to rigidities, whereupon the boom gives way to another recession. Such a pattern was evident in many of the Latin American countries' stabilizations of the 1960s and 1980s.

Kiguel and Liviatan (1989; see also Liviatan 1989) argue that the latter pattern characterizes stabilizations based on the exchange rate. The recession—according to this line of argument—is a necessary outcome of the slow buildup of credibility with a pegged exchange rate. In order to build up such credibility the economy has to follow a path of real appreciation. Real appreciation, however, teaches the private sector not to increase prices or wages while relying on the authorities to accommodate by devaluing. However, this process inevitably results in a loss of output. We will argue here that a "second" recession, somewhat delayed, can also occur after credibility has been built up.[7]

The Israeli stabilization program has so far reduced inflation, not to Western levels, but to an annual rate of 16–20%. Such inflation is not sustainable without realignments in the exchange rate. Indeed, between

July 1985 and December 1989 the exchange rate was cumulatively devalued by about 32% against the dollar (54% against the basket of Israel's major trading partners' currencies). Discrete devaluations took place at the beginning of 1987, at the end of 1988, at the beginning of 1989, and (a small one) in June 1989.

The real appreciation, led by wage increases, eroded profitability in the business sector, as can be seen in table 7.2. Real labor costs per unit of output increased 20% from before the stabilization until 1989,[8] and in the manufacturing sector the rise reached 25%. Although the effect of rising real wages was the most prominent one, aggregate supply and profitability were also negatively affected by two other components: taxation and costs of finance (see table 7.2), to be taken up in turn.

Stabilization processes are often followed by a sharp increase in tax collection. Such an increase stems from the disinflation effect (the inverse Olivera-Tanzi effect). In Israel, gross tax collections increased from an average of 43% of GNP during the high-inflation period (and 38% in 1984) to 48% in 1986. Such an increase encompasses a sharp increase in both direct effective tax rates and indirect ones. Direct effective rates in the business sector increased from a low of 18.4% in 1984 (25% on average

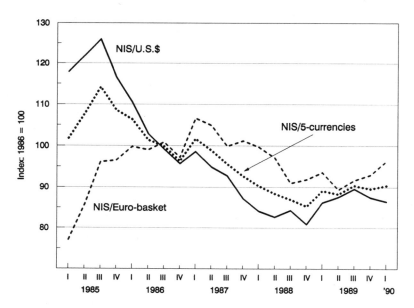

Figure 7.4
Relative prices of industrial production.

during 1982–1984) to a peak of 33.3% in 1986, and have stayed more or less stable ever since. The sharp increase in net indirect taxes, from 4% of GNP in 1980–1984 to 10% in 1986–1990, should be divided between firms and households, but it also contributed to the squeeze in firms' profit-ability. The high effective rates—an outcome of statutory rates set during the inflationary period (which at the time were translated into lower effective rates due to the inherent lags)—became "too" high from a growth-inducement point of view and were recently reduced.[9]

The development of interest rates completes the profitability picture. High real interest rates are a common feature of post-stabilization periods. They can stem from a deliberately tight monetary policy to support the disinflation process; they can be the unintentional outcome of the interaction between expected and actual inflation; or they may reflect the problems of conducting monetary policy during disinflation periods.[10] Moreover, high interest rates are an important ingredient of monetary policy that supports a fixed exchange rate facing occasional and brief speculative attacks.

Real interest rates—at a record high during the first few months after the July 1985 stabilization—decreased later, but remained high (the marginal real rate averaged about 35% on average during 1986–1987). Since 1988 these rates have come down significantly, and by mid-1989

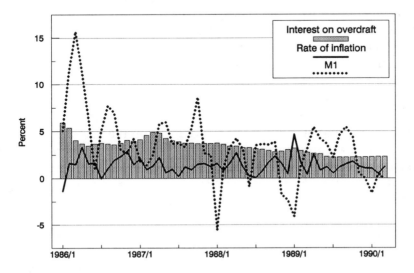

Figure 7.5
Interest rates, money growth and inflation.

they were not much higher than in the industrialized countries. However, the difficulties arising from the 5-year cumulative financial burden were quite marked. While interest rates were not the dominant cause of the financial crisis, they did contribute to financial difficulties in a number of sectors. It should be stressed that such high rates did not prevail in all the sectors. Manufacturing, for example, faced relatively lower rates thanks to a large component of subsidized export credit. For a detailed discussion of financial issues see section 3.

Finally, we come to the most significant development that has been taking place in the business sector since stabilization: structural adjustments and the forced rise in efficiency (through restructuring and labor shedding) in face of the new macroeconomic environment.

The July 1985 program dramatically changed the economic environment in Israel, and the ensuing drastic decline in inflation required firms to adopt a pattern of conduct very different from the one prevailing hitherto. During the inflationary era, firms could overinvest (thanks to cheap government credit) and ignore inefficient real activities. High inflation enabled firms and households to achieve high profits mainly through successful financial manipulations. Low inflation brought to light a set of real inefficiencies, necessitating a structural adjustment. Moreover, the government's new attitude toward fiscal balance meant not only a reduction in current public activities and expenditures, but also a sharp decline in the government's willingness to bail out faltering private firms,[11] thus gradually forcing firms to bear the responsibility for their own activities. Although on a macroeconomic level there is so far only slight evidence of increasing efficiency, on a more disaggregated level (sub-branches and some major conglomerates) we observe a substantial real increase in productivity after 1986.

Table 7.4 presents productivity figures for the total business sector as well as for the manufacturing sector. We focus on the manufacturing sector because it represents about 1/3 of the business sector, and because its data are the most readily available. In the aggregate business sector there was an increase in productivity after the stabilization, but it disappeared in 1988 and 1989. In the total manufacturing sector we note an increase in productivity in 1989; some of the sub-branches have particularly higher rates, and in two major conglomerates (the trade-union-owned Koor industries and the Israel Aircraft Industry)—which encompass 16% of manufacturing—we can trace the accelerated increase in productivity throughout the period 1986–1989.

The case of the Israel Aircraft Industry (I.A.I.) is of particular interest because the cancellation of the Lavi aircraft project at the end of 1987, a very painful government decision taken after a bitter debate, signaled a major turning point in government policy. I.A.I. subsequently fired 5,000 of its 21,000 employees but managed to recover its 1986 output by the end of 1989, while the share of exports in total output increased from 60% to 80%. Koor reduced its 1985 workforce of 34,000 by over 10,000 while increasing productivity 20% over the period 1986–1989. The reduction in employment of these two conglomerates alone accounts for almost half of the total reduction in manufacturing employment in 1987–1989 (which amounted to 10%—see table 7.4).

Figure 7.6 presents the number of bankruptcies and liquidations[12] in the past few years. It shows the increase in the number of bankruptcies after the disinflation, followed by a decrease in 1986–87, and demonstrates the sharp rise in 1988–89. It seems that the firms' response to the changes that followed stabilization varied among different sectors, sub-branches and individual firms. On the one hand, many firms ran into major difficulties, some of which necessitated bankruptcy proceedings or major restructuring using mass firing of labor.[13] On the other hand, the average figures imply that other firms were at the same time expanding both employment and output. Similar conclusions can be drawn from the evidence provided by Regev (1989) on job turnover in the manufacturing industry. According to Regev's data, the number of job turnovers was higher in the years following the stabilization than in the four preceding years.

The above-mentioned restructuring process has very little to do with the slow credibility buildup and the difficulties arising from real appreciation. Moreover, the adjustment to other changes (such as the increase in effective tax rates and high interest rates) are also independent of the credibility issue. Other countries, whose stabilizations have been very successful and which achieved credibility quite rapidly, also went through a structural change causing a recession, which usually lagged a couple of years behind the disinflation stage. Each country displays its own restructuring features resulting from the specific change in the macroeconomic conditions that accompanied the stabilization programs. Garber (1982), for example, has pointed out the emergence of a sharp recession in Germany two years after the 1923 stabilization; in May 1925 output began to slow down, the number of bankruptcies surged, and unemployment expanded.[14] In Germany of the 1920s, unlike Israel,

Table 7.4
Rate of increase of productivity.

	1985	1986	1987	1988	1989
Business sector					
Product	2.9	4.1	7.0	0.0	1.6
Labor input[a]	0.1	2.2	3.8	0.3	1.4
Labor productivity	2.8	1.8	3.0	−0.3	0.2
Real[b] wage		10.0	8.5	2.1	−2.5
Manufacturing					
(diamonds excluded)					
Product	2.9	3.7	4.9	−3.1	−1.9
Labor input	−0.2	2.0	0.0	−4.6	−5.8
Labor productivity	3.1	1.7	4.9	1.7	4.1
Real[c] wages		12.6	11.4	2.5	0.2
Food					
Product	−1.0	13.7	12.8	−1.5	−3.2
Labor input	−9.0	8.8	6.2	−1.2	−3.3
Productivity	−0.4	4.5	6.3	1.3	-0.1
Real[e] wages		18.6	12.9	5.1	−5.7
Textiles					
Product	0.3	5.2	3.9	−12.6	1.3
Labor input	−4.5	3.7	2.7	−13.6	−9.1
Productivity	4.9	1.6	1.1	−1.2	11.4
Real[e] wages		23.6	9.3	8.2	1.5
Metal Products					
Product	0.9	0.9	3.4	−1.7	−4.0
Labor input	−3.2	1.3	−6.6	−4.8	−7.2
Productivity	4.3	−0.5	10.7	3.8	3.5
Real[e] wages		14.1	7.2	−0.5	−1.2
Electronics and Transport					
Equipment					
Product	10.1	−3.3	−3.2	0.8	−5.0
Labor input	5.1	−3.4	−4.3	−3.5	−5.4
Labor productivity	4.7	0.1	1.2	4.4	0.4
Real[e] wages		10.5	13.2	4.4	5.3
Chemical and Oil Products					
Product	0.0	1.8	11.4	0.8	5.7
Labor input	3.6	2.9	2.3	0.1	−1.9
Productivity	−3.5	−1.0	9.1	0.8	7.7
Real[e] wages		10.7	21.5	4.6	−0.6
Transport Equipment					
Product	4.9	−3.7	−9.1	−19.9	6.4
Labor input	9.6	−5.5	−10.4	−17.0	−2.1
Productivity	1.3	2.0	1.4	−3.5	8.7
Miscellaneous					
Product	16.8	3.6	−10.7	2.3	7.0
Labor input	0.0	6.1	−2.2	−4.6	−4.5
Productivity	16.8	−2.4	−8.6	7.2	12.0

Table 7.4 (continued)

	1985	1986	1987	1988	1989
I.A.I.					
Product			−7.1	0.9	6.8
Labor input[f]			−5.6	−14.8	−4.6
Productivity			−1.6	15.8	11.8
Koor					
Product[d]	2.6	−10.0	−7.7	−6.5	−3.0
Labor input[f]	0.2	−2.1	−7.1	−16.1	−10.2
Productivity	2.3	−8.1	0.6	11.5	8.0

Source: Central Bureau of Statistics, I.A.I. and Koor.
a. Working days.
b. Nominal wages deflated by GDP prices.
c. Wages deflated by wholesale prices.
d. Change of products measures by change in sales.
e. Wages deflated by the corresponding component of prices.
f. Number of workers.

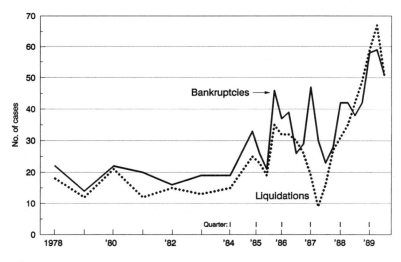

Figure 7.6
Bankruptcies and liquidations (1978-84: Annual data; 1985-89: Quarterly data).
Source: Administrator General, Ministry of Justice.

inflation declined instantaneously and the exchange rate remained unchanged for a long period with no substantial real appreciation (lack of inflationary inertia could be a major factor here). Similar recessions were recorded in other European stabilizations.[15]

The extent of the financial difficulties in Israel became apparent only gradually. In the first stage after disinflation, various firms managed to refrain from major changes and adjustments by relying on more and more credit (see Piterman 1989).[16] Some of them may have been expecting government help at some point; the abstention from such intervention, which would have been typical in the 1970s, became apparent only with the passage of time. For a more extensive discussion see section 3.

On top of the above-mentioned factors, it seems that in the Israeli case favorable conditions prevailing during 1986–87, both internally and externally, temporarily postponed the need for the restructuring. On the one hand, the consumption boom in this period accelerated domestic demand; on the other hand, an increase in foreign demand (due to an acceleration in world trade and to a change in the exchange rate of the dollar against the European currencies) made Israel's exports to Europe—the major market—more competitive.

The external conditions are, of course, exogenous, but internal developments in consumption demand are often cited as characterizing post-stabilization periods. Kiguel and Liviatan (1989) attribute this phenomenon to an initial lack of credibility of the program. They view the consumption increase as advanced purchases to forestall the bad times expected in the immediate future. We argue that the consumption surge can be given a different, more optimistic interpretation. When a stabilization program succeeds in correcting fundamental factors, there will be an increase in perceived permanent income and wealth, which in turn will manifest itself in an increase in both consumption and investment. In the Israeli case, the signs of success at the beginning of 1986 (i.e., the dramatic decline in inflation), the elimination of the government deficit, and other imminent reforms were responsible for the increase in current consumption (excluding nondurables) and in investment both in 1986 and in the first half of 1987. Part of this increase could also be a response to a cyclical downturn in 1984–85, when real wages declined. This drop in the real wage was more than compensated for by the considerable increase in real wages in 1986 and 1987. However, in the second half of 1987 and the beginning of 1988 signs of a turnaround began to show, some related to delayed effects of the stabilization and some due to political developments.[17] There followed a decline in consumption, less so in current consumption and more so in durables (which tend to fluctuate more anyway).

Finally, let us repeat the observation made in the previous section on the steep rise in unemployment, which lagged behind the drop in output growth: This was the combined effect of the labor-shedding process and of an unprecedented increase in labor participation rates.

3. Financial Factors in the Stabilization and Restructuring Process

The period since 1985 has witnessed considerable changes in the real cost, composition, and financial burden of credit in the economy.[18] As table 7.5 shows, average real short-term interest rates were quite high both before and shortly after stabilization—particularly on free-market credit, whose share has been growing steadily.[19] While there was quite a sharp drop in 1986, real rates climbed quite sharply in 1987 (owing to considerable monetary restraint that temporarily accompanied the January 1987 devaluation) and then came down again in 1988 and 1989, with the gradual relaxation of monetary restraint. By 1989 both nominal and real rates had dropped drastically.

As columns 4 and 5 of table 7.5 show, development of the real cost of credit differed across sectors: agriculture faced a much steeper rise than the average for the economy—and vice versa for the manufacturing sector (compare 1985 or 1987 with 1983 in columns 1, 4, and 5). Comparison of the interest rates on directed credit with the free-market rate (columns 2 and 3) and analysis of the change that has taken place in the share of free credit by sector (columns 6–8) provide an explanation of this development. Before 1985, both agriculture and manufacturing (as well as services and trade, not shown here) were granted substantial amounts of credit at low (negative real) interest rates from the public purse, for both exports and domestic consumption. Since 1985 only production for exports could still obtain subsidized credit, and this on far less attractive terms. With manufacturing a relatively more export-based sector (nearly 50% of its output is exported, versus 20–25% for agriculture), its relative reliance on directed credit has been higher and the drop in its share has been less than in agriculture.

The real interest burden on a sector is the product of the interest rate and the ratio of credit to output. As columns 9–11 show, this ratio has been fairly stable over time both for manufacturing and for the economy as a whole, but has risen steeply in agriculture (while for services and

Table 7.5
Real interest rates, changes in directed credit, and credit ratios, 1983–1989.

	Real interest rates on total short-term credit					Percentage share of directed credit			Total short-term credit per output		
	Whole economy										
	Total credit (1)	Free credit (2)	Directed credit (3)	Agriculture (4)	Manufacturing (5)	Whole economy (6)	Agriculture (7)	Manufacturing (8)	Whole economy (9)	Agriculture (10)	Manufacturing (11)
1983	5.1	8.3	-0.5	-0.6	4.6	36.8	51.2	75.0	24.8	30.7	30.8
1984	24.2	25.3	22.4	22.6	31.8	39.8	56.5	76.8	22.6	26.3	28.3
1985	17.3	26.4	1.3	16.8	9.0	40.3	51.7	76.1	25.6	28.9	28.1
1986	10.2	17.5	-6.5	11.2	1.0	33.0	34.9	66.4	26.6	35.9	27.6
1987	19.7	26.2	0.1	19.9	10.1	26.6	28.3	59.3	31.5	49.1	30.1
1988	14.4	18.9	-2.8	14.7	6.8	21.3	23.2	54.1	35.0	68.2	34.3
1989	10.5	10.0	11.1	9.9	11.1	18.0	16.8	50.1	39.3	66.8	36.7

Sources:
Column 1: Bank of Israel *Annual Report 1988.*
Column 2: based on Ben-Rawe 1989.
Columns 6–8: based on Ben-Rawe 1989.

trade, not shown here, it has fallen steadily after stabilization, presumably due to economies in inventory requirements).

In agriculture, more than in manufacturing, there has been a long-term increase in the credit-to-output ratio since the early 1970s, one of the main results of inflationary distortions in the economy. Excessive investments in the 1970s were financed by cheap long-term credit (at highly negative real interest rates[20]) rather than from own accumulated profits, which in turn were squandered on alternative current uses (including private consumption). The government had already stopped handing out unindexed loans in the beginning of the 1980s: with the 1985 stabilization, public long-term lending was virtually stopped. While the growth in net real capital stock in agriculture, for example, came to a halt already in the early 1980s, the existing debt had to be recycled increasingly in the form of short-term debt at high real interest rates—a familiar 1970s phenomenon reminiscent of the Third World debt problem. The financial leverage ratio of total outstanding debt to the net capital stock in agriculture rose in the course of the 1970s from around 20% to 50% and subsequently increased to 90% by 1987 (see Kislev et al. 1989).

In the first stage of stabilization the mere sharp reduction in nominal interest rates created a one-time automatic "debt-rescheduling" effect resulting from the fall in the relative interest-payment burden or the rise in the average loan-repayment period.[21] But once this adjustment has been made, the real financial burden starts to bite. In agriculture, the first major financial crisis occurred in the moshav (co-operative) movement, and subsequently in the two biggest kibbutz (collective) movements. Both types of organization have so far been marked by highly diffuse mutual responsibility for individual credit creation. In the (cooperative) moshav movement, centralized credit and bookkeeping arrangements relieved the individual farming unit of the burden of strict accountability. In the kibbutz movement this "soft budget constraint" marked the relationship of individual kibbutzim (collectives) to the central bodies of the whole movement, which got their funds from the government or the banks.

In the kibbutz movement, the internal mutual reliance systems helped to delay the crisis but also magnified the size of the cumulative debt to over 10% of GNP (their share in GNP is only half of that).[22]

In both cases the government participated in a scheme of debt relief and debt rescheduling worked out jointly with the banks and the borrowers. The moshav movement's debt amounted to $1 billion, of which 40% was to be written off by the banks and various other agencies and the rest to be rescheduled, primarily by the government. This scheme is still being gradually implemented on an individual-moshav basis. The kibbutz debt-relief program involves a $1 billion write-off, two-thirds of which was taken up by the banks and one-third by the government. In addition, $1.5 billion will be rescheduled through government floating of bonds. The remaining $1.5 billion is borne by the kibbutz movement, which has also undertaken severe internal restraining measures. Part of the program involves a radical change in the mutual reliance system and a shift to individual-kibbutz financial planning, with a link to a commercial bank which will henceforth enforce the control of credit.

We have concentrated our discussion on agriculture, but it is important to stress that some restructuring and debt-rescheduling schemes between banks and enterprises have taken place in the manufacturing sector—most notably the above-mentioned case of the Koor industrial conglomerate, which is owned by the Histadrut trade union. Here, too, the government participated in the recovery program, but so far only with a relatively modest share of $50 million.

We end this section with a brief mention of the reform process in the financial markets in recent years. The process of disinflation increased relative demand for unindexed short-term assets, whose share in total private assets quadrupled during the period 1984–1987. This in itself increased the liquidity of the banking system, since the liquidity (reserve) ratios on unlinked assets were lower than those on other assets. The drop in the government deficit also enabled a substantial increase in domestic credit expansion, through a sharp reduction (and unification) of mandatory liquidity ratios on unlinked assets (see table 7.6).[23] This process, combined with a relaxation of limitations on foreign-exchange-linked credit, brought about a reduction in interest rates. Similar developments have taken place in the capital market. Mandatory reserves on long-term linked assets traditionally had to be invested in long-term government bonds or non-marketable government deposits. Capital-market reform has taken the form of a reduction, since 1987, in these reserve ratios, a gradual increase in the marketability of the domestic national debt,[24] and the opening up of the capital market to the free floating of private bond issues. The consequences of these steps can be seen in the narrowing of interest-rate gaps in the capital market as well as in a decline in the average rate on private bonds (for details see Ben-Bassat 1989).

The real yield on government securities has dropped sharply, from 6–7% in 1985 to below 2% in 1989, while a parallel process has taken place

Table 7.6
Selected liquidity ratios for non-linked and linked assets, 1984–1989
(percentages).

	Short-term non-linked assets			Long-term linked assets		
	Demand deposits	CDs	Time deposits (2–3 months)	Index-linked saving schemes	Pension funds	Provident funds
1984	45	17	14	75	92	92
1985	60	43	38	75	92	92
1986	48	38	20	75	92	78
1987	38	38	20	55–65	92	78
1988	26	26	16	55–65	93	78
1989	21	21	12	55–65	93	72
Size of asset in 1988 (% of GNP)	(3.2)	(4.9)	(3.8)	(29.0)	(29.4)	(55.8)[a]

Sources: Piterman 1989 and Bank of Israel data.
a. Includes life insurance.

in the cost of private bond issues. Likewise, the market for mortgages has opened up, and as a result the real cost of mortgages has dropped from 11–12% in 1987 to 5–6% in 1989. Though this process of liberalization and reform in the financial markets is not yet complete, the economy has come quite a long way since 1985. The real cost of capital is now much closer to international levels. It also seems that debt write-offs[25] and reschedulings have passed their peak.

4. Inflation and the Wage-Exchange-Rate Policy Game

The relatively low inflation attained as a result of the stabilization program stayed at a more or less stable rate through 1986–1989, thereby consolidating one major achievement of the program. However, no real further progress was made in closing the gap between domestic price inflation and that prevailing in the Western economies. While CPI inflation remained more or less stable, other prices, especially wages and the exchange rate, did not.

In the past four years wages increased at much higher rates than prices, causing the real wage to cumulatively increase by about 30%, thus substantially reducing profitability. Only in 1989, with unemployment at 9%, do we see a turning point: wages increased at a lower rate than prices, resulting in a mild reduction in real wages and a more substantial one relative to labor productivity (see figure 7.7).

With the July 1985 program a stable-exchange-rate regime was announced. However, no absolute commitment to an exchange-rate peg was made, and in the past four years a number of devaluations took place[26]: one in the beginning of 1987, another (two-step) devaluation at the end of 1988, and finally a small one in June 1989. Table 7.7 shows the average change in the exchange rate over the period and its varying behavior over time.

Table 7.7 presents data for the inflation rates, breaking down the consumer price index into tradable and nontradable goods and services. The rate of change of nontraded goods' prices was much higher (25% on average per year and slightly decreasing over time), while the inflation of traded goods' prices remained more stable at about 12% per year, regardless of the timing of the devaluations. This is one measure[27] of the decline in the comparative advantage of production for exports (and import substitutes) largely accounting for the poor export performance in 1988 (see section 2).

Two intriguing questions emerge: (a) Why did the inflation rate remain apparently stuck in the past four years in spite of the varying conditions? In particular, exchange-rate behavior varied during this period, as did the macroeconomic conditions (an expansion of aggregate demand in the first two years and a recession in the last two). (b) Why did wages increase so much? Was it an unintentional overshooting, reflecting mistakes of inflationary expectations of workers and employers? Or was it, rather, an exogenous increase—and if so, what could be the reason?

These questions are interrelated, and at least part of the answer to both lies in the role of expectations. We believe that inflationary expectations play an important role in explaining the "wage-exchange-rate-price" complex. They affect wage behavior through their role in wage contract negotiations, and they also affect the price-setting mechanism, especially for non-traded goods and services.[28] Tradable goods and services are less affected by expectations, since competition is probably higher in that sector, in spite of impediments to free imports.

The rate of inflation can be viewed as the outcome of a "game" played by the public "against" the government.[29] The rules of the game allow for the government's declarations with regard to its future policy—in particular the exchange rate when the economy operates under a pegged-

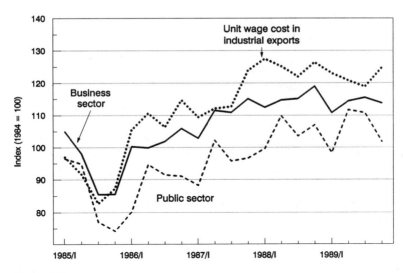

Figure 7.7
Real wage per employee.

Table 7.7
Wages, prices, and exchange rates (average percent change).

	1986	1987	1988	1989
Nominal Wages				
Business sector	66.0	30.7	21.7	18.0
Manufacturing	63.4	32.0	20.4	21.3
Commerce, restaurants, hotels	70.2	27.6	22.9	16.9
Financial and commercial services	67.6	23.7	25.8	13.4
Personal and other services	18.5	34.5	23.7	14.5
CPI	48.1	19.9	16.3	20.2
Wholesale prices	45.1	18.5	17.5	21.0
Tradables[a]	42.6	14.1	11.5	12.5
Nontradables[a]	46.1	24.7	20.7	22.8
Nontradables, excluding housing	64.1	34.5	24.4	20.8
Exchange rate[b]	45.0	16.0	2.4	16.1

Source: Central Bureau of Statistics.
a. Excluding fruit, vegetables, and controlled goods and services.
b. Versus currency basket.

exchange-rate regime. The public assesses the credibility of these declarations and forms its inflationary expectations accordingly. The expectations will, in turn, affect the setting of prices and the negotiations for wage contracts, while the government has to assess this behavior and determine its future policy.

It should be noted that such a game determines the average inflation rate itself, not *relative* prices, which are related to macro conditions. However, as experience and theory show, in the wake of exchange-rate-based stabilizations, such a game will usually result in a real appreciation as government credibility is gradually built up. We believe that such a model is appropriate in explaining the Israeli inflation, although we are aware that this is a mere hypothesis. In what follows we will try to support it with a few theoretical considerations and some empirical evidence.

Let us present the background for this game after the July 1985 stabilization program. A major component was the government's declared policy with regard to the exchange rate. With the implementation of the stabilization program, a stable exchange rate was announced. However, there was no strict commitment to a fixed exchange rate. On the contrary, the behavior of the exchange rate was tied to future developments in wages, i.e., it was announced that the exchange rate would not remain absolutely fixed if wages did not "behave." Indeed, after the 1986 upsurge in real wages a devaluation was carried out in January 1987, as part of a broader policy package involving an agreed wage concession (see Bruno and Piterman 1988). After January 1987, a somewhat tighter announcement was made, stating that devaluations would not automatically accommodate future wage increases (see *The National Budget 1988*); however, it was understood that realignment, though rare, would occur if the circumstances (e.g., sharp loss of competitiveness) warranted such action.

The Bank of Israel's notion was to gradually lengthen the periods between step-wise alignments and reduce the size of devaluations until nominal wages and prices stabilized. Rather than adopt an extreme once-and-for-all pegged-exchange-rate stance and at the same time avoid the other extreme of automatic accommodation to wage behavior, such an intermediate strategy was expected to induce wage discipline through the gradual buildup of government credibility. According to this scheme, the Bank of Israel advocated another alignment of 6-7% in March 1988, 14 months after the preceding one. However, with elections approaching, the Minister of Finance adopted a "wait and see" attitude: at no stage during most of 1988 was it made clear to the business sector that there would be no devaluation. At the same time no alignment was in fact made until after the elections, in December 1988, 23 months after the previous alignment, and only after very heavy capital outflows. The postponement dictated a larger devaluation than that of January 1987, thus the previously planned gradualist exchange-rate-adjustment scheme was not followed, undermining the credibility of exchange-rate announcements.

In January 1989 a ±3% band around the new exchange rate was introduced to enable greater flexibility in monetary policy. That, too, may have been misinterpreted by the strong and rather vocal export lobby as signaling a more flexible export-oriented exchange-rate policy. Moreover, there were inconsistent announcements by various policy makers. Some advocated more flexibility, others advocated a harder stance; this made the public's task in evaluating the government's intentions even more difficult.

A large part of the reason for the inconsistency of declarations over time lies in the underlying differences of view among policy makers (and their private advisors). There is an obvious conflict between the key role of a stable *nominal* exchange rate as a nominal anchor and the time-honored pledge to keep the *real* exchange rate from appreciating. The first was stressed by the Bank of Israel; the second has usually directed the exporters' lobby and played a more important role with the Ministry of Finance.

There are other factors in the government's policy and actions, besides the exchange rate, that affect the process of expectations and credibility formation—in particular, fundamentals such as the budget deficit or the government's willingness to bail out ailing firms. Indeed, since July 1985 the government's policy with regard to such fundamentals has changed considerably. Another important factor affecting inflationary expectations is government action regarding subsidy cuts and other prices under its control. After the implementation of the program and until the end of 1988 the government refrained from pushing up these prices, and their average annual increases were lower than the average inflation. However, since January 1989 their rates have exceeded other rates of change (excluding housing; see figure 7.8).[30]

After the implementation of the stabilization program, the public assessed the new conditions and formed new inflationary expectations.

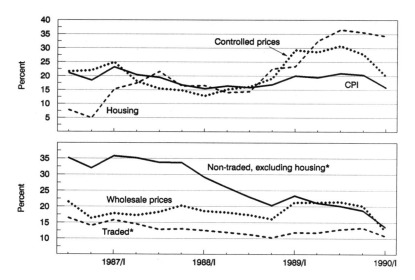

Figure 7.8
Selected price indexes, 1986-1989 (annual percentage change of last four quarters).
(* Excluding fruit, vegetables, and controlled goods and services.)

It seems that fundamental factors and the evaluation of the government's declarations and actions, together with tight monetary policy, were sufficient to bring inflation down to about 20%, but no further.[31]

Various studies suggest that a major element in determining expectations may be lagged inflation, thus indicating that the formation of expectations has a partial adjustment element. Since inflation remained more or less stable, it also had a reinforcing stabilizing effect on expectations.[32]

A moderate inflation rate that remains more or less stable after a stabilization program is not a unique Israeli phenomenon; it is shared by other recent successful stabilization experiences, such as in Chile and Mexico, where a pegged-exchange-rate regime was implemented with stabilization. It seems that in those countries, too, the inflation rate can be the outcome of a similar game in which the credibility of the government is tested and inflationary expectations adjust gradually (see Kiguel and Liviatan 1989). Only after full credibility is achieved, especially when fundamental factors are consistent with a fixed exchange rate with no alignments, will inflationary expectations converge to Western rates.

The steady and gradual decrease in velocity of circulation of deposits (see figure 7.9) suggests that the credibility buildup was rather slow, and the tightening of declarations after 1987, together with other fundamen-

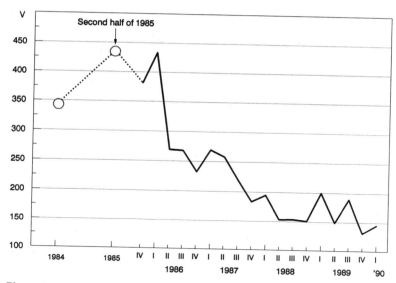

Figure 7.9
Velocity of circulation.

tal government policies, contributed to this trend. However, the declaration by the new Finance Minister, in January 1989, and the apparent shift in targets (more export-oriented than before, resulting in an additional small realignment in June 1989 and a different attitude toward controlled prices) may have hampered credibility in the exchange rate as a nominal anchor.

The expectations argument and the slow credibility buildup can only partly explain why wages increased as much as they did in 1986–1988. Since the exchange-rate policy declared in July 1985 signaled that if wages were to increase excessively realignment would follow, it could very well be that firms did yield to workers' demands more than they would have done had the declaration been a somewhat "harder" one.[33] Indeed, after the tighter declaration of January 1987 there were lower nominal wage hikes, although higher than price increases. One could also interpret the fall in real wages in 1989 as a sign that the gradual learning process is finally beginning to bear fruit.

In spite of the previous argument, the explanation of nominal wage behavior since 1987 remains incomplete. An additional explanation of the surge in real wages has to do with the institutional structure of wage contracts in Israel, on the one hand, and the restructuring process, on the other. The institutional factors include economy-wide arrangements such as across-the-board wage increases stimulated by wage hikes in the large public sector (see figure 7.7),[34] too slow an adjustment in COLA arrangements, or the minimum wage law, which compelled firms to raise wages above the level warranted by market forces. The restructuring process and the downward rigidities in the labor market make it difficult to reduce wages in firms that have run into difficulties, whereas firms that are doing well may increase real wages according to productivity. The two together result in a ratchet-like increase in average wages.[35] Note that although we present several arguments that may explain an increase in wages, we are not sure that these provide a full answer. Finally, theoretical considerations (see Helpman and Leiderman 1988) suggest that an exogenous shock to wages will result in steeper price increases if firms have monopolistic power. However, the evidence from a cross-section analysis of the manufacturing sector does not support this hypothesis (in contrast with the case of Mexico, presented elsewhere in this volume).

We end this section by pointing out one positive feature of the inflation profile that seems to be emerging from the data for 1989. If we exclude the housing sector from the price index, the wage and price increases in non-traded goods and services seem to be gradually converging toward those of tradable goods.[36] The latter has been more or less stable for the past three years, in spite of the irregularity of devaluations. These developments suggest that with an ongoing slack in the labor market, the inflation rate (excluding the housing sector) may be heading downward, provided the prices of controlled goods are kept within the bounds of average inflation. However, housing prices are most likely to continue rising at higher rates, owing to the immigration wave from the Soviet Union.

5. What Lies Ahead?

We have discussed in great detail the causes of the Israeli recession in the past two years, emphasizing that it can, at least in part, be attributed to the restructuring process in the economy. In this concluding section we will try to assess where the economy is heading in the near future.

The most recent economic indicators suggest that somewhere in the beginning of 1990 the economy started very slowly to move out of the depths of the recent recession. Higher growth rates in the near future could be expected on the basis of the improved aggregate supply conditions—the sharp reduction in real interest rates and the reduction in per-unit labor costs. The latter trend could continue, given the slack in the labor market. To this one should add a likely cyclical upturn in private consumption and housing demand, as well as a planned increase in investment in infrastructure, a long-neglected area.

On top of the improved supply and demand conditions there is an extremely important additional factor: immigration from the Soviet Union. Experience has shown that in the first year of absorption an immigrant contributes mainly to a net increase in aggregate demand (mainly for housing), and only later does that person participate in the increased supply to the labor market. A large immigration wave will stimulate economic activity, but a higher rate of activity may be a temporary phenomenon and can by no means ensure transition to sustainable growth. The latter depends on the continued restructuring process as well as on the systematic pursuit of the various reforms mentioned, not the least of which has to do with a further cut in the size of the government's expenditure and the extent of its involvement in the economy.

One problem that may still plague policy makers (and politicians) is the recent sharp increase in unemployment. Although its increase may have come to a halt, a relatively high level of unemployment is likely to linger on as the increased output growth may be accompanied by a substantial increase in productivity. Structural factors are also likely to persist (e.g., the rise in participation rates).

Another issue that emerged in 1989 and is likely to intensify with the advent of large immigration is the pressure on the housing market. Though conditions exist for a further reduction in inflation in the rest of the economy, acceleration of housing prices, given present CPI-linked COLA agreements on wages, may push wages and prices upward if proper moderating measures are not undertaken.

An important indicator of sustainable growth is the level of new capital formation so as to ensure that capacity at least keeps up with output growth. For some time, output can draw upon unutilized capacity, but ultimately the surest guarantee of renewed growth is a suitable flow of investment spurred by the producers' own profit incentives and not by excessive government support, as was the case in the 1970s.

The aging of capital stock, part of which is now obsolete, indicates the existence of an even more serious problem in terms of *net* investment (after discards). This is even more disturbing in view of the fact that technological innovation is usually embodied in new equipment. A rough estimate of the gross investment necessary for capital stock to keep pace with a 5–6% growth in business-sector GDP suggests that investment should rise from its current level of 18.5% to at least 21–23% of GNP within a few years.

What is holding back investment today? In the past, it could be argued that limitations on domestic savings and on foreign borrowing were the effective limits on investment. This, we have seen, is no longer the case. Nor do the present lower rates of interest hinder new investments. The reasons for the sustained lower rate of investment in the business sector have to do with the low profitability and higher effective tax rates already mentioned (see section 2 and table 7.2) as well as with economic and political uncertainty. There has recently been a surge of interest on part of some large foreign investors, but so far it has taken the form of financial portfolio investments rather than new real capacity buildup. Renewed economic activity and improved profitability are likely to bring about an endogenous increase in investment, but that remains to be seen.

Acknowledgments

We would like to thank Stan Fischer, Mordechai Fraenkel, Elhanan Helpman, Nissan Liviatan, Zalman Shiffer, and the participants of the Research Department's seminar at the Bank of Israel for illuminating comments on an earlier draft. Galit Gonen and Rimona Cohen provided able research assistance.

Notes

1. The detailed developments in the period until mid-1987 were analyzed in Bruno and Piterman 1988 and in the subsequent Bank of Israel Annual Report for 1987, published in May 1988. A longer-term view of the crisis and the reform process was recently given in Bruno 1989.

2. Given the highly concentrated Israeli banking system (five banking groups comprising the bulk of banking activity), strong direct "moral suasion" had to be applied by the Bank of Israel in May 1989.

3. See Bruno and Piterman 1988 and Cukierman 1988.

4. This study is based on annual observations for the period 1962–1988. An additional long-run effect on the output supply side comes from reduced potential capacity due to very high real interest rates in the pre-stabilization period, estimated by Lavi (1989) at 0.5% per annum but ignored here.

5. By 1989 relative prices had changed direction, and exports eventually started growing again.

6. This stage of adjustment can be rather short, as testified by the orthodox stabilizations of European hyperinflations in the 1920s (Sargent 1982).

7. The issue of exchange-rate and wage-formation credibility is taken up in greater detail in section 4.

8. We compare the average real labor cost per unit of output during 1982–1984 to the labor cost in 1989. The gap between real wage increases and productivity growth gradually narrowed between 1986 and 1988 (the annual figures being, respectively, 6%, 4%, and 1%). In 1989 real unit wage costs actually fell. Thus a gradual learning process has occurred (see also section 4).

9. The Finance Ministry has recently reduced corporate taxes and has extended the reform in income taxation, offset by a 1% higher value-added tax.

10. See Fischer 1986 and Bruno and Piterman 1988.

11. Only in major financial crises such as in the agricultural sector did the government step in (see section 3).

12. The data collected here do not distinguish between the sizes of different firms.

13. We have data suggesting that the number of afflicted firms increased sharply, but we do not present them here since the method of estimation is somewhat inconsistent over time.

14. Between May 1925 and the low point of April 1926 industrial production dropped 17% and the unemployment rate rose from 3.5% to over 20% (see Garber 1982, tables VIII and X).

15. In Austria and Poland of the 1920s we find a similar recession a few years after successful stabilization (see Wicker 1986). See also Siklos 1989 on Hungary in the 1940s.

16. Koor Industries, for example, used an ill-fated foreign loan of over $100 million (floated through Drexel Burnham at over 13% interest) only to postpone its crisis from 1986 to 1988. In spite of considerable progress in output and employment restructuring, Koor has not yet recovered from its financial difficulties.

17. It is also possible that the public realized that the government was not as determined as before to proceed with the planned reforms, as elections were approaching.

18. For an analysis of the first phase see Bruno and Piterman 1988. For a more detailed and updated analysis of financial factors in the stabilization process see Piterman 1989.

19. Additional disaggregation into shekel and foreign-exchange-linked credit shows particularly high real interest rates right after stabilization—an average rate of 82% in the second half of 1985 (see Bank of Israel, *Annual Report 1988*, table VIII-9).

20. Litvin and Meridor (1983) have estimated the average rate for the 1970s at *minus* 17%, which implies a grant-equivalent amounting to one half of investment.

21. This was recently pointed out by Piterman (1989). Assuming that principal is rolled over while interest payments are paid on a current basis, the average repayment period of short-term debt (i.e., the ratio of principal to the interest rate) rose from 5.5 months in the first half of 1985 to 10.6 months in the second half and to 31.9 months in 1986. It has stayed more or less the same in 1988 (29.2 months). In other words, this interest-rate illusion is a one-time effect. Such "rescheduling" can be effective in the long run only if the real rate of interest is lower than the profit rate.

22. Only 30% of the increased debt between 1984 and 1988 is to be ascribed to above-"normal" long-term interest rates. The rest stems from the refinance of past investment (part of which has to be written off) and collective consumption uses (such as improved housing conditions). It should be pointed out that the kibbutz movement derives only 45% of its income from agriculture, the rest coming from manufacturing and services.

23. The table and the discussion are based on Piterman 1989.

24. The share of marketable bonds in total new government indexed bond issues has increased from 4% in 1984 to 63% in 1988 (see Ben-Bassat 1989).

25. The substantial write-offs eliminated commercial banks' profits in 1988. The profit rate for 1989 remained a low 4% on average.

26. From the introduction of the stabilization program until August 1986, the exchange rate remained fixed against the dollar, resulting in an unplanned depreciation of the shekel against a wider basket of currencies. Therefore, since August 1986 the exchange rate was pegged to a basket of Israel's principal trading partners' currencies.

27. This index relates only to CPI, whereas a more adequate index should relate to the GDP deflator. However, we do not have a disaggregation of the GDP price index into tradables and non-tradables. For an alternative indicator of unit labor costs see table 7.1. This indicator rose 9.5% in 1988 and declined 4% in 1989.

28. Those not controlled by the government.

29. See, for example, Cukierman 1988 and Horn and Persson 1987.

30. In Israel controlled prices encompass about one-fifth of the CPI index. However, empirical studies suggest that they have a significant signaling effect (see Melnick 1989). Moreover, when a budget deficit emerges there is a strong political incentive to cut subsidies rather than tangle with individual ministries over a cut in their share of the expenditure pie.

31. As often mentioned (see Bruno and Piterman 1988), it may very well be that the unplanned devaluation in the first half of 1986 (due to the pegging of the shekel to the dollar) caused inflation to go down to 20% and not to a lower rate.

32. See, for example, Gottlieb et al. 1985 and Offenbacher 1985.

33. The fact that governments "tie their own hands," as in the European Monetary System (EMS), has certainly helped bring about a faster convergence of inflation in traditionally inflation-prone European countries (Italy, France). It is important to note that in this case, too, that substantial real appreciation took place and that the process of inflation convergence took several years. See Giavazzi and Giovannini 1989.

34. For example, the I.A.I, which ran into trouble in 1987, was forced to increase wages due to institutional arrangements (specifically, the link between the I.A.I.'s wages and the public-sector wage agreements).

35. For a more detailed analysis of wage policy and wage behavior during the first and second phases of the disinflation see Artstein and Sussman 1988.

36. The relative convergence of wages can be seen in table 7.7 by comparing wages in the service and commerce industries with the total for the business sector. For prices, the absolute gap between the two sectors has been gradually falling from about 20% in 1986–87 to 15%, then 10% and 6% by the third quarter of 1989.

References

Artstein, Yael, and Zvi Sussman. 1988. Wage Policy During Disinflation: The Israeli Stabilization Program of 1985. Bank of Israel Research Department Discussion Paper no. 88.07.

Bank of Israel. 1988. *A Plan for the Resumption of Growth and the Lowering of Inflation.* (In Hebrew).

Ben-Bassat, Avraham. 1989. Capital Market Reform, Goals and First Results. Bank of Israel Research Department Discussion Paper no. 89.08.

Ben-Bassat, Idit. 1989. Price Indexes for Tradable and Nontradable Goods. Bank of Israel Research Department Discussion Paper no. 89.11.

Ben-Rawe, Yoram. 1989. The Interest Rate Burden of Short Term Credit on Industries, 1983–1988. Bank of Israel Research Department Discussion Paper no. 89.07.

Bruno, Michael. 1989. Israel's Crisis and Economic Reform: A Historical Perspective. NBER Working Paper no. 3075.

Bruno, Michael, and Sylvia Piterman. 1988. "Israel's stabilization: A two years' review." In *Inflation Stabilization: The Experience of Israel, Argentina, Brazil, Bolivia, and Mexico*, M. Bruno, G. Di Tella, R. Dornbusch, and S. Fischer, eds. (MIT Press).

Cukierman, Alex. 1988. "The end of the high Israeli inflation—An experiment in heterodox stabilization." In *Inflation Stabilization: The Experience of Israel, Argentina, Brazil, Bolivia, and Mexico*, M. Bruno, G. Di Tella, R. Dornbusch, and S. Fischer, eds. (MIT Press).

Fischer, Stanley. 1977. "Long term contracts, rational expectations, and the optimal money supply rule." *Journal of Political Economy* 85 (no. 1): 191–205.

Fischer, Stanley. 1986. "Exchange rate versus money target in disinflation." In *Indexing, Inflation, and Economic Policy*, S. Fischer, ed. (MIT Press).

Garber, Peter M. 1982. "Transition from inflation to price stability." In *Carnegie-Rochester Conference Series on Public Policy* 16.

Giavazzi, F., and A. Giovannini. 1989. *Limited Exchange Rate Flexibility: The European Monetary System*. MIT Press.

Gottlieb, Daniel, Rafi Melnick, and Sylvia Piterman. 1985. "Inflationary expectations in Israel: A multiple indicators approach." *Journal of Business & Economic Statistics* 3 (no. 2): 112–117.

Helpman, Elhanan, and Leornardo Leiderman. 1988. "Stabilization in high inflation countries: Analytical foundations and recent experience." In *Carnegie Rochester Conference Series* 28.

Horn, Henrik, and Torston Persson. 1987. "Exchange rate policy, wage formation and credibility." *European Economic Review* 32 (no. 8): 1621–1636.

Kiguel, Miguel A., and Nissan Liviatan. 1988. "Inflationary rigidities and orthodox stabilization policies: Lessons from Latin America." *World Bank Economic Review* 2 (no. 3): 273–298.

Kiguel, Miguel A., and Nissan Liviatan. 1989. The Business Cycle Associated with Exchange Rate Based Stabilization. Mimeograph.

Kislev, Yoav, Zvi Lerman, and Pinhas Zusman. 1989. Experience with Credit Co-operatives in Israeli Agriculture. Center for Agricultural Economic Research, Rehovoth, Working Paper 8902.

Lavi, Yaacov. 1989. Interest Rate Effect on Investment in Israel: 1962–1988. Bank of Israel Research Department Discussion Paper no. 89.08.

Litvin, Uri, and Leora Meridor. 1977. "Policy measures and their effect on exports and real exchange rates." In *Israel Economic Papers*, N. Halevi and Y. Kop, eds. (Jerusalem: Israel Economic Association and Falk Institute). (In Hebrew.)

Litvin, Uri, and Leora Meridor. 1983. "The grant equivalent of subsidized investment in Israel." *Bank of Israel Economic Review* 54 (April): 5–30.

Liviatan, Nissan. 1989. Israel's Stabilization Cycle with Some Reference to Latin American experience. Mimeograph.

Melnick, Rafi. 1989. Forecasting Short Run Inflation in Israel 1983–87: An Evaluation. Bank of Israel Research Department Discussion Paper No. 89.06.

Offenbacher, Edward K. 1985. "Empirical research on money demand in Israel." *Bank of Israel Economic Review* 60: 3–16.

Piterman, Sylvia. 1989. Economic Stabilization in Israel: Financial Difficulties in the Adjustment Process to Low Inflation. Mimeograph.

Regev, H. 1989. *Job Turnover, Productivity and Efficiency in Israeli Manufacturing Firms During the 1980s*. Jerusalem: Central Bureau of Statistics. (In Hebrew.)

Sargent, T. J. 1982. "The end of four big inflations." In *Inflation: Causes and Effects*, R. E. Hall, ed. (University of Chicago Press).

Siklos, Pierre L. 1989. "The end of the Hungarian hyperinflation of 1945–1946." *Journal of Money, Credit and Banking* 21 (no. 2): 135–147.

Taylor, John. 1979. "Staggered wage setting in a macro model." *American Economic Review Papers and Proceedings* 69: 108–113.

The National Budget 1988. Jerusalem: Ministry of Finance, Ministry of the Economy and the Bank of Israel. (In Hebrew.)

Wicker, Elmus. 1986. "Terminating hyperinflations in the dismembered Habsburg monarchy." *American Economic Review* 76 (June): 350–364.

Comments by Stanley Fischer

The Bruno-Meridor paper brings us up to date on developments in Israel's economy four and a half years after the implementation of its heterodox stabilization program. Whereas economic performance in the first two years, discussed at the Toledo conference, was superb, the next two and a half years were marked by a serious recession and continuing inflation at around 20% per year.

The authors' goal is to account for both the 1988–89 recession and the continuation of high inflation. Their thesis is that a period of recession is inevitable some time after an exchange-rate-based stabilization, which by its nature results in a real appreciation after the fixing of the exchange rate. As they explain: "Real appreciation, however, teaches the private sector not to increase prices or wages while relying on the authorities to accommodate by a devaluation."

While there is much else of interest in the paper—particularly the very important analysis of the long-term effects of high real interest rates and the discussion of the beginnings of a restructuring of Israeli industry—I will concentrate on the issue of the inevitability of recession. I will also briefly discuss the continuation of the 20% inflation.

Heterodox Stabilization

The analysis on which the 1985 heterodox stabilization program in Israel was based was that *both* the real and the nominal equilibria of the economy had to be changed, and that they could be shifted simultaneously with very little loss in output. The hope was to adjust monetary and fiscal policy to ensure a sustainable real equilibrium, which would also be consistent with a sustainable low inflation rate, and to use wage and price controls to avoid the unemployment problems that typically occur when inflation decelerates.

Three variables were seen as needing adjustment if Israel was to emerge from its economic crisis: the fiscal deficit was too large, the real wage was higher than the economy could sustain, and a real devaluation was needed.

There was some uncertainty about the real exchange rate, for a significant depreciation had taken place at the end of 1983 and the current account was in reasonably good shape. It was also generally agreed that once the inflation rate had been reduced, a major economic restructuring that would reduce the role and the size of government would be needed for growth to resume.

Although there had earlier been discussion of the possibility that the Israeli inflation was a "bubble," that was not the general view—nor would it have been a plausible one—by 1985. It is important to emphasize that the authors of the stabilization plan did not believe that the problem was simply to move the economy from a high-inflation equilibrium to a low-inflation equilibrium, with no change in the real equilibrium; rather, the analysis was that the real equilibrium of the economy had to be changed.

The announced program was a tough one, intended to cut the budget deficit by at least 5% of GNP. Subsidies were cut sharply, and some government spending cuts were announced. The currency was devalued and the exchange rate fixed, at least for a time. Wages and prices were allowed a one-time adjustment and then frozen at levels that caused a significant reduction in the real wage.[1] Government employment was to be cut.

The effects of the first stage of the stabilization plan lasted only six months. In the business sector, the real wage was back up to its pre-stabilization level within six months; in the public sector too, wages rose rapidly after six months. The cuts in the public-sector work force came to an end in the last quarter of 1985. By mid-1986 public-sector employment was well above its level at the time of stabilization (figure 7.2).

It is hardly an exaggeration to say that by early 1986 only one of the three real factors which had been assumed to underlie the economy's difficulties had been changed—the fiscal deficit had been cut by as much as 8% of GNP, chiefly as a result of the combination of subsidy cuts and the Tanzi effect on government revenues. It is also only a slight exaggeration to say that by early 1986 the heterodox phase was over: wages were not controlled, and prices were reasonably rapidly decontrolled. From 1986 on, orthodox stabilization was necessary.

The roots of the difficulties faced in 1988 and 1989 lie in the six-month period after the stabilization plan; indeed, they can be traced to a very early decision, in mid-July 1985. At that time the Histadrut and the employers' association reached a new wage agreement, ratified by the government, that indexed wages and provided for nominal wage increases of 4% a month for three months starting at the end of 1985. In effect, the agreement assumed that the real wage needed to be cut for only six months. Equally important, by failing to drop wage indexation, and maintaining central bargaining, the agreement signaled that there would be no change in the method of wage determination in the economy.[2]

The signal was thus given early on that on the wage front it was back to "business as usual" with regard to the method of wage determination and the level of the real wage. Once that signal had been given, the analysis of the Bruno-Meridor paper falls into place. After that, there was indeed no alternative to teaching the private sector a lesson through continued tight money, high real interest rates, and currency appreciation: a recession was inevitable if the inflation rate was to be kept low.

The Alternative

How inevitable was the recession, the result of the need to maintain pressure on aggregate demand through monetary policy? The answer requires a judgment on the political possibilities. From an economic viewpoint, the equilibrium that was being reached early in 1990 could have been reached soon after the stabilization. If the real wage had not been allowed back to its earlier level, and especially if the further increases in 1986 and 1987 had been prevented,[3] the recession of 1988–89 need not have happened. Nor need the period of high real interest rates have been so long.

Politically, the government was at its strongest shortly after the stabilization. Had it been willing to stage a confrontation with labor at that time, it might have succeeded in reducing inflation at a lower long-run cost than the country ultimately paid. The basic assumption in 1985 was that in the face of a clearly perceived national economic emergency, the social partners would agree to make the needed real adjustments in the economy without the further pressure of a recession. Of course, it would have taken tough bargaining to reach such an agreement. As the attempt was not made, we cannot know whether such a change would have been possible if the government had been willing to be tougher at the early stages.

Further, Israeli fiscal policy was essentially immobilized after the stabilization. In the face of the wage pressure, the government could, in principle, have undertaken a restrictive fiscal policy, in particular cutting back government expenditures. That would have taken some of the pressure off monetary and exchange-rate policy, permitting lower real interest rates earlier. However, after the stabilization the battle was always to prevent an increase in the budget deficit: fiscal policy held on, fortunately successfully, by its fingertips.

A Success in Any Case

Even if the stabilization could have been done better, and no doubt it could have been, the overall program has been a success. The inflation rate is down to 20% per annum rather than 20% per month. The budget deficit is at a sustainable level, and budgetary discipline has essentially been maintained. The external situation has not been a problem since 1985, except at times when a near-term devaluation was likely.

There were times when the program could have gone off track. Early in 1986 the government was under pressure to "go for growth"—which meant an easing of fiscal policy. It resisted that temptation. It has mostly hung tough in negotiations on bailing out victims of the financial crisis. At the end of 1987 the government took the tough decision not to produce the Lavi fighter plane—a decision which, as the authors point out, was followed by major increases in productivity in the aircraft manufacturing industry. This fiscal discipline was essential to the maintenance of low inflation, and the government deserves much credit for it.

While fiscal discipline was maintained, exchange-rate policy kept counter-inflationary pressure on the private sector. It would have been better to agree in 1985 that the real wage should not increase unless productivity did, and to end wage indexation. Then, in all likelihood, the real interest rate could have been reduced more rapidly and many of the difficulties analyzed in the Bruno-Meridor paper would have been avoided.

Continuing Inflation

The continuation of inflation at about the 20% level is one of the most interesting and puzzling common post-stabilization features. Aside from inflationary momentum, and the reliance on seignorage as a means of financing the government, it is difficult to understand the reasons for the inflation. And since the seignorage revenues are reasonably small, it would seem that a further fiscal correction could remove the inflation.

Even without understanding why the inflation continues, it is possible to discuss policies that would be needed to end it. The choices are similar, on a reduced scale, to those faced at the time of the original stabilization. The government has to make the fiscal adjustments needed to enable it to manage with the seignorage revenue corresponding to low, single-digit inflation. It then faces the choice between orthodox stabilization that will produce a further recession (the 1988–89 recession did not reduce the inflation rate) and a heterodox program.

The heterodox element would be a new type of wage agreement that ends wage indexation and keeps the rate of nominal wage increase low. The exchange rate could then be held constant (against a basket), and fiscal and credit policy could be used to ensure consistency of aggregate demand and supply. At the same time, it is important to pursue more vigorously the needed structural adjustments in the economy, which have been taking place only very slowly since 1985.

A heterodox approach is preferable to continuing the orthodox stabilization program that is perforce being followed now. However, that does not ensure that it will happen.

Notes

1. Strictly speaking, wage agreements are reached between the Histadrut and the industrialists, and ratified by the government. However, in the circumstances of mid-1985, the government was sure to take a major role in any wage negotiation.

2. This point has been emphasized by Emmanuel Sharon, who, as Director-General of the Ministry of Finance, played a key role in the stabilization program.

3. The extraordinary behavior of the real wage in Israel may be seen from the fact that the increase in the real wage in Israel from 1984 to 1989 exceeds the increase in each of the major OECD economies; while the Israeli real wage in the business sector rose over 20%, the real wage in the U.S. business sector rose 2.5% and that in Japan 14%.

General Discussion

Some of the participants were concerned about the discrete adjustments in the exchange rate. Guillermo Ortiz pointed out that such a regime may seem to hurt credibility, and that a crawling peg, as in Mexico, seems preferable. Jacob Frenkel answered that a crawling peg has its disadvantages since it loosens the nominal anchor. He added that one should distinguish between credibility that stems from fundamentals (such as the budget) and credibility with nominal variables. The former seems more important. Don Patinkin noted that the importance of the credibility issue is rather exaggerated. He attributes more importance to the cooperation the government got from the private sector, which had become fed up with the adverse consequences of high inflation. Patinkin also pointed out that the credibility issue became popular only recently, and he wondered whether this could stem from the fact that governments became less credible by attempting tasks they never undertook before. Peter Bernholz disagreed: he thinks governments are no different than before, but there is a big difference compared to the gold-standard era, when even unstable countries were forced into discipline by the regime itself.

Some participants addressed the hike in real interest rates and pointed out that such a phenomenon characterized many countries that had undergone stabilizations. However, there were some differences. Miguel Kiguel distinguished between developments in Latin America and Israel. In the former deposit rates rose after stabilization, whereas in the latter lending rates increased. Sweder van Wijnbergen pointed out the differences between Mexico and Israel: In the former, the high real rate reflects mostly the risk premium on nominal debt, whereas in Israel no such phenomenon occurred. Guillermo Ortiz and Don Patinkin asked whether the high interest rate had significant redistributive effects.

8   Mexico Beyond the Debt Crisis: Toward Sustainable Growth with Price Stability

Guillermo Ortiz

After the outbreak of the debt crisis in 1982, Mexico, like most other indebted countries in Latin America, endured several years of stagnation and high inflation. At the end of 1987, Mexico implemented a "heterodox" stabilization program that has lasted over two years with minor modifications. The program can be credited with important achievements. Inflation was brought down from an average annual rate of 225% in the last quarter of 1987 to less than 20% in 1989. A recession was avoided after the shock program, and economic growth has picked up in recent months. This is all the more remarkable since the program was implemented under adverse external conditions and practically no external financing.

A distinct feature of the Mexican stabilization program is that structural policies were vigorously implemented in addition to the macroeconomic and incomes policies adopted. In particular, trade liberalization, deregulation, and the privatization of public enterprises seem to have played an important role in improving expectations and increasing economic efficiency.

The success of the program has given rise to new problems. The rise in aggregate demand (a feature observed in other cases of heterodox stabilization), the appreciation of the exchange rate, and the effects of trade liberalization have caused a rapid increase in imports. Interest rates in real terms have remained at very high levels since the program was launched, and the relative price of controlled goods has deteriorated. There is also the question of the speed and timing of the lifting of price controls. These are some of the challenges to be faced in the near future.

This paper reviews the Mexican stabilization experience of the past two years. Section 1 provides the background to explain the rise in inflation after the onset of the debt crisis. Sections 2 and 3 deal with the first results of the program and some of the more relevant aspects of the stabilization strategy. Section 4 analyzes recent developments and current challenges. The final section presents some conclusions.

1. Background: The Debt Crisis and the Adjustment Period, 1983–1987

Compared with other debtor countries in Latin America, Mexico's experience with high inflation is relatively recent. From the mid 1950s until the early 1970s, inflation remained stable, at a level comparable with that observed in the United States and other industrialized countries. Double-digit inflation became chronic after 1975, but remained under 30% (annual rate) until 1982. In that year—which marked the unraveling of the debt crisis—the exchange rate was devalued 466%, bringing about a discrete jump in inflation and a deep recession the following year.

The initial conditions facing the new administration of President Miguel de la Madrid can be summarized as follows: a total lack of credibility in government policies after several failed stabilization programs announced since mid 1981; severely strained relations with the private sector after the nationalization of the banking system; the payment

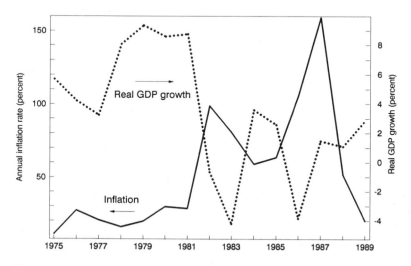

Figure 8.1
Inflation and real GDP growth, 1975–1989. Sources: Inflation—Banco de México; GDP growth—Secretaría de Programmación y Presupuesto.

of Mexdollar deposits in pesos at a substantially lower exchange rate than the one prevailing at the time in the free market, and the imposition of exchange controls (August–September 1982); acute instability in the financial markets (reflected in capital flight and disintermediation in the domestic banking system) and inflationary pressures resulting from the devaluations and internal imbalances; a high fiscal deficit (17.7% of GDP); and a stock of internal debt amounting to 23% of GDP (versus 15% in 1978). On the external front, Mexico had a current-account deficit, substantial payment arrears on the private-sector debt, and a huge total foreign debt. In addition, the financial arrangements that had been concluded with foreign creditors clearly indicated that a large negative resource transfer would exist in the foreseeable future.

The adjustment process followed since the eruption of the foreign-debt crisis can be divided into three stages. The first comprises the period from 1983 to mid 1985. The second begins with the oil shock of 1986, concluding with the stock market crash of October 1987. The third stage includes the two faces of the current stabilization program: the Pact for Economic Solidarity (Pacto de Solidaridad Economica, PSE) and the Pact for Stability and Growth (Pacto para la Estabilidad y Crecimiento Economico, PECE). The third stage is the main subject of this paper; it will be dealt with in a separate section.

The Initial Phase: 1983–1985

The immediate policy objectives of the economic program launched by the new administration at the end of 1982 (and supported by the IMF) were to abate inflation and to prevent the large-scale bankruptcies and unemployment that might result from the implementation of the adjustment program. To reduce inflation required correction of the fiscal imbalances, stabilization of the foreign-exchange markets, and a wage policy that would not fuel inflationary expectations.

The reduction of the fiscal deficit was the key element of the adjustment program. The main quantitative target was a reduction of the PSBR (Public Sector Borrowing Requirements) from 17.6% of GDP in 1982 to 8.5% in 1983, and to less than 4% in 1985. In the event, the adjustment undertaken in 1983 turned out to be much more severe than anticipated, making apparent the difficulties inherent in implementing a stabilization program in a country facing large resource transfers abroad. In particular, inflation and exchange-rate depreciation—and thus, inflationary pressures for the coming year—turned out much higher than anticipated. Consequently, compliance with the nominal targets of the program entailed a much sharper real adjustment than the adjustment originally contemplated. Thus, in 1983 the PSBR/GDP was indeed almost halved with respect to the 1982 levels; however, GDP fell 5% against an initial projection of zero growth. Although inflation was reduced from the levels of the previous year, it was still higher than the programmed target (80% vs. 55%).

Despite the significant fiscal correction of 1983 and a strict monetary policy aimed at accumulating foreign reserves, both the devaluation and the drastic corrections of public-sector prices reinforced the inertial element of inflation, rendering the process of stabilization more costly. In particular, the productive system had become overly dependent on the subsidies implicit in official prices, including the exchange rate, which had prevailed for many years. The sudden reduction of these subsidies led to a process of readjustment of relative prices reflected, in the short run, in inflationary pressures. In this context it is not surprising that difficulties were encountered in complying with the nominal fiscal targets. The deviations from the fiscal targets became more pronounced in 1985—as a result of rapid credit expansion to the private sector, an incipient revival of public investment, and declining oil prices—and the IMF program was interrupted. The authorities attempted to strengthen the fiscal situation and to correct an emerging deterioration of the balance of payments in mid 1985. However, the earthquakes that hit Mexico City in September 1985 and the sharp fall in international oil prices at the beginning of 1986 aggravated an already difficult situation.

The early demise of the 1984 recovery revealed the vulnerability of the economy to external shocks. As soon as the external environment turned less favorable and the economy began to grow, the balance of payments—and the general climate of expectations—deteriorated rapidly. This episode also uncovered the true dimensions of the debt overhang and the difficulties of implementing stabilization policies in a context of falling terms of trade and, more generally, of changing relative prices.

Figure 8.2 illustrates the magnitude of the fiscal effort undertaken. The primary balance of the public sector shifted from a negative 3.5% of GDP in 1982 (the figure for 1981 was –8%) to an average +4.8% in 1983–1987.

The counterpart to the drastic fiscal adjustment was an equally notable overshooting of the balance-of-payments targets. As seen in figure 8.3, the cumulative current-account surplus for the period 1983–1987 was

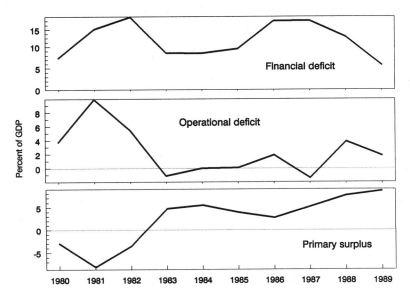

Figure 8.2
Financial deficit, operational deficit, and primary surplus, 1980–1989. Source:
Dirección Feneral de Planeación Hacendaria, Secretaría de Hacienda y Crédito
Público.

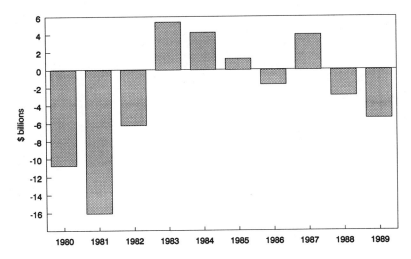

Figure 8.3
Current account. Source: Banco de México.

approximately $14 billion despite the fall in the terms of trade (table 8.1). This should be compared with a projected cumulative deficit of US$8 billion contemplated in the annual programs.

An important feature of the Mexican adjustment program was the adoption, from the outset, of structural policies. With respect to the public sector, in addition to (and as a result of) the correction of the fiscal imbalance, the government implemented a program of divestiture of public enterprises. In 1985, an ambitious and comprehensive program of trade liberalization was initiated. In 1982, virtually all imports were subject to non-tariff barriers; by the end of 1987 only 20.3% of the value of imports was subject to quantitative restrictions. At the same time, tariffs were reduced from a maximum level of 100% in 1982 to 45% in 1987.

The Oil Shock

The oil price shock of early 1986 forced a reconsideration of the economic program and a reordering of priorities. It soon became apparent that the magnitude of the shock was much greater than previously envisaged, and of a more permanent nature. Thus, the immediate concern of the authorities was to protect the balance of payments rather than to arrest inflation or sustain growth, and to avoid a depletion of foreign-exchange reserves. The program adopted included a very active exchange-rate policy, a tightening of credit policies, an increase in interest rates, and additional budget cuts and revenue measures. On the external front, the program included an arrangement with the IMF, debt scheduling with commercial banks and the Paris Club, and additional financing from

Table 8.1
Terms-of-trade index.

1980	100.0
1981	97.7
1982	85.2
1983	77.8
1984	76.3
1985	72.2
1986	52.0
1987	57.5
1988	52.0

Source: Banco de Mexico.

banks and multilateral sources. Structural policies aimed at reducing public-sector growth and at fostering trade liberalization were also considered an essential element of the program.

The magnitude of the oil shock was staggering: oil revenues declined by US$8.5 billion, equivalent to 6.5% of GDP, 40% of total export receipts, and 26% of public-sector revenues. Of course, economic activity suffered a severe decline and inflation accelerated (GDP fell 3.8% and CPI growth jumped from 64% in 1985 to 106% in 1986). These results were largely unavoidable given the magnitude of the exchange-rate depreciation (35% in real terms during 1986) and the fact that the economy had to absorb internally the total impact of the oil-price fall. Employment, on the other hand, did not suffer a significant decline, and major bankruptcies were avoided. On the positive side, the balance-of-payments results were quite remarkable, and financial intermediation strengthened significantly.

Developments in the first nine months of 1987 were quite positive, with the exception of the behavior of inflation. Economic activity began recovering in the second quarter of 1987, the balance of payments strengthened considerably, and financial savings also grew in real terms. This situation was, however, drastically modified after the stock market crash in October. A price correction of the Mexican stock market, which began in early October (after very large increases since mid 1986), turned into a crash prompted by the fall in Wall Street and other world stock markets. In a "flight to safety" reaction, investors switched from stocks to dollar-denominated assets, pressing the foreign-exchange market. The authorities decided to withdraw from the market in mid-November and to avoid reserve losses while preparing a comprehensive anti-inflationary program.

2. The Pact for Economic Solidarity

The stock market crash and the ensuing financial crisis fundamentally altered the economic strategy for 1988. It is paradoxical that a financial crisis should have occurred when international reserves were at a historical peak (at the end of 1987) and the balance of payments was recording a substantial surplus. But there is also little doubt that the inflationary environment amplified the nervousness of financial markets. Once more it became apparent that, in times of high inflation, expectations are extremely volatile and can easily destabilize what appeared to be an otherwise sound financial situation.

The crisis again brought the inflation problem to the forefront. The relatively good behavior of the economy in 1987—particularly the notable strengthening of the balance of payments and the spectacular rise of the stock market—had given many observers (and some members of the administration) the impression that the economy could function well at the existing inflation levels. However, the drastic change in expectations that took place in a matter of weeks made apparent the inherent fragility of the economic situation. It also underlined just how close Mexico was to hyperinflation: at the end of 1987, the annual inflation rate was above 150% and accelerating, and most forecasts for 1988 predicted an inflation rate of over 200%.

What was the cause of the rise of the rate of inflation in 1987? The immediate cause was the lagged effect of the very active exchange-rate policy applied in response to the oil shock of 1986. But this is just one manifestation of a more general problem faced by Mexico and other indebted countries in the presence of a debt overhang. This is closely associated with the fiscal dimension of the debt problem. To the extent that external debt obligations represented commitments of the public sectors in the debtor countries, governments faced the additional problem of extracting resources from the public to finance the debt service. Clearly, the different sectors of society tend to resist the government's attempts to levy additional taxes or to gather resources by increasing the real price of goods and services produced by public enterprises. Governments have had to resort to the inflation tax as a means of overcoming the resistance of society to the internal transfer of resources to the public sector.

In a way, inflation has played a "catalytic" role in the resource transfer effected by indebted countries, realized mostly through the reduction in real wages. These reductions, in turn, have often been brought about by abrupt exchange-rate depreciations. To the extent that nominal wages do not adjust immediately to abrupt exchange-rate depreciations, export competitiveness is temporarily improved. In addition to its impact on production costs, the fall in real wages dampens domestic demand, liberating domestic production for exports. In addition, if formal or informal indexation mechanisms are present, inflationary impulses tend to replicate themselves. These effects may help to explain why it has proved so difficult to implement successful stabilization programs in indebted countries, even though these countries often have large external surpluses.

The emergency program adopted after the oil shock led to an improvement in the balance of payments. The current-account surplus, the disbursement of some new money from commercial banks, and some capital inflows raised the level of reserves above US$14.5 billion in September ($10 billion higher than the figure recorded a year earlier). Thus, from a balance-of-payments perspective, the "initial conditions" that existed for the launching of the anti-inflation program were most appropriate. Regarding relative prices, although some distortions still existed with respect to public prices, as seen in figure 8.4, "controlled" prices (a concept including all publi-sector prices and some important private prices) rose about 20% in excess of non-controlled prices. This facilitated the utilization of several nominal anchors.

On December 15, 1987, President Miguel de la Madrid announced the Pact of Economic Solidarity (PSE), which was jointly signed by the government, labor, agricultural workers, and the private sector. The main objective was to stabilize the economy while avoiding a sharp recession. The pact's main features were as follows:

• An increase of the public sector's primary surplus by about 3 percentage points of GDP, through a reduction of expenditures of 1.5% of GDP (from 22% to 20.5%) and revenue measures consisting mostly of increases of prices and tariffs of public enterprises yielding about 1.5% of GDP. To

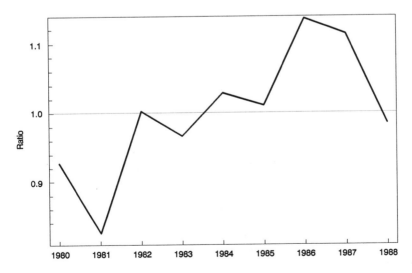

Figure 8.4
Controlled/noncontrolled prices. Source: Banco de México.

this effect, energy prices were raised about 85% in December, as were telephone rates, urban transportation, basic foodstuffs, etc. The new prices were to remain fixed until the end of February.

· A tightening of monetary policy. Tight credit ceilings were announced at the beginning of the year; commercial banks were given lending ceilings for January 1988 equal to 90% of the outstanding average balance existing in December 1987. This ceiling was further reduced to 85% in February.

· Trade-liberalization measures were implemented far ahead of schedule. Maximum tariffs were lowered from 45% to 20%, and practically all import permits (except those related to the agricultural sector and the automobile and pharmaceutical industries) were eliminated.

· After an initial depreciation of the controlled exchange rate of about 22%, with which a virtual unification was again attained, the exchange rate was to remain stable until the end of February.

· Wages were raised a cumulative 38% in December and on January 1, remaining fixed until the end of February.

The backbone of the program was the fiscal correction. In the short run, the fiscal overshooting was estimated to be sufficient to cover the bulging of real interest payments on domestic debt (stemming from the transitory high real interest rates) so as to achieve an operational balance. In the longer term, the primary surplus would also suffice to cover all interest payments on external debt, real interest payments on domestic debt, *plus* the loss of the inflation tax resulting as inflation lost momentum. These were the fundamentals.

The main "hetero" component of the program was, of course, the agreement between the different sectors to establish a path for key prices and to review this path in a concerted fashion according to rules.

The rapid decline in inflation allowed the lengthening of the period between agreements, introducing a more ambitious strategy for fighting inflation. Thus, within the framework of the negotiations held in March, May, August, and October 1988, minimum wages, the prices of public goods and services, controlled private prices, and the exchange rate were kept unaltered during the rest of the year.

The unveiling of the pact was received with widespread skepticism, not least since the initial impact of the price alignments and the exchange-rate depreciation was to almost double the inflation rate of December

1987 and January 1988 with respect to the average of the previous few months (14.8% and 15.5% in December and January, respectively). In addition, the presidential election, scheduled for July 1988, generated uncertainty as to whether the government's commitment to follow the austere fiscal program would hold. However, as inflation began to slow down and the public finance figures showed that the fiscal surplus was on track, the program began to gain credibility. The financial markets reacted favorably to the March 1988 arrangements: the stock market rose significantly, and large capital inflows were recorded. Nominal interest rates fell substantially, responding to the capital inflows and to the expectation of a substantially lower inflation rate in the months ahead; yet, as explained in the following section, real rates remained quite high.

3. Economic Stabilization: The Results of the Pact

Mexico's stabilization program included both orthodox or "fundamental" elements and "heterodox" features, consisting mainly of incomes policies through social accord and the utilization of nominal anchors to break inertial forces and to curb inflationary expectations. In this respect, the program has some features in common with those implemented in Argentina, Brazil, and (particularly) Israel. But unlike in Argentina and Brazil, the fundamentals were kept in place: monetary and fiscal policies remained tight. In addition, and as a result of the government's keeping its own commitments, the path of wages and other key prices was maintained close to the original targets.

Inflation in Mexico had an important inertial component that emerged from the built-in wage indexation mechanisms, which had become more pervasive with the passage of time; from the existence of the highly concentrated markets, which partly canceled wage adjustments (Alberro 1987); and from the negative and volatile expectations of economic agents associated with the debt overhang. To eliminate inflation in these circumstances, in addition to fiscal and monetary restraint, a change in indexation mechanisms is needed. In the Mexican and Israeli cases (Bruno and Piterman 1988) this problem was tackled by reaching social agreements.

A distinct feature of the Mexican experience was that the stabilization program was accompanied by important structural policies, beyond those undertaken in previous years. With the announcement of the pact, the trade-liberalization program was brought further ahead of schedule and was also considered an essential element of the anti-inflation strategy that would operate by imposing the discipline of international prices on domestic producers. The privatization program, implemented since the beginning of the de la Madrid administration, was also reinforced in 1988 in connection with the effort to strengthen the financial position of the public sector. The third leg of the process of structural change was the deregulation of economic activity. Although this program was also launched in 1983, only since the beginning of the current administration has it been applied on a significant scale.

Economic Activity in 1988: First Results

The basic objectives of the Pact for Economic Solidarity, lowering inflation and avoiding a sharp recession, were fully achieved. In 1988 the annual rate of inflation (51.7% measured by the CPI) was the lowest since 1982. The average monthly inflation rate in the second half of 1988 was 1.2%, compared with 9% in the second half of the previous year. Real GDP increased 1.1%, close to the 1.5% observed in 1987. Whereas in 1987 exports constituted the main source of demand expansion, the policy mix of the stabilization program contributed to a surge in private internal demand. Private consumption increased 2% in real terms in 1988, and private demand expanded 10.9%. Exports, however, grew only 2.7%, compared with 10.1% the previous year. The results were achieved despite adverse external conditions: a 10% deterioration of the terms of trade; a 3-percentage-point rise in the average interest rate of the external debt; and poor weather conditions, which had the double effect of a bad agricultural year and a considerable rise in grain imports. In addition, and in contrast with the Israeli experience, the Mexican program was implemented without external financial support; on the contrary, the country experienced substantial negative resource transfer.

The external shocks, combined with the overall economic uncertainty associated with the stabilization process itself, led to a sharp rise in domestic real interest rates, which had a drastic impact on public finances. Real interest payments on domestic public debt rose from –0.7% of GDP in 1987 to 7.7%. This increase more than compensated for the adjustment of the primary balance (7.6% of GDP); the operational balance then turned into a deficit of 3.5% of GDP (from a surplus of 1.4% observed in 1987).

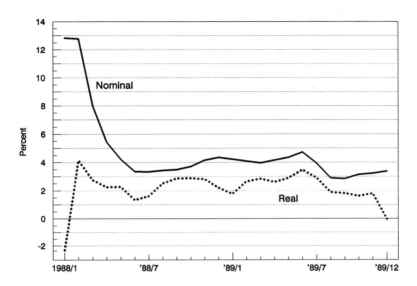

Figure 8.5
Real and nominal interest rates, 1988–1989.

The extremely high interest rates that prevailed in 1988 (figure 8.5) entailed a substantial resource transfer to the private sector. Although the higher income was reflected in a larger amount of private savings, this was insufficient to cover the borrowing requirements of the public sector and the private demand for credit, which also showed an unexpected rise. Thus, the initial rise in international reserves brought about by the sharp credit contraction imposed at the beginning of the program was reversed, and the international reserves declined after April. The other side of the coin was, of course, a deterioration of the current account, explained by the rise in private expenditures (particularly the recovery of private investment), the increase in international interest rates, and the once-and-for-all effect of the trade liberalization (table 8.2).

The fall in oil export receipts was compensated for by the dynamic behavior of non-oil exports, particularly manufacturing exports. The surge in imports, on the other hand, is probably explained for the most part by the opening of the economy, the exchange-rate appreciation, and the recovery of private investment, working through several channels. First, the opening of the economy had a direct effect on previously protected industries that saw their market shares threatened and thus had to upgrade investment to sustain their competitiveness. Second, to

Table 8.2
Aggregate supply and demand, 1981–1989 (real % change from preceding year).

	1981	1982	1983	1984	1985	1986	1987	1988	1989
Aggregate supply	9.8	−5.2	−6.6	4.4	3.1	−4.3	1.9	3.8	4.4
GDP	8.8	−0.6	−4.2	3.6	2.6	−3.7	1.6	1.4	2.9
Imports	17.7	−37.9	−33.8	17.8	10.9	−12.4	5.0	38.0	20.7
Aggregate demand	9.8	−5.2	−6.6	4.4	3.1	−4.3	1.9	3.8	4.4
Private consumption	7.4	−2.5	−5.4	3.3	3.6	−2.3	−0.2	2.5	6.0
Public consumption	10.3	2.0	2.7	6.6	0.9	1.5	−1.2	−0.3	−0.6
Private investment	11.5	−15.1	−22.1	7.9	12.2	−10.4	6.8	10.9	9.5
Public investment	22.5	−18.8	−36.0	4.1	0.9	−14.2	−13.4	−5.3	−3.6
Exports	11.6	21.8	13.6	5.7	−4.5	3.2	10.1	2.7	3.1

the extent that the opening of the economy was perceived as a permanent policy change, the export- and import-competing industries benefited from a boom in long-run investment projects (Snchez 1988). Third, the (repressed) demand for imported consumer goods (which increased 150.3% between 1987 and 1988), which had accumulated in the course of the prolonged closed-economy phase, was finally released. And fourth, a certain portion of previously unregistered imports (contraband) was imported through legal channels.

An alternative explanation for the surge in imports and the rise in investment—one that contradicts some of the previous arguments—is related to the uncertainty surrounding the permanent nature of the trade-liberalization policy and the success of the stabilization efforts. If opening up the economy is perceived as a policy that will have to be reversed because of a balance-of-payments crisis associated with the failure of the program, there will be an incentive to build up speculative stocks of imported goods. Likewise, there will be a wide gap between the *ex ante* and the *ex post* real interest rate. The *ex ante* real rates could have been perceived as low or even negative if inflation was expected to rise to previous levels. If this was the case, then some of the investment projects may have been undertaken on the assumption of an *ex ante* low real rate of interest. However, the expectation of high inflation in the future is usually accompanied by uncertainties surrounding relative price changes that could reverse the anticipated gains from new investments. It would then be difficult to conclude that this could be a valid general explanation for the rise in private investment in 1988, which continued strongly through 1989, as discussed in the following section.

The rise in private investment in the context of an extremely tight monetary policy brought about the development of an informal credit market in the second half of 1988. Since the authorities refused to allow nominal (and real) rates to rise when a strong credit demand became apparent, an extensive informal credit market developed in which firms and other large investors with excess liquidity would lend to other firms directly or through financial intermediaries not subject to reserve requirements.

The development of this informal credit market clearly hampered the effectiveness of credit ceilings, mostly because its expansion came about at the expense of traditional instruments. In view of these circumstances, in October 1988, commercial banks were authorized to subscribe bankers' acceptances and to grant guarantees on commercial paper with the sole limitation of compliance with the proper capitalization requirements and observance of a 30% liquidity coefficient on the resulting liabilities. Since the interest rates and the maturities of those instruments were freely determined by the market, these measures amounted to a complete liberalization of interest rates. These measures were of great importance. The first impact was a rechanneling of funds from the informal market and from traditional instruments to bankers' acceptances. The share of the latter in total bank deposits increased from 1.8% in September to 48.7% in December. But the main effect was the substitution of traditional instruments of monetary policies (credit ceilings and reserve requirements) for open market operations. This, in turn, has considerably deepened financial markets and paved the way for a thorough process of modernization of the financial sector.

The Role of Nominal Anchors and Shortage Problems

Throughout the duration of the PSE, the nominal exchange rate remained practically fixed and several important private and public prices were frozen. Yet no generalized shortage problems were observed (table 8.3); in fact, despite the price controls, production increased. There is little doubt that the fixing of the exchange rate played a crucial role in the stabilization process. The most obvious reason is that in the tradable-goods sector internal and external prices are directly linked; thus, stabilizing the exchange rate also stabilizes the domestic prices of these goods. A second reason is that foreign imports are also utilized in the nontradable-goods sector; once again, stabilizing the exchange rate reduces costs.

The authorities managed to sustain a virtually fixed exchange rate throughout 1988 despite the substantial real appreciation observed, particularly in the first months of the year. A key element was, of course, that parity was initially supported by more than US$13 billion in reserves. In addition, the devaluation effected prior to the launching of the pact implied a substantial initial margin for a subsequent real appreciation that was fully expected. Third, the exchange rate was supported by the pursuit of consistent monetary and fiscal policies, although in retrospect the increase in the primary surplus was insufficient to prevent a rise in the operational deficit and a loss of reserves.

As mentioned earlier, despite the application of price controls, production actually increased. Helpman (1987) has argued that under certain conditions price controls do not necessarily create distortions and can even stimulate production. This is the case under imperfect competition. In a simple monopoly, with constant marginal costs, a price set between the monopoly's price and the marginal cost raises production. Helpman argues that the hypothesis of monopolistic competition cannot be rejected.

In a series of regressions of the shortage index (table 8.3) against the concentration index in Mexico, it was found that the shortage index of a cross-section of industries was negatively correlated with the degree of

Table 8.3
Shortage index, 1988.

January	10.0
February	7.0
March	6.0
April	6.0
May	3.0
June	9.0
July	12.0
August	5.0
September	11.0
October	13.0
November	9.0
December	9.5

concentration in these industries. That is, larger shortages occurred in less concentrated (or presumably more competitive) industries. This is consistent with Helpman's results, and it lends support to the view that price controls work better in monopolistic or oligopolistic industries.

The Role of Trade Liberalization

It is not easy to assess clearly the independent contribution of the trade-liberalization measures adopted with the pact to the reduction of inflation. A first consideration is that trade liberalization was already underway at the time the program was launched, although maximum tariffs were cut substantially (from 40% to 20%) in connection with the program. A second point is that the arbitrage of foreign prices should be most effective in competitive sectors where there is a large number of firms and relatively few barriers to entry, in the same manner that price controls can yield better results in monopolistic or oligopolistic industries. In the case of Mexico, there seems to be a high degree of concentration in many industrial sectors.

Nonetheless, the large increase in imports recorded after the tariff reduction probably did have, to some extent, the intended effect of imposing the discipline of foreign prices on domestic producers. The exchange-rate appreciation also helped to stabilize domestic prices. One indicator that suggests the effectiveness of the exchange-rate stabilization combined with the tariff-reduction measures is the behavior of the Producer Price Index (PPI), which is more heavily weighted with traded goods. As seen in figure 8.6, the growth rate of the PPI declined much faster than the CPI. The average increase in the second half of 1989 was only 2.9%.

A second indicator that can be used to gauge the contribution of trade liberalization to the reduction of inflation is the behavior of the relative prices of some products in competitive industries with many partici-pants—such as textiles and clothing, which fell in mid 1988 as imports began exerting pressure on domestic producers. It is possible, then, that in these sectors foreign price arbitrage was a significant factor in rapidly breaking inflationary inertia. Profit margins, on the other hand, which had risen substantially in 1982–1987—a rise probably associated with the observed fall in real wages that was not fully translated to lower prices due to protection—appear to have fallen after the price freeze and the tariff reduction. The existence of high profit margins before the stabili-

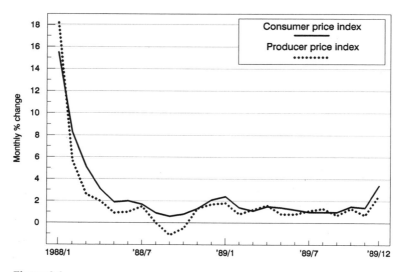

Figure 8.6
Consumer and producer price indexes, 1988–1989.

zation program was announced undoubtedly allowed firms to comply with price controls—or price guidelines—and to better cope with foreign competition.

Thus, although it is difficult to attribute a precise contribution to the deepening of the trade-liberalization process of the reduction in inflation, it may have played an important role in increasing supply in competitive sectors and in abating inflationary expectations. As Ize (1989) notes, in oligopolistic sectors, where price controls have kept prices from rising, foriegn competition will also play a useful role in the future (when price controls are lifted or become ineffective) by preventing rapid increases.

4. Recent Developments and Current Challenges

Toward the end of 1988 it was clear that the results of the PES had been quite satisfactory. Inflation had been reduced over 100 percentage points with respect to the previous year, and economic growth had not fallen perceptibly. Aggregate demand and supply rose 3.3%, revealing a high growth of imports (35% in US dollar terms), and international reserves had declined by US$7 billion.

In the design of the economic strategy for 1989, it was clear that the consolidation of the stabilization program and the resumption of economic growth required assured external financing for a moderate current-account deficit over the medium term. Given the level of international reserves, it was not possible to sustain a further substantial drain.

In December 1988 the incoming administration of President Salinas established the second phase of the stabilization program: the Pact for Stability and Growth (PECE). The new pact was designed and negotiated with different sectors along the same lines as the previous one. Some moderate adjustments were made to public prices utilized as inputs in the production process, and the exchange rate began depreciating at a daily rate of 1 peso per US dollar, resulting in an annual nominal depreciation of about 16%. Minimum wages were raised 8%, indicating continued moderation of wage demands and sending the appropriate signals to the public. An important new development was the government's commitment to renegotiate the external debt.

The new pact, although giving priority to consolidate the gains made in the inflation front, sought to establish the basis for renewed and sustainable economic growth after seven years of stagnation and severe deterioration of living standards. Fiscal policy was to be strengthened: the primary balance was targeted to reach 7.3% of GDP (an increase of about 2 percentage points with respect to 1987). Monetary policy was entering a new phase. With the liberalization of interest rates and the elimination of reserve requirements and credit ceilings, the only policy instrument was open market operations. The challenge, then, was to finance the public-sector borrowing requirements exclusively through bond issues in financial markets. This was one more reason for aiming at a stronger primary surplus. In addition to the strict implementation of domestic policies, the success of the PECE depended crucially on the elimination of the debt overhang and the reduction of resource transfers. As mentioned above, it is now widely recognized that the consequences of the debt overhang for Mexico and most other debtor countries in Latin America had been disastrous.

Table 8.4 presents the most relevant numbers resulting from the debt negotiations. The basic result is that resource transfers, which on average represented 5.5% of GDP from 1982 to 1988, will be reduced to 2.4% on average for the years 1989–1992. There has been ample discussion in the international press and in academic circles as to whether this agreement will be "sufficient" to help Mexico reestablish a sustainable growth path.

Table 8.4
Savings of the Mexican external-debt renegotiation on the current account—commercial banks (millions of U.S. dollars).

	1990	1991	1992	1993	1994
Interest reduction[a]	2,252.2	1,501.0	1,501.0	1,501.0	1,501.0
New money	756.0	648.0	648.0	0.0	0.0

Sources: Direccion General de Planeación Hadendaria. Secretaría de Hacienda y Credito Publico.
a. In 1990 includes $751.2 million correspondent to the retroactive of 1980.

At this stage, rather than contributing to the debate, it is perhaps more useful to examine the first results.

Developments in 1989

Economic developments in 1989 were, in general, quite favorable. The annual rate of inflation sank from 51.7% to 19.7%. Preliminary estimates indicate a GDP growth of 2.5–3% versus a program target of 1.5%. The higher growth rate was also reflected in higher imports and in a current-account deficit that exceeded the program's targets. For the second consecutive year, imports rose at an extremely high rate (54.7% in 1988 and 26.2% in 1989), reflecting a continuation of the trends and effects discussed in the last section: trade liberalization, another bad agricultural year, and (mainly) an increase in aggregate demand.

One of the most significant developments during the year was a clear favorable turn of expectations. This was reflected in increased consumer confidence, higher private investment, and capital inflows. Several factors contributed to the improvement of expectations. Undoubtedly, the renegotiation of the external debt was a key development. The confidence-building effect of the negotiation was probably as important as the financial effects of the reduced resource transfers on the restriction of economic growth. The mere announcement of the agreement precipitated a decline of domestic interest rates of about 20 percentage points (from nominal levels of about 55%) as well as some capital inflows. Other external factors which had a positive impact were higher petroleum prices and the continued expansion of industrialized economies. On the domestic front, the strict adherence to the economic program was of paramount importance in consolidating the credibility of the new administration. Fiscal policy remained on track, allowing monetary policy to remain tight; the exchange-rate rule announced in December 1988 was observed; and structural policies were pursued vigorously.

The primary surplus of the public sector increased about 2 percentage points of GDP, reaching a record level of 8% in 1989. Domestic interest rates were higher than projected for the year as a whole, despite the sharp decline observed after the announcement of the signing of the financing package for 1989–1992 with commercial banks. The PSBR declined from about 12% of GDP in 1988 to 6.2% in 1989, and the operational deficit dropped from 3.5% of GDP to less than 2% (see table 8.5). Since the public sector received practically no external financing, the financial deficit was covered primarily through the issuance of government securities placed with the public. This was made possible by the strong rise in private-sector financial savings (20% in real terms), reflecting the effects of financial liberalization and improved confidence.

Regarding structural policies, an important agreement was reached to begin dismantling the protection for the automotive sector (one of the last

Table 8.5
Main economic variables.

| | | 1989 | |
	1988	Program target	Estimated
Real growth (%)	1.1	1.5	2.5
Inflation	51.7	18.0	19.7
Public finances (as a percentage of GDP)			
Financial deficit	11.9	6.7	6.2
Operational deficit	3.5	2.8	1.8
Primary surplus	7.6	6.7	7.8
Financial variables			
Real exchange rate (percentage change)	−23.2	−3.8	0.7
Financial real savings (rate of growth)	5.0	9.3	20.5
Real financing to private sector (% change)	9.5	4.2	45.9
Balance of payments ($ billions)			
Current account	−2.9	−4.8	−5.6
Imports	18.9	20.7	22.9
Non-oil exports	13.9	16.0	15.2

Source: Secretaría de Hacienda y Credito Público y Secretaría de Programación y Presupuesto.

protected sectors in the economy), further integrating this industry with world production. Foreign-investment rules were also considerably liberalized. The largest airline was privatized, and the privatization of the telephone company (the second largest firm in Mexico after PEMEX) was announced, in addition to the sale of a number of smaller public enterprises. Other important measures included an ambitious deregulation program, fiscal reform, and a "financial package" aimed at opening and modernizing the financial sector.

The importance of structural policies should be underscored. Although, as mentioned earlier, it is difficult to assess precisely the quantitative contribution of structural policies to economic stabilization and/or to the resumption of economic growth, its impact on expectations and on economic efficiency in Mexico has been fundamental.

More favorable expectations precipitated a rise in private expenditure on both consumption and investment. Consumption expenditures rose in response to a higher disposable income, after several years of decline. In turn, income increased because of a rise in employment and industrial wages. Minimum wages increased on an annual basis (5.2%) but still declined in average terms (6.5%). Average industrial wages increased 2% (see table 8.6). Another factor pushing consumption was the resource transfer to the private sector, implied by the payment of high real interest rates on domestic debt, which represented 6.9% of GDP. In this case, the income or wealth effect implied by the resource transfer seems to have dominated once again the substitution effect implied by the higher interest rates.

Table 8.6
Manufacturing wages (1978 pesos).

1981	6,281.9
1982	6,300.2
1983	4,564.8
1984	4,354.6
1985	4,351.2
1986	3,892.8
1987	3,884.1
1988	3,774.4
1989[a]	3,840.2

Source: Dirección General de Planeación Hacendaria. Secretaría de Hacienda y Credito Público.
a. January–May.

After increasing 10.9% in real terms in 1988, private investment is estimated to have risen 9.5% in 1989. The increase in private investment in the context of extremely high real interest rates continues to pose quite a puzzle. One explanation that was previously mentioned is that the perceived difference between the *ex ante* and the *ex post* interest rate, caused by the expected rise in the rate of inflation, implies a lower *ex ante* real rate, which constitutes the relevant factor for investment decisions. It is doubtful, however, that this perceived difference could hold for extended periods (see figure 8.5).

A more plausible explanation for the continued expansion of private investment is that many firms that were heavily indebted at the outset of the debt crisis in 1982 were able to substantially reduce their outstanding debt to both domestic and foreign creditors. For example, the external debt of the private sector, which amounted to US$25 billion in 1982, is currently estimated at less than US$ 6 billion. Regarding domestic debt, the enterprise sector as a whole is a net creditor of the financial system. Thus, firms (particularly large firms) with surplus cash and a much-improved balance sheet have invested heavily, stimulated by foreign competition and based on favorable expectations of future domestic sales, exports, and lower interest.

Current Challenges

Why have interest rates remained so high? What are the prospects for an early reduction to a more sustainable level? Two sets of factors can be used to explain the level and the trends of domestic interest rates: expectations and fundamentals. In the early part of the stabilization program, as explained earlier, the external shocks and the overall uncertainty associated with the stabilization process itself produced a sharp rise in interest rates. At that stage, during the second and third quarters of 1988, the dominant factor explaining the high levels of real interest rates could have been a lack of credibility regarding the sustainability of the pact—and thus a large gap between *ex ante* and *ex post* interest rates.

With the passage of time and the gain in credibility of the stabilization program, the explanation for the continued high interest rates should be more related to the behavior of "fundamentals"—the supply and demand of loanable funds—than to the state of expectations. It is true, on the other hand, that the uncertainty surrounding the negotiation of the external debt persisted through the first half of 1989. That this was an important factor influencing the behavior of interest rates is evident from the steep fall in nominal rates that followed the announcement of an agreement. Yet, although lower than in the first two quarters, real rates remained high in the second half of 1989.

Table 8.7 provides some evidence on fundamentals. Regarding the sources of funds, the growth of domestic financial savings in real terms rose rapidly from 5% in 1988 to 20.5% in 1989. However, foreign borrowing of the public sector fell short of the program's target. In 1989, the protracted nature of the external-debt negotiations caused a delay in disbursement to the extent that the net foreign borrowing of the public sector was actually negative (US$–0.3 billion), compared with US$7 billion contemplated in the program. On the uses side, although the public-sector borrowing requirements remained in line with the program's projections, the rise in the demand for credit of the private sector was totally unexpected. Private credit rose an estimated 45.5% in real terms versus a program projection of 4.2%. An indeterminate but probably

Table 8.7
Financial flows in Mexico (trillions of Mexican pesos).

	1988	1989 Program target	Estimated
Total sources of funds	44.4	45.3	61.0
Growth of M4	48.2	27.5	59.3
Percentage real annual growth	5.0	9.3	20.5
Foreign borrowing by public sector	−3.0	17.2	−0.7
Billions of U.S. dollars	−1.3	7.0	−0.3
Other deposits	−0.8	0.6	2.4
Total use of funds	44.4	45.3	61.0
Public sector borrowing requirements	47.2	32.5	30.0
Percentage of GDP	11.9	6.7	6.2
International reserves accumulation	−15.7	2.7	−4.6
Billions of U.S. dollars	−6.9	1.0	−1.8
Commercial bank credit to private sector	13.0	10.1	35.7
Percentage real growth	9.5	4.2	45.9

Source: Dirección General de Planeación Hacendaria. Secretaría de Hacienda y Credito Público.

substantial portion of this increase represents the rechanneling of funds from the informal credit market to the financial system after the financial liberalization at the end of 1988, and consequently does not represent a "real" demand for funds. Yet another part of this increase corresponds to end-of-year window-dressing operations of commercial banks. However, despite those adjustments, the increase in private credit demand was enormous, representing a continuous and substantial pressure on financial markets.

The future persistence of high real interest rates poses a serious threat to the stabilization program and to the prospects of sustained non-inflationary growth. First, it would imply that margins obtained from the foreign-debt negotiation could not materialize. The impact in public finance stemming from the reduced resource transfers would be compensated (perhaps more than compensated) by the rise in domestic interest payments. Second, the economic recovery would eventually be aborted as private firms would accumulate debt at an unsustainable pace, posing an additional danger to the stability of banks and the financial sector. Third, the probably negative redistributive effects of the resource transfer implied by high real interest rates would be exacerbated.

What are the prospects for a reduction in real rates? To the extent that the program for 1990 (which envisages a continuation of fiscal and monetary discipline and a deepening of the structural change) remains on track, the credibility of the government will be further enhanced, and expectations should allow for a fall in rates as savers demand a smaller risk premium. The final signing of the restructuring of the public debt should improve expectations. In addition, and more important, the conclusion of the agreement will provide in 1990 a gross interest relief of some US$2.2 billion, as well as new money from commercial banks in the order of US$850 million. Private credit demand, on the other hand, is expected to increase 18.3% in real terms, representing a significant decline in relation to 1989's real growth rate.

A second major issue that will have to be faced in the near future is the "landing" of the pact; that is, the gradual lifting of price controls and the correction of relative prices. As seen in figure 8.4 above, the controlled/noncontrolled price ratio has fallen substantially since the end of 1987 (17%), despite the fact that controlled prices represent 36% of the price index. The fall in this index is explained mostly by inertia, by the backward adjustment of the prices of (mostly) nontradables, and by initial negative expectations regarding the duration and success of the pact. The current level of this price ratio is similar to that prevailing in 1982. Apart from the possible emergence of economic distortions, a further deterioration of this index will imply additional resource losses from the sale of public goods and services.

In December 1989 the government and the various sectors of society agreed to extend the PECE though July 1990. Within this framework, the peso continues to depreciate at a daily rate of 1 peso per US$, implying an annual depreciation rate of 14.5%. Minimum wages were increased 10%, and public sector-prices and tariffs have been adjusted by an average 7.5%. The wage and price increase caused a cumulated one-time increase in prices, in December 1989 and January 1990, of 7–8%. The controlled-to-noncontrolled price ratio after these adjustments is expected to be only 4% higher. This illustrates the difficulties of correcting relative prices in a substantive manner in the framework of the pact, which establishes precisely a path for key prices and incomes. It would be unrealistic to expect that the relative prices of public goods and tariffs can be raised substantially in the future while abiding by current agreements. Corrections will have to be made gradually, and other variables—mostly on the supply side, such as productivity—will have to provide the necessary room for the implementation of the adjustments.

Regarding the "landing" of the pact, it could prove all the more difficult to lift price controls in a situation of rapidly growing demand. Aggregate demand is estimated to have increased 4.4% in 1989 (0.6 percentage points higher than the increase registered in 1988). The growth in demand was especially strong during the first half, and the latest available information presents a mixed and somewhat contradictory picture. On the one hand, private sector demand for credit was unusually strong in the last quarter of 1989. On the other, production data, inventories, and polls on business intentions suggest a slowdown in economic activity and aggregate demand in recent months. Whatever the cause, it seems clear that fiscal policy will have to remain very tight— especially in the first half of 1990—so as to mitigate aggregate demand and thus to facilitate the conditions for the lifting of controls.

On the positive side, since most goods subject to price controls are tradables, trade liberalization has already modified the structure of relative prices. Although there are some cases of domestically controlled prices being below international prices, this does not seem to be the general rule. In addition, a number of price controls apply to industries with a monopolistic or oligopolistic structure, which respond positively to price controls in terms of market efficiency. To the extent that this is true, the deterioration of relative prices would appear to be less severe, implying that one can proceed gradually with the lifting of controls.

5. Conclusions

One of the most damaging consequences of the debt crisis has been the macroeconomic instability resulting from the resource transfer. The internal transfer from the public to government required to effect the external transfer has led to inflation and to recurrent balance-of-payments crises in Mexico and other debtor countries. Indexation mechanisms, which inevitably arise in inflationary processes, tend to exacerbate inflation and to make all the more difficult the implementation of stabilization programs. Mexico's experience during the adjustment years 1983–1987 illustrates these difficulties.

The Mexican stabilization program followed a three-pronged strategy. First, orthodox demand-management measures were aimed at raising the fiscal primary surplus and restricting the supply of credit. Second, a heterodox package of incomes policies and nominal anchors was established through a social agreement directed to break the formal and informal indexation rules, and thus to break the inflationary inertia, as well as to generate stabilizing expectations. And third, a structural adjustment program including the privatization of state-owned enterprises and trade liberalization was implemented. The objective of the third prong was to increase economic efficiency and to impose the price discipline of external competition. In the second stage, the stabilization program introduced two additional elements: the negotiation of the external debt and the vigorous pursuit of economic deregulation. The purpose was to eliminate the debt overhang—one of the fundamental causes of inflation—and to elicit a supply-side response in terms of higher productivity.

The program has succeeded in reducing inflation and in establishing the conditions for the restoration of economic growth. Excess demand has implied a surge in imports and a loss of international reserves, spurred by an appreciation of the real exchange rate and by the effects of trade liberalization. A notable feature of this whole process has been the revival of private investment in a context of high real interest rates. In turn, private credit demand—associated with the higher investment— has been accommodated by the financial markets, which have responded positively to deregulation and to interest-rate liberalization. On the other hand, the rise in real interest rates has probably had a perverse effect: it has fueled rather than tempered the rise in aggregate demand due to the income effect stemming from the resource transfer to the private sector. Excess demand has also provoked a deterioration of the relative price of controlled and tradable goods.

The persistence of high interest rates and the deterioration of some relative prices constitute the main challenges for the consolidation of the stabilization program. The negotiation of the external debt has provided new breathing space and also improved expectations. The government has also gained enormously in credibility. It will be necessary, however, to pursue strict fiscal discipline and to continue the structural policies, particularly deregulation. The bet is that gains in efficiency and productivity will offset the exchange-rate appreciation and allow for an increase in exports and a gradual recovery of the relative price of tradable goods. The relaxation of price controls must be implemented within an austere fiscal environment. Monetary policy, on the other hand, has a limited role to play in the current circumstances: it can influence the capital account and the level of reserves through higher interest rates, but at the same time it will probably induce a deterioration of the current account. Thus, fiscal policy and structural measures are the more effective instruments with which to influence demand and supply.

Perhaps the most solid conclusion of the Toledo Conference was that the failure of the first heterodox programs launched in Latin America was due to the fact that fiscal policy was not implemented with sufficient vigor at the appropriate time to reduce existing imbalances. In Israel, where the program has succeeded, the fiscal effort played a key role not only in reducing macroeconomic disequilibria but also in enhancing the government's credibility. Heterodox programs work where the fundamentals are in place. The prospects in Mexico are now brighter: the negotiation of the external debt, the credibility gained by the government, and the steady pursuit of current policies should result in the consolidation of the stabilization program and the renewal of sustainable growth.

Acknowledgment

I wish to thank Alejandro Rodríguez for his very helpful assistance and comments.

Notes

1. As in other countries in the region, the 1982 crisis was caused by expansionary fiscal and monetary policies implemented in the preceding years, which, in the context of an appreciating exchange rate, led to unsustainable balance-of-payments deficits and to the accumulation of a large foreign debt. The events that precipitated the Mexican debt crisis have been amply documented. See, for example, Aspe and Córdoba 1984, Gil Díaz 1984, and Ortiz 1985.

2. The deposits in dollars in Mexican banks were called Mexdollars.

3. In 1983–1984 the government privatized, merged, liquidated, or transferred to local governments approximately 750 out of 1,550 state-owned entities existing in 1982.

4. Despite the fall of oil income and the substantial amortization of the private debt (US$2 billion), net reserves declined only US$1.1 billion and gross reserves actually increased. The balance-of-payments outcome reflected a rapid increase in non-oil exports (41%), a decline of imports (13.5%), and capital inflows induced by tight credit policies.

5. The balance of the adjustment process initiated in 1983 has positive and negative aspects. On the positive side, as a result of the structural measures implemented in the external sector, Mexico's trade structure was greatly diversified. In 1987, manufactures represented 48% of total exports, compared with 14.2% in 1982. The average growth rate of non-oil exports from 1983 to 1987 was 21.7%. In addition, spurred by external competition, the economy as a whole became more competitive and export-oriented.

6. To the extent that exchange-rate depreciations are unexpected and/or the exchange rate overshoots its equilibrium level (leading to expectations of a future real appreciation), the government can affect a once-and-for-all reduction in its real domestic debt even under conditions of full capital mobility. See Ize and Ortiz 1986.

7. The most important controlled private prices are those of the basic basket, which contains 77 goods. Around 40 of them are related to food (eggs, meat, milk, sugar, tortillas, etc.).

8. This was probably the case with respect to the textile industry.

9. A cross-section regression between the concentration index ($CONCEN$) for fourteen products of the basic consumption basket and the average shortage index (S) of 1988 for the same products gave the following result:

$S = 14.5 - 0.1071CONCEN$

(9.2) (-5.05)

$R^2 = 0.6798$; D.W. $= 1.78$; F $= 25.5$.

The analysis suggests that the larger the industrial concentration, the lower the shortage.

10. For instance, the deregulation of the transport sector resulted in cost reductions of 25–30% on some of the most heavily utilized routes.

11. Debt reduction was greatly facilitated by FICORCA. This was a facility established at Banco de Mexico in 1983 to help firms spread the exchange-rate losses resulting from devaluation. This facility involved no government guarantees or subsidies, while providing an incentive for foreign creditor banks and firms to engage in medium-term debt-restructuring agreements. In the event, private firms obtained very substantial debt discounts for early repayments.

12. In the time that has elapsed since the conference in Jerusalem and the revision of this paper, some important developments have taken place in Mexico. In May 1990, President Salinas tabled a bill in Congress proposing a constitutional amendment to allow for the privatization of commercial banks (nationalized in 1982). The bill was approved. Also in May, the PECE was extended through January 1991, with some moderate public price adjustments. Gasoline prices were raised 9.7%, exchange-rate depreciation was reduced from 1 peso to 80 cents a day, and no increase to minimum wages was granted. The renewal of the pact was made possible in no small measure by the reduction in nominal interest rates that followed the announcement of the impending bank privatization. In June, the initiation of talks which may lead to a free-trade agreement with the United States (and eventually with Canada, leading to a North American free-trade zone) was announced. Financial markets have reacted favorably to this piece of "news." Since inflation is running somewhat higher than in 1989 (25% annually), the reduction in nominal rates has implied a sharp reduction in real rates, somewhat reducing the concerns expressed in this paper.

13. Some important subsidies were also reduced substantially, such as corn tortillas and transportation in Mexico City.

References

Alberro, J. L. 1987. "La dinámica de precios relativos en una economía inflacionaria" [The dynamics of relative prices in an inflationary economy]. In *Los Planes Heterodoxos de Estabilización [Heterodox Stabilization Plans]* (Edición Especial de Estudios Económicos, El Colegio de México).

Aspe, P., and J. Córdoba. 1984. Stabilization Policies in Mexico (1983–1984). Mimeograph, MIT.

Bruno, M. 1986. The Israel Economy, the End of the Lost Decade? Mimeograph, Hebrew University of Jerusalem.

Bruno, M., and S. Piterman. 1988. "Israel's stabilization: A two-year review." In *Inflation Stabilization: The Experience of Israel, Argentina, Brazil, Bolivia, and Mexico,* M. Bruno et al., eds. (MIT Press).

Bruno, M., G. Di Tella, R. Dornbush, and S. Fisher, eds. 1988. *Inflation Stabilization: The Experience of Israel, Argentina, Brazil, Bolivia, and Mexico* (MIT Press).

Gil Díaz, F. 1984. "Mexico's path from stability to inflation." In *World Economic Growth*, A. Harberger, ed. (San Francisco: Institute for Contemporary Studies).

Helpman, E. 1987. Macroeconomic Effects of Price Controls: The Role of the Market Structure. NBER Working Paper no. 2434.

Ize, A. 1989. Trade Liberalization, Stabilization and Growth: Some Notes on the Mexican Experience. IMF Working Paper.

Ize, A., and G. Ortiz. 1986. "Fiscal rigidities, public debt and asset substitution: The case of Mexico." *IMF Staff Papers* 31, No. 2.

Ortiz, G. 1985. "Economic expansion, crisis and adjustment in Mexico (1977–1983)." In *The Economics of the Caribbean Basin*, M. Connolly and J. McDermott, eds. (Praeger).

Ortiz, G. 1989. "The IMF and the debt strategy." In *International Monetary Fund in a Multipolar World*, Catherine Gwin and Richard Feinberg, eds. (Washington, D.C.: Overseas Development Council).

Rodríguez, A. 1988. Ortodoxia, Heterodoxia e Inflación Inercial [Orthodoxy, heterodoxy and inertial inflation]. Mimeograph.

Sachs, J. 1989. "Strenghtening IMF programs in highly indebted countries." In *International Monetary Fund in a Multipolar World*, Catherine Gwin and Richard Feinberg, eds. (Washington, D.C.: Overseas Development Council).

Sánchez, García S. 1988. Penetración de mercados, movimientos del tipo de cambio y dinmica de las exportaciones: El caso de México [Market penetration, changes in exchange regimes and the dynamics of exports: The case of Mexico]. Mimeograph, MIT.

Sargent, T., and N. Wallace. 1981. "Some unpleasent monetarist arithmetic." *Federal Reserve Bank of Minneapolis Quarterly Review* 5 (no. 3): 1–17.

Secretaría de Hacienda y Crédito Público. 1989. "The use of price controls as a stabilization strategy." Inedit Document. "Un Modelo Simple de Crecimiento e Inflación" [A simple model of inflation]. Mimeograph. "La Renegociación de la Deuda Externa" [The renegotiation of the external debt], Dirección General de Planeación Hacendaria.

Simonsen, M. H. 1988. "Price stabilization and incomes policies: Theory and the Brazilian case study." In *Inflation Stabilization: The Experience of Israel, Argentina, Brazil, Bolivia, and Mexico*, M. Bruno et al., eds. (MIT Press).

Comments by Fernando Clavijo

Guillermo Ortiz has written a very comprehensive and enlightening review of Mexico's stabilization experience since 1982. Since the Toledo conference focused on that period, I will skip most of the second part of the paper, which covers the years preceding 1987.

Considering the magnitude of the oil shock of 1986, the overall results of the new program adopted were better than expected. The author suggests that the negative effects resulting from the oil shock of 1986 were largely unavoidable, and that the economic policy implemented in that year was correct. I fully agree with him. I also share with him the need to emphasize that the most urgent priority in the event of an adverse shock of such magnitude was to avoid a depletion of foreign-exchange reserves, even if it was achieved at the expense of higher inflation.

I do not share his views, however, when it comes to the analysis of policies adopted in 1987. The policy dilemma was either to maintain the real exchange rate at the level attained in 1986 or (from what the author calls a short-term macroeconomic perspective), to correct, to some extent, the exchange-rate overshooting, in order to moderate inflationary pressures and to stimulate economic activity through a higher level of real income. It seems to me that the stronger-than-expected balance-of-payments situation at the end of 1986, together with other developments in the economy at the beginning of 1987, required a reordering of priorities for 1987.

Moreover, unlike the author, I would consider the option of correcting the exchange-rate overshooting—thereby moderating inflationary pressures—not only from a short-term perspective. With the benefit of hindsight, one can posit that 1987 was a clear case in which the option of decelerating inflation at the expense of a weaker balance-of-payments outcome should have been considered from a medium-term perspective.

I tend to believe, along with Beristain and Trigueros (1989), that in 1987, when the economy was in a better position (oil prices recovered that year) and foreign capital started to pour in, the real exchange rate had to be lower than in the previous year, and it was precisely the attempt to maintain it at the level of late 1986 that brought about serious inflationary pressures.

This is important because it was the acceleration of inflation, the stock market crash, and some other events in the financial and foreign-exchange markets that led to the decision to adopt the Pact (a heterodox program was, of course, widely discussed among policy makers in Mexico in 1987). Indeed, the author himself points to the "paradoxical [fact] that a financial crisis should have occurred when international reserves were at a historical peak (at the end of 1987) and the balance of payments was recording a substantial surplus. But there is also little doubt that the inflationary environment amplified the nervousness of financial markets."

In addition to the necessary initial conditions of the Pact of Economic Solidarity mentioned by the author, I believe that the following points should not be overlooked.

· The financial positions of most of the big enterprises at the end of 1987 were very comfortable in comparison with 1982. Profits were at the highest level (with some exceptions, such as in the textile and steel sectors). The leverage ratio of the private sector had been substantially reduced. The ratio of total liabilities to total assets declined in most sectors by more than 40% from 1982 to 1987.

· An important reduction in public-sector expenditures had been achieved. The non-interest component in relation to GDP in 1987 was 6 percentage points lower than in 1982.

· According to some sources, the Olivera-Tanzi Effect was estimated to be more or less the equivalent of the inflation tax.

The Pact of Economic Solidarity

In his discussion of the outcome of this pact for 1988 and developments during 1989, the author provides some empirical evidence which might explain why there were no serious shortage problems, and assesses the role of trade liberalization in the inflationary process.

Based on a negative correlation between the degree of industrial concentration and the sectoral shortage index, he argues, as does Helpman (1987), that under imperfect competition price controls do not necessarily create distortions and may even increase production. As for the role of trade liberalization, although acknowledging that it is difficult to assess its contribution to the reduction of the rate of inflation, the author tends to support the thesis that, overall, it has been helpful. This position is at odds with some empirical evidence, presented by Ten Kate and De Mateo (1989a,b), which suggests that the level of nominal protection provided by the real exchange rate since 1987 was so high that price arbitrage was not as effective as has been claimed.

The main macroeconomic indicators summarized in table 8.5 of the paper indicate how successful the pact has been. Again, I broadly agree with the author's assessment of macroeconomic results. It must be mentioned, however, that in 1988 capital outflows contributed to the decrease of foreign-exchange reserves, thereby somewhat undermining credibility at the beginning of the program. Nevertheless, given the good results for the first year, private capital poured in early in 1989, contributing to the investment burst as well as strengthening the credibility of the pact.

Finally, when it comes to the analysis of implemented policies, two facts seem to have been overlooked by the author. On the one hand, the government was apparently betting on the expansion of private-sector demand; this is why the financial liberalization took place at the end of 1988 and the commercial banks' reserve coefficient was reduced (from 52% to 30%) early in 1989. On the other hand, as in other heterodox disinflation episodes, a burst of private consumption and investment should have been expected. Therefore, it is striking that the target for the rate of growth for 1988, shown in table 8.5, was rather on the conservative side.

References

Beristain, J., and I. Trigueros. 1989. "The Mexican adjustment strategy." Revised version. Paper prepared for the conference *Latin American Adjustment: How Much Has Happened?*, Institute for International Economics, Washington, D.C.

Helpman, E. 1987. Macroeconomic Effects of Price Controls: The Role of the Market Structure. NBER Working Paper no. 2434.

Ten Kate, A., and V. F. De Mateo. 1989a. "Apertura commercial y estructura de la protección en México. Estimaciones cuantitativas de los ochenta [Trade openness and the structure of trade protection in Mexico. Quantitative estimates of the eighties]." *Comercio Exterior* 39 (no. 4): 312–329.

Ten Kate, A., and V. F. De Mateo. 1989b. "Apertura commercial y estructura de la protección en México. Un análisis de la relación entre ambas [Trade openness and the structure of trade protection in Mexico. An analysis of their mutual relations." *Comercio Exterior* 39 (no. 6): 497–511.

Comments by Sylvia Piterman

The 1987 Toledo conference included a session on "Lessons from Mexico." At that time Mexico was still trying to stabilize without any heterodox element in its policy; it had undergone a substantial fiscal adjustment, real wage decreases, real devaluation, and structural changes. The paper presented at that conference by Francisco Gil Díaz and Raul Ramos Tercero concluded that an anti-inflationary strategy in Mexico obviously has to include a fixed-exchange-rate regime, because of the openness of the Mexican economy. But the authors questioned the usefulness of a price freeze. Moreover, they wrote that the failure of the Argentine and Brazilian freezes had discouraged others from trying the same policy.

A few months after the Toledo conference, Mexico launched the program described here in detail by Guillermo Ortiz. This program included all the main heterodox ingredients (on top of the fiscal adjustment): a social pact, the fixing of the exchange rate, and a price freeze. Nevertheless, it cleverly avoided other countries' mistakes, considerably increasing its probability of survival after learning "the lesson from Mexico."

Now, two years after the Mexican stabilization, we can summarize the main differences between Mexico's program and other programs, and especially between the Mexican and the Israeli program. Perhaps these differences will permit Mexico to avoid some of the difficulties encountered by the Israeli stabilization effort today.

Fiscal Adjustment

First of all, the fiscal deficit was adjusted in Mexico some years before the plan. In this sense Mexico is more similar to Chile, which made the real adjustment some years before it started to anchor the price level.

Structural Reforms

If we look at the 1987 Mexican program, it seems that the main difference between it and other heterodox experiments is the extent of the structural changes implemented in addition to fiscal, monetary, and incomes policies.

Ortiz mentions these structural changes several times in his paper, paying special attention to the role of trade liberalization and pointing to evidence of the effects of liberalization. These effects would seem to be present in every price system anchored by the exchange rate, even without any change in the level of trade restrictions.

To assess the impact of trade liberalization and other reforms, we have to compare the effects of similar policies with or without such reforms—for example, to compare Mexico's PSE and a former, similar stabilization effort, which did not include liberalization measures. It is also possible to compare Mexico's PSE with the Chilean experience, which included structural reforms and liberalization.

I think it would be very interesting to include a detailed description of the reforms in the paper and to try and analyze its effects on the stabilization process. Perhaps these reforms, even though they endanger the program (by leading to rapid import growth in the short run), can help prevent the business cycle and the phase of growing unemployment connected with the stabilization process.

Real Wages

Another important difference between the Mexican experience and most other experiences is Mexico's success in the stabilization of real wages. During 1981–1987 real wages in the manufacturing sector decreased 40 percent, but they remained stable in 1988 and 1989, in spite of the pressures that were certainly present given the drop in wages up to 1987. The development of wages in Israel was quite different (see figure 8.C1).

Wage stabilization in Mexico probably helped in preventing the erosion of profitability, and it may help the economy to break out of the business cycle characteristic of the stabilization process.

The Dynamics of Inflation Slowdown

The dynamics of inflation slowdown also differed in Mexico. In Argentina, Israel, and Brazil, there was a price shock and an attempt at immediate stabilization of the price level. In Mexico, the social pact included a path for the slowdown of inflation. In figure 8.C2 we see that the convergence to low inflation was slower in Mexico than in the other countries. What are the real effects of a gradual versus a rapid convergence? Is it easier for the economy to disinflate over several months instead of disinflating abruptly?

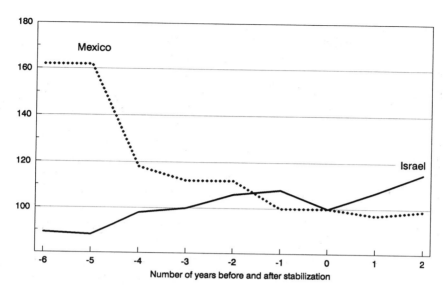

Figure 8.C1
Real wages in industry before and after stabilization. (Index: year of program
implementation = 100.)

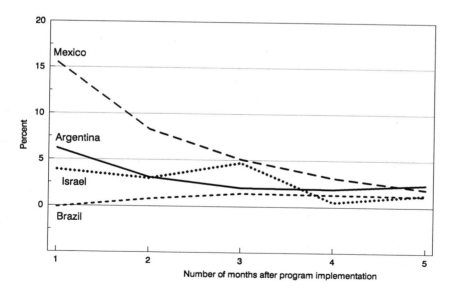

Figure 8.C2
Inflation slowdown after stabilization.

The External Position of the Economy

I also want to comment on the external position of Mexico before and after the program, in comparison with the external position of Israel. Ortiz writes that, in contrast with the Israeli experience, the Mexican program was implemented without external financial support. This is true, but if we look at figure 8.C3 we see that the level of international reserves in Mexico immediately before the program was extremely high. Therefore, at that time Mexico did not seem to need external support. Israel's external situation was very weak when it launched its program, and it was not known that there would be a substantial improvement in the terms of trade and a huge repatriation of capital.

It is also interesting to note Mexico's enormous loss of reserves in the year after the program, which was due to the increase in the import surplus. The fact that the Mexican stabilization program survived in spite of this loss is due partly to expectations that external financial support for Mexico would be coming early in 1990.

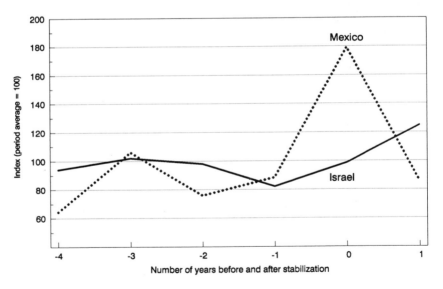

Figure 8.C3
Foreign currency reserves before and after stabilization.

The Real Interest Rate

Finally, let me comment briefly on high real interest rates prevailing for a long period after stabilization and appearing together with rapid credit expansion, a phenomenon which Ortiz describes as "a puzzle."

Two factors, frequently ignored in trying to solve the puzzle, should be stressed. First, the rise in real interest rates occurs together with a rapid decrease in nominal interest rates. It seems that the increase in real interest rates is felt only in the long run, whereas the decrease in nominal interest rates is felt immediately—as it improves the cash flow of firms, which are then ready to borrow at the new interest rates. Secondly, the increased liquidity of banks due to the increase in local-currency deposits raises the supply of credit (to firms and consumers) and eases credit rationing. The latter, after the stabilization program, apparently leads to a sharp reduction in "shadow interest rates" and could be one of the factors explaining the ensuing growth of credit, financing consumption, and economic activity, in spite of very high measured interest rates.

General Discussion

Some of the participants addressed the sequence in which Mexico's policy measures were implemented. The Mexican stabilization program was implemented in two stages. The first involved the traditional orthodox part combined with structural reforms, thus correcting fundamentals before launching the "hetero" part of stabilization. Sebastian Edwards believes that this sequence contributed to the success of the policy; only in cases of hyperinflation does one need to stabilize before embarking on structural reforms. Michael Bruno wondered whether a stepwise policy would have helped to prevent the second recession that hit Israel, whose stabilization program had been implemented in one step. Zalman Shiffer asked about the existence of distortions at the firm level in Mexico resulting from the inflationary era. Such distortions were mentioned by Peter M. Garber, and occurred in Israel.

The question of the remaining inflation was also raised. Rafi Melnick noted the similar rate (~20%) prevailing in countries with successful stabilizations and wondered, along with other participants, about the possible causes of this phenomenon.

Vittorio Corbo pointed out the various ways in which policy makers have chosen to deal with real appreciation in the successful stabilization countries. In Mexico they preferred to implement a crawling peg; in Israel they preferred to devalue from time to time; in Chile, between 1978 and 1982, the policy was not to devalue at all. He believed that lessons could be drawn from comparing the three cases.

9 Premature Liberalization, Incomplete Stabilization: The Özal Decade in Turkey

Dani Rodrik

In late 1979, Turkey was in the throes of a foreign-exchange crisis, with widespread shortages, negative growth, and inflation in triple digits. A decade later, Turkey had a comfortable balance-of-payments position and considerable foreign reserves. Exports and foreign-exchange receipts from tourism and other services were buoyant. The economy had achieved a remarkable transformation from an inward-oriented outlook to an outward-oriented one, and had undergone significant liberalization in the areas of trade and finance.

However, there remain some disturbing similarities with the late 1970s. Despite favorable external terms of trade, inflation is around 70% and the public-sector budget is out of control. Though not as severe, a recession grips Turkish industry. Perhaps most ominous, labor and business groups alike have lost much of their confidence in the ability of the government to set things straight. A round of further trade and foreign-exchange liberalization, launched in the summer of 1989 and billed as the government's new weapon against inflation, has alienated all but the rentier groups and has had scarcely any effect on prices.

In evaluating the Turkish experience of the 1980s, one has to confront the apparent paradox of a tremendously successful external adjustment pitted against severe internal imbalances. As is by now well recognized, dealing with a debt crisis of the sort that Turkey had in the late 1970s requires two sorts of adjustment: an external adjustment entailing a net transfer of resources from the domestic economy to foreign creditors, and an internal adjustment entailing a net transfer of resources from domestic residents to the public sector (which bears the external debt). Turkey was considerably more successful on the former front than on the latter. As we shall see, Turkey's inflation experience can be explained in large part by the needs of public finance: public-sector deficits have been financed at the margin by the inflation tax.

Two aspects of the Turkish stabilization of the 1980s pose puzzles. First, how was the initial reduction of inflation in 1981–82 accomplished at no apparent cost to growth, and, in fact, at a time when growth picked up considerably? Second, what accounts for the persistence of inflation and the two jumps in its level in 1983–84 and 1987–88? The account that follows will focus on these puzzles. Some remaining structural problems and policy dilemmas are discussed at the end of the paper.

1. Background

Turkey's economic troubles date back to 1977, when a public-sector-led investment boom collapsed as a consequence of a foreign-exchange crisis. By 1978, Turkey found herself mired in a severe debt crisis and an extended series of negotiations with foreign creditors, for whom this would prove a dress rehearsal for the more generalized outbreak of 1982. After two years of muddling through, Turkey showed some signs of successful adjustment in the first half of the 1980s. But more than ten years after the crisis, Turkey is deeper in debt and macroeconomic stability remains elusive.

The reasons for Turkey's debt crisis of 1977 were essentially twofold. First, expansionary fiscal policy in the wake of the first oil shock wreaked its usual havoc on macroeconomic balances, at a time when restraint would have been the more prudent policy. As table 9.1 shows, public investment rose from 7.0% of GNP (in 1973) to 13.1% (in 1977), while domestic savings stagnated. The counterpart in the external balances was a turnaround from a surplus of 2.2% on the current account to a deficit of 6.9%. Yet the crisis could have been averted, or at least

Table 9.1
Investment-savings balances, 1973–1977 (percent of GNP).

	1973	1974	1975	1976	1977
Investment					
Private	11.1	10.0	10.3	13.1	11.9
Public	7.0	10.8	12.2	11.6	13.1
Domestic savings					
Private	11.6	11.0	8.5	11.2	11.7
Public	8.8	7.4	9.0	8.1	6.4
Foreign savings (current-account deficit)	−2.2	2.3	5.0	5.4	6.9

postponed, if Turkey's foreign-borrowing strategy had not been inherently destabilizing. After 1975, a major part of foreign inflows were attracted under the infamous "convertible Turkish lira deposits" (CTLD) scheme. The scheme provided a public exchange-rate guarantee to private borrowers, effectively ensuring that the borrowers would pay Swiss or German interest rates on loans denominated in Turkish currency, irrespective of Turkish inflation or devaluation. The mad scramble for foreign borrowing lasted for about two years, until foreign banks refused to roll over credits and the Turkish government ran out of foreign reserves. By the end of 1977 the implicit subsidy on foreign borrowing was costing the government around 2% of GNP, and it would rise even farther as the subsequent large devaluations entailed even greater capital losses on the CTLD debt.

Between mid 1977 and early 1980, a string of weak governments were unable to arrest the deterioration of the economy. Two IMF stand-bys ended in failure. The foreign-exchange constraint led to shortages, which, together with excess liquidity, resulted in rising inflation. Inflation reached 120% annually in early 1980. Nominal devaluations lagged behind domestic prices, leading to real appreciation (see figure 9.1). One positive outcome in this period was a substantial restructuring of the external debt, including the bulk of the CTLDs, which were consolidated

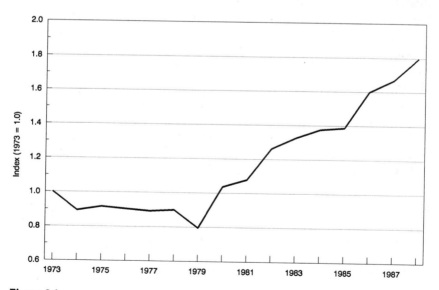

Figure 9.1
Real exchange rate.

and converted into long-term liabilities. A summary of this restructuring and the background political situation is provided in Celasun and Rodrik 1989.

2. Early Results of the 1980 Stabilization

In January 1980, a clear break with the half-hearted measures of the past was signaled by an economic package that went considerably beyond those that had recently been undertaken. The package included a large devaluation (from TL 47.1 to TL 70 to the US$), export subsidies, an increase in interest rates, and substantial price increases for state enterprise products and a promise to abolish most government subsidies. Perhaps more important than the specific measures was the clear enunciation of a new approach favoring exports, outward orientation, and liberalization. The program was the handiwork of Turgut Özal, the undersecretary to the prime minister in the minority government of Demirel, which had taken over in late 1979. So closely was Özal identified with the "January 24 package" that when the military took over in a bloodless coup in September 1980 (in response to the increase in political violence) he was asked to continue overseeing the economy.

With the exception of a 16-month interregnum in 1982–83, Özal has indeed remained at the helm. He became prime minister after the November 1983 elections. He then launched a second round of measures aimed at deepening the process of outward orientation. These included substantial import liberalization and a relaxation of controls on the capital account of the balance of payments. Domestic residents were allowed to open foreign-currency deposit accounts with domestic banks. The import liberalization has since suffered some setbacks, as revenue and protection requirements have forced the government to impose and manipulate some highly discretionary specific import duties. Similar setbacks have occurred in financial liberalization, as interest-rate controls have alternately been lifted and re-imposed in response to financial crises. After a long delay, the process of privatizing state-owned enterprises was also launched in late 1988. In November 1989, having lost much popular ground in the general and local elections of 1987 and 1989 respectively, Özal had himself elevated to the presidency by a reluctant Parliament. The economic transformation that Turkey underwent under his guidance identifies the 1980s quite clearly as the Özal decade.

Özal's policies hinged on an exceptional restructuring of key relative prices within the economy. The real value of the Turkish lira was kept on a downward path, with a daily crawl on a PPP-plus basis. The initial real devaluation of January 1980 was therefore not only maintained but steadily reinforced. The weakness of labor unions in the aftermath of the September 1980 coup was used to entrench (and exacerbate) the reduction in real wages that had taken place in the preceding inflationary period. While wage repression may not have been a direct policy goal, it facilitated stabilization by taking cost pressures off the private and public sectors. The considerable flexibility exhibited by the real exchange rate and by real wages in the 1980s is a critical component of the account that follows.

From the very beginning, Özal put heavy emphasis on output recovery alongside stabilization. The two prongs of the growth strategy in the early 1980s were public investment and export encouragement. As table 9.2 shows, in the first few years of the program public investment took an uncharacteristic turn for a stabilization episode: it rose by 2–3 percentage points of GNP. Moreover, the structure of public investment was shifted away from manufacturing (which might have simply crowded out private investment) and toward infrastructure (which is possibly complementary to private capital).

Table 9.2
Macroeconomic indicators, 1978–1980.

	GNP growth (%)	Inflation (%)	Merchandise exports (mil. $)	Percent of GNP			
				Current account	Investment		External debt
					Total	Public	
1978	2.9	52.6	2,288	−2.6	18.5	9.5	32.7[a]
1979	−0.4	63.9	2,261	−2.1	18.3	9.5	31.2[a]
1980	−1.1	107.2	2,910	−5.5	21.4	11.5	27.2
1981	4.1	36.8	4,703	−3.5	21.5	13.2	26.1
1982	4.5	25.2	5,746	−2.1	20.3	12.0	29.8
1983	3.3	30.6	5,728	−3.5	20.6	10.2	32.6
1984	5.9	52.0	7,133	−2.8	19.3	9.7	39.5
1985	5.1	43.4	7,958	−1.9	20.8	11.4	47.2
1986	8.1	29.4	7,457	−2.6	24.5	13.4	53.1
1987	7.4	32.0	10,190	−1.4	25.4	13.3	56.1
1988	3.4	68.4	11,662	2.1	23.6	10.3	53.3

a. Converted to domestic currency at black-market exchange rate.

On the export side, the encouragement took several forms. First, as mentioned above, the exchange rate was maintained on a depreciating path, with an implicit PPP-plus rule to provide a healthy margin of competitiveness to domestic producers. Figure 9.1 shows the steady real depreciation of the Turkish lira after 1980, an experience unparalleled in modern Turkish history. By 1988, the real lira had depreciated by more than 100% relative to its level in 1979. Second, exporters were provided with a dazzling array of subsidies, including credit at sub-market rates and tax "rebates" only loosely linked to actual tax payments. The *ad valorem* equivalent of these subsidies amounted to 20–25% in the early 1980s, with some reduction after 1984 (see Milanovic 1986, table VII.4).

Exports responded quickly and, one would guess, beyond the wildest dreams of Özal himself. Within two years, exports doubled (from $2.3 billion in 1979 to $4.7 billion in 1981), and stood at $8 billion dollars by 1985 (table 9.2). Despite widespread allegations (and evidence) of overinvoicing, the increase in exports remains spectacular even when one adjusts for the "fictitious" component, and continues to baffle skeptics. Thanks to exports and public investment, growth also recovered quickly. After negative growth in 1979 and 1980, the Turkish economy settled on a growth rate of 4–5%, with occasional dips and overshoots (see table 9.2).

As table 9.2 shows, the stabilization program brought inflation down from its peak of 107% in 1980 to a more reasonable level of 25% in 1982. In 1980 Turkey was still an economy with few sources of inflationary inertia: real wages had proved downward flexible in 1978–79, and even more so with the military at the helm. The trick in bringing inflation down was thus aggregate demand restraint, of which a healthy dose was applied in 1980–1982. As we shall see below, despite the rise in public investment, the adjustment in public-enterprise prices, real-wage cuts, and output recovery allowed the public-sector deficit to come down from 10% of GNP in 1980 to 5.4% and 6.0% in 1981 and 1982, respectively. Monetary restraint took the form mainly of increases in interest rates. With the liberalization of bank deposit rates in mid 1980, depositors began to face something they were unaccustomed to: positive real interest rates. Demand for broadly defined money increased considerably as a result, with the M2/GNP ratio rising from 15% in 1980 to 23% in 1982 (see figure 9.5). This remonetization of the economy played a crucial role in controlling inflation, leading Rüşdü Saracoglu, the current governor of the central bank, to comment that "interest rate policy. . .

was perhaps the single most important factor in lowering the rate of inflation" (Saracoglu 1987). But other changes in relative prices also helped by reducing aggregate demand: real-wage cuts, a deterioration in agriculture's terms of trade (as price-support programs were deemphasized), and public-sector price increases all implied a transfer of real income from the private to the public sector, with a corresponding cutback in expenditures by the former and the deficits of the latter (Celasun and Rodrik 1989).

What then allowed Turkey to bring inflation down in such a short time, and in the context of a growing economy, where so many other countries have failed? Part of the answer has to do with the single-minded dedication with which sharp changes in relative prices (exchange rates, interest rates, public-sector prices, real wages) were imposed on a society rendered temporarily docile by military rule. These changes in relative prices were the counterpart to the fiscal and monetary contraction of 1980–1982, as they allowed the public-sector deficit to be cut and private absorption to be reduced. And the military's role was not altogether malicious: the alleviation of the intense cycle of political violence that had prevailed prior to September 1980 endowed the new regime with an initial period of goodwill and public confidence. This breathing spell allowed Özal to implement a set of radical policies which would have been unimaginable in normal times.

But a large part of the answer has to do with the external balance. Compared with other countries going through their crises after 1982, the Turkish government was initially granted exceptionally favorable terms on the external-debt front. The foreign-exchange constraint was allevi-ated practically overnight in 1980, not only because of the government's policies but also because of generous inflows from official and multilateral sources. The Turkish public sector consequently never experienced a sharp turnaround in net resource transfers from abroad, and therefore had less need for inflationary finance at home.

Tables 9.3 and 9.4 show the net resource transfers (NRT) to Turkey during the 1980s. In table 9.4, estimates of the breakdown of the total NRT between the public and private sectors are provided. Because of the nature of the assumptions made in calculating this breakdown, these numbers are less reliable than the aggregate figures shown in table 9.3. Nonetheless, interesting conclusions emerge. First, in aggregate terms it is not really until 1985 that the Turkish economy started to generate net resource transfers abroad of any sizable magnitude; there are large net

Table 9.3
Net resource transfers to Turkey (percent of GNP).

	Current account	Interest payments	Net resource transfers	Net resource transfers to 17 HICs
1980	−5.5	1.0	4.5	
1981	−3.5	2.0	1.5	
1982	−2.1	2.7	−0.6	0.8
1983	−3.5	2.8	0.7	−2.8
1984	−2.8	3.2	−0.3	−4.8
1985	−1.9	3.3	−1.4	−4.2
1986	−2.6	3.7	−1.1	
1987	−1.4	3.7	−2.2	
1988	2.1	3.9	−5.9	

Table 9.4
Sectoral distribution of the net resource transfer (NRT) (percent of GNP, unless otherwise indicated).

	PSBR (1)	Share financed by foreign borrowing[a] (2)	Public net foreign borrowing[b] (3)	Public foreign interest payments[c] (4)	NRT Public[d] (5)	NRT Private[e] (6)
1980	10.0	0.355	3.55	0.85	2.7	1.8
1981	5.4	0.628	3.39	1.76	1.6	−0.1
1982	6.0	0.495	2.97	2.42	0.5	−1.1
1983	5.2	0.239	1.24	2.59	−1.3	2.1
1984	6.5	0.516	3.35	2.78	0.6	−0.9
1985	4.9	0.153	0.75	2.81	−2.1	0.7
1986	4.5	0.536	2.41	3.08	−0.7	−0.4
1987	8.3	0.345	2.86	3.12	−0.3	−2.0

a. Source: OECD 1987–1988.
b. Column 1 *times* column 2.
c. Total interest payments (from table 5), *times* the share of public debt in total external debt.
d. Column 3 *minus* column 4.
e. Total NRT (table 5) *minus* column 5.

inflows, especially in the first two years of the adjustment program. Note that 1985 comes five years after the start of the adjustment program, and eight years after the initial debt crisis. Other heavily indebted countries did not enjoy this luxury; as table 9.3 shows, they were forced to generate a NRT of 4–5% of GNP almost as soon as their debt crisis hit in 1982.

Since the relationship between external-debt service and domestic inflation is intermediated by the public-sector budget, of more interest is the NRT undertaken by the public sector. Here, table 9.4 again shows a quite favorable picture, especially in the early years of adjustment. It is only in 1983 that the Turkish public sector first makes a positive NRT, and the magnitudes thereafter are not particularly large. Over the 1980–1987 period as a whole, the public sector is a net recipient of NRT from abroad (of 0.1% of GNP).

We see now the key difference between Turkey and other highly indebted countries. These countries had to substitute inflationary finance for external finance when their debt crisis hit. In Turkey, although this was also the case in 1978–79, from early 1980 on the Özal program coincided with an alleviation of the external-finance constraint. The squeeze on fiscal balances was correspondingly smaller, and the resort to the inflation tax less pronounced. I will return to the budget-inflation nexus later on.

What then accounts for the fact that Turkey was given, in Lance Taylor's (1990) words, a "long leash" by international finance institutions in the early 1980s? Here the story becomes political. Around 1979–80, Turkey's geopolitical importance to the Western alliance was highlighted by a series of crises: the Turkish threat to move closer to the Soviet Union, the Iranian revolution, and the Soviet invasion of Afghanistan. The fragile political situation within Turkey added to the worries. These prompted a rescue operation launched by the leading OECD countries in early 1979.

Turkey consequently became the recipient of medium- and long-term loan commitments in 1979–1981 that were on average twice as large as in 1975–1978 (the latter covering mostly the period prior to Turkey's debt crisis, in which capital was flowing in smoothly), and of public commitments three times as large (Celasun and Rodrik 1989, chapter 9). The World Bank extended five consecutive Structural Adjustment Loans, the most ever made to a single country. The IMF helped out with a three-year stand-by in June 1980, rewarding Turkey with 625% of Turkey's quota at the time—the largest multiple awarded by the IMF until then. These flows were facilitated by the obvious redirection of economic strategy sought by Özal. They were also easier to come up with in an international environment in which Turkey was the only large country in a debt crisis. But the significance of Turkey's renewed strategic importance cannot be underestimated.

To summarize this section: The fight against inflation was won in 1980–1982 with considerable assistance from external creditors. Capital inflows from public sources postponed the need for a drastic fiscal retrenchment and reduced the recourse to the inflation tax. Some reduction in public deficits did take place, mainly through relative-price changes which benefited the public sector at the expense of the private sector. Economic activity did not suffer as the reduction in domestic absorption was counterbalanced by exports, which received hefty and sustained encouragement.

3. Inflation in the 1980s

As the second column of table 9.2 indicates, the successful campaign against inflation was rather short-lived. Figure 9.2 provides more details on price developments since 1980. After reaching the low 20s, the inflation rate rose again in 1983, reaching 50–60%. In 1985 and 1986

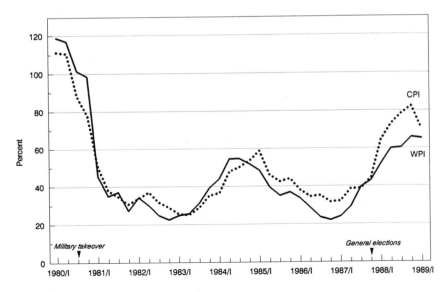

Figure 9.2
Inflation rate.

inflation slowed down again, only to pick up in 1987. Currently, inflation ranges around 60–70%, a level higher than any since 1980. As seen, there is some evidence of a political cycle at work. The sharp fall in inflation in late 1980 is, as discussed above, partly associated with military rule. The accelerations of inflation in 1983 and in 1987 coincides with general parliamentary elections.

What accounts for the inability to bring inflation down? As noted above, inertial factors were relatively unimportant in the early part of the decade and, as the large variability of inflation would suggest, have not played an important role since then (with the possible exception of the last year or so). This would suggest that the monetization of public-sector deficits is the primary culprit.

Tables 9.5 and 9.6 provide the relevant data for an analysis of seignorage and the inflation tax in this period. Seignorage here refers to the revenue raised by the monetary authorities by issuing non-interest-bearing liabilities, i.e., base money (MB). On the central bank's balance sheet, the increase in MB is the counterpart to the domestic credit extended by the central bank to the treasury (and public enterprises), once we regroup net foreign assets of the central bank under public-sector foreign borrowing. Table 9.5 shows the computation of the monetary base, while table 9.6 calculates seignorage revenues (as a share of GNP) as given by the increase in MB in a given year divided by that year's GNP. The inflation tax, in turn, refers to the increase in nominal (base) money which individuals have to accumulate to keep their real balances constant (see below). This is also calculated in table 9.6. Since part of the money base (required reserves held by commercial banks) pays interest, the revenues derived by the government by issuing money should net these payments out, and this is also done in table 9.6. The difference between seignorage and inflation tax arises from changes in real money demand, which in turn may be the consequence of financial liberalization or *changes* in the inflation rate, real income, and interest rates. This difference is sometimes referred to as the non-inflationary component of seignorage, as it is the increase in money demand that is consistent with a zero inflation rate.

As these tables show, the Turkish public sector has consistently relied on revenues from seignorage and the inflation tax on the order of 1.5–3.0% of GNP, even in low-inflation years. Notice also that high-inflation periods do not necessarily generate larger seignorage, as the higher levels of inflation in these periods result in substantial erosion in the real demand for money and reduce the base of the tax. For example,

Table 9.5
Monetary base[a] (TL billions).

| | Currency[b] | Deposits with CB[c] | | | Monetary base[d] | GNP |
		Commercial banks[e]	Other financial institutes	Other sectors		
1979	144	261	0	27	432	
1980	218	299	0	58	575	4,435
1981	281	416	1	135	833	6,554
1982	412	533	1	103	1,049	8,735
1983	548	704	1	141	1,394	11,552
1984	736	1,150	4	145	2,035	18,375
1985	1,011	1,518	0	41	2,570	27,789
1986	1,415	1,740	7	208	3,370	39,310
1987	2,275	2,431	2	45	4,753	58,390
1988	3,426	5,382	31	390	9,229	102,443

a. All stocks are at year-end.
b. Currency in circulation minus cash in CB vaults.
c. Excludes deposits of public sector.
d. Sum of first four columns.
e. Includes import deposits.

Table 9.6
Seignorage and inflation tax (percent of GNP).

	Seignorage (ΔMB/GNP)	Inflation[a]	Inflation tax[b]	Interest paid on required reserves[c]	Adjusted seignorage[d]	Adjusted inflation tax[d]
1980	3.2	94.9	9.2	0.22	3.0	9.0
1981	3.9	24.2	2.1	0.51	3.4	1.6
1982	2.4	24.8	2.4	0.67	1.8	1.7
1983	3.0	40.9	3.7	0.79	2.2	2.9
1984	3.5	66.7	5.1	1.10	2.4	4.0
1985	1.9	38.2	2.8	0.62	1.3	2.2
1986	2.0	24.4	1.6	—	2.0	1.6
1987	2.4	49.0	2.8	—	2.4	2.8
1988	4.4	69.6	3.2	—	4.4	3.2

a. WPI inflation during year.
b. Column 2 *times* MB_{-1}/GNP.
c. Source: World Bank 1988.
d. Interest paid is subtracted.

total seignorage in 1981 surpassed the level in 1980 even though that in 1981 was one-fourth of that in 1980. A quick comparison of the annual inflation rates with the consolidated public-sector deficit (the latter is shown in table 9.4, column 1) will show a broad correlation between the two.

Now let us pursue the logic of the public-finance view of inflation. Assume that fiscal deficits are financed *at the margin* purely by money creation (i.e., seignorage) and that other financing items do not respond systematically to the deficit. Then the public-sector budget identity can be expressed as

$$d = m(\Delta MB / MB) , \tag{1}$$

where d is the deficit-to-GNP ratio, m stands for the share of base money in GNP, and other financing items are ignored for notational simplicity. In any given year, let the proportional change in demand for base money $(\Delta MB/MB)$ depend on inflation and real income in the following manner: $\Delta MB/MB = \pi + \mu n$, where π is the inflation rate, n is the real growth rate of GNP, and μ is the income elasticity of demand for base money. Then we can rewrite (1) as

$$d = m(\pi + \mu n) . \tag{2}$$

This expression shows the combinations of m, π, and n that are consistent with an exogenous level of the deficit. Note that $m\pi$ stands for the inflation tax. Solving for π, we get an explicit formula that captures the essence of the public-finance view of inflation:

$$\pi = (d/m) - \mu n . \tag{3}$$

This highlights four important determinants of the inflation rate. First, and most obvious, is the deficit. An increase in the deficit of one percentage point of GNP will increase the inflation rate by $1/m$ percentage points. Given the Turkish average for m in the 1980s of around 0.10, this amounts to a 10-percentage-point increase in π.

A second important determinant, as this example already illustrates, is the monetization of the economy, and more specifically the ratio of base money to GNP. As we shall see, financial liberalization during the 1980s has resulted in a considerable decline in m, exacerbating the inflationary consequences of a given deficit. Finally, real growth of income and the income elasticity of demand have predictable effects on inflation via their effects on money demand.

Can an equation like equation 3 explain much of the Turkish inflation in the 1980s? As a purely descriptive exercise, we can estimate a simple regression of the form

$$\pi = \alpha_0 + \alpha_1[(d/m) - \mu n] + \varepsilon. \tag{4}$$

Brushing a whole host of econometric and interpretation problems aside and limiting ourselves to a "naïve" public-finance view, we can think of α_0 as the "trend" or "inertial" inflation rate. The prediction of the public-finance view of inflation would be that α_1 is statistically indistinguishable from unity. The results of the regression are reported in table 9.7, where different values of μ (ranging from 1 to 5) have been tried to generate the right-hand-side variable. Notice that period-average m's have been used here (by taking the geometric mean of two year-end MBs) to correct for changes in the level of base money during the relevant year.

The results are quite consistent with the public-finance view. Regardless of the value of μ used, the intercept coefficient emerges as statistically insignificantly different from zero. This would suggest that whatever inertial forces may have been at work, they were insufficiently powerful

Table 9.7
The relationship between public deficits and inflation, 1980–1988.[a]

Equation	μ	α_0	α_1	R^2	d.f.
(1a)	1.0	0.04 (0.20)	0.65 (0.30)	0.40	7
(1b)	1.0	—	0.71 (0.09)	0.40	8
(2a)	2.0	0.04 (0.19)	0.70 (0.28)	0.48	7
(2b)	2.0	—	0.76 (0.09)	0.40	8
(3a)	3.0	0.05 (0.18)	0.73 (0.25)	0.55	7
(3b)	3.0	—	0.81 (0.09)	0.54	8
(4a)	4.0	0.08 (0.16)	0.74 (0.22)	0.61	7
(4b)	4.0	—	0.87 (0.09)	0.59	8
(5a)	5.0	0.12 (0.15)	0.73 (0.20)	0.65	7
(5b)	5.0	—	0.92 (0.09)	0.60	8

a. Figures in parentheses are standard errors.

over the entire period. Moreover, although the point estimate for α_1 is always less than unity, it is statistically significantly different from zero but not from unity. On the basis of this simple test, we cannot reject the hypothesis of a one-for-one link between public-sector deficits (appropriately scaled) and inflation. The clear implication is that at the margin deficits are (nearly) completely monetized. Note also that the regressions do best with relatively high income elasticities of demand for base money. Demand elasticities of 4 or 5 are too high to be credible. Even if we rule these cases out, the fiscal view, as captured by this regression equation, appears to "explain" around 50% of the variation in inflation over the 1980s.

Figure 9.3 compares the actual inflation rate with the inflation rate predicted by the above framework. Since α_1 is statistically indistinguishable from unity, the predicted inflation rate is computed simply as $[(d/m) - \mu n]$, with μ fixed at 3.0. We see that the simple public-finance view does an adequate job of capturing some important turning points in inflation: the sharp reduction in 1981, the increase in 1984, and the jump after 1986. It does less well in some other respects: the predicted inflation is significantly higher in 1981 and 1982, and significantly lower in 1984; the actual inflation rate increases sharply in 1988 whereas the prediction is a steep fall.

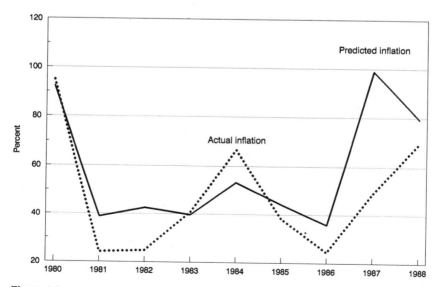

Figure 9.3
Predicted and actual inflation.

As emphasized above, two key variables that go into the public-finance view of inflation are the public-sector deficit (d) and the base money/GNP ratio (m). Let us take a closer look at each.

4. Public-Sector Balances

Table 9.8 displays the consolidated public-sector accounts in the 1980s. In Turkey, the two major components are the consolidated government budget and the accounts of the State Economic Enterprises (SEEs). Since 1984, however, Özal has also created a large number of special funds which disburse money in a rather discretionary way and are largely beyond the purview of the parliament. These funds are financed by special earmarked taxes (such as specific import duties) and by borrowing through so-called revenue sharing certificates, and have usually been running surpluses (see table 9.8). The importance of these funds can be gauged by considering that their revenues amount to one-fourth of the regular budgetary revenues.

As table 9.8 shows, after an initial decline in 1981, the aggregate public deficit has hovered around 5–6% of GNP during most of the 1980s. The magnitude of this deficit can be put in perspective by noting that this is just about the same level of deficit that obtained during the boom years 1973–1977. The considerably larger deficit of 1980 was in large part attributable to the second oil shock and the contraction of real activity. Once allowance is made for the special factors that pushed the 1980 deficit up, the magnitude of fiscal adjustment in the 1980s is hardly exemplary.

Several forces interacted to limit the magnitude of fiscal retrenchment. As mentioned above, the presence of generous capital inflows in the initial years of the program made a drastic retrenchment superfluous. In addition, the adjustment of income-tax brackets (in response to bracket creep) and the lowering of tax rates in late 1980 led to a reduction in direct tax revenue in the early 1980s: direct taxes fell from 11.7% of GNP in 1980 to 6.5% in 1985. Some of this loss was made up later, with the introduction of the value-added tax in 1985. Third, revenue enhancement on the part of public enterprises relied almost exclusively on price adjustments rather than on productivity increases. These price adjustments became politically more difficult as time went on. The available evidence shows no discernible trend in labor productivity of the SEEs (World Bank 1988b, pp. 82–84). The price adjustments, in turn, were typically delayed and

Table 9.8
Public-sector balances[a] (percent of GNP).

	1980	1981	1982	1983	1984	1985	1986	1987	1988	1989[b]
General government	-3.3	-0.8	-2.0	-2.6	-4.2	-1.7	-1.2	-3.9	-3.6	-3.1
Cons. budget	-3.7	-1.8	-2.8	-2.6	-5.3	-2.8	-3.6	-4.2	-3.7	-3.5
Local admin.	0.2	0.2	0.1	0.0	0.2	0.2	-0.2	-0.4	-0.4	-0.1
Revolving funds	0.2	0.8	0.7	0.0	0.4	0.4	0.4	0.2	-0.2	-0.0
Special funds	—	—	—	—	0.5	0.5	2.1	0.5	0.7	0.5
State Economic Enterprises (SEE)	-6.7	-4.6	-4.0	-2.6	-2.3	-3.2	-3.3	-4.4	-2.8	-2.4
Total public sector	**-10.0**	**-5.4**	**-6.0**	**-5.2**	**-6.5**	**-4.9**	**-4.5**	**-8.3**	**-6.4**	**-5.6**
Sources of financing (per cent of total)										
Net foreign borrowing	35.5	62.8	49.5	23.9	51.6	15.3	53.6	34.5	41.0	20.2
Net domestic borrowing	64.5	37.2	50.5	76.1	48.4	84.7	46.4	65.5	59.0	79.8
Of which:										
Central Bank	34.3	20.0	12.7	11.2	11.1	25.6	14.7	11.9	n.a.	n.a.

a. Negative numbers indicate deficits.
b. Provisional.

bunched after elections, helping to generate the political inflation cycle displayed in figure 9.2. The acceleration of inflation in late 1987 and early 1988 can be attributed in large part to the effect of delayed increases in SEE prices (Central Bank 1989).

The cycle is reinforced by the pressure on the Central Bank to provide easy credit to popular sectors prior to elections. In the second half of 1987, for example, "the Central Bank was obliged to increase credits extended to the public sector significantly, in particular to the Soil Products Office, and to the state-owned Agricultural Bank, which extends credits to farmers" in preparation for the November general elections (OECD 1987–88, p. 38). As John Waterbury has stressed, Özal's politics has two faces: on the one hand, it aims to enhance economic efficiency and public-sector finances; on the other, it relies on the traditional mechanisms of "coalition maintenance through state patronage." The first is what "Özal wishes to show the donor community, the EC, and international business;" the second reflects the payments he has to make to ensure the dominance of his center-right coalition (Waterbury 1989, pp. 6–7).

After 1983, the toll of earlier inadequate fiscal adjustment began to be exacted in sharply rising debt service. By the second half of the 1980s, interest payments on external *and* internal debt became a major force pushing deficits up. As figure 9.4 shows, interest payments out of the consolidated budget rose from 1% of GNP in 1981 to 5% in 1988. Interest payments now amount to about a third of all current expenditures (inclusive of transfers). Significantly, domestic interest payments have begun to outstrip payments on the external debt since 1987. This reflects a deliberate decision, made after 1983 (as the official capital inflows started to slow down), to increase resort to domestic debt finance as a non-inflationary alternative. Table 9.9 shows that new issues of public debt took off after this date, to the point that the public sector now completely dominates the capital market. Government paper is now bought primarily by commercial banks, who can hold it as part of their liquidity requirement. The bulk of public debt carries a maturity of one year or less, so new debt is now issued primarily to roll over the old debt. While the recent acceleration of inflation has pushed the interest rates on public debt to negative levels in real terms, the real (after-tax) return on public securities averaged around 10–20% in 1985–86, generally above corresponding rates offered by the private sector (Akyüz 1990).

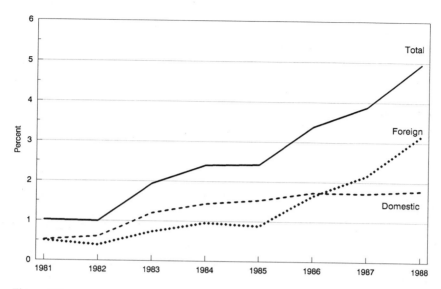

Figure 9.4
Government interest payments as percentage of GNP.

Table 9.9
Issues of public debt.

	Public-debt issue		Allocation of government bonds and Treasury notes (percent)			
	Percent of GNP	Percent of all issues	Banks	Public sector	Private firms	Individuals
1980	1.7	65.5				
1981	2.1	76.6				
1982	0.9	37.9				
1983	2.3	69.9				
1984	4.7	92.0	43.4	26.9	26.2	3.5
1985	6.1	93.8	51.6	22.1	23.6	2.7
1986	7.8	91.8	69.9	26.4	2.7	1.1
1987	10.3	89.8	77.7	18.1	4.0	0.2
1988	8.9	88.8	90.5	6.7	2.8	0.0

Source: Hazine ve Diş Ticaret Mustesarligi, as reported in *Cumhuriyet*, September 12, 1989, p. 12.

In Sargent-Wallace (1982) fashion, earlier bond financing now threatens fiscal balances and makes inflationary finance more likely, in two ways. First, the interest burden adds to the deficit, and increases the pressure on the central bank to finance the public sector. Second, the presence of a large unindexed debt increases the temptation to erode it by generating a sudden, unanticipated inflation. Since maturities are short, however, the room for the latter is limited.

5. Trends in Money Balances

As pointed out above, the re-monetization of the economy played a crucial role in reducing inflation in the early 1980s. This can be seen clearly in figures 9.5 and 9.6, which illustrate the sharp increase in M2 between 1980 and 1983, in real terms and as a share of GNP. The primary role was played here by interest-rate reform, and the corresponding sharp increases in interest on time deposits after 1980. The reduction in inflation reinforced to some extent the process of re-monetization. In a careful econometric study of money demand in Turkey, Anand and van Wijnbergen (1988) document the sensitivity of time deposits to nominal interest rates and to expected inflation. Notice from figures 9.5 and 9.6 that MB and M1 were rather stagnant in this period, suggesting that a considerable portfolio shift from currency and demand deposits to time deposits took place as a consequence of the reform. Nonetheless, base money held its own until 1983.

It is after 1983 that we see a definite erosion in the ratio of base money to GNP. This was a response to the substantial relaxation of foreign-exchange regulations in December 1983. A key factor in this respect was the decision to allow residents and non-residents to open unrestricted foreign-exchange deposit accounts in domestic banks. It is hard to underestimate the psychological impact of this reform in a country where hitherto persons could be held criminally liable for possessing even small change in dollars. Indeed, Özal's aim was to demystify the dollar and the Deutschmark. But the reform also had the predictable consequence of setting into motion a portfolio diversification away from domestic money balances and toward foreign currency. By the end of 1986, foreign-exchange deposits by residents had grown from zero to almost half of all time deposits, and to 16% of *all* financial assets, including government securities (Akyüz 1990, table 6). Clearly, not all of the growth in these deposits came at the expense of domestic money. But

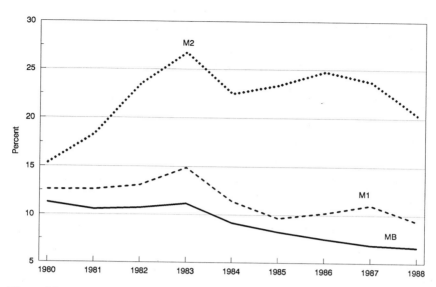

Figure 9.5
Money/GNP ratios: MB, M1, and M2.

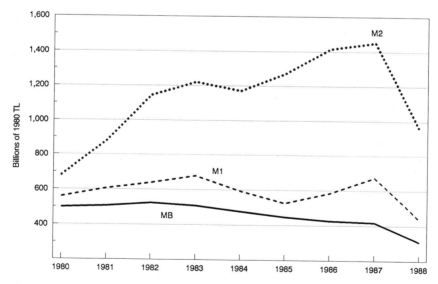

Figure 9.6
Real stocks of MB, M1, and M2.

the stagnation of (or decline in) the principal monetary ratios after 1983— in the context of falling inflation until 1987—strongly suggests considerable substitution. Recent work at the World Bank (1988a) uncovered evidence of a structural shift in the demand for currency and demand deposits after 1983, which shows up mainly as a reduction in income elasticities.

Indeed, the steady erosion in the MB-to-GNP ratio after 1983 (figure 9.5) is indicative of an ongoing process of dollarization (or, perhaps more appropriate, DM-ization), rather than a one-time portfolio diversification. This is consistent with the experience with dollarization in Mexico and Peru, where the process tends to be spread out over time and cumulative (Dornbusch and Reynoso 1989). In the words of Dornbusch and Reynoso (1989, p. 26), "the shift [into dollar deposits] can be well approximated by a combination of a traditional portfolio choice model based on relative rates of return and a dynamics that is represented by the logistic process." In other words, diversification into foreign-currency deposits appears to be subject to a learning curve. A serious implication is that a return to local-currency assets is no longer guaranteed (or complete) once the macroeconomic environment stabilizes.

For obvious reasons, the reduction in the stock of MB is disturbing from the standpoint of inflation control. The inflation cost of the financial liberalization can be gauged by the following simple exercise. In 1988, the average stock of MB stood at 6.6% of GNP, down from 11.2% in 1983. Had the public-sector deficit remained constant at its 1983 level of 5.2% of GNP, it follows from equation 3 that the inflation rate would have been 32.3 percentage points higher in 1988 than in 1983 on account of the erosion in MB alone. This amount corresponds roughly to the actual difference in the inflation rates in the two years, which is not surprising since the deficit in 1988 was only slightly higher than that in 1983. In other words, the difference in the levels of inflation between the two years is almost completely accounted for by the demonetization brought about by the capital-account liberalization. This would seem a high price for demystifying foreign exchange.

6. Some Additional Dilemmas

Exchange-Rate Policy

On the exchange-rate front, the government's policy until very recently has been to achieve a trend real depreciation, which amounts to following a PPP-plus rule. The outcome for the real exchange rate was shown in figure 9.1, and more detail is provided for the period since 1983 in figure 9.7: an occasional real appreciation aside, the real exchange rate has indeed depreciated steadily. The policy had an important signaling effect on top of its direct effect of rendering exporting and import-substituting more profitable: it clearly distinguished the Özal administration from its predecessors by demonstrating commitment to an outward orientation.

It is difficult to see why the need for a policy of real depreciation should persist almost an entire decade (Rodrik 1990). There are many costs imposed by continuous (and therefore anticipated) real depreciations. First, in an economy like Turkey's they tend to depress real wages. Second, they tend to keep real interest rates higher domestically than abroad, thanks to arbitrage. Third, they tend to increase the real burden of the public sector's external debt, necessitating a larger fiscal retrenchment than otherwise. Finally, a PPP-style rule threatens to leave the economic system without a nominal anchor, allowing the inflation rate to drift.

Until recently, the central bank appears to have weighed these considerations as less important than that of maintaining (and increasing)

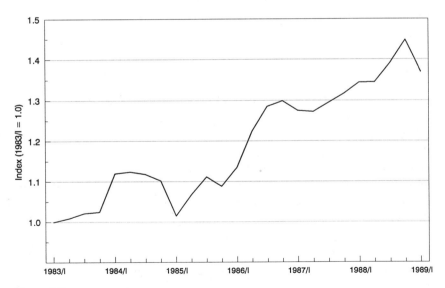

Figure 9.7
Real exchange rate (quarterly index).

external competitiveness. Since late 1988, the central bank has slowed down the rate of crawl of the lira. This appears to be linked to the sluggishness of the inflation response to a considerable weakenening of demand in the second half of 1988. A current-account surplus of $1.5 billion in 1988 must also have provided some confidence for fighting inflation with the nominal exchange rate. In any case, during the twelve months following September 1988 the lira has depreciated (in nominal terms) by 33% against the dollar and by 23% against the DM. Since the inflation rate in this period was over 70%, a considerable real *appreciation* is involved (see the value for 1989:I in figure 9.7).

Judging by the behavior of market participants, and by the absence of a substantial premium in the black market, the current path of the nominal exchange rate appears sustainable in the short run. But as the Southern Cone countries discovered a decade ago, controlling inflation via the exchange rate is a risky business over the medium to the longer run. In the absence of sufficient fiscal retrenchment, consistent with lower inflation, one of two things are likely to happen: continued real appreciation, with damaging consequences for the export drive and real activity; and a sudden collapse of the exchange rate, exerting further upward pressure on inflation. One interpretation of the central bank's current strategy would be that it is aimed at indirectly achieving the retrenchment needed by forcing exporters to agitate in favor of fiscal cuts.

Investment in Manufactures

One of the surprising features of the export boom, which is largely based on manufactures, is the absence of an underlying investment drive. Initially, that was to be expected, as the industrialization of the 1960s and the 1970s set up a substantial manufacturing capacity, which the foreign-exchange crisis had rendered idle. This capacity was heavily dependent on protected domestic markets, which explains the substantial realignment of relative prices needed before Turkish costs could be brought down to world levels. The subsequent export boom relied on this capacity, leading to such anomalies as the iron and steel sector—the epitome of Turkish import substitution—becoming a major exporter.

As figure 9.8 shows, public investment in manufacturing steadily declined after 1980. This was consistent with the redirection of public capital formation toward areas that do not compete with the private

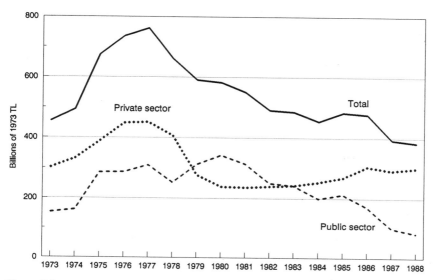

Figure 9.8
Manufacturing investment.

sector, such as infrastructure. The expectation was that private manufacturing investment would offset this fall once the economy started growing. Figure 9.8 shows that this expectation was not borne out. After a sharp fall during the crisis years 1977–1980, private manufacturing investment was very slow to recover. Between 1980 and 1988 the trend in real capital formation in manufacturing has been sharply downward in aggregate, and only moderately upward for the private sector. The rising trend in overall investment (table 9.1) reflects capital formation in other areas— mainly housing and, to a lesser extent, tourism. In 1988, total manufacturing investment still stood at only two-thirds its level in the peak year of 1977.

The reasons for this disappointing performance are not entirely clear. An important part of the explanation must have to do with the prevailing atmosphere of macroeconomic instability. As discussed above, both inflation and the real interest rate have been quite variable, and Conway's (1988) work demonstrates that manufacturing investment is quite sensitive to uncertainty in these variables. In addition, the level of real interest rates has tended to be higher than at any time in recent memory. This discourages investment not only through its effect on the cost of capital, but also through its negative impact on the balance sheets of highly leveraged firms. Trade policy has aggravated the environment of uncertainty by emitting inconsistent signals: import duties and export subsidies have been frequently and arbitrarily manipulated. Investors found refuge in the comparatively safe sector of housing, for which there is seemingly insatiable demand.

Income Distribution

No account of the Turkish stabilization experience would be complete without some reference to its distributional consequences. As we have seen, the early stabilization effort relied heavily on relative-price adjustments. These adjustments have since been either frozen or continued. The net result has been a regressive redistribution of income from popular sectors (wage and salary earners and farmers) to profits, rents, and interest income.

Table 9.10 shows the extent of the redistribution that has taken place since the late 1970s. In 1988, the real wage and the agricultural terms of trade both stood at barely over half their levels of 1973; aggregate per-capita income, meanwhile, had increased by more than a third. This has

Table 9.10
Distributional indicators (1973 = 100).

	Real per capita GNP	Agricultural terms of trade	Real wages
1973	100.0	100.0	100.0
1974	104.7	90.5	97.7
1975	110.1	105.5	105.4
1976	116.4	112.8	121.7
1977	118.5	117.0	124.2
1978	119.4	96.3	122.6
1979	116.5	78.4	101.5
1980	112.9	69.8	72.2
1981	114.4	69.3	64.8
1982	116.2	63.2	64.6
1983	116.9	61.2	67.3
1984	120.2	63.7	61.0
1985	124.9	58.9	54.8
1986	131.3	56.5	54.4
1987	131.8	60.8	55.1
1988	139.2	54.1	54.6

Source: Özmucur 1989, table 2.

gone alongside a rather striking realignment of factor shares in national income. Agriculture's share has fallen from 24% (1980) to 16% (1988). The share of wages and salaries has gone down from 27% to 14%. Meanwhile, profits, rents, and interest income now constitute 70% of national income, up from 49% in 1980. While these nominal shares are no doubt distorted by inflation—only a small part of interest payments represent real income gains to asset holders—they do reflect a dismal reality with respect to distribution (see Boratav 1990 and Özmucur forthcoming for more detailed information).

While income distribution is important in its own right, it also has implications for the likelihood of successful adjustment in the near future. Fiscal retrenchment becomes more difficult when major popular sectors already feel that they have paid more than their due. The pressure prior to elections to direct resources toward rural areas has already been noted. Public-sector wage settlements have also come under similar pressure recently. It is difficult to be optimistic about the capacity of the Turkish political system to deliver the kind of social contract that will be needed to conquer inflation once and for all.

7. Concluding Remarks

In the early 1980s, the early timing of her debt crisis, along with the geopolitical conjuncture, provided Turkey with an opportunity that no other large country has enjoyed. Inflows of foreign capital in these early years cushioned the fiscal squeeze and allowed a relatively painless reduction in inflation alongside a process of export-oriented growth. Export expansion was, in turn, facilitated by the temporary suspension of normal politics, which allowed a substantial restructuring of relative prices with scarcely any opposition. The capital inflows and the military interregnum were, of course, not to last. In the best of all possible worlds, the outward-oriented reforms would have taken sufficient root by the mid-1980s to allow the public sector to undertake the delayed retrenchment at no great cost to output.

The Özal government, which took power in November 1983, chose to pursue a curious mix of liberalization and patronage politics. On the one hand, a substantial amount of trade and financial liberalization was undertaken. As argued above, the financial liberalization itself proved rather disastrous for inflation and macroeconomic stability; the jury remains out on import liberalization. On the other hand, the scope of government activity was considerably enlarged via extra-budgetary funds, which could be used (or abused) for discretionary purposes. External finance was replaced by domestic borrowing, at terms highly disadvantageous to the public sector. Somewhere down the line, the private sector's confidence in Özal began to erode, reaching a nadir in August 1989 when, in a desperate move to control inflation, Özal reduced import duties on a wide range of consumer goods. It is now clear that the opportunity afforded by the favorable conjuncture in the early 1980s was missed.

Aside from the deeper structural problems mentioned at the end of the paper, inflation remains the unsolved problem of the 1980s. As this paper has shown, a simple-minded public-finance view of inflation does a respectable job of explaining why inflation has remained high on average, as well as explaining the timing of its jumps. There is little evidence of systematic cost-push or inertial influences during most of the 1980s. More recent experience, however, suggests that Turkish inflation may be taking on some Latin American characteristics. For one thing, it has become more difficult to get labor to accept real-wage cuts. Secondly, inflationary expectations have become seriously ingrained. Third, the severe squeeze on industrial activity since the second half of 1988 has brought to the fore cost-push effects: entrepreneurs react to reductions in demand by wanting to raise their prices since their average costs rise in recessions. Finally, the feedback between the exchange-rate rule and prices tends to fuel inflation, something that the current policy of slowing the crawl is attempting to tackle. These factors may explain why inflation has continued to rise since 1987 despite the prediction, based on the public-finance view, that it would fall (see figure 9.3).

Whatever the role of inertial elements, fiscal reform will have to be at the core of any serious attempt to reduce inflation to reasonable levels. The large role of interest payments in current expenditures does not allow much room for reduction on the expenditure side (at least in the consolidated government budget). But the tax intake is still too low (less than 25% of GNP, versus 40% in Europe) and that is perhaps one of the two areas (the other is the improvement of the performance of public enterprises) where the most substantial gains can be made. There is a large pool of unreported income that needs to be brought into the tax base. With respect to financial liberalization, unfortunately this cannot be undone: once the genie of dollarization is out of the bottle, it is impossible to stuff it back in. This leaves a credible, radical package of fiscal consolidation as the only solution. The alternative, as the experience of the 1980s has demonstrated, is a series of a successively higher inflation plateaus, with accompanying deterioration in the performance of the economy.

Notes

Note on sources and calculations: Unless otherwise noted, the main sources for the tables are the standard statistical publications of the Central Bank and the State Planning Organization. In general, all monetary, balance-of-payments, and debt statistics come from the annual reports or quarterly bulletins of the Central Bank. Data on sectoral saving-investment balances and the public-sector accounts come from the State Planning Organization, occasionally via the OECD Economic Surveys for Turkey. The real-exchange-rate series is calculated as an equally weighted geometric average of the bilateral real exchange rates *vis-à-vis* the United States and West Germany, using WPI.

1. For a detailed account of the crisis and the role of the CTLD scheme, see Celasun and Rodrik 1989, chapter 2.

2. See Anand, Chhibber, and van Wijnbergen 1990.

3. Overinvoicing results from the overt subsidies mentioned above. Using partner-country trade statistics, it is possible to put some rough orders of magnitude on the extent of overinvoicing. My calculations (Rodrik 1988) suggest an overinvoicing rate of around 11% in the period 1981–1987. But once one allows for the *under*-invoicing during the later 1970s (on the order of 4%), the growth rate of "real" exports is reduced only marginally.

4. For a more detailed account of the international political background, see Celasun and Rodrik 1989, chapter 9.

5. Öniş and Özmucur (1989, p. 63) estimate an OLS regression linking the inflation rate to the public-sector deficit for the period 1972–1988. They find that a one-percentage-point increase in the ratio of the deficit to GNP is associated with a 5.67% increase in inflation (with a standard error of 2.52).

6. The available econometric evidence on the structure of money demand in Turkey suggests the presence of a structural break in the mid 1980s, with higher income elasticities earlier than later. See World Bank 1988a, Anand and van Wijnbergen 1988, and Kopits 1987.

References

Akyüz, Yilmaz. 1990. "Financial system and policies in Turkey in the 1980s." In *The Political Economy of Turkey: Debt, Adjustment and Sustainability*, T. Aricanli and D. Rodrik, eds. (Macmillan).

Anand, Ritu, Ajay Chhibber, and Sweder van Wijnbergen. 1990. "External balance and growth in Turkey: Can they be reconciled?" In *The Political Economy of Turkey: Debt, Adjustment and Sustainability*, T. Aricanli and D. Rodrik, eds. (Macmillan).

Anand, Ritu, and Sweder van Wijnbergen. 1988. Inflation, External Debt and Financial Sector Reform: A Quantitative Approach to Consistent Fiscal Policy with an Application to Turkey. NBER Working Paper no. 2731.

Boratav, Korkut. 1990. "Inter-class and intra-class relations of distribution under 'structural adjustment': Turkey during the 1980s." In *The Political Economy of Turkey: Debt, Adjustment and Sustainability*, T. Aricanli and D. Rodrik, eds. (Macmillan).

Celasun, Merih, and Dani Rodrik. 1989. "Debt, adjustment and growth: Turkey." In *Developing Country Debt and Economic Performance: Country Studies*, Jeffrey Sachs and Susan Collins, eds., vol. 3 (University of Chicago Press).

Central Bank. 1989. *Annual Report 1988*, Ankara.

Conway, Patrick. 1988. The Impact of Uncertainty on Private Investment in Turkey. Department of Economics, University of North Carolina.

Dornbusch, Rudiger, and Alejandro Reynoso. 1989. Financial Factors in Economic Development. NBER Working Paper no. 2889.

Kopits, George. 1987. Structural Reform, Stabilization, and Growth in Turkey. IMF Occasional Paper 52, Washington, D.C.

Milanovic, Branko. 1986. Export Incentives and Turkish Manufactured Exports, 1980–1984. World Bank Staff Working Paper no. 768, Washington, D.C.

OECD. 1987-1988. *Economic Surveys: Turkey*. Paris.

Öniş, Ziya, and Süleyman Özmucur. 1989. The Inflation Problem and Policies to Prevent Inflation in Turkey. Bosporus University. (In Turkish.)

Özmucur, Süleyman. 1989. "Social aspects of Turkish liberalization, 1980–88." In *Political Economy of Turkish Liberalization, 1980–88*, T. Nas and M. Odekon, eds. (Lehigh University Press).

Rodrik, Dani. 1988. "How much of the Turkish export boom is fictitious?" *Toplum ve Bilim* 42, Summer. (In Turkish.)

Rodrik, Dani. 1990. "Some policy dilemmas in Turkish macroeconomic management." In *The Political Economy of Turkey: Debt, Adjustment and Sustainability*, T. Aricanli and D. Rodrik, eds. (Macmillan).

Saracoglu, Rüşdü. 1987. Economic Stabilization and Structural Adjustment: The Case of Turkey. Paper presented at World Bank and International Monetary Fund Symposium on Growth-Oriented Adjustment Programs. Washington, D.C.

Sargent, T., and N. Wallace. 1982. "Some unpleasant monetary arithmetic." *Quarterly Review*, Federal Reserve Bank of Minneapolis.

Taylor, Lance. 1990. "Turkish experience: Summary and comparative notes." In *The Political Economy of Turkey: Debt, Adjustment and Sustainability*, T. Aricanli and D. Rodrik, eds. (Macmillan).

Waterbury, John. 1989. Export-led Growth and the Center-Right Coalition in Turkey. Princeton University.

World Bank. 1988a. *Turkey: External Debt, Fiscal Policy and Sustainable Growth*. Washington, D.C.

World Bank. 1988b. *Evaluation of Structural Adjustment Lending in Turkey*. Washington, D.C.

Comments by Sweder van Wijnbergen

The author starts with an insightful survey of recent economic history in Turkey. He brings out important differences between Turkey's "post-debt-crisis" experience and the Latin American experience over the corresponding period. While Turkey experienced roughly similar increases in debt/output ratios, the sources of that increase were very different. In Latin America we find low growth offsetting the gains made through draconian cuts in trade deficits; Turkey had witnessed continued growth and continued access to capital markets and thus could sustain much larger deficits on its current account. The author explains this by the "long leash" on which the international organizations kept Turkey; there is something to this, but I think it is incomplete. A substantial part of the external flows that financed Turkey's external current-account deficits came not from the OECD or the World Bank but from Turkish guest workers in Western Europe. Turkey can claim credit for creating an economic environment in which its nationals found it profitable to send their money home, in rather striking contrast to the widespread capital flight that has plagued almost all Latin American countries over the post debt crisis period.

The author argues the relevance of the public-finance approach, Phelps style, in understanding Turkish inflation. He presents some empirical results that seem to support this approach, and concludes that fiscal deficits had a lot to do with inflation in Turkey and, conversely, that getting rid of inflation in Turkey requires a fiscal cutback. While I share his views of the usefulness of the public-finance approach to inflation and of the need for more restrictive fiscal policy in Turkey, I doubt that the evidence he presents would convince a non-believer.

First of all, what are the facts? The author talks about incomplete stabilization, high triple-digit inflation earlier on, then a sudden decline to 40–50%, even 30% initially, some relapse in 1985, another decline, and then things get out of hand. But the picture would look very different had he presented the two years before 1980; Turkey was really not in a sustained period of triple-digit inflation. The inflation rate before 1980, like the one afterward, was in the 50–70% range. Looking at year-to-year inflation rates may be misleading in the case of Turkey because of the rather discontinuous way in which public-sector prices are adjusted. Typically there are, at times, very large public-sector price adjustments, after which nominally fixed prices are maintained until the pressure builds up for another very large increase. This arithmetically shifts measured inflation back and forth over time, keeping it artificially low when public-sector prices are frozen and creating artificial peaks when public prices are adjusted. This practice introduces much more variance in measured inflation than is really there. For example, most of the 109% inflation in 1980 happened in the first two months, when there was a very large devaluation and a very large increase in public-sector prices. If one averages out these price increases, in 1980–1983 inflation was 46%, in 1984–1988 it was 44%, and in the years of the late 1970s it was also around 40–50%. It is arguable that Turkey is not an example of incomplete stabilization but a case of no stabilization at all.

I have some doubts about the model itself. The public-sector deficit needs to be financed one way or another. If one brings in debt issue, the budget constraint underlying the paper's equation becomes an identity and is not very helpful. Where the Sargent-Wallace approach yields real information is where one brings in sustainability limits on debt issue and then asks what, for given primary deficit or surplus and sustainability limits on debt issue, is the sustainable inflation rate within Turkey's financial structure. It is more a medium-term consistency approach than a way of tracking inflation from quarter to quarter.

Second, I think the exercise is done with a bit too much simplicity. In particular, the inflation tax base has moved around a lot in Turkey because of extensive reform in the financial sector. The author brings that up, by the way, in an interesting observation where he argues, rightly in my view, that the introduction of foreign-exchange deposits, by undermining the base for the inflation tax, has raised the steady-state inflation rate by about 20 percentage points. This is a good point, but there was a whole lot that went on beyond that. I think that serious analysis of the inflation tax means going beyond running base money on inflation. One needs to assess, for example, how the central bank's regulatory policy on things like reserve requirements shifts base money demand around for any level of inflation.

For example, consider the puzzle, mentioned by the author, that real base money did not decline in spite of higher inflation. What happened at the same time is that the central bank raised reserve requirements from 15% to 40%, thereby more than offsetting declining cash balances by a substantial increase in the other component of base money—commercial banks' demand for reserves.

There is a second issue where more detailed base-money demand would have helped, and this is maybe more a policy issue. The author argues that the financial liberalization in Turkey was premature. There was indeed a substantial liberalization of interest rates, unfortunately not followed by an equal improvement in the bank-supervision systems. One can argue that the crash in 1982–83 was due not so much to the liberalization *per se* as to the failure to beef up the regulatory and supervision system. From a macroeconomic point of view, was this financial liberalization really such a bad idea as the author makes it out to be? He mentioned that a higher time-deposit rate would drive people away from cash, reducing base-money demand and increasing the sustainable inflation rate for given fiscal policy. It is true that an increase in time-deposit rates leads to shifts from cash and demand deposits into time deposits, and since reserve requirements are now less than 1, that will reduce demand for base money. But it will also draw other assets, that have no impact on base money, into time deposits and thereby raise demand for base money. My analysis of money demand in Turkey[1] suggests that the second effect in fact dominates. Higher time-deposit rates raise rather than lower base-money demand, because so many assets are shifted from outside the banking system into time deposits that the negative effects of shifts away from currency are more than offset.

Finally, the author should have been more careful in the choice of the deficit measure used. To establish the link between inflation, base money, and fiscal deficits, one needs to consolidate the balance sheets of the central bank and the public sector. This is important in Turkey, since the central bank's contribution to the consolidated public-sector deficit is not only substantial but also varied, with estimates ranging from 0.6% to 0.2% of GDP. But with flaws like this, why does the author produce such impressive results? The explanation lies in his running inflation on a deficit measure that includes nominal interest payments; the real debt erosion taking place through inflation is counted in the deficit, instead of in the "below the line" capital account, where it belongs. In a country with a non-indexed internal debt of 10% of GDP and inflation rates around 60–70%, inflation is a big component of normal interest payments, and that is a big component of the variation in the deficit. So his model is not very far from running inflation on itself. Of course, including the left-hand-side variable in a somewhat transformed way on the right-hand side greatly improves the regression's "fit," but it does not increase its predictive power, since one has to predict the right-hand side too.

In discussing the real exchange rate, export performance, and income distribution, Rodrik criticizes the impact of the real depreciation that took place over the first seven years of the 1980s for its impact on real wages and questions, for that reason, the sustainability of the Turkish economic program. But was there an alternative? *A priori* one might think there was, since the period is characterized by gradual fiscal expansion, which increases demand for Turkish goods; if one starts from equilibrium, such a policy would have supported appreciating rather than depreciating real exchange rates. But Turkey did not start from commodity-market equilibrium in 1980–81. There was a big recession in 1981, with a very high degree of overcapacity. The real depreciation shifted world demand toward Turkish goods; this is the main explanatory factor behind the high increase in exports.[2] It also explains, in combination with initial excess capacity, why all this could take place without a major increase of investment in tradable sectors, one of the puzzles the author mentions. The increase in competitiveness had such a large impact on exports precisely because all this unused capacity was just waiting to be used. From that point of view I think it is very hard to criticize Turkish exchange-rate policy in most of the past decade. If moving toward a real exchange rate that establishes a balance between the supply of and the demand for Turkish goods implies a cut in real wages, that is regrettable, but there is not much one can do about it.

Of course, if Turkey were to run into capacity constraints, this policy would not remain sustainable. The only way room can be made for increasing exports in the face of aggregate capacity constraints is through restrictive fiscal policy. This can work either directly, by reducing public expenditure on Turkish goods, or indirectly, by reducing private demand for Turkish goods. If capacity constraints would become binding, the easy road to high growth through high export growth spurred by improved competitiveness would be closed.

Notes

1. See Ritu Anand and Sweder van Wijnbergen, Inflation, External Debt and Financial Sector Reform: A Quantitative Approach to Consistent Fiscal Policy with an Application to Turkey, NBER Working Paper No. 2731, 1988.

2. For empirical evidence see Ismail Arslan and Sweder van Wijnbergen, *Turkey: Export Miracle or Accounting Trick?*, World Bank PRE Working Paper No. 370, 1990.

General Discussion

Some participants addressed the liberalization policy accompanying the disinflation policies in Turkey. Persio Arida questioned the economic rationale for capital liberalization, whereas Nadav Halevi pointed out that premature liberalization (of the capital market rather than of trade) caused inflows of capital and appreciation. He added that, as in Israel in 1977, the introduction of foreign-exchange deposits influenced inflation. However, if the public was faced with both inflation and devaluation, capital would probably be smuggled abroad.

The implications of "Europe 1992" on Turkey's economy were raised by Assaf Razin. Dani Rodrik responded by emphasizing that export markets and capital availability would be affected.

10

The Yugoslav Path to High Inflation

Velimir Bole and Mitja Gaspari

Since the beginning of the 1980s the Yugoslav economy has been suffering from almost continuously accelerating inflation. Although the country has experienced rapid price increases (15–30% annually) before, the trends of the 1980s can be compared to the experience of other countries: accelerating inflation, budget financing problems, greater indexation of the economy combined with greater "rationality" of price expectations, and unsuccessful attempts at stabilization.

It seems plausible to assume that Yugoslavia was able to maintain a "natural" rate of inflation of some 10–30% annually because of shortcomings of the economic policy as well as because of its distinctive economic system, with all its admitted shortcomings (social ownership, the way enterprises and the public-sector deficit were being financed, wage-cost pressures, and so on). What is less clear is the way in which the characteristics of this system and this policy contributed to accelerating inflation, especially since 1982. Was there a sort of "shocks and accommodations" mechanism at work here (see Bruno and Fischer 1986), or does the blame lie with the *de facto* deficit of the public sector? As we will see in what follows, both factors were active in explaining the mechanism of inflation (in particular since 1987), with operational deficits taking place especially in the "high-inflation" phase.

We will try to show that Yugoslavia's present crisis (of which high inflation is only one feature) stems from an inward-looking investment strategy that was financed by an enormous inflow of foreign capital in the second half of the 1970s, combined with a total lack of response by economic policy to the first oil-price crisis. On top of that came the second oil crisis, creating an even greater need for massive inflows of foreign capital in the late 1970s and a rapidly growing foreign debt which almost tripled in the second half of this decade.

Under the conditions described above, high inflation was triggered by the sharp worldwide rise in interest rates and by the abrupt squeezing of the hard-currency credits extended to the more indebted countries in the early 1980s, which made it impossible for the economy to import the raw materials and goods necessary for normal functioning as well as to service its huge debt. A devaluation of the dinar was introduced as well as a partial rationing policy in order to curtail the supply of goods and services for domestic markets and rechannel it to foreign markets; these steps, and the rigid economic structure, served as a trigger for the escalating price dynamics observed since 1982.

We suggest that the mechanism of high inflation was affected by shocks and accommodation and that only after 1987 did a high public deficit also become an important factor in accelerating inflation. We will also test the proposition that sudden changes in exchange-rate policy and in wage and price regulations are the most common shocks affecting the Yugoslav economy, and that they added fuel to the already high inflation rates. In addition, as the "rationality" of expectations improved, so too did the accommodation of shocks (through indexation and "dollarization"). We further suggest that in the first two phases of inflation (between 1982 and 1987), the inflation-accelerating mechanism cannot be reduced simply to terms of "fiscal" versus "balance-of-payments" issues.

Formally, neither the federal nor the state (or local) budget in Yugoslavia can show a deficit; there can be no formal public debt, foreign or domestic. However, there has been an undeniable (though hidden) actual deficit. We estimate its magnitude at greater length in section 3. The hidden deficit is an outcome of the formal losses of the central bank, which in Yugoslavia also operates as a treasury. The deficit was being financed through printing money. However, the evidence suggests that the drastic increase in actual public deficits occurred only after the price takeoff, and only then did the deficit hamper price-stabilization policies.

The evidence suggests that a "shocks and accommodation" approach provides a reasonable description of the inflationary process in the 1980s and that some economic measures taken had a significant impact on the acceleration of inflation: the exchange-rate and interest-rate policies in 1983/1–1984, monetary policy between 1985 and 1987, and wage policy since the middle of 1988. With the progress of indexation after 1984, the inflationary impact of shocks also increased greatly, especially since 1987.

Some evidence will be presented to show that the "rationality" of businesses' and households' inflationary expectations increased significantly after 1987. Our data suggest that the dollarization of the economy has increased considerably, especially since 1988/I, and that this can explain the recently observed "strange" changes in the demand for real balances.

In what follows, we briefly describe the economic performance and policies implemented before the "trigger" year of 1982 (section 1) and present a survey of the economy since 1982 (section 2)—including some statistical tests of the strict exogeneity of the main economic variables connected to inflation. Section 3 is devoted to estimates of the operational (inflation-adjusted) deficit of the public sector in 1987–1988. In section 4 we analyze relevant parameters of the estimated equations of demand for real balances, including some implicit estimates of the scope of indexation and dollarization in the economy.

1. Policy Measures and Performance in the Late 1970s

At least three new exogenous factors that came into play in the period 1973–1975 have had a long-term effect on the economy of Yugoslavia: the rapid oil-price increase in 1973, the constitutional changes of 1974, and the decision to push forward the economy's technological development in 1975.

The constitutional changes of 1974 afforded greater freedom to individual republics—but without a "penalty clause." This meant that pressure would often be exerted on the central government (or, rather, on the central bank) to step in and rectify any deleterious outcome of the consequences of any republics' policy failing to achieve the desired results. Since this was done via the republics' representatives lobbying of the federal government, the central bank's interventions were not necessarily based on economic criteria. Indeed, given the heterogenity of the problems encountered by the various republics (and consequently their solutions), it would have been very difficult to formulate a rational overall federal economic policy to offset the various republics' mismanaged policies. In particular, federal intervention, and the corresponding lack of any learning experience on the part of the republics, was extremely costly, contributing a great deal to the government's hidden deficit, in particular through subsidies to agriculture and to export via "selective" credits from the central bank. In addition, there were also expenditures due to direct grants to various enterprises as a part of the "non-budget" expenditures of the federal government.

The consequences of the constitutional changes of 1974 and their effect on the hidden deficit did not initially contribute to accelerative inflation, but rather to the country's mounting foreign debt. The economy's growing debt was also substantially affected by a policy decision (in 1975) to stimulate technological development in order to improve the supply of goods and services in the domestic market. Achieving this goal called for a massive expansion of investment as well as an increase in imports, especially of equipment and machinery (see Cemovic 1985).

Table 10.1 summarizes some common indicators for 1972–1982; additional data (for subperiods) appear in table 10.2. The intensification of investment activity is immediately evident from columns 1 and 2 of table 10.1, and the consequences of radical policy decisions are revealed by table 10.2.

The numbers in both tables are calculated from official data, and it should be borne in mind that they use the material definition of "social product," i.e., they exclude health, educational, financial, housing, and other services. We therefore concentrate more on rates of change than on absolute values.

Note, in particular, the increase in the share of fixed investment, from 30.2% in 1972–1974 to 33.6% in 1975–1979, and the even more dramatic increase in imports of equipment and machinery (from 20.2% to 24.9% in the same periods). Both fixed investment and imports later declined (to 28.8% and 18.6% respectively) as the hard-currency credit squeeze tightened and oil prices started soaring again.

The third factor contributing to accelerating prices in the 1980s was the rising price of oil in 1970s. The real increase (relative to retail prices) in the domestic prices of crude oil and of petrochemical products was 52.1% in 1974 and 53.8% in 1979. Although enormous, these price increases still did not reflect the degree to which the economy depends on imported oil. Total oil supplies were not immediately affected by the first oil crisis (price increase), since more than 25% of this supply was produced domestically at the time (31% in 1973–1975 and 29% in 1976–1979). Moreover, in 1975 slightly less than 25% of total supplies came from the Soviet Union (rising to 44% in 1980) at relatively favorable—though gradually increasing—prices.

While the oil crises had only a moderate impact on the domestic prices of fuel (especially the controlled price of gasoline) and petrochemicals,

Table 10.1
Selected economic indicators, 1972–1982 (annual percentage change in constant prices unless otherwise indicated).

	Gross social product[d] (1)	Gross fixed investment (2)	Retail prices (3)	Trade balance[a] (4)	Current-account balance[b] (5)	Total debt[c] (6)	Average real wages (7)
1972	4.3	3.1	16	−0.97	0.42	3.60	0.7
1973	4.9	2.2	19	−1.46	0.49	4.27	−4.5
1974	8.5	9.1	26	−3.43	−1.18	4.77	5.6
1975	3.6	9.7	26	−3.59	−1.00	5.89	−1.2
1976	3.9	8.2	9	−2.48	0.17	7.00	4.5
1977	8.0	9.5	13	−3.84	−1.58	8.41	1.9
1978	6.9	10.5	13	−4.18	−1.26	10.47	7.3
1979	7.0	6.4	22	−6.57	−3.66	13.46	1.7
1980	2.3	−5.9	30	−5.67	−2.29	17.33	−11.7
1981	1.4	−9.8	46	−5.31	−0.75	19.53	−4.5
1982	0.5	−5.5	30	−3.78	−0.46	18.73	−3.9

Sources: *Statistical Yearbook* (1984), Federal Statistical Office, Belgrade; Bulletin of the National Bank of Yugoslavia (1979, 1981), National Bank of Yugoslavia, Belgrade; Cemović 1985.
a. *Vis-à-vis* the convertible currency area (billions of US$).
b. Billions of US$.
c. To the convertible currency area (end-of-year figures, billions of US$).
d. Gross domestic product excluding "nonproductive" services.

Table 10.2
Shares in GSP and imports (constant prices).

	1972–1974	1975–1979	1980–1982
Private consumption	54.8	53.7	51.2
Gross fixed investment	30.2	33.6	28.8
Share of imported equipment and machines out of total imports	20.2	24.9	18.6
Average annual growth rate of imported oil	24.2	9.9	−10.3
Average annual increase in (dollar) price of imported oil	85.8	10.5	26.0

Source: *Statistical Yearbook* (1984), Federal Statistical Office, Belgrade.

domestic demand for these products rose considerably between 1972 and 1979. Formally, therefore, the average aggregate price elasticity of imported oil was neither negative nor small. Oil imports more than doubled between 1972 and 1980, although oil import prices increased tenfold in the same period![1]

What was the effect of this import-driven development on trade, the current-account balance, and total debt? Columns 4–6 of table 10.1 show a clear worsening of the balance of (hard-currency) trade by 1979, when the trade deficit peaked at $6.6 billion—quite a "respectable" deficit for an economy whose annual hard-currency exports totaled about $5 billion and whose GNP was around $45 billion. At the same time the total hard-currency debt grew by some 30%. And while the trade and current-account situation improved somewhat in the beginning of the 1980s, the hard-currency current-account deficit in 1981–82 was still around $1.4 billion (see *Central Bank Annual Report* for 1982). Given this deficit and the outstanding hard-currency debt, aggravated by the worldwide credit squeeze and soaring interest rates in world financial markets, Yugoslavia's position became untenable in 1982. The stage was set for inflation to take off.

2. From High Inflation to Hyperinflation: 1982–1989

At least three subperiods can be discerned in the evolution of Yugoslavia's inflation from 1982 onward. The first lasted until the fourth quarter of 1984 and was characterized by very active (sometimes inconsistent) economic policy. The second subperiod, from early 1985 to the end of 1986, saw less frantic activity, especially in 1986, under the influence of the new "programmed inflation" theory: the sliding exchange rate was curbed, wages were increased, interest rates (already negative) were further reduced, and money was pumped into the economy. In the third subperiod (beginning in the first quarter of 1987), a radical amendment of accounting techniques precipitated widespread indexation, resulting in a drastic reduction of the sensitivity of relative prices (and of exports) to changes in wages and the exchange rate. Moreover, since 1987 the government has been unable to maintain any restrictive measure for more than two months.

Tables 10.3 and 10.4 present the relevant data on the performance of the Yugoslav economy since 1982. Detailed data (quarterly and monthly rates of growth) on some important variables (prices, wages, exchange rate, and money) are relegated to the appendix (table 10.A1).

Table 10.3
Selected economic indicators, 1983–1988 (annual percentage change in constant prices unless otherwise indicated).

	1983	1984	1985	1986	1987	1988
1. Gross social product	−1.3	2.0	0.5	3.6	−1.0	−1.6
2. Gross fixed investment	−9.7	−9.7	−3.7	3.5	−3.9	−3.0
3. Retail prices	38	55	77	91	118	199
4. Trade balance[a]	−2.2	−1.7	−1.6	−2.0	−1.1	−0.6
5. Current-account balance[b]	n.a.	0.8	0.3	0.3	1.1	2.2
6. Total debt[c]	19.6	19.6	18.2	19.2	20.5	18.7
7. Average real wages	−12.1	−5.9	3.7	12.6	−6.7	−8.0
8. Operational public-sector deficit[d]	n.a.	7.4	2.8	2.8	10.5	5.8

Sources: *Statistical Yearbook* (1988), Federal Statistical Office, Belgrade; *Index* (1989/10), Federal Statistical Office, Belgrade; Bulletin of the National Bank of Yugoslavia (1989/5), National Bank of Yugoslavia, Belgrade; Annual Report of the National Bank of Yugoslavia, National Bank of Yugoslavia, Belgrade.
a. *Vis-à-vis* the convertible currency area (billions of US$).
b. *Vis-à-vis* the convertible currency area (billions of US$).
c. To the convertible currency area (end-of-year figures, billions of US$).
d. Percentage of gross social product.

Table 10.4
Shares in GSP, 1982–1988 (percentages, in constant prices).

	Private consumption (1)	Public sector material expenditure (2)	Gross fixed investment (3)
1982	50.6	8.2	26.5
1983	50.2	7.9	24.2
1984	48.7	7.7	21.4
1985	48.5	7.8	20.5
1986	48.9	7.9	20.5
1987	49.6	7.8	19.7
1988	48.5[a]	8.1[a]	19.4

Source: *Statistical Yearbook* (1989), Federal Statistical Office, Belgrade.
a. Estimate.

Curtailing Domestic Demand and Stimulating Exports: 1982–1984

As noted, the subperiod 1982–1984/III was characterized by intensive, though sometimes erratic, economic-policy efforts to restructure final demand in response to the balance-of-payment crisis. The means to this end were stimulating exports (primarily via a more active exchange-rate policy and export subsidies as well as easier access to imported inputs) and curbing other imports. The dinar was devalued (by 23% against the US$), imports (except imported inputs) were severely restricted, gasoline (followed later by other goods) was rationed, foreign travel was taxed, and a limit was set on withdrawals from foreign-currency accounts. In addition, investment in fixed capital was directly controlled and re-strictions were imposed on enterprises' wage policy and on public-sector expenditures (at this time prices were already controlled).

As shown in table 10.3, the above measures were fairly successful; they had little effect on inflation, but the trade and current-account balances improved significantly. Furthermore, table 10.4 shows that investment in fixed assets dropped (its share in GSP fell from 26.5% to 21.4% between 1982 and 1984); the shares of private consumption[2] and public expendi-tures in goods declined too, although much more moderately. Note that the really drastic changes in domestic demand were achieved in 1983–84 through direct rationing rather than by changing relative prices.

But owing to the extreme rigidity of relative prices, the reduction and restructuring of domestic demand had an inevitable effect on inflation. Price controls led to a rigid price structure and a low elasticity of demand with respect to the prices of "import-intensive" goods (such as petro-chemical products), thus preventing exchange-rate policy from fully affecting imports and domestic demand and necessitating a drastic change of the exchange rate to achieve the same results. However, because of the mark-up price-formation mechanism, the rising cost of hard currency was pushing the general price level up while, at the same time, relative-price changes were quite small.

Furthermore, price controls were lifted for six months (in the second half of 1983), reimposed for three months, and relaxed and reimposed again, and so on, interchangeably, until May 1988. This practice led firms to anticipate future price controls by raising prices at every opportunity by more than would have been warranted by the simple mark-up mechanism. Price controls were thus being rendered less and less effec-tive, and each relaxation was accompanied by a higher inflation plateau—a clear example of economic shock. A similar "stop-go" policy governed the economy's exchange-rate policy and affected exporters' behavior (it lowered the exchange-rate elasticities of exports).

In order to examine the exogenous elements in the determinants of the inflation rate during the period in which inflation accelerated, we present in table 10.5 the results of tests run on hypotheses of strict exogeneity for the exchange rate, wages, and the discount rates (see Hendry and Richard 1983). Specifically, the results are F-values derived from Granger causality tests between inflation on the one hand and base money, the exchange rate of the German mark (DM), wages, and the discount rate on the other hand.[3] The subperiods were chosen so as to represent specific price-control phases and therefore do not correspond accurately to the subperiods referred to earlier.

The results of such causality tests are open to various interpretations. Speaking loosely, a significant F value is sometimes taken to indicate that variable A caused variable B. More accurately, a significant F value permits the rejection of the hypothesis of no feedback from A to B (ignoring the prior history of B). One can also say that a high F value permits rejection of the hypothesis that A is not strictly exogenous to B. Our choice of interpretation will be dictated by our needs; we may sometimes have to adopt a simple heuristic interpretation.

The figures for 1983/1–1984/5 reveal Granger causality from the exchange rate of the DM to inflation as well as some feedback in the

Table 10.5
Results of strict exogeneity tests (F values).[a]

	Base money	Exchange rate	Wages	Discount rate
Hypothesis A: No feedback from variables to prices				
Jan. 1983 – May 1984	1.9	*5.7*	0.5	**3.5**
June 1984 – May 1986	3.65	0.2	2.4	*5.3*
June 1986 – Dec. 1987	1.3	1.7	1.0	2.1
Jan. 1988 – June 1989	0.2	0.3	**3.4**	2.2
Hypothesis B: No feedback from prices to variables				
Jan. 1983 – May 1984	1.3	*5.5*	0.0	0.1
June 1984 – May 1986	**2.7**	0.9	*7.9*	0.8
June 1986 – Dec. 1987	*6.1*	1.4	**3.2**	*5.7*
Jan. 1988 – June 1989	2.2	1.0	*7.1*	**3.7**

a. Figures in italics are significant at 0.1 level of significance; figures in bold typeface are significant at 0.05 level of significance.

reverse direction. The F values do not permit rejection of the hypothesis that the discount rate was strictly exogenous to inflation. On a purely heuristic level we can say that neither the money base nor wages (Granger-) caused inflation in this period, nor were they strictly exogenous to inflation. Therefore, we conclude that the evidence suggests that the factors that triggered inflation after 1982 were the rate of interest and, especially, the exchange-rate policy.

Policy Slackness: 1985–1986

The policies implemented in 1982–1984 were reversed in 1985: a great deal of money was injected into the economy, interest rates were brought down (especially after 1985/II), the exchange rates of hard currency were curbed, and wages rose. Real wages rose until the third quarter of 1986 (for 3.7% in 1985 and 12.6% in 1986; see table 10.3, line 7) and were still considerably higher, even at the end of 1987, than they were in 1985/I, in spite of the imposition of strict wage controls in the first quarter of 1987. Although inflation gathered considerable momentum in 1985–86 (retail prices increased 77% in 1985 and 91% in 1986; see table 10.3, line 3), demand for real balances went up as lot of new money was pumped into the economy. It is also worth mentioning that in 1985–86 the real appreciation of the exchange rate considerably reduced the operational (inflation-adjusted) public-sector deficit.

External conditions also improved after 1985: the interest rate on the external debt started to decline, the dollar was weakening, and world oil prices dropped. All these external factors alleviated the adverse effects of economic policy slackness after 1984 on economic performance (notably the current account and the balance of trade), but inflation nonetheless continued to accelerate.

Table 10.5 shows that in the period from June 1984 to May 1986 both the money base and the discount rate Granger-caused inflation. It is also worth noting that it was only in this period that the monetization of the hidden deficit had a sizable exogenous impact on the acceleration of inflation. The data in this table also clearly show that the interest-rate policy significantly affected inflation; however, detailed evidence in table 10.A2 reveals that it in fact curbed inflation. Thus (heuristically speaking again), the money base was the only economic-policy variable that contributed significantly to the acceleration of inflation in this period of uncontrolled prices. Furthermore, the figures for this period permit us to reject the hypothesis that price increases had no feedback effect on the money base and wages: the printing of money and wage payments were considerably affected by price movements. As wages in the two following periods (June 1986 to December 1987 and January 1988 to June 1989) were also significantly influenced by inflation (see table 10.5), it seems plausible that once wage controls were lifted in mid-1985 wage indexation contributed a great deal to strengthening the inertial momentum of price movements. The same rationale applies to interest-rate policy after May 1986 and to monetary policy from early 1985 to the end of 1987.

Indexation and Price Thaws after 1986

Accounting techniques in the Yugoslav economy were thoroughly revamped in the first quarter of 1987, and a new law made it mandatory for firms and all institutions in the "nonproductive" sector (schools, hospitals, etc.) to revalue all balance-sheet entries (excluding liquid or near-liquid assets, but including own capital). Different items had to be reevaluated by different price indexes (being independent of contracted interest rates). However, no entry had to be increased for the revaluation. Capital was increased (at the end of the revaluation operation) by the difference between the revaluation of assets and sources (liabilities and capital) when the latter was positive and unchanged when negative. In the latter case total business costs were increased by the difference. Other items of the balance sheet (except capital) were left unchanged by new mandatory operation of revaluation.

The new accounting law promoted widespread use of the "indexation" clause. After 1987, for example, contracts were as a rule made on the basis of official (monthly) rate of revaluation for financial assets, so enterprises tried to offset (pure bookkeeping) differences in revaluations which by the new accounting principles increased business costs (when revaluations of sources were greater then revaluations of assets)! Leaving aside any other unfavorable results of the new accounting system, what is of importance to us here is its disastrous effect on inflation. Not only did it spur widespread indexation; it made income statements subject to the evaluation of balance-sheets, and what is worse, it explicitly added inflation-generated losses on the firms' own capital to operating costs. This now placed enterprises firmly in the same boat as the commercial banks. However, since controls on interest rates were more effective than those on the prices of goods and services, the resulting pressure on banks was stronger than that on the firms (reinforced by sizable losses incurred by the banks themselves). The new accounting principle, combined with the ever-increasing sophistication of households with respect to price expectations, resulted in a total collapse of the last built-in "brakes" on inflation in the economy, with every price acceleration caused by a short-term (even random) shock being perpetuated by the indexation promoted by the new accounting system.

The "shocks and accommodation" mechanism of price acceleration (see Bruno and Fischer 1986) became very effective after June 1987: the brief freeze on wages at the end of 1987/I, the price freeze, and the reshuffle of relative prices and wage control at the end of 1987 gave inflation another boost. In addition, the operational deficit rose in 1987, probably owing to the drastic increase in the primary deficit (as the government increased subsidies to certain sectors, using so-called "nonbudget expenditures"; by 1988 such nonbudget expenditures were almost as high as budget expenditures). A manifestation of the shocks can be seen in the zig-zags of economic policy; it is difficult to find a single 6-month span in which exchange-rate, interest-rate, and wage policies remained unchanged!

In an attempt to stabilize the economy, price controls were put into effect again at the end of 1987; these barely survived for two months, after which price increases were back to over 7% a month (see table 10.A1). The authorities therefore had to implement a third stabilization program.

The new stabilization program enacted in June 1988 was fairly well prepared, and was dubbed the "Three Nominal Anchor" package of policy measures. It provided highly restrictive guidelines for the growth of nominal wages, credit, and public-sector expenditure, while at the same time drastically *cutting* price controls. The dinar was devalued by 23% and import restrictions were relaxed substantially. All these measures were taken under the auspices of the IMF. However, the government went along these lines only for a short while (which came as no surprise, given its past record and credibility). A month and a half after the new program was launched, the restrictions on nominal credit were lifted; this was followed by the elimination of the remaining anchors (in the last quarter of 1988), and by October 1989 the economy was effectively operating without any economic policy.

In the first quarter of 1989 imports were liberalized significantly, i.e., restrictions on imports were lifted and import taxes were reduced, but although this move was hailed by the country's enterprises it failed to bring about any noticeable change in the economy. Imports did not even go up in dollar terms until 1989/III, probably because the new exchange rate set after the above-mentioned 23% devaluation (and subsequent adjustments according the PPP principle) was too high to make imports attractive.

Nor did the liberalization have any effect on inflation, whereas the reduction in import taxes (in 1988 accounting for some 80% of total customs duties) aggravated the problem of financing the budget. In early 1989 wages began catching up with and then overtaking inflation, promptly hiking the monthly rate of inflation from 15% to 30% (see also table 10.A1). Since the lag in tax collection remained more or less unchanged, the steep increase in prices generated an enormous Tanzi effect. To illustrate, the lag in collecting turnover tax between January 1988 and June 1989 is estimated to exceed two and a half months, and the lag in collecting other taxes was even greater (see Mencinger 1989). How serious is the effect of such a lag on the deficit can be demonstrated by the fact that the average quarterly ratio of turnover tax over aggregate final demand (less investment into inventories) fell from 10.2% in 1988/I–III to 9.3% in 1989/I–III (the turnover tax alone accounted for about 22% of total tax revenues in 1989).

The statistical data in table 10.5 suggest that in the period between June 1986 and December 1987 none of the policy variables investigated can be said to have Granger-caused inflation, whereas there appears to have been a significant feedback effect from inflation to the money base, to wages, and to the discount rate. Accordingly, the 1987 alteration of the accounting system seems to have been accompanied by (and even to have enabled) a shift to non-accommodating macroeconomic policies. Such accommodation went hand in hand with rising prices. Table 10.5 presents additional evidence suggesting that lifting all wage controls at the end of 1988 gave another boost to price dynamics. Moreover, it seems (see table 10.5) that the discount rate and wages were influenced during the last period by price dynamics. As for the exchange rate and the money base, it appears that an almost perfectly accommodating monetary policy and adherence to the PPP rule in adjusting the exchange rate make it impossible to discern any feedback (or "causality") from prices to these two variables.

3. The Fiscal Deficit and Money Creation[4]

In order to understand the impact of the fiscal deficit and money creation on inflation in Yugoslavia, we must first define the terms "public sector" and "public-sector deficit," and the way this deficit was being financed.

Yugoslavia's (narrowly defined) public sector—i.e., the federal budget—did not have much of a deficit until 1987, regardless of whether or not the nominal income statements of the National Bank of Yugoslavia (henceforth referred to as NBY or "the central bank") and the National Banks of the separate republics and autonomous provinces are included (see Tait 1989). It should be noted that the budgets of local governments (republics, autonomous provinces, and municipalities) *must* balance out, and that these bodies have no access to domestic or foreign credit (other than the central bank's).

The main source of the public sector's real deficit is the subsidization of specific economic sectors through "selective credits" extended by the national bank system in order to promote exports and agriculture. Another source is the creation of negative net wealth in the central bank's balance sheet, stemming from its foreign-currency-denominated debt (to the rest of the world and to Yugoslav residents), i.e., from the uncovered exchange losses arising from the net foreign-exchange indebtedness. The public sector's deficit therefore has to be calculated carefully and does not correspond to any measure appearing in the official data.

In the 1980s this fiscal deficit was financed largely by net foreign borrowing and by printing money. The focus was eased by the relative inelasticity of the demand for (broadly and narrowly defined) monetary aggregates with respect to the inflation rate, at least until the end of 1986. Another important source of deficit financing, in the absence of an explicit domestic public debt, was the deferment of federal budget obligations from one fiscal year to the next.[5]

One can therefore infer that the fiscal budget of the (narrowly defined) Yugoslav public sector does not represent the whole budget, and that one must apply the "stock of indebtedness approach" (see Anand and Wijnbergen 1989) in order to take into account all the sources creating the deficit. This approach starts with changes in the net indebtedness of the public sector as an indicator of trends in its fiscal deficit. Nonetheless, we still must take into account certain features specific to the circumstances prevailing in Yugoslavia.

Subsidies given through real negative interest rates (see Sokoler 1987) are also available from the central bank to commercial banks; thus, the central bank's selective credits substitute for public-sector expenditures. Therefore we treated these selective credits as credit to the public sector. As the central bank cites its negative net wealth in all periods as the difference between subsidized interest on credits it extends in dinars and the interest due on foreign loans received, we regard the monetization of such accrual of negative net wealth (i.e., the NBY's accumulated losses) as the way of financing public-sector expenditures. Finally, the increase in net foreign debt is included in the flows of financing the federal budget deficit.

Thus, Yugoslavia's public-sector deficit is composed of the difference between primary revenues and primary outlays, *plus* the negative balance of interests on foreign-currency assets and liabilities of the central bank, *minus* revenue from nominal interest on net dinar assets of the central bank. Of course, the interest payments (both domestic and foreign) have to be adjusted to real terms (net of domestic and foreign inflation, respectively).

The deficit is financed by increasing the foreign debt of the central bank, issuing money base (the inflation tax and increasing real money base), *less* the growth of the central bank's credit to commercial banks. Again, repayment of (real) principal (included in nominal interest payment) is deducted, since we are dealing with the operational deficit.

No reliable data on the primary deficit are available, nor is it possible to detect some of the sources used for financing this deficit. There are some hidden forms of taxation that offset some of the federal budget expenditures, and we have already noted the recourse made to budgetary arrears.

Table 10.6 gives figures for the past two years, which should be regarded only as indicators of scale rather than as the basis for a discussion of the deficit's inflationary effect.[6] The figures show that the inflation tax has been a predominant source of financing the operational deficit in 1987–88. Although the primary deficit was much lower in 1988 than in 1987, the inflation tax remained high and even increased. Real increases in net foreign liabilities of the NBY was an important source of deficit financing in 1987, but declined in 1988 thanks to a new stabilization program designed to replenish net foreign-exchange reserves. (The latter decline was only partly offset by the increase in inflation tax.)

As the new stabilization program failed to implement a restrictive monetary policy, the effect of a decrease in the real value of additional credit to the commercial banks fell between 1987 and 1988.

The central bank's foreign liabilities (reckoned in dollars) did not vary significantly after 1983, possibly implying that exchange-rate-related

Table 10.6
Inflation-adjusted public-sector fiscal deficit and its financing, 1987–1988 (percentage of GSP).*

	1987	1988
Financing the deficit		
Real drop in dinar credit to commercial banks	2.3	1.1
Real increase in net foreign indebtedness of the central bank	3.1	−1.8
Revenue from monetization[a]	5.1	6.5
Of which:		
Inflation tax[b]	6.2	7.2
Increase in real money base[c]	−1.1	−0.7
Total financing	10.6	5.8
Interest expenditures		
Real interest on net foreign liabilities	2.1	2.8
Real interest on net dinar assets of the central bank	2.0	2.5
Total interest expenditures	4.1	5.3
Estimated primary deficit	**6.4**	**0.5**

Source: National Bank of Yugoslavia and authors' calculations.
* The editors draw the readers' attention to the fact that in this study the definition of the "deficit" is not the conventional one; it includes the capital gains and losses of the central bank.
a. Defined as $[(\Delta M)/P]/GSP$; M — money base.
b. Calculated as a difference $a - c$.
c. Defined as $[\Delta(M/P)]/GSP$; M — money base, P — price index. See Anand and Wijnbergen 1989, pp. 25, 26.

reductions in deficit financing were at least partly offset by issues of dinar reserve money also before 1987. Table 10.3 shows that the slackness of the exchange-rate policy was accompained by a decline in the country's operational deficit in 1985 and 1986. It should be remembered that from June 1984 to May 1986 the money base had a feedback effect on inflation (see table 10.5).

Generally speaking, one observes an improvement in the fiscal stance during 1988, although inflation continued to accelerate. It therefore seems that other factors (such as the wage explosion after 1988/III) were at work.

Table 10.6 also demonstrates that expenditures on interest payments increased between 1987 and 1988.

4. The Demand for Real Balances and the Financing of the Public-Sector Deficit

In the preceding section we saw that the public sector was running a large deficit in 1987 and 1988, largely financed by the inflation tax. This is why the magnitude of the semi-elasticity of demand for real (base) money and its persistence are so important in connection with the monetization of the public sector's deficit.

We will try to address empirically some additional important issues related to the financing of the public sector's deficit and the demand for real balances. Thus, we present estimates of the demand for real balances by households and businesses, as well as the demand for real money base, and discuss the stability implications of financing the public-sector deficit, the optimal inflation tax, commercial banks' interest rates, and the effect of dollarization on the demand for real balances.

Suppose the demand for real balances has a standard semi-exponential (Cagan) form:

$$h_t = a \exp(-\alpha \Pi^*_t) , \tag{1}$$

where h stands for real balances per unit of GNP, α is the semi-elasticity of demand for real balances on expected prices, and Π^* is the expected rate of inflation in the next period.

Assume further that inflationary expectations are formed according to an adaptive mechanism,

$$\Pi^*_t - \Pi^*_{t-1} = \beta(\Pi_t - \Pi^*_{t-1}) , \tag{2}$$

where β is the coefficient of adaptation.

From the government budget constraint it follows that in a steady-state the rate of inflation, the public-sector deficit (d), the growth rate of output (n), the volume of bonds (b), and the money base (h) are interconnected by the relation

$$\Pi = [d - n(b + h)]/h . \tag{3}$$

Of course, d, b, and h are calculated per unit of GNP. It is a well-known fact (see Bruno and Fischer 1987) that in the steady state a deficit can be financed by printing money at two different (equilibrium) rates of inflation. However, which of the two equilibrium points (implied by equations 1 and 3) is stable depends on the product of α and β. It can easily be shown (see Bruno 1989) that the high-inflation equilibrium point is stable if $\alpha\beta$ is greater than 1. At the high-inflation equilibrium point the economy reacts rather strangely to changes in the public-sector deficit, which makes it all the more important for policy makers to know whether $\alpha\beta > 1$.

Shifting changes in the demand for real balances are also of importance to commercial banks, since collecting part of the inflation tax (on demand deposits) is a major source of financing their huge balance-sheet losses. According to some estimates (see Mates 1985), the nonperforming assets had already exceeded the banks' total assets by 20% in 1984. Thus, nonperforming loans and off-balance-sheet items implied that losses exert continuous pressure on the banks' interest-rate spread. The effect of such pressure depends on the specific location of the economy on the Laffer curve at a given rate of inflation: if the economy is situated on the left side of the curve, increased inflation will *mitigate* the pressure on interest rates, and vice versa if the economy is situated on the right side.

The problems entailed in identifying and specifying the demand-for-money equation are well known (see, for example, Cooley and LeRoy 1981). Furthermore, the assumption, made above, about the adaptive nature of inflationary expectations could be disputed as being too "mechanical," or too *ad hoc*, or even on the grounds that such expectations are not strictly rational. Be that as it may, table 10.5 indicates that one cannot reject the hypothesis about the adaptive nature of inflationary expectations (see also Sargent and Wallace 1973). Since Bruno (1989) has already suggested that the coefficient of adaptation depends on inflation, we have estimated the demand for real balances separately for two subperiods (see table 10.7).

In the Cagan specification of demand for real balances, expected inflation represents the expected opportunity cost of holding money. However, as accelerating inflation usually generates increased dollarization in the economy, it seems reasonable to seek some measure of the opportunity cost in a combination of inflation with exchange-rate dynamics. Such a measure could be written as

$$\psi\,ER^* + (1 - \psi)\Pi^* , \tag{4}$$

where ER^* represents anticipated developments in the exchange rate and ψ is its weight. By assumption, expected opportunity costs are also adaptive. But in the steady state, when defined as above, they coincide with actual price dynamics. This approach could provide additional

Table 10.7
Parameters of the demand-for-money model.

	Semi-elasticity (1)	Coefficient of adaptation (2)	Coefficient of dollarization (3)
June 1986 to December 1987			
Businesses (M1)	−5.43	0.56	0.01
	(1.57)	(0.15)	(0.09)
Households (M1)	−3.66	0.36	0.00
	(1.99)	(0.21)	(0.00)
Money base	−5.53	0.19	—
	(2.24)	(0.08)	
January 1988 to June 1989			
Businesses (M1)	−3.08	0.69	0.21
	(0.61)	(0.24)	(0.15)
Households (M1)	−2.09	0.76	0.44
	(0.37)	(0.28)	(0.17)
Money base	−3.28	0.25	—
	(1.46)	(0.14)	

Figures in parentheses are standard errors.

insight to the usual practice of viewing exchange-rate dynamics as the sole measure of inflationary expectations in a high-inflation context. In addition, Yugoslav households (like households in other high-inflation countries) own foreign-exchange-linked deposits: thus, viewed from the angle of households' demand for real balances, the proposed measure of opportunity costs takes on additional significance in that such foreign-exchange-linked deposits can be seen as a close substitute for money. By the same token, the "weight" of the exchange rate (ψ) can also be viewed as a measure of the economy's degree of dollarization.

Table 10.7 presents some interesting parameters of the demand of households and businesses for real balances and real money base. Additional parameters and standard errors appear in table 10.A4. The figures reveal that the semi-elasticities of demand for real balances were considerably higher in the earlier than in the later period. This is not surprising: widespread indexation of the economy was set off by the 1987 revamping of the accounting system, inducing both households and businesses to rethink their portfolio policies. Because of an almost nonexistent active interest-rates policy before 1987, it is hardly possible to evaluate decision making regarding financial assets at that time.

Therefore, there is evidence of a sharp reduction of money illusion reflected by the difference between the semi-elasticities of the two subperiods.

It is clear from table 10.7 that the semi-elasticities of business demand for real balances exceed those of households, and both are smaller than the semi-elasticity of demand for money base. This implies that the rate of inflation at the maximum level of inflation tax collected by the central bank is less than "optimal" from the commercial banks' point of view. Either way, when inflation topped 40% monthly in the second half of 1989, the rate was definitely higher than optimal for both the central bank and commercial banks. Hence, any further rise in the inflation rate will inevitably reduce collections of inflation tax by both the central bank and the commercial banks.

Column 2 of table 10.7 gives estimated coefficients of adaptation. It should be borne in mind that the model of demand for real balances treats the opportunity cost of holding money as the weighted sum of inflation rates and the growth of the exchange rate, so that the estimates presented here do not correspond to results obtained by using the usual (Cagan) hyperinflation-induced demand for money. The evidence supports the hypothesis that the adaptation coefficient is an increasing function of the rate of inflation. We observe that since early 1988 the "rationality" of price expectations (especially that of households) has risen. The adaptation coefficient of demand for real money base also increased substantially, although the product of the estimated values of semi-elasticity and the adaptation coefficient is still smaller than unity.[7] We can conclude that the evidence fails to unequivocally support the hypothesis that the "stable high-inflation equilibrium" approach can adequately describe events in the Yugoslav economy in 1988–89 with respect to the ways in which the public-sector deficit was financed.

The fact that a dramatic switch occurred in the behavior of households and businesses after 1987 is further illustrated by the estimated values of the coefficient of dollarization. While the weight of the exchange-rate dynamics did not significantly affect the opportunity cost of holding money in 1986/6–1987/12, we observe a steep rise in the coefficient of dollarization for the period 1988/1–1989/6. This implies that households regard exchange-rate dynamics as being almost as important as the rate of inflation. With respect to the demand for real money base, the coefficient of dollarization was insignificant in both periods analyzed here, so we reestimated the equation without the dollarization effect.

Figure 10.1 includes the monthly values of real money base as well as real money held by firms and households after 1988/1. The surprising finding is that the demand for real balances in 1989 suddenly leveled off and even started to increase—just as inflation was turning into hyperinflation! One possible explanation for this phenomenon is that the increase in the supply of money led to increased money holdings. But the fact that the money base was lagging two months behind household demand for real balances when the latter started leveling off refutes this explanation. Alternatively, this may be a "reform effect" (see, for example, Anderson, Bomberger, and Makinen 1988), that is, an anticipated stabilization of the economy leading to unexplained increases in the demand for real balances. Such an explanation could be supported by the government reshuffle of March 1989, which then proceeded to take some popular measures. In our opinion, however, the "strange" behavior exhibited by the demand for real balances after 1989/3 was induced by the fact that such behavior is also determined by the exchange rate. And when the sliding exchange rate was curbed after 1989/2 this is likely to have contributed to the increase in the demand for real balances from 1989/3 onward.

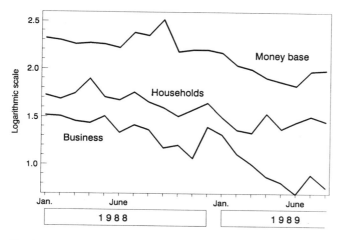

Figure 10.1
Real money balances, 1988-1989.

Appendix

Table 10.A1
Growth rates of some important variables (percentages).

		Retail prices	Exchange rate of DM	Wages	Money (M1)
Quarterly averages of monthly growth rates					
1983	I	2.8	7.2	−1.0	0.3
	II	2.6	3.0	4.7	0.8
	III	5.9	5.4	2.1	3.0
	IV	5.0	4.0	9.0	2.2
1984	I	1.8	1.4	0.5	2.0
	II	3.3	2.7	4.9	2.2
	III	5.2	4.9	0.9	4.0
	IV	4.5	3.8	12.3	4.0
1985	I	6.6	7.0	3.4	1.2
	II	3.7	4.7	3.1	1.3
	III	4.2	5.1	4.8	4.3
	IV	5.8	5.5	14.9	6.2
1986	I	6.7	4.8	3.2	3.8
	II	5.8	9.2	6.9	5.1
	III	4.9	1.9	2.7	8.2
	IV	4.8	5.0	18.2	8.5
1987	I	7.4	8.8	−0.4	3.5
	II	6.9	6.2	4.7	3.2
	III	8.7	9.8	7.7	6.7
	IV	11.6	19.4	15.7	10.8
1988	I	5.4	3.6	6.8	5.3
	II	9.9	15.6	4.0	7.0
Monthly growth rates					
1988	7	11.5	8.9	7.5	20.4
	8	16.0	12.0	14.2	13.2
	9	14.6	10.8	11.3	3.7
	10	17.7	21.6	12.4	13.1
	11	14.5	18.8	32.9	15.6
	12	13.3	12.5	30.8	22.6
1989	1	14.6	10.3	−23.0	7.4
	2	22.8	19.8	38.8	4.6
	3	17.1	22.0	28.2	6.9
	4	26.2	22.1	34.6	28.3
	5	23.5	25.5	10.1	12.3
	6	30.3	20.0	44.0	24.4
	7	31.3	37.8	28.1	48.3
	8	28.4	28.3	39.2	28.0

Table 10.A2
Discount rates regressed on inflation rate.

	1983/1– 1984/5	1984/6– 1986/5	1986/6– 1987/12	1988/1– 1989/6
r	0.02	0.25	0.16	0.53
d^a	—	0.18	−0.32	−0.20
a_0	0.36	0.04	−0.22	0.00
	(3.6)	(6.1)	(−2.9)	(0.0)
a_1	−0.00	0.00	0.00	−0.00
	(−3.8)	(3.7)	(2.8)	(−0.1)
a_2	−0.00	−0.01	0.00	−1.36
	(−0.0)	(−0.3)	(0.1)	(−5.3)
a_3	0.01	−0.06	−0.00	1.33
	(0.8)	(−2.1)	(−0.0)	(5.4)
a_4	−0.30	−0.04	0.04	0.18
	(−3.4)	(−5.1)	(5.1)	(2.5)
a_5	0.03	−0.06	0.02	0.02
	(2.3)	(−3.2)	(0.5)	(0.4)
a_6	0.03	−0.02	−0.06	0.03
	(1.9)	(−1.3)	(−1.9)	(1.2)
R^2	0.93	0.92	0.98	0.98
F^b	3.5	5.3	2.1	2.2

Figures in parentheses are t statistics.
Parameters a_i denote: a_0 intercept, a_1 parameter at time trend, r, a_2, a_3, a_4 parameters for distribution of current and lagged inflation rates and a_5, a_6 parameters of first two forward inflation rates (see Sargent and Wallace 1973).
a. Parameter obtained as the first-order serial regression coefficient of LS residuals.
b. F values refer to test for existence of feedback from discount rate to inflation.

Table 10.A3
Inflation rate regressed on discount rate.

	1982/1– 1984/5	1984/6– 1986/5	1986/6– 1987/12	1988/1– 1989/6
r	0.92	0.10	0.02	0.02
d^a	−0.22	−0.44	−0.36	−0.33
a_0	−0.05	0.36	20.17	−52.88
	(0.7)	(2.0)	(1.5)	(−2.6)
a_1	−0.00	0.00	−0.22	0.44
	(−2.0)	(0.6)	(−1.6)	(2.6)
a_2	−81.07	−4.10	0.27	0.28
	(−1.2)	(−2.0)	(0.1)	(0.8)
a_3	84.12	−0.47	2.02	−0.76
	(1.3)	(−0.9)	(1.8)	(−2.8)
a_4	1.52	−0.29	−8.23	20.94
	(0.7)	(−1.6)	(−1.4)	(2.5)
a_5	−3.21	1.44	1.42	0.00
	(−0.5)	(0.6)	(0.8)	(1.5)
a_6	2.07	−2.15	2.00	0.00
	(0.4)	(−1.2)	(2.2)	(0.9)
R^2	0.45	0.36	0.82	0.93
F^b	0.1	0.8	5.7	3.7

Figures in parentheses are t statistics.
Parameters a_i denote: a_0 intercept, a_1 parameter at time trend, r, a_2, a_3, a_4 parameters for distribution of current and lagged discount rates and a_5, a_6 parameters of first two forward discount rates (see Sargent and Wallace 1973).
a. Parameter obtained as the first-order serial regression coefficient of LS residuals.
b. F values refer to test for existence of feedback from inflation to the discount rate.

Table 10.A4
Demand for money.

	1986/6–1987/12			1988/1–1989/6		
	Businesses	Households	Money base	Businesses	Households	Money base
f	0.11 (0.40)	0.00 (0.01)	—	0.52 (0.24)	0.89 (0.30)	—
d	−0.24 (0.21)	−0.42 (0.31)	−0.39 (0.26)	0.12 (0.28)	−0.24 (0.30)	−0.24 (0.30)
a_0	0.26 (0.33)	0.55 (0.32)	0.52 (0.20)	1.04 (0.84)	0.80 (0.41)	0.63 (0.34)
a_1	0.37 (0.14)	0.35 (0.15)	—	0.05 (0.21)	0.52 (0.18)	—
a_2 Semi-elasticity (α)	−5.43 (1.57)	−3.66 (1.99)	−5.53 (2.24)	−3.08 (0.61)	−2.09 (0.37)	−3.28 (1.46)
a_3 Coef. of adaptation (β)	0.56 (0.15)	0.36 (0.21)	0.19 (0.08)	0.69 (0.24)	0.76 (0.28)	0.25 (0.14)
R^2	0.84	0.60	0.87	0.86	0.83	0.82

Figures in parentheses are standard errors.
Log of real balances is regressed on log of volume of transactions and expected opportunity cost of holding money (convex combination of exchange rate and inflation); parameters denote: a_0 intercept, a_1 elasticity on volume of transactions, $[1 - 1/(1 + f^2)]$ weight of exchange rate in a measure of opportunity cost of money (Ψ) and d first-order serial correlation coefficient (see, for example, Zellner, Huang, and Chau 1965).

Acknowledgments

The authors thank anonymous referees for helpful suggestions which improved the presentation of this paper and eliminated some errors.

Notes

1. Over two-thirds of all oil-driven power plants in Yugoslavia were built *after* the first oil crisis and before 1982.

2. Private consumption includes only direct payments of households.

3. An appendix elaborating the methodology can be obtained from the authors upon request.

4. The editors draw the readers' attention to the fact that in this study the definition of the "deficit" is not the conventional one; it includes the capital gains and losses of the central bank.

5. In practice, the NBY made the necessary payments and informally debited the budget—i.e., the transaction was not recorded in the balance sheet of NBY.

6. Rough estimates of the total operational deficit in previous years are presented in table 10.3.

7. For the discrete-time case the condition $\alpha\beta > 1$ is substituted by $\beta(\alpha + \frac{1}{2}) > 1$ (see Friedman 1978). The less stringent condition does not hold for the second period either. However, taking into account distribution of estimators for α and β, it is possible to reject hypothesis that $\beta(\alpha + \frac{1}{2}) > 1$ at the 0.1 level of significance.

References

Anand, R., and S. van Wijnbergen. 1989. "Inflation and the financing of government expenditure: An introductory analysis with an application to Turkey." *World Bank Economic Review* 3 (no. 1): 17–38.

Anderson, R. B., W. A. Bomberger, and G. E. Makinen. 1988. "The demand for money, the `Reform Effect' and the money supply process in hyperinflations." *Journal of Money, Credit and Banking* 20 (no. 4): 653–672.

Bruno, M. 1989. "Econometrics and the design of economic reform." *Econometrica* 57 (no. 2): 275–306.

Bruno, M., and S. Fischer. 1986. "The inflationary process: Shocks and accommodation." In *The Israeli Economy: Maturing through Crises*, Y. Ben-Porath, ed. (Harvard University Press).

Bruno, M., and S. Fischer. 1987. Seignorage, operating rules and the high inflation trap. NBER Working Paper.

Cemović, M. 1985. *Why, How, and How Much Credits Did We Take*. Institute for Promotion of Trade, Belgrade. (In Serbo-Croatian.)

Central Bank. 1982. *Annual Report*.

Cooley, T. F., and F. S. LeRoy. 1981. "Identification and estimation of money demand." *American Economic Review* 71: 825–844.

Friedman, B. M. 1978. "Stability and rationality in models of hyperinflation." *International Economic Review* 19: 45–64.

Hendry, D. F., and J. F. Richard. 1983. "The econometric analysis of economic time series." *International Statistical Review* 51: 111–148.

Mates, N. 1985. Problems of Accumulated Losses in the Financial System. Unpublished paper. (In Serbo-Croatian.)

Mencinger, J. 1989. "Taxes and inflation." *Economic Outlook of Yugoslavia* (September): 29–42. (In Serbo-Croatian.)

Sargent, T. J., and N. Wallace. 1973. "Rational expectations and the dynamics of hyperinflation." *International Economic Review* 14 (no. 2): 328–350.

Sokoler, M. 1987. "The inflation tax on real balances, the inflation subsidy on credit, and the inflationary process in Israel." *Bank of Israel Economic Review* 59: 1–26.

Tait, A. A. 1989. IMF Advice on Fiscal Policy. IMF Working Paper no. 87.

Zellner, A. D., S. Huang, and L. C. Chau. 1965. "Further analysis of the short-run consumption function with emphasis on the role of liquid assets." *Econometrica* 33 (no. 3): 571–581.

Comments by Neven Mates

The authors have identified in their paper the shocks that, in their opinion, led to an increase in inflation in different periods during the 1980s. For the first two periods they are certainly right regarding the shocks they mention. I find their opinion that the main cause of runaway inflation in the third period (beginning with 1987) was the introduction of a new accounting system unacceptable, or far-fetched at least. The new accounting system provided for indexation of all credits and ensured real positive interest rates on deposits and credits for the first time. One may view this as an increase in the capital costs of firms that pushed inflation further. However, this period was also marked by considerable political instability in the country, no wage restraint, and an expansive monetary policy. I would give these factors much greater weight among possible causes of increased inflation in that period than I would give the influence of the new accounting system.

In the analyses of inflationary processes I would focus more attention on the mechanism of monetary policy.

In my opinion, the most important problem concerning the functioning of the central bank arises from the government's attempts to achieve too many goals through the activity of this institution. In this way, the central bank has been burdened with many non-monetary functions. By means of favorable credits at low interest rates, or simply through the issuing of high-powered money, the central bank subsidized agriculture, promoted exports, financed surpluses in "clearing" trade with Eastern European countries, compensated commercial banks for foreign-exchange losses on household savings, financed the federal government's temporary deficits, etc. All these activities were carried out to the detriment of the primary function of the central bank.

There were also several methodological problems in monetary planning which were not solved successfully. The National Bank of Yugoslavia never tried to estimate the demand for money under conditions of rising inflation. Instead, the inflation rate for the coming year was estimated and money targets set by the deduction of some "percentage of restrictiveness." At the same time very optimistic forecasts were made considering "clearing trade," foreign-exchange losses, budget deficits, and so on. The whole amount of the available increase in loans from the National Bank of Yugoslavia was then earmarked for "selective loans." In this way, "refinancing ratios" for selective credits were determined.

Rising prices of agricultural products, value of exports in domestic currency, etc., were, in the course of the year, automatically followed by increases in the volume of credit for selective purposes given by the banks. Forecasts of favorable monetary effects of net reserve positions, clearing trade effects, and the monetization of exchange-rate losses often proved too optimistic. At the same time, fixed percentages of refinancing facilities provided by the central bank resulted in an unplanned increase in its loans and in the money base. The scaling down of these refinancing rates often proved impossible to carry out. The rights once granted proved difficult to revoke. The monetary planning was then repeated by the National Bank, and a much higher rate of inflation was planned and accommodated. The problem was that the mechanism of selective credits did not usually leave the central bank any room for discretionary decisions that could have corrected undesirable developments during the year.

Finally, the specific form of the public-sector deficit played an important role in the inflation process. As these authors say, the government budget did not usually show a deficit, but the central bank was accumulating losses, and it was also very active in parafiscal lending activities. This process also has some self-enhancing characteristics. In the early 1980s the government was compelled to change the real exchange rate, but this could have been achieved by a smaller nominal devaluation. However, the first devaluation was not followed by serious anti-inflationary measures. Interest-rate policy was too inert, and monetary policy was expansive. Inflation spurred in this way created large losses for the central and commercial banks on account of net foreign-exchange liabilities and loans with fixed interest rates. Inflation thus fueled itself by destabilizing government and banking-system finances. This is the reason why it is not enough to identify shocks in specific periods; it is also important to show how the absence of anti-inflationary measures after the depreciation of the dinar at the beginning of the 1980s (which was certainly unavoidable) started the self-enhancing process of inflation.

To get some idea about the amount of losses and of deficit spending through parafiscal activities of the central bank, it is helpful to make the following calculation.

From 1980 to 1988 the cumulative losses of the central bank grew from 1 billion to 14 billion US dollars. In addition, the parafiscal activity of the central bank cost the government its whole potential revenue from high-powered money creation.

There are several methods of estimating total revenue from money creation, but we resort here to a rough approximation. We calculated the real value of monthly high-powered money growth for the whole period from 1980 to 1988. This was done by dividing the monthly increase of high-powered money by the current exchange rate of the dinar to the US dollar. On the basis of this calculation, we estimate that the total revenue from money-base creation in the nine-year period amounted to $14 billion. If we add to this revenue the increase in the central bank's losses, the total public deficit was $27 billion. If we estimate the gross domestic product to have been around $55 billion per year, this results in an average parafiscal deficit of 5.5 percent of the GDP in the period 1980–1988.

This was the cost of parafiscal operations by the central bank through selective loans, an inadequate interest-rate policy, the taking over of exchange-rate losses of commercial banks and firms, etc.

Finally, it is also important to be aware of the special institutional position of banks in the Yugoslav economic system. Banks have not been really independent, profit-oriented financial institutions. After the constitutional reform of 1971, they were organized as a "service" of the labor-managed enterprises. Every founder, i.e., enterprise, had only one vote, regardless of its equity share. This formal right to manage banks was, however, only of relative significance. Particularly great influence on the management of a bank was usually exercised by a small number of founders, who had their representatives on the bank's managing board, and by local political circles (government, party, etc.), which exercised great influence on the election of the bank's director. Since the enterprises were net debtors, and the local political structures were primarily interested in crediting the local economy as much as possible, banks were in fact managed by big debtors. The losses caused in this institutional setup had to be covered sooner or later by the government. In the last few years part of these losses in the banks was covered through the inflation tax, which was partly appropriated by banks. These institutional characteristics of the Yugoslav economic system also played a very important role in the inflationary processes.

Comments by Domenico Mario Nuti

Yugoslavia's hyperinflation record is quite respectable. It went from what Bole and Gaspari call a "natural" rate of inflation of 15–30% a year before the 1980s to 2,500% a year in 1989. Its accumulated external debt to banks in the BIS area was about $8 billion, which, just recently, was retraded in the secondary market at 52.8¢ to the dollar, halfway between Mexico's (39.5¢) and Chile's (65.8¢) averages. Together with the official debt, the total rises to almost $20 billion, or close to two years' worth of Yugoslav exports.

The paper by Bole and Gaspari makes a valuable contribution to our understanding of the fundamental sources of this domestic and external imbalance and of the problems entailed in its stabilization. The authors draw a careful distinction between system-specific and policy-specific factors in the Yugoslav experience. This is important especially for the sake of comparison, and I would like to reemphasize the specific features of the Yugoslav system, deriving from its unique brand of associationist or self-managed socialism.

Yugoslavia is largely a market economy, with a well-articulated banking system (167 banks at the last count), open to trade, and with a convertible currency. However, it presents the following systemic peculiarities:

The central bank, while not obliged to grant automatic credit for plan fulfillment as in Soviet-type systems, nevertheless has an important fiscal (and not monetary) function—redistributing resources across the economy in place of the state budget. Thus the Bank provides subsidized credit to specific enterprises, sectors, and regions, and incurs losses for such subsidies and for bad loans granted in the implementation of government policies. In particular, the central bank absorbs foreign-exchange losses as intermediary for foreign loans—because it fails to charge domestic enterprises for the foreign-exchange risk when lending internationally borrowed funds.

According to Yugoslav law, the budget (whether federal, state, or local) simply cannot have a deficit. Thus, formally, there is no public debt, domestic or foreign. This debt is tucked away in the banking system—not only in the central bank, but also in other banks, owned by self-managed enterprises—and becomes a channel for the collectivization of losses.

An important contribution of the paper is the attempt to uncover and estimate the scale and dynamics of the public-sector deficit. This is reconstructed from the identifiable sources of its financing (table 10.6) following a modified version of the stock-of-indebtedness approach of Anand and Wijnbergen. The inflation tax appears to be the dominant source of finance.

I have reservations about two aspects of this calculation. First, when the real interest rate is negative, it is regarded in its entirety as a subsidy from the banking system to the enterprise sector. But if this is indeed regarded as a subsidy, it comes from the public, not (or not entirely) from the banking sector. The banks' subsidy, if any, is that part of their cost and normal profit which is not covered by the margin between their lending and borrowing rates. Second, regardless of the interest rate charged on loans, there are still hidden subsidies, namely that part of the bank portfolio which should simply be written off and which will not be written off without greater enterprise discipline in cases of liquidation and bankruptcy. The government budget deficit is therefore under-recorded to the extent of the increase in the amount of bad loans. In the course of the discussion Gaspari recognized that bad loans made by Yugoslav banks to the enterprise sector were of the order of $10 billion, rising to $18 billion if exposures through guarantees, commitments, and contingencies are included (this also happened in Spain, but on a much smaller scale). In Yugoslavia, future recapitalization would be necessary and would take several years, say $3 billion a year for six years. In spite of this under-recording, the budget deficit reached 10.5% of GNP in 1987 and fell to 5.8% in 1988, although the primary deficit fell from 6.4% to 0.5%.

The authors argue that the fiscal function of the central bank was enhanced by the constitutional changes of 1974, which gave greater financial autonomy to individual republics of the Yugoslav federation, but in practice cast the central bank in the role of "government of last resort," i.e., in the role of validating individual republics' choices through offsetting their mistakes, preventing them from learning from those mistakes and from negotiating some kind of Nash equilibrium between themselves. Yet a major feature of the Yugoslav economy and society has been precisely the continued presence of corporatist and neocorporatist social pacts at all levels (local, republican, federal). The real problem seems to have been not the opportunity to play a game but the adoption of noncooperative strategies on the part of the players.

Another important systemic feature of Yugoslavia is the ownership regime. Until 1965 national capital outside the relatively small private sector belonged to the state. Since then, after constitutional changes and economic reform, *de jure* and *de facto* national capital literally does not belong to anybody. Yugoslav enterprises are in the anomalous position of having no owners, since the state is no longer the owner and workers have only temporary usufruct, not ownership—i.e., they can share value added but cannot appropriate the increase in enterprise present value, whether due to reinvestment or success. (The only parallel in a market economy seems to be that of the Trustees Savings Bank in the United Kingdom at the time of its transformation into a joint stock company; cooperatives also exhibit partial propertylessness, i.e., for the part of their capital over and above what can be distributed to members.) Ludwig von Mises argued that you cannot have markets without private property; I think a regime of competitive bidding for the use of state property can go a long way, but not with the Yugoslav property system. This is the fundamental source of all kinds of rigidities, and even of possible perverse responses, to the extent that enterprise members are selfish enough to maximize value added distributed per man, and strong enough to get away with it.

In theory, the Yugoslav enterprise should pay out only what it earns. In practice it is monopolistic and treats labor earnings as a cost, like any wage-contract capitalist firm, adjusting prices to match. Even if we ignore the niceties of the so-called Illyrian Firm, as the theoretical model of a self-managed firm has been called in the economic literature, the Yugoslav enterprise is bound to respond sluggishly to price increases because this raises the value of the marginal product of labor by less than its average revenue (since nonlabor costs are never entirely indexed to the price of the product), thus discouraging supply expansion through greater employment.

If this is the case, inflation will not evoke a supply response, and devaluation will not work. With fairly inelastic demand for imports and inelastic supply of exports, such as is bound to result from the microeconomics of Yugoslav enterprises, a devaluation worsens terms of trade without promoting net exports. This may explain one of the authors' findings: the trade-promotion ineffectiveness and the inflationary effect of exchange-rate devaluation. This and other findings derive from Granger causality tests, subjected to sharp criticism but neatly employed.

An interesting result is the estimate of an "index of dollarization" (or, rather, DMarkization) of the Yugoslav economy. This is the coefficient of the exchange rate in the estimate of demand for real balances. In 1988–89, with respect to 1986–87, the index rose from 1% to 21% for business and from 0% to 44% for households. This is a measure of the opportunity cost of foreign exchange and should not be interpreted literally as a share of hard-currency transactions in total transactions. However, it reflects well the effects of indexation and hyperinflation.

With respect to the centrally planned economies of Central and Eastern Europe, now in transition toward a market mixed economy, Yugoslavia exhibits greater similarities than one might have expected: overambitious investment, unstoppable labor earnings, and fiscal re-distribution. It avoided repressed inflation at the expense of open inflation and hyperinflation. At the risk of oversimplifying or forcing the evidence provided by the authors, I draw both positive and negative lessons from Yugoslavia for other Central and Eastern European countries: the way to effective reform passes first through hyperinflation, then through the austerity of balanced budgets and monetary discipline backed by wage restraint; it is only then that interest and exchange-rate policies can be used with any degree of confidence and flexibility.

General Discussion

The decentralized operation of Yugoslavia policy was addressed. Mario Blejer asked about the prospects of active fiscal policy as long as enterprises can obtain unlimited credit to pay taxes and are not compelled to repay loans. Haim Barkai pointed out that enterprises in Yugoslavia can actually print their own money, since they know that any excess expenditure will eventually be accommodated by the central bank.

Sebastian Edwards emphasized the potential role of trade liberalization in 1988. He inquired as to the real effect of the failure of three nominal anchors and trade liberalization.

Some participants asked whether any major changes occurred with the implementation of the recent disinflation policy in December 1989. Stanley Fischer pointed to the need for steps to ensure that the central bank would close its "open gates." Mitja Gaspari responded by outlining some of the major features of the new program introduced in December 1989:

· The exchange rate of the new dinar was fixed at Din 7 per DM, to remain unchanged until June 1990.

· The Dinar will be convertible by domestic residents at the new rate, starting in January 1990.

· Wages are to be pegged to the exchange rate. They were calculated in December in terms of DM, and will be frozen at an average level (DM800 per month). Some room for adjustment within the fixed average is to be left, as long as the wage bill remains unchanged.

· The exchange-rate anchor and the wage anchor are accompanied by a partial freeze on prices of key items representing 20% of the retail price index. These prices had been raised in real terms prior to the freeze.

· A strict monetary policy was announced restricting the rate of change of net domestic assets, forbidding selective credits by the National Bank, and pegging the discount rate and bank loan rates (at 24% and 35% respectively).

· Losses of the National Bank are to be transformed into public debt, thus preventing hidden deficits in the future.

11

Panel Discussion: What's New Since Toledo?

Michael Bruno (moderator), Guido Di Tella, Jacob Frenkel, Stanley Fischer, and Nissan Liviatan

Michael Bruno

Quite a few of those present at this meeting were active participants in a conference held in Toledo in June 1987. At that time five countries were represented; four of them (Argentina, Brazil, Bolivia, and Israel) had just gone through the first stage of a stabilization process, and the fifth (Mexico) was preparing for stabilization.

The first point that I would like to make, which comes out of our very fruitful discussion in the past two days, is that the experience since Toledo has been much more varied than could have been anticipated at that time. Let me mention the main changes observed across countries before coming to the main questions that are worth discussing in this panel.

First, Argentina and Brazil, after the apparent success of 1986–87, spiraled from high inflation into hyperinflation. One hypothesis raised at the previous conference was that unless stabilization of high inflation can be sustained, there comes a point at which it will turn into hyperinflation. Unfortunately, the facts support this hypothesis. At some point, persistence and inertia disappear and the process becomes highly unstable. The question, of course, is: Where do these countries go from here? This issue was discussed yesterday, and I would like to revert back to it today: Are we dealing with a new economic regime or a failed stabilization? The concept of credibility and its (complete) loss was mentioned frequently in connection with these two countries' experience.

Second, Mexico and Israel. Mexico, which has carried out one of the most successful heterodox stabilization programs, has moved from correcting fundamentals to a successful heterodox program; Israel, rather unexpectedly, has moved into a slump and restructuring, exemplifying the problems that can emerge in the transition from stabilization to growth. These problems are also shared by Bolivia, whose stabilization has been remarkably successful, although in comparison with Israel it experienced hyperinflation and implemented an orthodox program to stabilize it. The question is: Must a sharp recession be an inevitable intermediate phase? The more one looks into hyperinflation experiences of the past—someone today called it "the Garber Phenomenon"—the more it seems that a second recession was common to most of the historical experiences. It remains to be seen whether Mexico will also join that club; perhaps not, because it made some of the structural corrections earlier on.

One characteristic common to the four successful stabilizations discussed in this conference (Bolivia, Chile, Israel, and Mexico) is that they are all still running annual inflation rates of 15–20%. How can one explain this?

Some of the countries in our sample, notably Israel, Mexico, Yugoslavia, and Turkey, have again illustrated the conflict between using the *nominal* exchange rate as a key anchor for the price system and maintaining a stable real exchange rate. This represents the tradeoff between price stability and trade account (and output) stability. Are there any additional lessons to be learned for stabilization from that experience? First, let me point out Chile's apparent success in avoiding this conflict in the past four or five years—a point that was briefly mentioned (too briefly in my opinion) in the discussion of Chile. Another familiar point that has come up in several countries' experience is the emergence of high real interest rates in the stabilization process and their effect, in the form of financial entanglements, on banking crises and so on. Many micro problems keep popping up, which, I think, are not fully taken into account in our macro approach to these experiences. This takes us closer to the structural change aspect of adjustment.

Finally, several new countries have in the meantime joined the high-inflation club, among them Turkey and, most notably, Yugoslavia. I fully agree with Mario Nuti's remark that had we held this conference six months later we would probably have included Poland. Some of us here have had superficial acquaintance with the Polish experience and found it very interesting. Unfortunately, more of it may be forthcoming as that part of the world changes its political structure. Are any more Communist-bloc countries likely to fall into the same pattern? Probably. The question that will then arise is: Will Eastern European inflation and stabilization be a variation on a familiar set of experiences and typology, or will they be of a new type for which some different approach will be required?

I will ask Guido di Tella to start the discussion and focus on the lessons of Argentina's and Brazil's recent experiences regarding the implications of failed (or, as we have called them, short-lived) heterodox programs. Where do we go from here? In a way, this takes us back to the main issues of yesterday's discussion. Jacob Frenkel will follow. He has been asked to take up the issue of supporting nominal anchors relating to the varied experience of our eight participant countries, and possibly to that of some others, such as EMS-type pegging of exchange rates. He also wishes to talk about the phenomenon of high real interest rates. Each one of the panelists, within the ten minutes allocated to him, is free to choose his own topic. Stan will be third, and will take up the problem of the transition from stabilization to structural change and to sustainable growth. In this context the particular problem of institutional reform in Eastern-bloc countries will also be mentioned. Rudi Dornbusch, who was supposed to join us, was unfortunately prevented from coming, and I am grateful to Nissan Liviatan for agreeing to participate at such short notice. Nissan is, of course, equally free to choose his own topic; let me just tell you that I had asked Rudi to round up this preliminary set of statements with some general policy lessons and implications for economic theory and methodology.

Guido Di Tella

As Stanley Fischer has said in this conference, economists have always understood that heterodox stabilization policies consisting purely of wage and price controls are not heterodox, they are absurd. They should be orthodox-plus policies, the *orthodox* part standing for at least a balanced budget and the *plus* part usually standing for some sort of price control or exchange-rate fixing.

This is the reason why I prefer to call these policies supra-orthodox, although they have not been perceived as such. Instead, they have been interpreted as offering a sort of tradeoff between fiscal austerity and price controls. Although this is a misinterpretation, it is loved by politicians, who tend to emphasize price and incomes policies rather than the "fundamentals." At least in Argentina and Brazil, heterodox tools were often used simply in order to postpone an adjustment, resulting in the later need for much more severe measures. In other instances, heterodox programs started with a weak set of measures, hypothetically enabling the attainment of the so-called fundamentals, but with a flimsy base and too little scrutiny of the realism of the measures and of the targets. Analysis and discussion (even by some outstanding economists) proceeded too rapidly, as if the fiscal deficit could easily be eliminated, forgetting that this is *the* crucial issue. Instead, the emphasis is placed on the beauty or consistency of the heterodox measures.

Whether we like heterodox measures or not, 90% of the problem is to get the fundamentals straight—especially the fiscal deficit. Thus the main thrust of analysis in a conference such as this should address this problem: the nature of the fiscal deficit, whether its cause is an abnormally low tax collection or an abnormally high expenditure, and the nature of the quasi-fiscal deficit. The size and structure of the income and expenditures of the government should also be analyzed, as should the taxes on which income is based: VAT, sales, direct, indirect, progressive, simple, collectible, the wage and interest component, whether the deficit originates in the central government or in decentralized agencies, the proportion of investment in total expenditure, the incidence of state enterprises and the impact of its prices and wages, the existence of subsidies to business or to consumers and the distributional consequences of the fiscal effort. It is no less important to analyze how income and expenditure flows are affected by such factors as anchors, credibility, changes in wage levels, rates of interest, and exchange-rate policies.

Another central issue is the definition of the fiscal deficit: Is it made on a cash or an accrual basis? Is it construed as a change in the public sector's financial debt or as a change in the net worth of the public sector? Would it be best to use a concept like the public-sector borrowing requirement? Should we use real or nominal terms, with or without adjusting for inflation? A proper definition, or, more appropriately, a proper set of definitions, and an understanding of the root of the fiscal problem, is central to an understanding of the measures, short-term or structural, necessary for reaching a fiscal balance and improving the chances of success.

However, some of the arguments advanced by learned economists have led to a misinterpretation of the importance of fiscal equilibrium. One of these is the argument concerning the automatic character of the fiscal improvement derived from an abrupt arrest of the inflationary process (the reverse Olivera-Tanzi effect). While this is true, it is not likely—or, at least, it is not necessarily true—that the effect, by itself, will wipe out the entire fiscal deficit, as believed to be the case in Brazil in 1985. Whether it does or not depends on specific elasticities, not on any *a priori* logical assertion.

Another argument in the same vein is the emphasis on the increase in monetization produced by stability, as a sort of cushion used to justify the temporary continuation of fiscal deficits. While most economists were clearly familiar with the once-and-for-all nature of the process, the politicians were not.

Finally, the identification of the two inflationary equilibrium levels has been used to explain how an economy can be forced from a higher to a lower level of inflation through purely administrative measures (i.e., price ceilings) with less seigniorage but also with a more moderate Olivera-Tanzi effect. While not denying the possibility of abating inflation through administrative means and anchors, one has to accept that they can generate imbalances and a need for future adjustments— particularly if an insufficient fiscal effort is made—giving rise to the cyclical inflationary pattern observed in many heterodox stabilizations. The exchange rate has been used as an anchor in some of the more successful stabilization programs, at the price of having it appreciate substantially; this is an intrinsic consequence of the policies pursued, given the existence of inertia aggravated by fiscal imbalance.

As Bruno has said in this conference, there is a conflict between using the nominal exchange rate as a key anchor for price stability versus maintaining real-exchange-rate levels as a way of ensuring trade imbalances and output stability. This conflict appears to result simply from inertia or, perhaps, from persistent fiscal imbalances.

It is probably true that the principal cause of the misunderstanding of the heterodox message is a matter of emphasis, since the fundamentals are always mentioned, though all too briefly. The authors adhering to this approach may have felt that they were belaboring the point, believing that most of the discussions should deal with other, more exciting (but in fact ancillary) problems, relishing the analysis of the endogenous character of the fiscal deficit and the diverse reasons why a fiscal crunch was neither so necessary, nor so intense, nor needed so soon. It is not surprising that the heterodox school has earned the reputation of fiscal leniency.

The Argentinian and Brazilian experience shows how fundamentals are just that: *fundamental*, and how the *fiscal deficit* plays a central role. The cyclical regime described by Kiguel and Liviatan is very accurate. This regime is the consequence of the mistaken view of the nature of the heterodox policy. When such a policy is used as a substitute for fiscal balance, the cyclical pattern becomes inevitable. We have executed "silly" heterodox plans, *hence* the cyclical "regime." Argentina has gone through the cycles of 1957, 1967, 1973, 1979, 1985, 1988, 1989, and 1990, a pattern stemming from the non-attainment of the fundamentals and an attempt to put off the day of reckoning through artificial and short-lived anchors.

A novelty has been the increasing use of forced demonetization, either as a consequence of forced refinancing of deposits (as in the case of the recent experience of Brazil and Argentina) or through forced price acceleration (as in Argentina's 1988 Primavera Plan), used more and more to restrain inflation later on, even without price or exchange controls. But low monetization and low confidence mean that fiscal deficits have even more explosive consequences price-wise, and that it is no longer possible to purchase time. This lies at the root of Teitel's view; small deviations may have tremendous consequences, seemingly out of proportion with the cause.

Any stabilization effort needs a solidly based fiscal balance and a tight monetary policy, to which we may or may not add price fixing. If the fundamentals are not attained, the omission will soon exact a stiff penalty, price-wise. This is the present situation in countries like Argentina and Brazil. Other matters may be treated, and they may be intellectually more stimulating, but they are in any case ancillary to the central issues.

Jacob Frenkel

In my remarks I focus on two main subjects. First, the analytical issues concerning the choice of nominal anchors during a stabilization program; second, the transformation from stabilization to growth and the role of the real interest rate in this respect.

To set the stage for the discussion, it is worth recalling some of the main lessons learned since the Toledo conference. First, the process of stabilization is a long one. While an initial fast reduction in the rate of inflation can be obtained, we have seen too many cases in which the early achievements were lost, policies were prematurely relaxed, and the inflation spiral accelerated. Expectations depend on the *credibility* of the policy measures and will not be adjusted to reflect the non-inflationary course of economic policy unless the policy makers have established a satisfactory track record and maintained it for an extended period.

Second, even in relatively successful stabilization programs—like the one represented by the Israeli experience—it seems to be very difficult to reduce inflation below the range of 15–20% per annum.

Third, it is very difficult to return to a satisfactory and sustainable growth path following the inevitable slowdown which accompanies the stabilization phase. For stabilization programs to succeed and for growth to resume, it is essential that some of the key economic variables—the real wage, the real exchange rate, and the real rate of interest—do not move significantly out of line.

Anchors

There are three sources of uncertainty, any one of which can provide a rationale for the use of nominal anchors: (a) The economic system is subject to uncertain exogenous shocks. (b) The behavior of economic agents and their reaction to the various shocks is uncertain. (c) The structure of the economy (i.e., the model) is uncertain. These three sources of uncertainty provide the analytical foundation for the use of nominal anchors in the stabilization program, and, depending on which of them is most prominent, they also determine which anchor (or anchors) should be used.

Consider, for example, the first source of uncertainty—uncertainty about the origin of the shocks. Here, prudence suggests that it would be useful to employ multiple anchors. Because of the uncertainty we do not know *ex ante* which one of the multiple anchors will be needed. Specifically, even though the fundamentals might be put in place, inertia and lack of complete credibility may put destabilizing pressures on labor markets, and/or goods markets, and/or the market for foreign exchange. Under these circumstances, the appropriate nominal anchors would be the price level, nominal wages, and the nominal exchange rate. Obviously, the success of such a multiple-anchors strategy presupposes that the fundamentals are in place. Therefore, the resultant levels of real wages and real exchange rates are consistent with the equilibrium of the economic system that would have prevailed had the course of economic policy (which is actually in place) been credible. Indeed, and under such circumstances, once the track record of an appropriate policy course is established, expectations will adjust to reflect the non-inflationary equilibrium. In that case, the removal of the anchors in due course will not be disruptive.

Consider next the second source of uncertainty—the behavior of economic agents. In this case, multiple anchors might be designed to secure political support from various segments of the economic system. Specifically, it is possible that in order to secure moderation of labor unions' demands and their support for anchoring the nominal wage, one would need to obtain the commitment of producers not to raise prices (i.e., anchoring the nominal price). To prevent price pressures associated with imported goods, the government might need to commit itself to maintain the nominal exchange rate intact. A social pact of this type restrains the behavior of economic agents and at the same time contributes to the stabilization effort. Again, the success of this strategy presupposes that the fundamentals are in place.

The third source of uncertainty concerns the structure of the economy. In this case, the equilibrium values of the key economic variables are also uncertain and, therefore, the anchors strategy might best be implemented through the adoption of a *band*, such as, for example, an exchange-rate band. This would still leave open the question as to whether intervention would take place only when exchange rates reached one of the boundaries, or whether it should also take place within the band.

Since credibility is one of the key factors governing the success of stabilization programs, it is important that the program should allow for mid-course corrections that do not destroy its credibility. In other words, the public should be informed on the basic contribution that the nominal anchors make but, at the same time, be aware that in an uncertain world occasional corrections might be necessary. With such transparency and clarity, mid-course corrections might actually enhance the credibility of the stabilization effort rather than signify its failure.

In the medium run the various nominal anchors should be relaxed. The first to be loosened should be the price anchor, and the (close) second should be the wage rate. One difficult question is: when is it safe to relax the anchors and be sure that the stabilization gains are permanent? In answering this question, one must compare the cost of premature removal with the cost of somewhat delayed removal. One of the most important considerations determining the cost of premature relaxation is that a mistake cannot be easily corrected. Once the anchors strategy failed, it would be more difficult to lend it credibility in the next stabilization attempt.

One of the puzzles characterizing the successful Israeli stabilization is the difficulty in lowering inflation below the 15–20% range. Why is the inflation so stubborn? The foregoing discussion of the three nominal anchors may provide a partial clue. One explanation involves the nominal wage anchor, the "wage creeping" explanation, according to which, because of seniority or promotion, wages kept on creeping upwards. The second explanation involves the nominal-exchange-rate anchor, according to which the recent devaluations of the Israeli shekel have contributed to the maintenance of the stubborn inflation. The third explanation involves the price anchor, according to which, because of a non-competitive environment in which prices are based on a mark-up process, any rise in the real wage is translated into a more significant rise in prices. This last explanation also underscores the importance of accompanying a stabilization effort by appropriate structural reforms designed to remove distortions and to enhance the competitiveness of markets.

The key assumption that the fundamentals have all been put in place is central to the entire nominal-anchor strategy. In its absence, reliance on nominal anchors can do more damage than good. In fact, it may transform high inflation into hyperinflation fueled by high pressures, which were suppressed along with nominal wages, prices, and exchange rates. Here, the "usual suspect" should be the budget deficit. Likewise, combatting inflation primarily through fixing the nominal exchange rate without removing the basic source of domestic price pressures may result in a real appreciation of the currency that harms export industries, worsens the balance of payments, and increases foreign debt.

Growth

The central difficulty faced by all "successful" stabilization efforts is the restoration of sustainable growth. Many stabilization efforts failed because, in an attempt to restore growth, fiscal and monetary policies were relaxed too soon. All stabilization efforts induce an initial slowdown of economic activity. In practically all cases this slowdown results in political pressures for a premature relaxation of policies. At the same time, the stabilization efforts are often associated with extremely high real rates of interest, which discourage investment and hamper growth. How can one overcome this? It is necessary to consider economic growth as an *integral part* of the stabilization program rather than as a second phase, which starts only after stabilization succeeds. This integrated perspective implies that the very *design* of a stabilization program should clearly reflect the fact that the sustainability of such stabilization (in terms of its desirability and in terms of the political support that it can secure) depends on whether or not it leads to a satisfactory growth performance. Accordingly, while it is useful to have positive real rates of interest, excessively high rates may endanger the stabilization effort.

Real interest rates should not be used as the main instrument arresting aggregate demand. The most effective policy instrument in this respect is the government budget. In fact, high interest rates may have a relatively small payoff in restraining aggregate demand; their main influence is in determining the *composition* of demand between spending on investment and durable goods and spending on less durable goods. Furthermore, since slow investment and growth may ultimately prove to be the Achilles' heel of the stabilization program, it is also useful to ensure that reductions in government spending affect primarily government consumption rather than government investment. This is all the more important in view of the evidence on the positive correlation between private-sector investment and public-sector investment (especially when the latter constitutes investment in infrastructure).

To conclude, a comprehensive assessment of the degree of success of stabilization efforts must address the issue of growth. Such an assessment must examine whether or not the policies adopted for stabilization are conducive to growth. This broader perspective implies that in designing the optimal policy package one must pay attention to the size and composition of government spending between consumption and investment as well as to the role of the real rate of interest in influencing private-sector investment.

Stanley Fischer

The Transition from Stabilization to Growth

In very-high-inflation economies, stabilization is the first essential step on the road to the resumption of growth. But that step itself involves two effects that tend to delay the resumption of growth: first, the reduction in aggregate demand resulting from fiscal correction and monetary tightening; and second, the high real interest rates that occur in the early stages of most stabilization programs.

The effects of the reduction in aggregate demand on growth can be offset by switching demand to net exports. This is one of the reasons why most stabilizations also involve a real devaluation—although the need for real devaluation differs among stabilizing countries, depending on the initial state of the current account. In the December 1989 Yugoslav stabilization, for instance, the current account was in substantial surplus and there was no clear need for a real devaluation.

Even so, it is necessary in any exchange-rate-based stabilization to take into account the real appreciation that will follow implementation of the initial stabilization measures. The currency has to be over-depreciated at the beginning, to leave room for the inertial inflation that is bound to continue in the next few months. Failure to plan for a real exchange rate that will still provide adequate export incentives after the first few months of the stabilization program is a recipe for prolonged slow growth.

There often comes a stage following a stabilization at which the two roles of the exchange rate—the nominal exchange rate as an anchor for the price level, and the real exchange rate as the relative price of traded goods, which determines the profitability of exports—conflict. The temptation is to hold onto the nominal exchange rate, for fear of the inflationary consequences of a devaluation; but it is usually wiser to worry more about the real exchange rate, to undertake a growth-enhancing real devaluation, preferably accompanied by a further tightening of fiscal policy that will sustain the lower exchange rate. In the Israeli case, several small devaluations have been accompanied by an agreement with the labor unions not to pass through the resulting inflation into wages.

The real-interest-rate problem is more difficult. Investment will not resume until real interest rates reach a reasonable level, and prolonged periods of high real interest rates create financial crises and bankruptcies even for firms that would be viable at reasonable levels of interest rates. Even so, the temptation to bring down the real interest rate very quickly has to be avoided. The view taken in the Cruzado Plan, that the real interest rate could be kept low from the start, has not generally been correct. The *ex post* real rate turns out to be high in successful stabilizations partly because *ex ante* there was a prospect of failure and of higher inflation than actually took place; further, in the early stages of a stabilization, the public is waiting to see whether the government really means it this time.

The real interest rate will tend to be lower the larger the fiscal correction, which is one reason to aim for fiscal overshooting at the beginning (another reason is that most governments do not undertake all the fiscal measures they announce); it will come down more rapidly the sooner the credibility of the stabilization program is established. This second factor, too, argues for fiscal overshooting.

The argument that the real interest rate is high *ex post* in successful stabilizations, partly because inflation is lower than expected, suggests the use of price-indexed loans in such situations. This is consistent with the fact that the real interest rate on old loans immediately following the 1923 German stabilization was in line with international rates, even though real rates for *Rentenmark* loans were extraordinarily high. However, the continuation of indexation following a radical stabilization is undesirable, and on balance it is probably preferable not to use the device.[1]

Real interest rates on nominal bonds should begin to decline as credibility is regained, but there is often a puzzling lag between the time at which most observers think that the situation has stabilized and the decline in real lending rates. This is in part due to inefficiencies in the financial system, which expands rapidly during periods of high inflation. To cover the costs of staying in business—which usually have been raised by the existence of bad debts—banks charge a large margin between borrowing and lending rates. Financial restructuring thus can help reduce the real interest rate. In addition, where the banking system is oligopolistic, pressure from the central bank may help push down margins quite rapidly—as the Bruno-Meridor paper argues has happened in Israel.

Beyond macroeconomic changes, the restoration of growth usually requires far-reaching structural changes in the economy. These naturally vary from country to country, but there are some common elements: fiscal reform as well as correction of the budget deficit; financial-sector reform; domestic regulatory reform; and in many, but not all economies, trade reform.[2] Here is where the World Bank comes in.

What is the right sequence of stabilization and structural adjustment measures? In general, in a very-high-inflation country, stabilization should come first. The benefits of measures such as trade-policy reforms or domestic deregulation are likely to be lost in the noise created by the relative-price distortions that always accompany high inflation. In addition, the risk that structural policy changes will be reversed, or not carried out at all, is much higher when macroeconomic conditions are unstable.[3] But there is no reason to be dogmatic: Mexico successfully began restructuring before instituting its inflation-stabilization program.[4]

The sequencing of structural adjustment measures depends on the individual country's circumstances. Some reforms, such as trade reform and domestic deregulation, are especially complementary and can usefully be carried out simultaneously, if the country has the administrative capacity. The general advice is to go for the big distortions and try to bring them down fast, provided, of course, the necessary tradeoffs—for example, between tariff reduction and budget balance—have been taken into account.[5]

Suppose that the government has proceeded resolutely with structural reforms after stabilization. What else? Certainly, the government should remove all distortions that discourage foreign direct investment. It should, to the extent possible, undertake productive infrastructure investments, those that complement private investments. But it will probably still take time before the confidence of private investors recovers. The government has to go through an uncomfortable period in which it has to maintain stable policies and incentives, and to wait.

Stabilization and Adjustment in Eastern Europe

All East European economies need to undertake fundamental structural reforms. Some of them, including Poland and Yugoslavia, also have to reduce inflation. Some that have not experienced inflation nevertheless face incipient inflation arising from a large monetary overhang.

The key question is whether inflation can be stabilized before the structural reforms are in place. In the very-high-inflation economies, it can, and it must. The stabilization will not necessarily reduce inflation to single-digit levels, but it is essential to try to maintain low inflation if the structural reforms are to have a chance of succeeding.

Inflation can only be controlled if the stock of money is controlled. This requires plugging gaps in the credit system. In most of the formerly socialist economies, the gap arises from automatic bank financing of enterprise losses; the commercial banks' losses are monetized through the central bank. Thus there will often be a large quasi-fiscal deficit in a country even when it reports a balanced budget. To prevent monetary growth, the central bank simply has to stop giving credit; enterprise losses will have to be covered out of the budget until the enterprise system can be reformed. One good use of foreign loans in such economies would be to finance an Enterprise Reconstruction Fund.

The effect of past monetary mismanagement, the monetary overhang, can be handled through asset sales and, in the early stages of reform, by raising the real interest rate on deposits to a non-negative level.

The sequencing of structural reforms in the transforming socialist economies has also to be tailored to the circumstances of each country. Trade reform and external-payments reform can play an important role in providing appropriate price signals for economies where relative prices have borne no relation to world levels, and should come early, if necessary with the assistance of an over-devalued (relative to its eventual level) exchange rate. In addition to trade reform, an essential step is enterprise reform. How such reforms should take place is not yet clear—whether there should be rapid privatization, and if so how, or whether there should be a period of recentralization of ownership, and if so how long that should last. Definitive answers do not exist, but experience will soon help sort the answers out.

Enterprise reform will have to be accompanied by the creation of a social safety net, as guaranteed employment is lost; in addition, many social services have in the past been delivered through the enterprise.

Accompanying these reforms is the need for accounting systems and much of the other infrastructure of a market system, including the creation of a modern financial system. Modern business practices can best be taught by example; for this and many other reasons, foreign direct investment has to be encouraged.

Despite the potential for chaos in the reforming East European markets, there are grounds for optimism. First, and most important, their governments and people want to make fundamental changes in the economy; there has, for instance, been less public protest over restrictive measures in Poland than in any other adjusting economy. Second, these economies are close to the European community, and have historical trading and communications ties with the rest of Europe. Third, they are welcoming foreign investment, and they are likely to get it. Fourth, the Soviet Union apart, these economies are small relative to the rest of Europe, and are likely to receive aid, both financial and technical, that is significant relative to their size.

No doubt there will be disappointments and setbacks as the economies of Eastern Europe are transformed, but in all likelihood they will be successfully transformed within a reasonable period of time.

Nissan Liviatan

When we ask ourselves what is new since the conference in Toledo, we should focus on the new economic developments and on the things which we thought we understood then but about which we have more doubts now.

One of the things we knew then is that in chronic-inflation countries there is a great deal of institutional inertia in the inflationary process and therefore stabilization can be facilitated considerably in the initial stage by heterodox policies. But it turned out that stabilization is taking much longer than we thought. If the question was only one of coordinating and synchronizing prices, wages, and other nominal variables, then (given appropriate fiscal adjustment) the incomes-policy phase should not have lasted more than two or three months. However, in Israel stabilization is already in its fifth year, and the economy has still not reached equilibrium.

The fact that inflation is low does not indicate that it has actually been stabilized, if it is supported by overvaluation (related to the exchange-rate policy) and unemployment, as is the case in Israel. The length of the stabilization process is one of the puzzles. Does it mean that a lengthy recession is unavoidable?

Another puzzle is the 15–20% plateau of annual inflation, or the "low inflation step" on which the economy of Israel has settled in the post-stabilization years.

We also thought that the exchange rate as a nominal anchor was very good policy. Now we doubt whether it was in fact a good policy, not only in the short run but also in the medium and the long run. Is it not desirable, as a rule, to switch nominal anchors in order not to put too much stress on the tradables sector?

The last issue, which is related to the experience of Argentina and Brazil, is that we did not realize how destabilizing heterodox policies can be in case of failure. It seems that one has to weigh very carefully the consequences of failure before embarking on a heterodox program when fiscal support is not assured.

In trying to deal with some of the foregoing issues, we should stress the role of credibility in the sustainability of the stabilization effort and in the readiness of the government to stand behind its nominal policy rules.

One reason for the length of the transition phase is that it takes a long time to establish credibility in the fiscal and nominal policies. A government facing adverse expectations is forced to compromise its policy targets (such as maintaining a fixed exchange rate) in order not to pay a high social cost in terms of overvaluation and unemployment. It takes a long time for the public to learn how far the government will go in its disinflationary policies. It is this sort of consideration that may explain the emergence of the phenomenon of a low inflation step.

The next question is whether the kind of recession that Israel experienced, following its heterodox program, is unavoidable. I am quite pessimistic about the ability to avoid the recessionary phase. This is because there seems to be no way in which the policy maker can prove his adherence to the nominal anchor except by demonstrating his readiness not to accommodate inflationary pressures (from the cost side) even at the cost of unemployment. This is quite a different issue from credibility in fiscal policies. Thus the public may believe that the government will persist in fiscal austerity but not that it is ready to resist wage demands at the cost of unemployment.

General Discussion

Sebastian Edwards: I think we have learned a great deal in this conference. The concept used most often was credibility. With the possible exception of Nissan Liviatan, very little was said about how we really go about establishing credibility, mainly from an institutional point of view. Once it is lost, how do we regain it? Credibility has been used to explain why some programs succeeded; it was used to explain why some other programs did not succeed. It was used to explain almost everything, but very little has been said on the institutional requirements, the kind of reforms needed and how do we really go about obtaining credibility once we lose it.

Don Patinkin: Stan said that inflation is a monetary phenomenon. This is one of the least meaningful statements that could be made about inflation. It is like saying that the price of potatoes is a potato phenomenon. [Interjection by Stan Fischer: "Sorry, Don. I went to school in the 1960s and I read *Money, Interest and Prices* and somehow I learned that M determines P. . . ." Patinkin's response: "To stabilize the price level you may fix *any* nominal quantity, and then all the other nominal magnitudes will be fixed."] Undoubtedly, when you have an inflationary process, you can see it in the money stock. But the question is: Why is the quantity of money increasing? Politicians always knew how to print money. Why do they sometimes do it at one rate and sometimes at another rate? What are the underlying considerations? When do they use taxes? When do they use seigniorage? I think that's the result of the other forces that generate inflation. Really, what we have to do is get at those forces.

Juan L. Cariaga: I was very glad to hear the wise words of Stan Fischer when he tells us that in order to restore growth you have to wait. In other words, lay down the foundations with stabilization and structural adjustment and wait for the restoration of growth. I think this is a lesson learned from Bolivia—don't listen to the impatient politicians who call for immediate growth and reactivation decrees. You will usually end up with a decree giving export incentives at the expense of the treasury, subsidized credit at the expense of the central bank, and cheaper imports at the expense of the public enterprises. This way you will end up jeopardizing the stabilization.

Peter Bernholz: I very much agree with Stan Fischer's remarks on the programs of Eastern Europe (and could add also China), but would add that the situation in East Germany and Russia is probably much worse than he mentioned. It is estimated that the total budget deficit in Russia amounts to 14% of the GDP, and we all know that this would mean hyperinflation, without corrective measures. Finally, a comment stimulated by Guido Di Tella's remarks: Isn't it more important to anchor politicians and central bankers than to anchor nominal magnitudes?

Guillermo Ortiz: Both Jacob and Stan mentioned that you should first stabilize and then take up structural reforms. The problem emerges because sometimes you need structural reforms to stabilize. Guido mentioned that we have to pay much more attention to the fiscal variables. It's very difficult to stabilize in a credible way if you have a public sector that owns money-losing enterprises and you are just cutting investments across the board without being selective. At least in the public sector you have to go deep into structural reforms before you stabilize. The same applies to trade liberalization. Once you stabilize at a certain exchange rate with a certain level of protection and you then want to liberalize, you may find the nominal anchors that you set for stabilization are not the ones that you would have set if you had liberalized first. The sequencing is not clear-cut. My second remark relates to high interest rates. There are two factors that explain high real interest rates. One is expectations, credibility problems, and so on, and the other is fundamentals. Fundamentals of supply and demand of funds. In the present circumstances, in some countries we are effectively cut off from international finance, and the resultant financial pressures of credit markets explain why interest rates are high. Perhaps the lesson here is that you have to do fiscal overshooting if you want to get interest rates down.

Yair Mundlak: A question was asked earlier whether political economy is science or art, and Nissan gave his answer. There is a more scientific answer, and this is that it is art, because had it been science the policies would have first been tried on dogs. But seriously, the dilemma can maybe best expressed in terms of an arbitrage equation of intertemporal optimization. We talk about governments to a large extent as social planners. The first-order condition in optimal growth would say that the marginal utility of consumption today equals the discounted value of marginal utility of consumption tomorrow. But the government has a different utility function, and two important attributes have to be added to the objective function: first, the political survival component; and second the rent-seeking element. When you add these you have a completely different game and the whole question of credibility becomes much more difficult.

Nadav Halevi: We agree on the basic issues of major inflations, such as getting the fundamentals right. But when you go into greater detail it seems to me that we are ignoring the differences in structures and in objectives between different countries and institutional forms. It is a little too hopeful to think that we can draw general truths without taking account of these differences.

Meir Heth: One aspect of structural adjustment that is quite often neglected or relegated to secondary importance by quantitative economists is institutional reform. Successful macro policies can bring about stabilization but may be inadequate to resume growth. To give just one or two Israeli examples: For public-sector reform it is not enough to cut public-sector budgets—you must also find ways to inject economic incentives in the provision of various social services. Another example is that of trade-union reform if one wants to introduce various changes in wage policy.

Persio Arida: It seems to me that Latin American experiences such as that of Argentina clearly show that the problem is not giving good or bad advice about fiscal policy but rather the response of the parties involved. For example, in Brazil all the proposals to promote fiscal adjustment were turned down by the president. The Summer plan and other proposals were announced very openly and then turned down by the Congress. Whatever the procedures, the political leadership was not prepared to conduct a tight fiscal policy.

Mario Nuti: The statement that inflation is a monetary phenomenon may have more meaning in the context of Eastern Europe than it has been given credit for. It is precisely monetary indiscipline that, as we now know, is the greatest drawback, the greatest failure of the system. I think that it is right to give primacy to monetary stabilization in the process of economic reform. However, I would be careful about transposing to Eastern Europe the experience of the stabilization of other countries. For instance, in the current stabilization program in Poland the anchors are the money wage, which is indexed on a very mild coefficient of 20% and 30% for the next few months, and the nominal rate of exchange, which has led to a drastic devaluation of the zloty, followed by a drastic daily revaluation. To me this makes absolutely no sense. There is the choice of real anchors of the quantity of real money, which is to fall by 30% throughout the year, and the target of a positive real rate of interest. The combination of these anchors is going to cost Poland more than is necessary in terms of unemployment and a fall in the standard of living. Therefore it might jeopardize the entire operation. I don't think that we should expostulate to the East the experience of other countries.

Michael Bruno: I would just like to remark that the revaluation going on in Poland may be a sign of confidence in the short run. The exchange rate in Poland does not really measure relative prices of goods but of assets, for foreign exchange is the only means of saving.

Zvi Sussman: As a part-time sailor, I would suggest that we learn a little bit more about the use of anchors from real sailors. You can lower an anchor which reaches the bottom and grips firmly, such as the control of the nominal exchange rate by the central bank. This is really an anchor which holds. But you can lower an anchor which just dangles in the water and doesn't do much. This applies, for example, to wage controls, because wages are determined within a very complex framework and fixing them is very difficult.

José Luis Machinea: I completely agree with what Persio Arida was saying. It would be very interesting, perhaps not this time but next time, to hear something about how those countries that were able to stabilize managed their political and social systems. There is an important difference in the political system in the case of Brazil, and especially in Argentina, in relation to other countries that were able to stabilize.

Final comments by Stan Fischer: The first thing we've learned since Toledo is that the stabilization process takes longer than expected. I don't think that people at that stage thought that a period of six months was sufficient, but I don't expect that they thought that it would take as long at it has been taking now. That refers both to the high interest rate and to the 20% inflation. We have got to look to a different set of countries to figure out how to get below the 15–20% barrier. We are now in the range of inflation rates that were being discussed in the early 1980s in the United States and in Europe, as part of the disinflation that took place then. Unfortunately, very few of those countries, if any (perhaps Italy), have disinflated without a recession.

The last thing we have learned, and which was brought home very strongly today, is that countries are very similar in many respects. I was thinking of the real-wage discussion looking at the Mexican program, thinking of what Yugoslavia will face in a few months when it renegotiates its wage contracts, and also thinking of the Israeli case. You see the similarities, but you must not be misled into thinking that you should give the same advice everywhere. At this stage it is absolutely clear that going to Argentina and talking about heterodox policies is a mistake. Together with Guido Di Tella I am willing to take a vow, and the vow is that neither you nor I nor any other economist should go to Argentina until they undertake a fiscal reform.

Notes

1. The tentativeness of the argument reflects the absence in the literature of a thorough analysis of either the issue or the record of the use of indexed loans in post-stabilization situations.

2. The exceptions are economies that have already undertaken trade reforms.

3. The World Bank does not make structural-adjustment loans (rapidly disbursing loans, which provide balance-of-payments support) when the macroeconomic situation is deemed unsatisfactory. Of course, this is not because it is opposed to structural adjustment, but because the chances the reforms will be successfully implemented in such conditions are low.

4. Note, however, that Mexico made its fiscal correction before attempting any major structural reforms.

5. I draw on work reported in the World Bank's forthcoming Second Report on adjustment lending, undertaken under the leadership of Vittorio Corbo.

Contributors

Persio Arida
Catholic University of Rio de Janeiro

Peter Bernholz
Institut für Volkswirtschaft
Basel, Switzerland

Mario I. Blejer
International Monetary Fund
Washington

Velimir Bole
Ekonomiski Institut
Ljublijana, Yugoslavia

Michael Bruno
Bank of Israel
Jerusalem

Eliana A. Cardoso
Fletcher School of Law and Diplomacy
Tufts University

Juan Cariaga
Inter-American Development Bank
Washington

Vittorio Corbo
World Bank
Washington

Sebastian Edwards
University of California
Los Angeles

Stanley Fischer
World Bank
Washington

Jacob A. Frenkel
International Monetary Fund
Washington

Mitja Gaspari
National Bank of Yugoslavia
Belgrade

Elhanan Helpman
Tel Aviv University

Daniel Heymann
CEPAL
Buenos Aires

Miguel Kiguel
World Bank
Washington

Leonardo Leiderman
Tel Aviv University

Nissan Liviatan
Hebrew University
Jerusalem

José Luis Machinea
Banco d'Argentina
Buenos Aires

Neven Mates
Economiski Institut
Zagreb, Yugoslavia

Leora (Rubin) Meridor
Bank of Israel
Jerusalem

Juan Antonio Morales
Universidad Catolica Boliviana
La Paz

Mario Nuti
European University Institute
Florence

Guillermo Ortiz
Ministry of Finance
Mexico City

Juan Carlos de Pablo
El Cronista Comercial
Buenos Aires

Sylvia Piterman
Bank of Israel
Jerusalem

Assaf Razin
Tel Aviv University
Tel Aviv

Dani Rodrik
John F. Kennedy School of Government
Harvard University

Andrés Solimano
World Bank
Washington

Simón Teitel
Inter-American Development Bank
Washington

Guido Di Tella
Embassy of the Republic of Argentina
Washington

Sweder Van Wijnbergen
World Bank
Washington

Index